AF598247

PARALLEL SYSTEMS AND COMPUTATION

PARALLEL SYSTEMS AND COMPUTATION

Proceedings of the 1986 IBM Europe Institute Seminar on Parallel Computing Oberlech, Austria, August 11–15, 1986

edited by

George PAUL

and

George S. ALMASI
IBM Research Division
T. J. Watson Research Center
P.O. Box 704
Yorktown Heights, NY 10598
U.S.A.

1988

NORTH-HOLLAND
AMSTERDAM • NEW YORK • OXFORD • TOKYO

ISBN: 0 444 70371 3

Publishers:

ELSEVIER SCIENCE PUBLISHERS B.V.
P.O. Box 1991
1000 BZ Amsterdam
The Netherlands

Sole distributors for the U.S.A. and Canada:

ELSEVIER SCIENCE PUBLISHING COMPANY, INC.
52 Vanderbilt Avenue
New York, N.Y. 10017
U.S.A.

LIBRARY OF CONGRESS
Library of Congress Cataloging-in-Publication Data

IBM Europe Institute--Seminar on Parallel Computing (1986 : Oberlech, Austria)
Parallel systems and computation : proceedings of the 1986 IBM Europe Institute--Seminar on Parallel Computing, Oberlech, Austria, August 11-15, 1986 / edited by George Paul and George S. Almasi.
p. cm.
Bibliography: p.
ISBN 0-444-70371-3 (U.S.)
1. Parallel processing (Electronic computers)--Congresses.
I. Paul, George, 1937- . II. Almasi, George S., 1938- .
III. Title.
QA76.5.I273 1986
004'.35--dc19 87-32270
CIP

PRINTED IN THE NETHERLANDS

PREFACE

The papers in this volume form the written proceedings of the 1986 IBM Europe Institute: Seminar on Parallel Computing, held in Oberlech, Austria, August 11-15, 1986.

The IBM Europe Institute, founded in 1982, was established to provide high-quality, advanced-level seminars and workshops for the European academic and scientific community. Each year the Institute consists of a series of one-week seminars. Each seminar focuses on a specific topic of scientific research of current interest. Attendees are invited from leading universities and other non-commercial research establishments in Europe, the Middle East and Africa; speakers are selected from leaders of the international research community and come from academic, government and industrial research establishments. The Institute seeks to promote information interchange among scientists from different countries and provides ample opportunity in the form of scheduled free-time, excellent meeting facilities and a general environment to foster cooperation and exchange of information and ideas between participants.

This seminar was the second in the Institute series dedicated to the topic of parallel processing. The first seminar, dedicated to highly parallel processing for both numeric and non-numeric or symbolic applications was organized by the editors in conjunction with the 1984 IBM Europe Institute, and was held in Davos, Switzerland, July 23-27, 1984. Selected papers from the first seminar were published in [1].

In contrast to the 1984 seminar, this seminar was primarily focused on parallel systems for numeric computation. The seminar was divided into five sections or topics:

- Parallel Programming Software and Environments
- Parallel Algorithms
- Survey of Parallel Processor Architecture
- Performance Analysis, Modeling and Applications
- Panel on Future Directions in Parallel Processing.

Each day of the meeting was divided into morning and evening sessions associated with these topics as indicated in the figure below. Breaks were included between all presentations and the afternoon of each day was left open to encourage informal discussions among participants.

All but four papers from the first four sections are included herein. Papers describing the parallel processor architectures presented in two of lectures not included here: "The IBM Research Parallel Processor (RP3): An Overview" by Dr. Kevin McAuliffe of the IBM T.J.

Watson Research Center and "The GF-11 Supercomputer" by Dr. Monty Denneau, also of IBM T.J. Watson, are published elsewhere [2] and [3]. The remaining two papers: "A Survey of Programming Language Features for Multiprocessing" by Dr. Brian Smith of the Argonne National Laboratory and "Message-Passing Models for Highly Concurrent Processing" by Professor Alain Martin of the California Institute of Technology are unfortunately unavailable for publication.

The fifth section consisted of an evening session dedicated to questions on future directions of parallel processing, which were directed to an invited panel, and to general discussion among the attendees. This session was tape recorded, but the resulting audio tape was unfortunately not transcribable. The invited panel consisted of Professor Dr. Wolfgang Giloi of the GMD-TUB Research Center for Innovative Computer Systems and Technology, Professor Roger Hockney of Reading University, Professor Robert Wilhelmson of the National Center for Supercomputer Applications at the University of Illinois at Urbana-Champaign, Dr. Jack Worlton of the Los Alamos National Laboratory, and the editors as moderators. The editors would like to express their appreciation to the panel for their participation and contribution to the meeting and to express their regret at not being able to include a transcription of this session in the proceedings.

The editors would also like to express their appreciation to Professor Roger Hockney, who helped organize and chair the meeting, to Dr. Herb Budd, Director of Scientific Programs -- IBM Europe, for inviting us to organize and chair this meeting, and to Mr. Lassi Hyvarinen, Manager of Education and Scientific Programs -- IBM Europe, and Mrs. Ingrid Tempe of his staff, who so ably arranged accommodations, meeting facilities, travel and other logistic details of the Institute thereby assuring the comfort of the speakers and attendees and contributing greatly to the overall success of the meeting.

George Paul
George S. Almasi

Yorktown Heights, NY

References

1. Almasi, G.S., and Paul, G., guest editors, "Special Issue on Parallel Processing", *Parallel Computing*, Volume 2, Number 3, November 1985.

2. Pfister, G.F., Brantley, W.C., George, D.S., Harvey, S.L., Kleinfelder, W.J., McAuliffe, K.P., Melton, E.A., Norton, V.A., and Weiss, J., "The IBM Research Parallel Processor Prototype (RP3): Introduction and Architecture", *Proc. of the 1985 International Conference on Parallel Processing*, August 1985.

3. Beetem, J., Denneau, M., and Weingarten, D., "The GF-11 Supercomputer", *Proc. 12th Annual International Symposium on Computer Architecture*, June 17-19, 1985 (108-113).

IBM EUROPE INSTITUTE: SEMINAR ON PARALLEL COMPUTING
Oberlech, Austria, August 11-15, 1986

Monday	Tuesday	Wednesday	Thursday	Friday
Morning Session: Parallel Programming Software and Environments Part I	Morning Session: Parallel Algorithms Part I	Morning Session: Survey of Parallel Processor Architecture Part I	Morning Session: Survey of Parallel Processor Architecture Part II	Morning Session: Performance Analysis, Modeling and Applications
Lunch Afternoon Open	Lunch Afternoon Open	Lunch Afternoon Open	Lunch Afternoon Open	Lunch Afternoon Open
Evening Session: Parallel Programming Software and Environments Part II	Evening Session: Parallel Algorithms Part II	Evening Session: Open	Evening Session: Survey of Parallel Processor Architecture Part III	Evening Session: Panel on Future Directions in Parallel Processing

Attendees at the 1986 IBM Europe Institute: Seminar on Parallel Computing

LIST OF CONTENTS

SECTION 3: SURVEY OF PARALLEL PROCESSOR ARCHITECTURE

SECTION 4: PERFORMANCE ANALYSIS, MODELING AND APPLICATIONS

SECTION 1
PARALLEL PROGRAMMING SOFTWARE AND ENVIRONMENTS

Parallel Systems and Computation
G. Paul and G.S. Almasi (Editors)

COMPILING FOR PARALLELISM: AN OVERVIEW

F.E. Allen

Computer Science Department
T.J. Watson Research Center
Yorktown Heights, NY 10598

The automatic restructuring of sequential FORTRAN programs to execute effectively on parallel processors is the subject of this paper. The restructuring involves both code and data and requires that dependence analysis be applied both within and across routines. The technology to accomplish this is discussed in the context of an experimental parallel translator (PTRAN).

1. Introduction

Sequential programs such as those written in FORTRAN specify a deterministic series of actions that use and modify data in storage. Writers of such programs have become accustomed to a computation model in which the stored data can be managed and manipulated quite explicitly. Users overlay data, reshape data across subroutine calls, put data in COMMON instead of passing them as subroutine arguments, organize references to them so that data referenced together are stored together, etc. Within the constraints of such a fixed storage model optimized by the user, FORTRAN compilers are able to produce remarkably good code for SISD (single instruction, single data) architectures, as well as for pipelined and vector machines.

The advent of parallel architectures has dramatically changed this model. In fact the major differences between the parallel and the SISD architectures and between the many varieties of new parallel architectures is the way storage is organized and how data accesses occur. Here are some examples:

1. A tightly-coupled 2- or 4-way 370 running one program from a single, virtual address space.
2. The RP3 at IBM Research having local and global memory.
3. CEDAR at the University of Illinois having local, shared (by a cluster), and global memory.
4. Bolt, Beranek and Newman's Butterfly and the various Hypercube architectures using message passing.
5. Distributed systems requiring message passing over generalized networks with rendezvous mechanisms.

For any of these machines (as well as many others) the user's old model of computation is no longer valid. The user must consider what parts of the computation can be executed in parallel, how to organize the data to correctly accomplish that, and how to estimate whether or not the communication overhead of these processes can be offset by the added parallelism. The old computation model now has new, orthogonal dimensions: the single, linear computation sequence becomes multiple computation sequences; the uniform address space on which arrays and vectors have been superimposed as convenient becomes segmented; the rules of storage accesses involve satisfying various protocols and residency requirements.

The established techniques (folklore and acquired wisdom) for writing efficient code are gone, turned around completely in some cases. For example, FORTRAN programmers usually try to order data accesses to match storage proximity. If these accesses are distributed across CPU's then costly cache coherency and other storage interlocks may occur during the execution.

The machines are not consistent with each other, making it more difficult than ever, if not impossible, to port programs from one system to another and have them continue to execute efficiently. SISD architectures differ largely in terms of scale: sizes of memory, speed of computation. Porting programs within the SISD class is often possible without change though some reorganization of storage and code is often necessary to accommodate the nuances of the system (compiler, operating system and hardware) to get the most efficient results. However, major structural changes are generally required to move programs between different parallel architectures, e.g. between loosely- and tightly-coupled architectures.

One response to the programming challenge of parallel architectures is to develop new languages having constructs and computational models compatible with these architectures. While we can learn a great deal from these languages, most require new technologies to support them. It is also premature: which languages are "best"?

Another response is to add constructs to existing, sequential languages to express parallelism. This is undoubtedly necessary but puts the burden on the user and does not solve the portability-for-efficiency issue.

Our response is to develop technology to automatically restructure sequential programs to run efficiently on parallel architectures. The purpose of this paper is to give an overview of the issues involved in automatically restructuring "dusty-deck" FORTRAN programs into processes to execute on multi-processors.

The automatic detection of parallelism, particularly for vectors, is not new. The pioneering work by Professor David Kuck at the Univ. of Illinois [11] has led to numerous systems including Kuck's powerful Parafrase system [12]. The work there [9][13][15][17] at Rice University [1], and elsewhere has contributed much to our understanding of the field. While we have extended the breadth and depth of previous techniques, the distinguishing feature of our work is its focus on restructuring the entire program including storage.

In order to develop and validate the technology for compiling for parallelism we are developing a parallel translator: PTRAN. The description of the PTRAN system in this paper forms the integrated framework for the approaches to compiling-for-parallelism given here.

PTRAN takes as its input "dusty-deck", FORTRAN 77 programs and is targeted to a tightly-coupled 2-,3-, or 4-way 370 running a system (MVS) capable of supporting multiple tasks from a single virtual address space. Features of PTRAN are:

1. Dependence analysis to detect data dependence at the element reference level. This is discussed in Section 3 of this paper.
2. Interprocedural analysis to determine data dependence between all of the routines associated with a given program. Section 4.
3. Code restructuring to form processes. Section 5.
4. Data restructuring to form parallelism and match the run-time system and architecture. Section 6.
5. A run-time system.
6. A user interface through an interprocedural data base.

In Section 7 we give the overall structure of the PTRAN system. It should be noted that this is work in progress, in fact work just started given the number of new techniques which must be invented.

Our results to date have been algorithms and it is expected that it will be some time before a complete implementation exists. It should be noted that most of our methods are relevant to other multiprocessing models even though our specific target is 370 MP.

Before giving an overview of the issues and the PTRAN approach, some further observations on the implications of compiling for parallelism are given.

2. Observations

2.1. Computational Model

We have already indicated the reasons for ***automatic*** restructuring of programs:

1. the disparity between the computational model provided by FORTRAN (and similar languages) and the computational models of parallel architectures;
2. the disparity between the computational models of different parallel architectures making effective portability essentially impossible;
3. the increased complexity facing users when developing applications for diverse parallel architectures.

Some of the implications automatic restructuring has on the design of a parallel translator are introduced in this section.

2.2. Finding Data Dependence

Computational independence requires data independence. Therefore the primary task of a parallel translator is to find and create independent data items and, when this is not possible, to organize storage and the computation so as to minimize synchronization and/or data copying. To do this it must determine as precisely as possible (and feasible) the

1. data and storage relationships at the element level;
2. the effects of subroutine calls;
3. the aliasing relationships in the program.

Consider the example in Figure 1.

```
R1:        create arrays A and B

R2:        DO I=1, 100
                C(2*I) = A(I) + B(I)
           ENDDO

R3:        DO I=1,100
                C(2*I+1) = A(I) + B(I)
           ENDDO

R4:        use array C
```

Figure 1. Regions R2 and R3 in the program can be concurrent processes.

Regions 2 and 3 in Figure 1 can be executed in parallel because only the even elements of C are modified in R2 while only the odd elements are modified in R3. To recognize this, a deep dependence analysis must be done.

In the example in Figure 2 (a), the outer loop can be transformed into multiple independent processes. The inner loop, the J loop, cannot be formed into independent processes without causing data synchronization at execution time. Section 3, dependence analysis, discusses the technology for recognizing these data relationships.

(a)	(b)
`DO I=1,1000`	`DOALL NP=1,1000`
	`(fork: I=process number)`
`DO J`	`DO J`
`A(J,I)=A(J-1,I)+B(I)*C`	`A(J,I)=A(J-1,I)+B(I)*C`
	`ENDALL (join)`

Figure 2. The outer loop in (a) can be formed into the concurrent processes shown in (b).

2.3. Expanding the Granularity of View

The traditional target of a compiler has been the SISD architectures exemplified by the 370s, CRAYs, VAXs and, more recently, RISC machines. Optimizing compilers for such computers concentrate on decreasing the number of instructions executed, selecting fast instructions and allocating the hardware resources, particularly the registers, so as to "optimize" the execution time of the compiled code. The units of purview of these optimizing compilers typically vary from the sub-expression, to the statement, to the basic block, to the loop, to varying loop nesting levels, and to the "global" level where "global" means ***subprogram*** (not the entire program). The granularity of the view of the traditional optimizing compiler was a reasonable match with the transformations being attempted. However to automatically restructure a program for most parallel architectures it is generally necessary to extend the compiler's view to the entire program. In other words it is necessary to extend global analysis to interprocedural analysis.

2.4. Automating the Information Flow

The traditional position of a compiler in a total system context is as a user service routine activated on command. The compiler takes the given source routines, transforms them as indicated and produces the requested output which can include considerable diagnostic and reference information. In this batch mode the information is re-created each time the routines are recompiled. Furthermore the user is the essential link between one compilation and the next and between one related routine and another. By capturing the entire program in a persistent database, this knowledge can be available to the user as well as to future compiles. Such compiler-derived information can be augmented with user-supplied information and with data collected by run time monitoring. This repository of information about the program is important in controlling complexity: it can be used as a guide to correct and effective modifications to the program by both the user and the system.

3. Dependence Analysis

3.1. Overview

Whenever two operands in a program might reference the same storage location the dependence relation must be recognized. This relation has been classified into three basic dependence types. For two references, S1 and S2, potentially referring to the same storage location and where S1 is potentially executed before S2 in the sequential program:

1. S1 and S2 are ***flow dependent*** if S1 writes data that S2 may read;
2. S1 and S2 are ***anti-dependent*** if S1 reads the same storage location S2 writes;
3. S1 and S2 are ***output dependent*** if they both write to the same location.

In Figure 1, the two occurrences of C would appear to have an output dependence. However on examining the relative values of the subscripts, the fact that the first occurrence stores into the even locations and the second into the odd can be determined. Increasingly elegant methods for performing dependence analysis continue to appear in the literature [1][2][6][17]. The basic idea is to formulate a linear equation involving the subscript sets of interest and then to determine whether or not the equation has an integer solution in the range of values of the subscripts. Returning to the example in Figure 1, let x represent I in the C subscript in region R2 and y represent the I on C in R3. We then ask if there is a integer solution to $2x = 2y + 1$ for x and y in the range of 1 to 100. Since no integer solution exists we know that a dependence does not exist.

In addition to determining the potential existence and type of dependence at the reference level, dependence analysis can determine the direction and distance of each component of the dependence relationship (Banerjee-Wolfe). The fact that a flow dependence exists in a loop is of interest but an important question is whether or not the dependence exists in the same iteration. Consider the example in Figure 2 (a). There is a dependence between the two references to A. Looking more deeply we discover that the I subscript dependence is on the same iteration of the I loop but that the J subscript dependence involves a flow dependence distance of -1: the A value being used in the current iteration was produced on the previous iteration and, by convention, the direction of the dependence is from the writer to the reader, hence the minus sign.

3.2 The PTRAN Approach to Dependence Analysis

Before performing dependence analysis, control and data flow analyses are performed using the available aliasing information. This gives the dependence analyzer a context in which to develop the dependence relationships. The dependence analyzer used is the Burke-Cytron method [6], a method that is faster and handles more cases than previous methods. The results of the analysis are encoded as distance vectors for use in subsequent transformations: in example (2a) a 2-element distance vector would record the dependence between the storing and the accessing of elements of A.

4. Interprocedural Analysis

4.1. Overview

Interprocedural analysis in its simplest form is used to determine the effects of a call on the calling routine and the aliasing relations propagated by calls to the called routine. Numerous approaches have been considered [3][5][7][8]. In its full form, the form needed to serve as a basis for effectively restructuring an entire program, interprocedural analysis should generate precise information with respect to array accesses and the extent of array overlaps [6][16]. Consider the example in Figure 3.

```
SUB P                                   SUB R (X,Y,L)
  COMMON C(10)                            COMMON C(10)
  DIM A(10,10)                            DIM X(L)

                                        DO   I=1,L
 DO  K =1,10                                 .
     .                                       .
   CALL R (A(1,K),B,10)                   X(I)=Y+C(I)
     .                                       .
 ENDOO                                       .
                                         ENDOO
 END                                      END
```

Figure 3. Interprocedural relationships

At the call of R in P it is useful to know how the arguments A and B and the data C in COMMON are affected by the call. Without that information the compiler must assume that all variables visible to the called routine are both modified and used. With detailed information about the effects of the call, including information about history-keeping variables, I/O activity, and other side effects, the compiler can, not only optimize in the presence of a call, but can consider forming processes. In the example in Figure 3 the K loop can become a DOALL loop with multiple executions of R occurring in parallel because each execution of R changes independent rows of A and does not use the results of previous executions.

In the called routine R, in the same example, it is important to understand the aliasing relationships between X, Y and C. Knowing that these are all independent allows the compiler to form processes from the I loop.

4.2. The PTRAN Approach to Interprocedural Analysis

The PTRAN interprocedural analysis is broken into three parts:

1. A basic interprocedural analyzer constructs the static call structure of the system, determines the effects of the individual procedures and then propagates these summary effects through the call graph. Since the results of this analysis are used as inputs to control and record data flow analysis, it must be done without regard for the internal flow in the routines. The result of doing the basic analysis is that the compiler knows which variables are defined and used at every call site and knows the potential externally-generated aliases at every procedure entry. This is described in [5].
2. A sophisticated interprocedural analyzer [6] then generates the precise information necessary to form processes. It follows a control and data flow analyzer. In the last example, the results of the basic interprocedural analyzer indicates that A was changed as a result of the CALL. However the sophisticated analyzer finds that different rows of A were being changed on each CALL and all CALLs could be done in parallel.
3. The Burke-Cytron dependence analyzer uses the results of the sophisticated interprocedural analyzer to recognize the cases in the example as well as other forms of aliasing (such as EQUIVALENCEd variables) in a uniform way: the underlying storage representation is used to determine when variables having different names, shapes and/or subscripts can potentially refer to the same storage location.

The examples in Figures 4, 5, and 6 indicate the breadth and depth of the Burke-Cytron analysis method.

```
DIMENSION A(10,10),VECTOR(100)
EQUIVALENCE (A,VECTOR)
...
DO I=1,99
   VECTOR(I) = A(10,10)
ENDDO
```

Figure 4. The references to VECTOR and A are independent so the loop can be formed into processes.

```
SUBROUTINE P (A,B)
                ...
                ...
          DO I = 1,N
                A(I) =
                     = B(I)
          ENDDO
```

Figure 5. Precise Aliasing Information: PTRAN can determine independence at the reference level in the presence of interprocedural aliasing.

```
DO I = 1,N
   CALL Q(A,I)
      =A(I)
ENDDO


SUBROUTINE Q(X,I)
      ...
      X(I) =
```

Figure 6. Interprocedural Subscript Analysis: PTRAN determines that the call modifies only A(I) rather than A so that the loop iterations can be executed in parallel.

5. Code Restructuring

5.1. Overview

Once a program has been analyzed to determine dependences and other relationships, parallel processes are formed within the constraints of the relationships. The formation of these processes involves data restructuring, the subject of the next section, and code restructuring. The basic purpose is of course, to improve the overall execution time by creating useful parallelism [10].

Maximal useful parallelism involves very dynamic partitioning, taking into account run-time parameters, branches, and system usage and configurations. However, the program can be statically restructured by the compiler to create heuristically useful units of work. Examples of such transformations [15] are loop unrolling and jamming (also called fusion), loop collapsing and loop interchange. Furthermore, the compiler can sometimes restructure the code to break dependences thereby decreasing run-time synchronization costs. The example in Figure 7 shows how the anti-dependence existing between references to A in the original loop can be broken.

```
    DO    I = 1, N
          A(I) = B(I) + C(I)
          D(I) = A(I-1) + E(I)
    ENDDO


BECOMES

    D(1) = A(0) + E(1)
    DOALL I = 2, N
          A(I-1) = B(I-1) + C(I-1)
          D(I)   = A(I-1) + E(I)
    ENDDO
    A(N) = B(N) + C(N)
```

Figure 7. Alignment to form independent processes.

5.2. *The PTRAN Approach to Code Restructuring*

Using the results of the dependence analysis potentially parallel units are identified and/or constructed. These units are then fused or broken to achieve a balance between the size and number of processes.

6. Data Restructuring

6.1. *Overview*

Again consider the example in Figure 1. While dependence analysis readily determines that regions 2 and 3 can be executed in parallel, the required and/or optimal organization of storage is far from clear.

1. On a tightly-coupled memory system with caching, references to neighbors may cause delays due to hardware cache coherency interlocks. In the example, considerable degradation might occur if regions 2 and 3 were executing simultaneously and cross-cache consistency were being kept on the stores into the elements of C. Strategies for solving the problem include fusing the loops then chunking them by the cache line size or running one of the loops backwards.
2. On a system with local and global memories such as the RP3, all of the data can be put in shared memory with some potential degradation in performance.
3. On a system with local, shared and global memories such as Cedar, all of the data can go in global memory or processor affinities can be established or data copying can be performed.
4. On a system without shared memories, the input data (arrays A and B) must be copied to local memories before execution and the results (the elements of C) merged after execution.

In summary, storage is restructured to accommodate the requirements of the hardware [14], to decrease execution time [4], and to break dependences.

6.2. The PTRAN Approach to Data Restructuring

Since PTRAN's initial target is a tightly-coupled 370 having hardware-maintained cache coherency, it does not have to choose the position of data in the memory hierarchy, but it does have to replicate data to break dependencies and to optimize the addressing to avoid hardware interlocks. The example in the next figure illustrates both points.

```
DO 1 I=1,100          DOALL NP=1,100

 T=
                      Tnp=

  =T
                      = Tnp

ENDDO                 ENDALL

   (a)                   (6)
```

Figure 8. Separate (process-private) T's are created for each process.

In order to create processes for the I loop in Figure 8, the dependence analyzer recognizes that process-specific locations for T must exist. Private storage is created for each process to contain the user and compiler temporaries needed for the lifetime of the process. It might be tempting to do "scalar expansion" on T to form a vector indexed by the process number. Scalar expansion is used in vectorizing compilers to break dependence in loops and is effective in that context: data-reference locality is important for most vector processors. However, to avoid cache coherency conflicts, it is important that PTRAN separate the addresses. Note that while the automatic detection of vector and process parallelism is the same, they have opposing requirements for the restructuring of code and data.

7. PTRAN Structure

The structure of the PTRAN system is given in Figure 9. A central feature of the system is the program data base. This repository contains partially translated subprograms, stubs describing missing routines, the static call structure of the system, the interprocedural summary information and other compiler-derived knowledge about the program. In addition it can contain directives and assertions from the user and run-time feedback information.

Another feature of the system apparent from Figure 9 and alluded to earlier in the paper is that the finding of parallelism is separated from the forming of processes. In this way the system can accommodate different architectures: run-time process costs and storage organization are accounted for in forming processes.

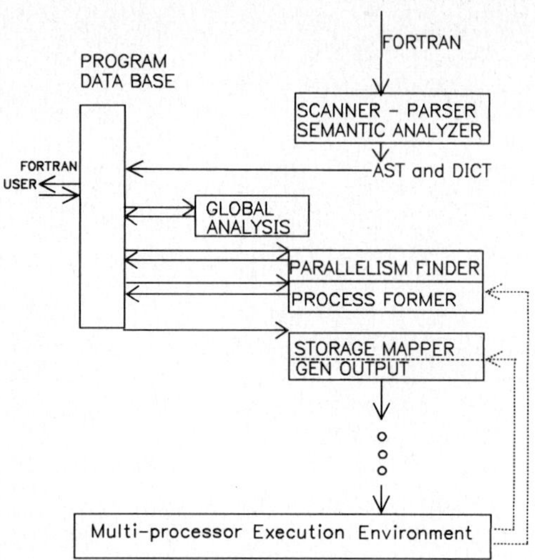

Figure 9. Structure of the PTRAN System

Summary

The new and disparate computational models of the multi-process architectures need new compiling technologies. An overview of a technology under development has been given in the context of a parallel translator, PTRAN, for FORTRAN.

Acknowledgements

Members of the PTRAN project are Michael Burke, Philippe Charles, Ron Cytron, and Jeanne Ferrante joined earlier by Mary Mace and in the summer by Todd Allen from the Univ. of Illinois and Susan Flynn from NYU. Without them and Cathy McCarthy who assisted with the preparation, this paper would not exist. Their contributions are deeply appreciated.

Bibliography

1. John R. Allen. *Dependence Analysis for Subscript Variables and Its Application to Program Transformations*, PhD thesis, Rice University, Houston, Texas 1983.

2. Utpal Banerjee. Data Dependence in Ordinary Programs, University of Illinois at Urbana-Champaign, 1976. M.S. Thesis.

3. John Banning. An Efficient Way to Find the Side Effects of Procedure Calls and the Aliases of Variables. *Conference Record of the Sixth ACM Symposium on Principles of Programming Languages*, pages 29-41, January 1979.

4. Michael Berry, Kyle Gallivan, William Harrod, William Jalby, Sy-Shin Lo, Ulrike Meier, Bernard Philippe, and Ahmed Sameh. Parallel Algorithms on the Cedar System, Center for Supercomputing Res. & Dev., U. of Ill., October 1986. CSRD Rpt. No. 581.

5. Michael Burke. An Interval Analysis Approach Toward Interprocedural Data Flow, IBM Research, 1984. Report RC11794.

6. Michael Burke and Ron Cytron. Interprocedural Dependence Analysis and Parallelization. *Proceedings of the Sigplan '86 Symposium on Compiler Construction*, 21(7):162-175, July 1986.

7. Keith Cooper. Analyzing Aliases of Reference Formal Parameters. *Conference Record of the Twelfth ACM Symposium on Principles of Programming Languages*, pages 281-290, January 1985.

8. Keith Cooper and Ken Kennedy. Efficient Computation of Flow Insensitive Interprocedural Summary Information. *Proceedings of the SIGPLAN 84 Symposium on Compiler Construction*, pages 247-258, June 1984. SIGPLAN Notices, Vol 19, No 6..

9. Ron Cytron. *Compile-time Scheduling and Optimization for Asynchronous Machines*, PhD thesis, University of Illinois at Urbana-Champaign, Urbana, Illinois 1984.

10. Ron Cytron. Useful Parallelism in a Multiprocessing Environment. *Proc. 1985 International Conference on Parallel Processing*, 1985.

11. David J. Kuck. *The Structure of Computers and Computations*. John Wiley and Sons, 1978.

12. D. J. Kuck, R. H. Kuhn, B. Leasure, and M. Wolfe. The Structure of an Advanced Vectorizer for Pipelined Processors. *Proceedings of CompSAC 80 (Fourth International Computer Software and Applications Conference)*, pages 709-715, October 1980.

13. Bruce R. Leasure. Compiling Serial Languages for Parallel Machines, University of Illinois at Urbana-Champaign, 1976. M.S. Thesis.

14. M. E. Mace and R. A. Wagner. Globally Optimum Selection of Memory Storage Patterns. *Proc. 1985 International Conference on Parallel Processing*, 1985.

15. David A. Padua and Michael J. Wolfe. Advanced Compiler Optimizations for Supercomputers. *Communications of the ACM*, 29(12):1184-1201, December 1986.

16. Remi Triolet, Francois Irigoin, and Paul Feautrier. Direct Parallelization of Call Statements. *Proceedings of the Sigplan '86 Symposium on Compiler Construction*, 21(7):176-185, July 1986.

17. Michael J. Wolfe. *Optimizing Supercompilers for Supercomputers*, PhD thesis, University of Illinois at Urbana-Champaign, Urbana, Illinois 1982. Report No. UIUCDCS-R-82-1105.

Parallel Systems and Computation
G. Paul and G.S. Almasi (Editors)

On the Application of Dependence Analysis and Restructuring Techniques to Parallel and Functional Languages

Ron Cytron

IBM T. J. Watson Research Center
P.O. Box 218
Yorktown Heights, New York 10598

This paper examines the interaction of dependence analysis and programming language constructs for three classes of programming languages: sequential, parallel, and functional. Dependence analysis is examined as a process by which a dependence equation is formulated and subsequently tested for appropriate solutions by a decision algorithm. This paper considers the effects of performing such analysis on each language class. Restructuring techniques that utilize dependence information are then examined for each language class.

1.0 Introduction

The advent of parallel processing has promoted research into the translation of programs, originally written for sequential machines, into a form suitable for execution on a parallel processor. Effective translation of sequential programs requires:

- Analysis to determine which operations must be executed in sequence and which operations can execute concurrently.
- Restructuring techniques to increase the consonance between a program and the resources of a parallel processor.

Dependence analysis of sequential languages has been examined in detail by Banerjee [1, 2], Wolfe [3] and Allen [4], and recent work has extended such analysis, utilizing summary information, to compute interprocedural effects [5].

Although programming in sequential languages has its advantages even for parallel processors, other programming languages have been proposed for such machines, notably *parallel* and *functional* languages. This paper examines the relationship between programming constructs in these languages and dependence analysis as originally formulated for sequential languages.

Restructuring translators such as *Parafrase* [6] utilize dependence information to optimize sequential programs for parallel processors. This paper examines a few transformations that are appropriate for parallel and functional programs. These transformations rely on the same thorough dependence analysis used for restructuring sequential programs.

2.0 Dependence Analysis

Most efforts at vectorization and parallelization look for concurrent operations with respect to iterations of a loop. Because references inside loops typically involve arrays, accurate dependence analysis must account for subscripted references. For example, classic data flow analysis would conclude that a definition of an array A reaches a use of A if a path exists from the definition site to the use site. Suppose the references actually consist of $A(2i)$ and $A(2i+1)$. By examining the subscripts, a simple test can determine the independence of the two references.

Precise dependence analysis also requires an understanding of interprocedural effects. One approach, taken by Huson [7], consists of procedure integration at call sites where interprocedural information is required. More recently, efforts have focused on utilizing summary information to capture the effects of procedure calls [8, 5, 9].

Following the approach of Burke and Cytron [5], this paper views dependence analysis in three parts:

1. The formulation of a dependence equation between two storage references. In terms of programming language constructs, the formulation of a dependence equation is relatively unaffected by the differences between sequential, parallel, and functional languages. Of interest are those statements that potentially reference the same storage locations.
2. The coupling of the dependence equation with a *context* in which the dependence should be tested. Here, the semantics of a given language dictate which contexts could support the dependence equation.
3. Deciding whether the dependence equation has solutions in its associated context. Although several decision algorithms exist, each is independent of language considerations and offers compromises between efficiency and accuracy.

Each of these aspects in considered in turn in the following sections.

Consider two statements S_x and S_y.

> A *flow dependence* exists from statement S_x to statement S_y if S_x computes and stores data that can subsequently be read by S_y.
>
> An *anti-dependence* exists between S_x and S_y if S_x reads data from a location into which S_y can subsequently store.

This paper considers only flow and anti-dependences, but dependence analysis is easily extended for input and output dependences, where the relationship between two uses or two definitions is of interest [10]. As with flow and anti-dependences, the context in which the dependence equation should be tested is governed by the choice of programming language (sequential, parallel, functional). A decision algorithm is then applied to the dependence equation in its chosen context.

2.1 Formulating a Dependence Equation

A dependence equation depicts the relationship between the access functions (subscripts) associated with "interesting" references. Two references are interesting if they potentially reference the same storage location. The scope of dependence analysis and the behavior of program references dictate which references are interesting:

- Scope of analysis: If the scope of dependence analysis is restricted to the intraprocedural level, then interprocedural aliasing and the effects of procedure calls cannot be accommodated. As a result, dependence analysis must assume that all locations visible from a call site are referenced. With respect to formal parameters, dependence analysis must assume that all parameters are aliased to each other and to all global variables. Through assertions, a user could specify the effects of procedure calls. Some languages preclude aliasing in certain situations: In Fortran, a variable cannot be modified where it is interprocedurally aliased with other variables.

- Behavior of references: If references to subscripted variables always remain within the declared extent of the variables, then dependence equations can be restricted to references of the same variable (or the variable's aliases if aliasing is accommodated) [5].

Suppose the statements S_x and S_y are surrounded by d normalized loops. (A normalized loop has an initial setting and increment of unity. Any iterative loop with constant increment can be normalized, and the references to the iteration variable can be adjusted accordingly [11].) Let $I = (i_1, i_2, ..., i_d)$ represent the iteration variables of the loops, where i_1 corresponds to the outermost loop and i_d to the innermost loop. A dependence (flow or anti-) between S_x and S_y implies that the execution of S_y must follow S_x with respect to the iterations of *some* of the d loops.

More formally, let S_x and S_y reference the variable A as shown in Figure 1, with subscript functions f and g at the definition and use of A, respectively. Consider an *instance* of statement S_x that executes when $I = X$ $(i_1 = x_1, i_2 = x_2, ..., i_d = x_d)$ and an instance of statement S_y with $I = Y$. The dependence equation that corresponds to the references is simply: $f(x_1, x_2,...,x_d) = g(y_1, y_2,...,y_d)$.

```
DO i1 = 1 TO N1
  ...
    DO id = 1 TO Nd
Sx:   A(f(i1,...,id)) = ...
Sy:        ... = A(g(i1,...,id))
     END
  ...
END
```

Figure 1. Normalized Loops with Array References.

If f and g are linear functions of the iteration variables, then the subscript functions can be written:

$$f(x_1, x_2,...x_d) = \sum_{k=1}^{d} a_k x_k + a_0 \qquad [2.1]$$

and

$$g(y_1, y_2,...y_d) = \sum_{k=1}^{d} b_k y_k + b_0, \qquad [2.2]$$

where a_k, b_k, a_0, and b_0 are integer constants. The dependence equation then becomes:

$$\sum_{k=1}^{d} (a_k x_k - b_k y_k) = b_0 - a_0 \qquad [2.3]$$

In this paper, as in extant work, subscripts are assumed to be linear functions of iteration variables.

2.2 Establishing a Context for a Dependence Equation

Consider the instances of iteration variables that appear in dependence equations as free variables. For the iteration variables $(i_1, i_2, ..., i_d)$, let the iteration vector $X = (x_1, x_2, ...x_d)$ be associated with statement S_x and $Y = (y_1, y_2, ...y_d)$ be associated with statement S_y. Following the notation of Wolfe, the iteration vectors X and Y can be summarized by the direction vector Z that reflects the sign of

$Y - X$, with each element z_k of the direction vector specifying the relationship between x_k and y_k for which the dependence holds [3].

1. If z_k = "=", then the dependence holds within the same iteration of loop k.
2. If z_k = "<", then the dependence holds from some iteration of loop k to a subsequent iteration.
3. If z_k = ">", then the dependence holds from some iteration of loop k to an earlier iteration.

The previous section shows how to formulate a dependence equation, but not all values assumable by the free variables of a dependence equation are "interesting" in the sense of supporting a dependence:

1. Iteration variables assume only integer values, so a dependence exists only if some solution to the dependence equation assigns integer values to the free variables.
2. An iteration variable typically iterates over a fixed range. A solution to the dependence equation must assign values to the free variables that lie within the range of their associated iteration variables.
3. A direction vector constrains the relationship between instances of iteration variables. A solution to the dependence equation must assign values to the iteration variable instances that respect a supplied direction vector. As described later, language semantics dictate an appropriate choice of direction vectors.

Consider the example of Figure 1 in the context of sequential languages, where two loops iterating from 1 to 10 surround the assignment statements. Note that a dependence exists only if a solution assigns integer values in the range (1,2,...,10) to the iteration vectors.

Now consider the appropriate direction vector constraints. For a flow dependence to exist, an instance of S_y must *subsequently* reference data stored by an instance of S_x. Values for the iteration vectors X and Y are *plausible* if the corresponding instance of S_x executes before the instance of S_y. Figure 2 shows solutions for plausible iteration vectors. The direction vectors are shown next to the iteration vectors. The iteration vectors shown in Figure 3 are implausible.

X	Y	Z
(1,1)	(2,2)	(<,<)
(3,3)	(4,3)	(<,=)
(2,5)	(3,2)	(<,>)
(8,9)	(8,9)	(=,=)

Figure 2. Plausible Direction Vectors: For a flow dependence in two loops from a sequential program.

X	Y	Z
(3,5)	(3,2)	(=,>)
(6,6)	(5,7)	(>,<)
(5,3)	(2,3)	(>,=)
(7,4)	(3,2)	(>,>)

Figure 3. Implausible Direction Vectors

Direction vectors can be combined in an intuitive manner. For example, "≤" implies that a dependence holds for "<" or "=". As a notational convenience, let "*" imply that no constraints hold between the pair of iteration values. ("*" designates the union of "<", "=", and ">".)

The semantics of sequential programming languages, in particular those associated with iterative loops, dictate which direction vectors are plausible. Section 3.0 discusses contexts relevant to parallel and functional languages.

2.3 Solving a Dependence Equation

This section describes various methods of obtaining solutions to the formulated dependence equation in its specified context. Following the approach in Burke and Cytron [5], a decision algorithm will initially be invoked under the most general of relationships between instances of an iteration variable (direction vector of (*,*,...,*)), and then subsequently invoked on more refined direction vectors until either independence has been shown or dependence has been shown with respect to a specific direction vector. For example, if two loops surround a pair of references, then decision algorithms are first invoked on the root of the tree shown in Figure 4. Refinement proceeds toward the leaves of the tree. If independence can be shown at any node, then further refinement of that node is unnecessary.

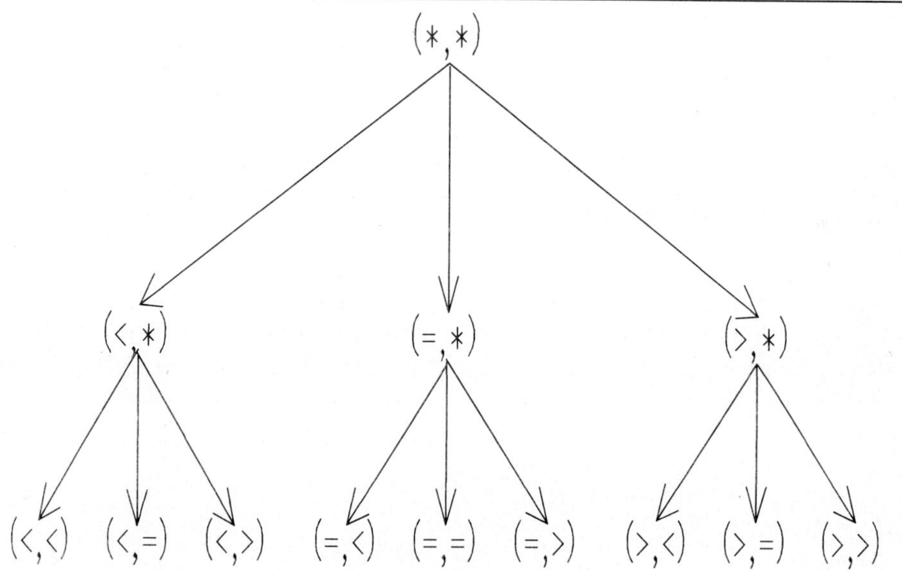

Figure 4. Direction Vector Tree for Two Loops

2.3.1 GCD Test

This test, based on diophantine theory [12, 13], determines if the dependence equation has any integer solutions. This section sketches how this test can be applied to a direction vector tree, such as the one shown in Figure 4. Consider the coefficients a_k and b_k for instances of the iteration variable i_k. The coefficients must stand as distinct terms of the dependence equation (multipliers of x_k and y_k) for any direction vector except "=". However, for the "=" direction vector, $x_k = y_k$ and the coefficients can be combined. Therefore, in refining direction vectors, the GCD test can be reapplied where an element of a direction vector becomes "=". For example, the dependence equation:

$$3x + 4y = 8$$

apparently has solutions for $x < y$ and $x > y$ (and therefore has solutions for "*"), but for $x = y$, the dependence equation becomes:

```
7x = 8
```

which has no integer solutions.

The following algorithm shows how the GCD test is applied to a dependence equation.

Input:

A dependence equation of the form shown in Formula [2.3].
A direction vector $Z = (z_1, z_2, \dots, z_d)$ as the context in which the dependence equation should be tested.

Output:

The decision as to whether the dependence equation has any integer solutions in its associated context.

for k:=1 to d do

if z_k="="

then $t_k = a_k - b_k$

else $t_k = \gcd(a_k, b_k)$

end for

if $\gcd(t_1, t_2, \dots, t_d) \mid (b_0 - a_0)$

then return DEPENDENCE

else return INDEPENDENCE

Note that the GCD test does not accommodate all information provided by the context:

1. The GCD test does not distinguish between "*", "<", and ">" direction vectors.
2. The GCD test does not restrict free variables to their respective iteration variable ranges.

The GCD test is therefore conservative and can only prove independence. For example, the GCD test proves independence in the loop of Figure 5. However, in the example shown in Figure 6, the GCD test cannot determine independence except for the "=" direction vector.

```
DO i=1 TO N
   A(2i)  =
                 = A(2i+1)
   END

Dependence Equation:
   2x  -  2y  =  1

 Direction Vector (*):
   GCD(2,2)  = 2 which does not
                    divide 1
          -->    Independence
```

Figure 5. GCD Test Shows Independence

```
DO i=1 TO N
   A(i) =
         = A(i+1)
   END

Dependence Equation:
   x - y = 1

 Direction Vector (*):
   GCD(1,1) = 1 which does
                 divide 1
        -->    Dependence

 Direction Vector (=):
   0 = 1

        -->    Independence
```

Figure 6. GCD Test Fails to Show Independence

2.3.2 Banerjee-Wolfe Inexact

This test was originally formulated by Banerjee [2] and subsequently extended to accommodate direction vectors by Wolfe [3]. In terms of the direction vector tree shown in Figure 4, Wolfe applies the inexact test in the context of each plausible leaf of the tree. A union is then taken over all leaves that fail to show independence to arrive at a single direction vector of sufficient generality to cover those leaves.

Burke and Cytron [5] modified the inexact test to allow testing in the context of any node of the tree shown in Figure 4. Where independence is shown, further refinement of a node is unnecessary. The tree is also convenient for summarizing the resulting set of dependence direction vectors. For example, if (<,*) appears in the set, then independence could not be shown for (<,<), (<,=), or (<,>).

In terms of its accuracy, the inexact test is also conservative: although the ranges of iteration variables are honored, the test does not guarantee integer-valued solutions. This test, in fact, can show independence in the example of Figure 6 for the direction vector (<) (where GCD failed to show independence), but cannot show independence in Figure 5 for the (*) direction vector. The details of this test are beyond the scope of this paper, but do appear elsewhere [2, 3, 5].

2.3.3 Exact Tests

An exact test honors all aspects of the context associated with a dependence equation. Banerjee and Wolfe provide an exact test for a single loop [1, 3]. Triolet [8] utilizes an algorithm due to Shostak [14] that determines whether a system of linear inequalities is *feasible*. As discussed in Burke and Cytron [5], exact tests are efficient for certain forms of subscripts. In the worse case, however, an exact test requires exponential time with respect to the loop nest.

3.0 Dependence Analysis and Language Semantics

This section describes the relationship between dependence analysis and sequential, parallel, and functional languages. In particular, the semantics of a given class of languages dictates which contexts are appropriate for dependence analysis.

3.1 Sequential Languages

This section considers ordinary imperative sequential languages such as Fortran. As was shown in Section 2.2, only a subset of all possible direction vectors are appropriate for loops that arise from sequential languages. Returning to the tree shown in Figure 4, those direction vectors to the left of and including the (=,=) direction vector correspond to situations in which statement S_x executes before statement S_y in the sequential execution. A flow dependence is only possible where this ordering is possible. Consider now an anti-dependence between S_y and S_x. Again, only the plausible direction vectors provide a situation in which S_y must complete before S_x. It might appear then that the leaves to the right of the (=,=) direction vector are irrelevant for dependence analysis of sequential languages. However, Burke and Cytron have shown that a flow (anti-) dependence under a plausible direction vector is equivalent to an anti- (flow) dependence under an implausible direction vector [5].

Thus, only a single test is required to disprove flow and anti-dependence, and dependence analysis can consider both sides of the dependence tree in Figure 4 for sequential languages. After analysis, a (potentially empty) set of direction vectors will hold for the dependence equation. Where a transformation distinguishes between flow and anti-dependences, elements of the set are easily identified as to their type (flow or anti-) of dependence.

3.2 Parallel Languages

This section considers dependence analysis for some parallel language constructs. First consider an "array" assignment statement, such as the one shown in Figure 7. When executed, the array assignment statement should appear as if all values of A are fetched before any value is stored. Such an execution would honor all anti-dependences yet disregard all flow dependences. This execution can be accomplished by executing all iterations and storing the results in the temporary T, as shown in the second program fragment of Figure 7. After all results are computed, the temporary T is copied to A.

Although the semantics of the array assignment statement can be achieved through temporaries, the space and time requirements of a computation can be decreased by performing the array assignment statement without temporaries. If the output of the array assignment statement is disjoint from its inputs, then no temporary is necessary. Consider the case where overlap exists between the output and inputs. If the statement is actually executed in parallel, then all fetches precede all stores, and the compiler need not test for any dependences. However, suppose this ordering of fetches and stores cannot be guaranteed at compile-time. For example, consider the sequential execution of the statement shown as the third program fragment in Figure 7. This execution fails to honor the anti-dependence. The fourth program fragment does honor the anti-dependence by reversing the order in which loop iterations are executed.

```
Original Statement:
   A(2::N) = A(1::N-1) + B(1::N-1)

Correct Sequential Execution using Temporaries:
   DO i=2,N
      T(i) = A(i-1) + B(i)
      ENDDO
   DO i=2,N
      A(i) = T(i)
      ENDDO

Incorrect Sequential Execution:
   DO i=2,N
      A(i) = A(i-1) + B(i)
      ENDDO

Correct Sequential Execution:
   DO i=N,2,-1
      A(i) = A(i-1) + B(i)
      ENDDO
```

Figure 7. An Array Assignment Statement

Where overlap exists between output and inputs, and where the use of temporaries should be avoided, a compiler must perform dependence analysis to determine if a given sequential execution of an array assignment statement fails to honor anti-dependences. Recall that for sequential languages, half of a direction vector tree (Figure 4) must be searched for both flow and anti-dependences. The array assignment statement of Figure 7 places no constraints with respect to indexing, but no flow dependences can be introduced when executing the statement. Thus, the entire tree must be searched. Any direction vector for which flow independence can be shown causes no problems for sequential execution of the array assignment statement. For example, if flow independence is shown for the direction vector (<,<), then the iterations (1,1), (2,2), (3,3), ..., (N,N) honor anti-dependences when executed sequentially.

Burke has demonstrated another use of dependence analysis: determining correctly-formed IDENTIFY statements in (a proposed) Fortran 8X language [15]. IDENTIFY statements must not yield "many-to-one" mappings between the host and identified arrays. Burke proposes a run-time test to analyze the subscript expressions, determining where such illegal mappings occur.

3.3 Functional Languages

Functional languages require programs to obey the single-assignment rule: a program cannot contain any output dependences. Without output dependences, a program cannot contain any anti-dependences unless it references uninitialized variables. Given that the single-assignment rule is followed, a dependence equation need not be tested in contexts of anti-dependence. However, a compiler could perform anti-dependence tests and issue compile-time diagnostics concerning the presence of (or potential for) anti-dependences.

4.0 Dependence Analysis and Restructuring Techniques

Although dependence analysis is typically used for restructuring sequential programs, this section provides some examples of transformations for functional programs. The first section describes a method for transforming nonfunctional programs (written in a language such as Fortran) into programs that obey the single-assignment rule of functional programming. The last section describes how copy operations that fail to increase the parallelism of a functional program can be eliminated.

Numerous sequential loop transformations are based on direction vectors: loop interchanging [3], alignment [16], loop fusion [3], loop distribution (vectorization) [6], and doacross [17]. The interested reader is referred to a survey by Padua and Wolfe [18] for an excellent overview of these techniques.

4.1 Creating Single-Assignment Programs

This section considers the transformation of programs into a form that obeys the single-assignment rule. Note that all anti- and output dependences could be eliminated by creating a new copy of a variable at each definition site. For structures larger than scalars, such copying can become very expensive. Based on the work of Ferrante [19], this section proposes a series of transformations that eliminates anti- and output dependences from a "structured" program. Each transformation accommodates one simple programming construct, but constructs of greater complexity can be accommodated by repeated applications of the simple transformations. For each construct, a bound is placed on the extra storage required to satisfy the single-assignment rule.

4.1.1 Straight-Line Code

Consider a fragment of code as shown in Figure 8.

```
     Before                          After
     ------                          -----

    a = expr1                     a1 = expr1
    b = a + ...                   b  = a1 + ...
        .                            .
        .                            .
        .                            .
    a = expr2                     a2 = expr2
    c = a + ...                   c  = a2 + ...
```

Figure 8. Straight-Line Code and Renaming

This code corresponds to a basic block with multiple definitions of some variable a. Using a well-known technique [20], instances of a are renamed to $a1$ and $a2$. All uses occurring between the definition of $a1$ and $a2$ must reference $a1$ and all uses after the definition of $a2$ must reference $a2$. Any number of variables within basic blocks can be renamed in this way.

Because the definitions lie along the same path, this transformation must create a new copy of each multiply-defined variable. However, the bound on the numbers of copies can be determined at compile-time and the space (names) can be preallocated. If the space were dynamically allocated at run-time, then some indirection would be required to locate the "current" value of a variable.

4.1.2 Multiple Reaching Definitions (No Loops)

Now consider a fragment of code as shown in Figure 9.

```
 Before                   After
 ------                   -----

a = expr1                a1 = expr1
if (c) then              if (c) then
   a = expr2                a2 = expr2
                         else
   fi                       a2 = a1
                            fi

                         birthpoint a2(a)
b = a                    b = a2
```

Figure 9. Multiple Reaching Definitions

Two definitions of *a* reach the statement that defines *b*. Distinct names cannot be chosen for the definitions of *a* because the proper value must flow to the definition of *b*. Cytron, Lowry, and Zadeck [21] provide a renaming algorithm based on the the idea of *birthpoints* [22]. A birthpoint occurs where multiple definitions reach a use. In this transformation, the renaming of the birthpoint variable is propagated back to its reaching definitions. Although multiple assignments appear in the code, single-assignment is preserved because only one branch is taken at run-time. The number of names is bounded because the number of birthpoints can be determined at compile-time.

4.1.3 Repeatedly Executed Statements

The above transformations accommodate multiple assignments to variables so long as no statement is executed twice. Now consider statements that appear in loops, as shown in Figure 10.

```
Before                   After
------                   -----

do while (c)             do while (c)
     = x                          = OLD x
  x =                      NEW x =
     = x                          = x
  enddo                    enddo
```

Figure 10. Statements in Loops

In general, a new copy of *x* is required each time a definition site for *x* is executed. Suppose the number of definitions of *x* can be determined at compile-time, perhaps through iteration variable analysis. Then the anti- and output dependences can be broken by *scalar expansion* [23]. The scalar is changed to an array with sufficient elements to hold each definition of the scalar. Where such information is unavailable, statements must dynamically create new copies of defined variables, as shown in Figure 10. A finite number of previous generations can be maintained through the "OLD" function:

```
NEW z = OLD y
NEW y = OLD x
```

maintains two old generations of x through y and z.

4.2 Eliminating Unnecessary Copying in Functional Programs

Consider now the goal of eliminating unnecessary uses of "NEW" from single-assignment programs. For example, consider the program shown in Figure 11.

```
for i:=1 to N do
  NEW x = x + A(i)
```

Figure 11. A Vector Sum

Each iteration of the loop causes a new instance of x to be created. This section discusses situations in which parallelism is not adversely affected by allocating a single location for all values of a variable. Recall that the single-assignment rule suffices to eliminate output (and therefore anti-) dependences, thereby increasing the parallelism of a program. (Note that the transformations discussed in Section 4.1 eliminate such dependences from programs that do not obey the single-assignment rule.) In the program shown in Figure 11, distinct instances of x do not contribute to the parallelism of the program fragment. Consequently, it would be reasonable to consider the reuse of x.

In general, consider some statement S that is "ready" to execute, in the sense that its inputs are available. Suppose S computes a value for variable x, and consider the set $R(S)$ of variables that are available when S is ready to execute. This set can be constructed recursively from the inputs to statement S: Since the inputs of S are available, the statements that computed those inputs must have their inputs available, and so on. If x (the output of statement S) is in $R(S)$ and if there are no other uses of x, then statement S can reuse the location for x, since the value stored there is no longer needed.

5.0 Conclusion

This paper has examined the role of dependence analysis for three classes of languages. Although dependence analysis has been well-established for sequential languages, with the goals of vectorization and parallelization, this paper has described the effects of parallel and functional languages on dependence analysis. Restructuring transformations, based on dependence analysis, have been described for these languages.

Acknowledgements

The author is grateful to Fran Allen, whose observations on the relationship of programming constructs to dependence analysis motivated the theme of this paper, and to David Kuck and David Padua who first demonstrated the need for dependence analysis outside the realm of sequential languages. The author is also grateful to Michael Burke, whose collaboration on a previous paper established the relationship of interprocedural information to dependence analysis. Most of Section 2 is borrowed from the paper coauthored by Michael Burke [5]. The author also thanks members of the PTRAN group at IBM Research and Todd Allen for their comments on this work.

Bibliography

1. Utpal Banerjee. Data Dependence in Ordinary Programs, University of Illinois at Urbana-Champaign1976. M.S. Thesis.

2. Utpal Banerjee. *Speedup of Ordinary Programs*, PhD thesis, University of Illinois at Urbana-Champaign, Urbana, Illinois 1979.

3. Michael J. Wolfe. *Optimizing Supercompilers for Supercomputers*, PhD thesis, University of Illinois at Urbana-Champaign, Urbana, Illinois 1982. Report No. UIUCDCS-R-82-1105.

4. John R. Allen. *Dependence Analysis for Subscript Variables and Its Application to Program Transformations*, PhD thesis, Rice University, Houston, Texas 1983.

5. Michael Burke and Ron Cytron. Interprocedural Dependence Analysis and Parallelization. *Proceedings of the Sigplan '86 Symposium on Compiler Construction*, 21(7):162-175, July 1986.

6. D. J. Kuck, R. H. Kuhn, B. Leasure, and M. Wolfe. The Structure of an Advanced Vectorizer for Pipelined Processors. *Proceedings of CompSAC 80 (Fourth International Computer Software and Applications Conference)*, pages 709-715, October 1980.

7. Christopher A. Huson. An In-Line Subroutine Expander for Parafrase, University of Illinois at Urbana-Champaign1982. M.S. Thesis.

8. Remi Triolet. *Contribution a la Parellisation Automatique de Programmes Fortran Comportant des Appels de Procedure*, PhD thesis, L'Universite Pierre et Marie Curie (Paris VI), Paris, France 1984.

9. Remi Triolet, Francois Irigoin, and Paul Feautrier. Direct Parallelization of Call Statements. *Proceedings of the Sigplan '86 Symposium on Compiler Construction*, 21(7):176-185, July 1986.

10. David J. Kuck. *The Structure of Computers and Computations*. John Wiley and Sons, 1978.

11. Bruce R. Leasure. Compiling Serial Languages for Parallel Machines, University of Illinois at Urbana-Champaign1976. M.S. Thesis.

12. H. Griffin. *Elementary Theory of Numbers*. McGraw-Hill, 1954.

13. A. M. Kirch. *Elementary Number Theory.* Intext, 1974.

14. Robert Shostak. Deciding Linear Inequalities by Computing Loop Residues. *Journal of the Association for Computing Machinery*, 28(4), 1981.

15. Michael Burke. A Test for Determining whether an IDENTIFY Statement is Many-to-One, IBM1986. Research Report RC12150.

16. David Alejandro Padua Haiek. *Multiprocessors: Discussions of some Theoretical and Practical Problems*, PhD thesis, University of Illinois at Urbana-Champaign, Urbana, Illinois 1979. Report No. UIUCDCS-R-79-99.

17. Ron Cytron. Doacross: Beyond Vectorization for Multiprocessors. *Proceedings of the 1986 International Conference on Parallel Processing*, 1986.

18. David A. Padua and Michael J. Wolfe. Advanced Compiler Optimizations for Supercomputers. *Communications of the ACM*, 29(12):1184-1201, December 1986.

19. Jeanne Ferrante. What's in a Name? Or the Value of Renaming for Parallelism Detection and Storage Allocation, IBM1986. Research Report RC12157.

20. Alfred V. Aho and Jeffrey D. Ullman. *The Theory of Parsing, Translation, and Compiling, Volume II.* Prentice-Hall, Inc., 1973.

21. Ron Cytron, Andy Lowry, and Ken Zadeck. Code Motion of Control Structures in High-Level Languages. *Conf. Rec. of the ACM Symp. on Principles of Compiler Construction*, 1986.

22. J. H. Reif and R. E. Tarjan. Symbolic Program Analysis in Almost Linear Time. *SIAM Journal of Computing*, 11(1):81-93, February 1981.

23. Michael J. Wolfe. Techniques for Improving the Inherent Parallelism in Programs, University of Illinois at Urbana-Champaign1978. M.S. Thesis.

Parallel Systems and Computation
G. Paul and G.S. Almasi (Editors)

EPEX – ENVIRONMENT FOR PARALLEL EXECUTION

David A. George
Prototype Systems
IBM T. J. Watson Research Center
P.O. Box 218 H4-D36
Yorktown Heights, NY 10598 USA

This paper describes a system that allows use of the standard environments of the IBM Virtual Machine/System Product High Performance Option (VM/SP/HPO), herein referred to as "VM", and the IBM Multiple Virtual Storages Operating System Extended Architecture (MVS/XA) to achieve parallel processing.

1.0 Introduction

Environment for Parallel Execution, or ***EPEX***, was intended to assist in the research of parallel systems by permitting development of applications that would run in parallel and to expose the system state of those applications using various simulation tools. EPEX provides (for a single user) the capability to activate multiple processes and supports direct memory sharing. Non-shared, local data is also permitted. Memory-based semaphores for inter-process communications to accomplish synchronization is also supported. EPEX supports the addition of user constructs (via subroutines) that represent emulated functions to be provided by other architectures thus allowing the user to evaluate mechanisms and techniques without recourse to actually building a hardware prototype first.

EPEX was conceived as a system to permit emulation of the architecture of the Research Parallel Processor Prototype (RP3) [1]. RP3 employs 512 microprocessors with 1000 to 2000 megabytes of storage, giving a sustained performance of 1000 MIPS and 800 MFLOPS for a wide range of applications. Interprocessor communications is achieved by a high bandwidth shared memory system that is implemented with state-of-the-art technology and design. EPEX emulates the RP3 environment on the native S/370 architecture providing a means to develop applications that actually utilize the core features of RP3, particularly in the area of data sharing and process coordination. The coordination used among the processes is exposed to the application program level and requires no explicit service by the operating system. Actual ***speedup*** is obtained when running applications under EPEX on the IBM 3081, 3084 and 3090 computers as they contain two or more central processing units.

In this paper a brief history is first discussed, thereafter the system implementation is discussed beginning with the core layer of the system for each of VM and MVS environments. Thereafter, a description of subroutines useful to our research at the IBM T. J. Watson Research Center is given, followed by a description of the high level interface called the ***Preprocessor***[5].

2.0 History

During the period 1981 to 1984, researchers in the Computer Science Department at the IBM T. J. Watson Research Center have performed experiments using S/370-168 computers coupled together in duplex (two-way) and as a triplex (three-way) using experimental modifications to the base design. The modifications were applied as temporary engineering changes that compromised proper machine characteristics for other experiments, hence the changeover process was difficult, error-prone and very time consuming. The author devised a VM environment suitable for emulating the hardware that exploited the simplicity of the VM debugging and control. In addition, various changes were devised for the VM operating system nucleus to support operation of virtual systems (i.e., use of dynamic address translation) such as MVS and VM running ***second-level***. The environment was configured very rigorously for particular users and exploited no more than a few virtual machines working concurrently as it was intended to provide a convenient alternative to scheduling precious machine time on the real hardware. Real hardware facilitated authenticating results, providing timing information and other demonstrations.

During the onset of the project to propose and build a massively parallel computer called the Research Parallel Processor Prototype (RP3), a new requirement for running applications was identified. The core system was incorporated into an all new design, a comprehensive environment for running application programs in a pseudo parallel machine environment. The EPEX system has many productive features as convenient resource scheduling and a high-level program language interface [2]. A similar core environment was later developed for MVS.

3.0 Core of EPEX

The system is comprised of independent ***invocations*** of the S/370 instruction stream: ***tasks*** in MVS (Figure 2) and ***virtual machines*** in VM (Figure 1), wherein each invocation has associated with itself two types of processor storage: private and shared. In VM, up to sixty-four virtual machines may actually be enjoined to perform a parallel program, however, it requires only two to take advantage of real-time speedup from a two-way MP, such as the IBM 3081. In MVS, EPEX is limited by the language environment and addressing region for the number of tasks. A practical limit is two tasks for EPEX-FORTRAN programs.

The invocations are referred to as ***processes*** in this paper. An initial number of processes is set by the user and the parallel job begins with all of them activated. Each obtains access to the shared memory and begins program initialization. Inter-process synchronization and communication is accomplished by memory-based semaphores.

3.1 Semaphores

Process control and inter-process communications is accomplished by sharing a portion of the storage addressing space. Via the memory, semaphores, shared variables that signal events or the assignment of a work element to a process are used. The semaphores are modified using the ***Compare and Swap*** (CS) instruction which permits support of a conditional alteration of storage based on the content. Furthermore, this is not a restricted (privileged) operation, hence this communications approach is direct and nearly instantaneous. Other shared variables are readily accessible to the independent processes.

EPEX has a private and shared memory configuration similar in construct to the RP3. In RP3, a single program technique has been proposed [7] as a reasonable means to allow programmers to construct programs that operate on separate tasks or virtual machines. All processes execute the same program in parallel, relying on memory-based semaphores for synchronization (i.e., relies on a shared memory architecture). Distribution of work is achieved via a dynamic process using the semaphores by processes that are created at the beginning of the execution of the parallel program. The processes remain in existence until the program execution is complete. The processes do not necessarily use the same copy of the program code, nor do they necessarily process instruction code at the same relative points within the programs (i.e., the MIMD model is supported). Following this model, programs may easily be written to perform a medium to coarse grain parallelism. Conventional program compilers are used to create the code and to define the common areas that contain the shared data and semaphores. A subroutine to perform the Compare and Swap instruction is provided in the EPEX package for supported languages. Common linkage and program object building techniques are used under the Conversational Monitor System (CMS) of VM and MVS.

Fine grain parallelism is generally achieved in single instruction multiple data machines. Vector arithmetic units are within this classification. EPEX permits usage of the vector capability of a processor, such as in the IBM 3090. Medium grain parallelism is the process of executing ***DO LOOPS*** by two or more processes. Each active processor obtains a share or chunk of loop indices to perform and overlaps its processing with the other processors. EPEX subroutines and the high-level preprocessor support easy usage of medium grain parallelism. Coarse grain parallelism is the term referring to disjoint invocations of subroutines or whole programs, available to the EPEX user. At this writing, the principle work has been done using the single program approach as it is easier to construct such programs.

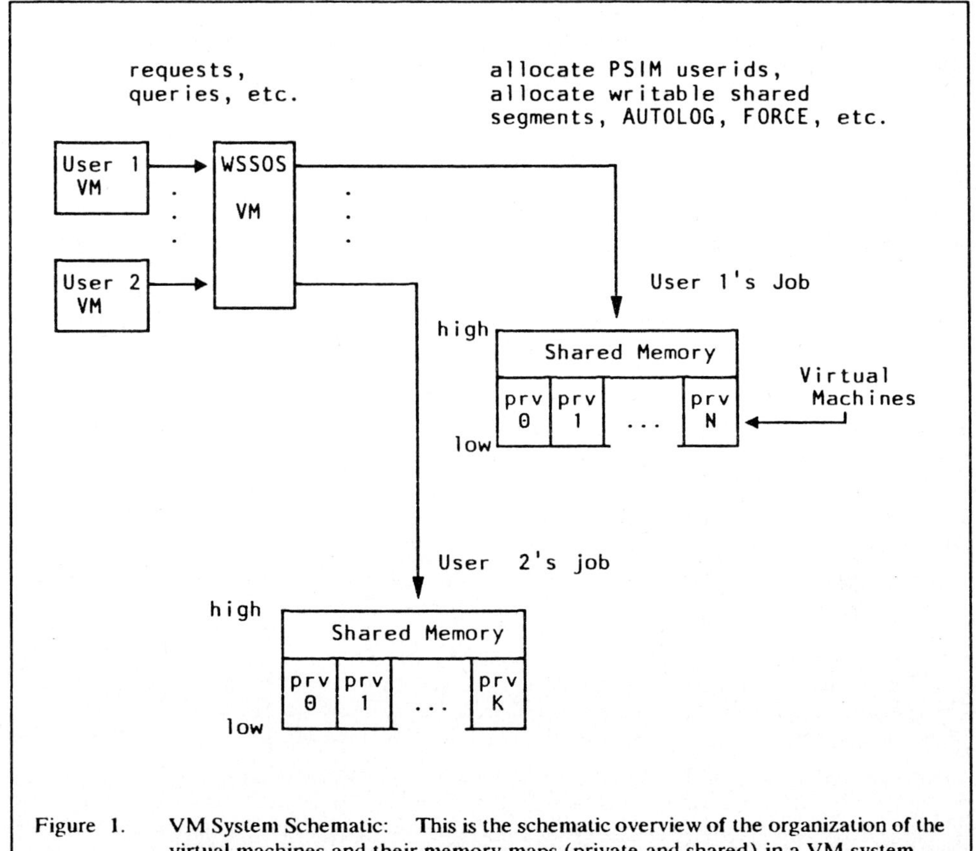

Figure 1. VM System Schematic: This is the schematic overview of the organization of the virtual machines and their memory maps (private and shared) in a VM system.

3.1.1 Parallel Forks

The process of distributing the work, either medium or coarse grain parallelism, is relatively simple to perform. One such method is to distribute an iteration loop (in Fortran, a ***DO***-loop). A single processor would simply use a symbolic location in memory (e.g., "I") to keep track of the iteration count. At each iteration, the content is updated by the loop increment and the process continues until the count exceeds some limit value. For an EPEX program, the symbolic location in memory is used as before (within a shared common area), however, it is updated by use of the Compare-and-Swap (CS) instruction (see later section for description of the RP3's Fetch-and-Ops). Each process attempts to update the value by the loop increment. If the CS is successful, the body of the loop is processed, providing that that limit value was not exceeded. The body of the loop must contain a process that will be correctly computed in light of the parallelism, such as the avoidance of calculation performed "in-place" in vectors [7]. Since other processes are attempting to update memory ("I"), some will find that the conditional change was unsuccessful, requiring a repeat attempt until the CS is successful. The overhead is not too great, requiring at the most that ***N-1*** processes would require only one retry.

3.1.2 Parallel Joins

The process of synchronizing the processes, such as the case of making all of them meet at a common point (i.e., ***parallel join***) before continuation into a process that requires all previous parallel compu-

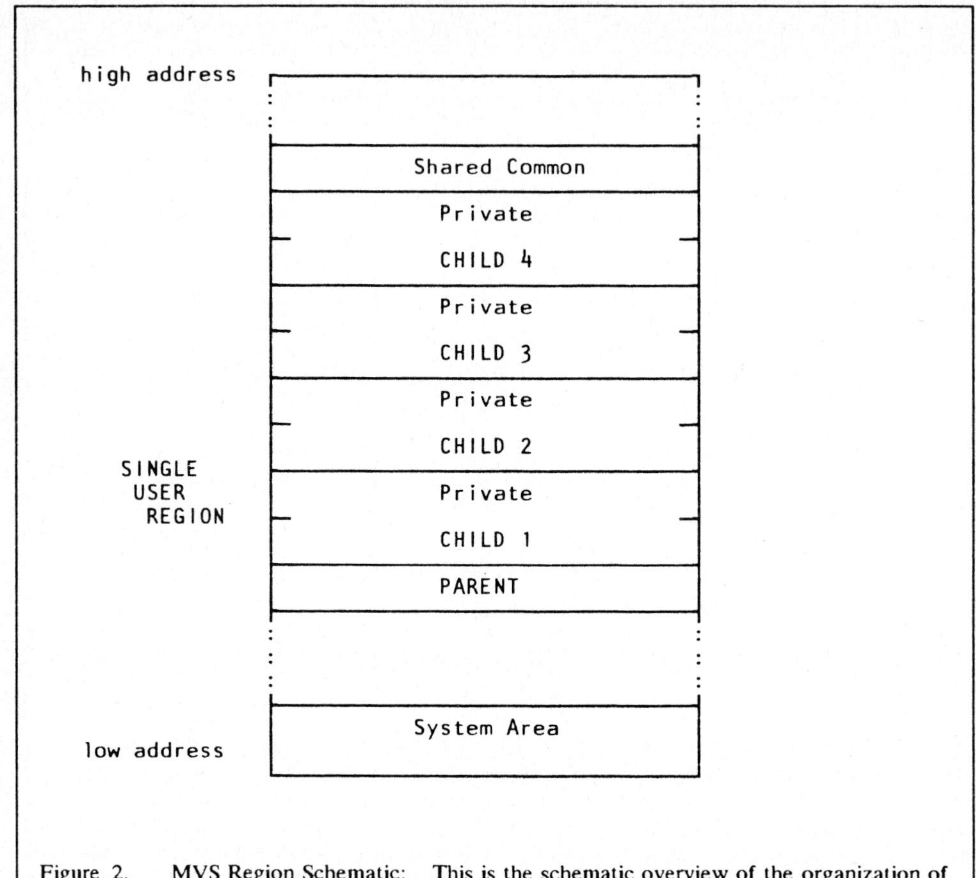

Figure 2. MVS Region Schematic: This is the schematic overview of the organization of the MVS tasks and their usage of memory (private and shared) running as a job in an MVS system.

tation to be completed is significantly more difficult to implement. A standard technique is to provide a mechanism for processor to processor interrupts, however this would necessitate operating system calls. Additionally, signaling methodology must generally be setup as ***list directed*** to handle the possibility of multiple concurrent events that require event posting. Signaling has been tried experimentally by A. Karp at the IBM Programming Center at Palo Alto using pseudo channel to channel adapters and other inter-virtual machine communications. At this writing it is not yet formally included in the EPEX package.

Another means to implement parallel joins is to simply allow a process to routinely check the content of storage (i.e., a ***spin loop***) to learn of the arrival of other processors to the join. A simple example is shown in Figure 3.

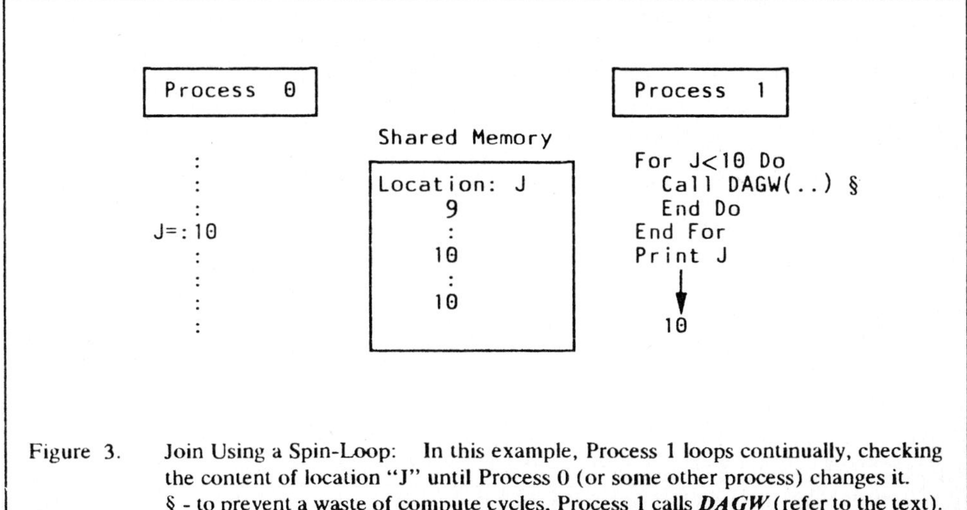

Figure 3. Join Using a Spin-Loop: In this example, Process 1 loops continually, checking the content of location "J" until Process 0 (or some other process) changes it. § - to prevent a waste of compute cycles, Process 1 calls ***DAGW*** (refer to the text).

To be acceptable in a time-sharing environment, a process should not simply use up CPU cycles in a spin loop. To avoid the wasted cycles, a special routine ***DAGW*** was developed. It requests a temporary drop in dispatching eligibility for a virtual machine or task that is long enough to allow all peers to have an opportunity to execute their piece of a time slice or relinquish their eligibility in the identical manner [4].

3.2 VM Core

The user prepares a program in two parts: one is the actual collection of main program and other subroutines, the other is a null program that contains only the declaration of the shared common areas (no instructions). These are compiled separately and link-edited into a storage segmentation that rigorously matches the boundaries of private and shared storage allocation that is planned by the user for his parallel job. Refer to Figure 7. The resultant operable module is thus made ready for subsequent execution with a user-provided EXEC procedure that invokes it after initializing the operational memory environment (obtaining the addressability and access to shared memory).

Although no modification to the VM system nucleus is required, a one-time task performed by the systems programmer is to define the Unprotected Named Shared Segments (called ***writable shared segments, or WSS*** herein) within the system name table, DMKSNT, an assembly file. Each entry of the table describes an area of memory allocation with an explicit name. WSSs are part of the overall support of addressing space for virtual machines, which is referred to as discontiguous shared named segments (DSS). DSSs are generally used to allow sharing common code and data that is expected to be handled as ***read-only***. Examples are the CMS nucleus, the CMS editor (XEDIT), compilers and interpreters. VM permits these named storage areas to be defined, initialized, and optionally to be specified as writeable.

A CMS EXEC-callable routine, DAGMEG4, is used to pass the request to load WSSs to the control program (CP) of the VM system. Parameters are first placed on the console stack, then the routine performs the desired diagnose call (a means to communicate with CP) to define the shared memory environment.

In VM, the virtual machines are invoked via the ***CP AUTOLOG*** command which also specifies the initial EXEC file for CMS to perform (refer to Figure 1). Generally, an EXEC is prepared that obtains the necessary storage, declares all CMS file definitions and and invokes the program. The Writeable Shared Segment Operating System (***WSSOS***) provides the user support in this task, simplifying the process as much as practical. Thereafter, the program code itself must contend with the other parallel executing processes to perform the work. When the program terminates, the EXEC resumes and performs ***house-keeping***, such as sending output to the user's private userid and logging-off the virtual machine, making it available for others to use.

In VM, DAGW supports the parallel join by permitting a drop in eligibility for the VM Scheduler to dispatch the requesting virtual machine. Consequently, virtual machines are dispatched in a ***round-robin*** fashion, thus eliminating the undesirable overhead that could result from ***spin loops***. This technique uses the same CPU Clock Comparator "hook" that MVS or VM operating systems employ when operating under VM. Explicit timer calls in VM would not obtain the desired result as they employ an intrinsic serialization within the MP environment of the Control Program of VM itself (i.e., diagnose calls generally imply building a request block for CP execution, obtaining storage for the block involves "lock" handling) thus defeating the potential for real speedup in EPEX execution.

3.2.1 Batch Monitor (Writeable Shared Segment Operating System)

WSSOS (see Figure 1) provides a means to initiate, inspect and terminate operation of "batch" virtual machines. A user communicates requests to WSSOS using panels from his own VM userid and actions are performed by the WSSOS service machine [3].

3.3 MVS Core

No modification or system installation change is required for EPEX to operate in an MVS region. As in the previous section about VM, the user prepares the program source in two parts: one is the user program including its declaration of shared commons, the other is a separate source listing containing only the shared common(s) (refer to Figure 7). Similar to VM preparations, the user supplies file definition statements (JCL) for the ***GO*** step. A multiple step job is submitted for the batch job that is comprised of steps to form a operable load module that contains multiple copies of the non-reentrable code, independent copies of local variables, and a single copy of the shared common areas. The resultant load module is joined to a ***parent*** task program that is first called when the ***GO*** step is begun (refer to Figure 2). The ***parent*** program spawns ***child*** tasks that perform the independent invocations of the S/370 instruction stream. Tasks are designated which file definitions to process for I/O to prevent multiple attempts to write output to the same file.

3.4 RP3 Emulation

As explained earlier, communication between the tasks or virtual machines is accomplished in EPEX by manipulation of items in the shared storage. Coordination is accomplished by use of both controlling variables and storage-based flags (semaphores). In the Research Parallel Processor Prototype, one such method for manipulation of shared variables is the Fetch-and-Operation type of instruction.

3.4.1 Fetch-and-Op Subroutines

The Fetch-and-Op subroutines emulate an atomic read-modify-write operation that is implemented in the hardware of RP3. Fetch-and-Ops are performed by the memory controller as a single transaction originating from the processor. The basic form of the operation is to send a data value and operation type to a specific word address in memory. The memory controller fetches the data in storage and returns that value to the processor, performs the operation, then stores the result to storage. Refer to Figure 4. Operations supported are:

IFNA integer addition

IFAND logical AND function

IFOR logical OR function

IFMIN data value sent by operation replaces storage if it is smaller than current value

IFMAX data value replaces storage if it is larger than the current value

I$WAP data value replaces storage unconditionally

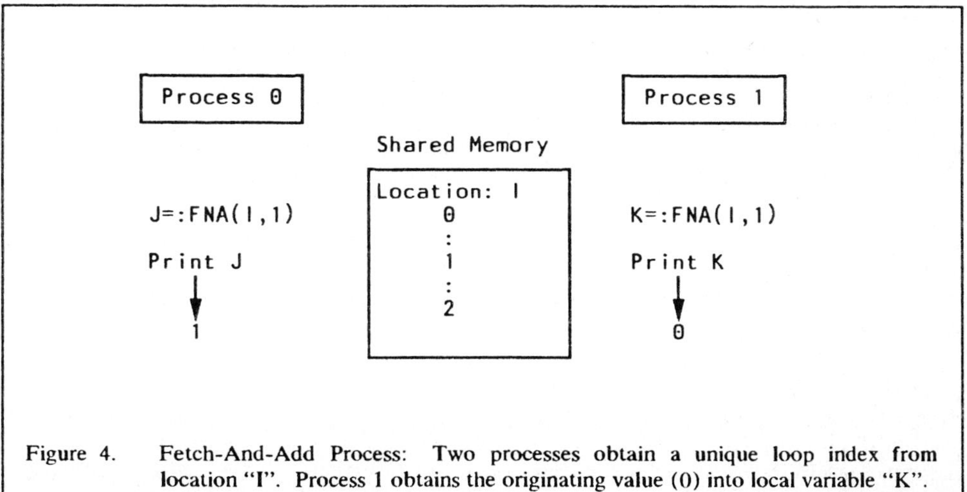

Figure 4. Fetch-And-Add Process: Two processes obtain a unique loop index from location "I". Process 1 obtains the originating value (0) into local variable "K".

4.0 Preprocessor

The ***Preprocessor*** extends a programming language with a set of high-level parallel constructs [5]. At this writing, the FORTRAN and C languages are supported independently. Also, the Preprocessor is restricted to operate only under VM/CMS. Refer to Figure 5 for an example of an EPEX-FORTRAN program.
The Preprocessor interface allows for extremely rapid conversions of existing programs to ***EPEX*** programs to obtain a relatively high degree of parallelism without taxing the skill or time of the programmer. A primary advantage is that both medium and coarse-grain parallelism can be easily achieved through the syntax of the macros (described in the following subsections) without the requirement to radically alter the original program. The Preprocessor is intended for general use for all individuals. Usage of the subroutines (described previously) is intended for expert usage or to develop extensions that might be incorporated into the Preprocessor at a later date.

The Preprocessor allows introduction of additional macro statements to the original source code which subsequently are converted into normal source code that includes additional processing statements that utilize some in-line code and the subroutines discussed previously. The EPEX macros are discussed in separate sections that follow:

4.1 Shared Data (Fortran)

Data structures that are to be shared among the processes are defined using @SHARED or @INCLUDE macro declarations. The syntax is similar to that used for ***COMMON*** statements in FORTRAN. Multiple occurrences of these statements may be placed within the EPEX program.

4.2 Distinguished Variables

The programmer may refer to the information supplied within particular reserved-name variables.

@MYNUM Provides the unique process identification for a VM virtual machine or an MVS task.

```
      @SHARED/VEC(100)
      @SERIAL BEGIN
       ...                      (code done by only
       ...                        one process, which
       READ INPF, ...              reads in data, etc.)
       ...
      @SERIAL END
      ...                       (Replicate code:  code which
      ...                         is done by all processes)
      ...
      @DO 100 I=1,100
       ...
       VEC(I) = FUNCT(I)        (code done using a unique
       ...                        value of variable I)
       IF (..) GOTO 30
       @SCRAM                   (method to escape loop)
  30  CONTINUE
       ...
 100  @DOEND
      ...
      @SERIAL BEGIN
       ...                      (one process performs
       ...                        report printing, etc.)
      @SERIAL END
      END
```

Figure 5. Example FORTRAN-EPEX Program: The FORTRAN statements have been removed to highlight the various EPEX statements discussed in the text.

@DAGW Global variable for allowing dynamic adjustment of the time interval that ***DAGWAIT*** uses as described previously.

@MAXWAIT Maximum number of loop iterations permitted for code to attempt obtaining a resource lock. The user's code might enter into deadlock or system load situations that require alteration of this variable.

@NUMPROCS A convenient means for determining how many processes were actually started for the parallel process.

4.3 Replicate Code Sections

Any section of code that occurs outside of sections declared for serial or parallel execution is referred to as ***replicate*** code. Every process, executing its own copy of the single program that is prepared by the user for entry into the Preprocessor, will execute that code. In general, a certain degree of local variable initialization must necessarily be done by each process, and this is the method to accomplish that.

4.4 Parallel Loops

@DO and @ENDO signify the parallel DO-loop. The statements may be labeled and are written consistent with the syntax of the language. If the actual processing to be performed within such a loop is too small to account for the relatively low overhead for distributing the work, a chunk of iterations can be implied by the loop rather than just one. Parallel ***joins*** implied by the @ENDO can be explicitly avoided by coding a ***NOWAIT*** parameter on the @ENDO. This permits a process to continue on with processing of code beyond the end of the do-loop, skipping the necessity of a "join". This permits a pipelining of the process of performing additional process (e.g., more do-loops) without requiring that all processes must await the arrival of all siblings at a common point in the code execution before continuing. @DO-loops may not be nested however they may be reused (i.e., may be within an ordinary do-loop). An additional usage counter, called a a "clock time" is used to control the proper consistency of code executions, particularly for the case where one process might fall way behind the progress of the parallel program and enter a @DO that was since completed and in the process of reuse. ***@SCRAM*** provides the way to exit parallel loops before normal completion.

4.5 Explicit Join

@BARRIER provides a means to make all processes wait at a particular location in the code until all have entered at the same place.

@WAITFOR is used to specify an explicit condition that must be satisfied before a process may continue. This is especially helpful to avoid a rigorous requirement that all processes running in parallel must perform the join process at only one particular statement location in the program.

4.6 Serial Execution

@SERIAL BEGIN and ***@SERIAL END*** define a section of program performed by only one virtual machine or task. Some "housekeeping" code must be done for every process, however, necessitating the ***replicate*** code described earlier. As described for the @DO, serial sections can be subsequently re-executed as the outer loop of processing iterates. Similarly, there is a provision to prevent a slow-to-arrive process from executing a serial section out of step with the progress of the parallel program.

5.0 Uses of EPEX

EPEX is generally useful for a broad range of applications. At the IBM T. J. Watson Research, some of these include algorithms such as Fast Fourier Transforms (1D, 2D), graphics and image processing and simulated annealing. Some applications include general modeling using Monte Carlo techniques (such as for a spin-lattice application), incompressible fluid flow, molecular dynamics, weather modelling, chip placement, and circuit simulation (including fault simulation).

Another use is directly applicable to the development of large scale multiprocessors. PSIMUL is a system that simulates the execution of parallel programs running on multiprocessors [8]. It provides detailed traces of memory access patterns and machine operations that can provide valuable insight into the predicted performance characteristics so that findings may be incorporated into the design of such systems at an earlier stage of the development. This "bootstrap" effect has benefited cache and network analysis work in RP3.

6.0 Conclusions

In this paper, the background, motivation and implementation of EPEX was explained. EPEX has been demonstrated as an effective means to acquiring real improvement in turnaround time for CPU-intensive jobs. Applications are easy to adapt or reprogram to take advantage of the medium to coarse-grain parallelism, requiring only a few days for the most complicated codes. First pass results on a dyadic (two processor) 3081 are typically 1.8 times the speed of the job when run conventionally (see Figure 6).

Moreover, EPEX represents a step in the development of inter-process communications using shared memory. Not only does EPEX provide insight to the development of applications for RP3, it provides a basis to model possible extensions to the architecture of massive multiprocessors.

$$\frac{\textit{virtual CPU time for original serial code}}{\textit{longest virtual CPU time of any of the processes}}$$

	1P	2P
FFT	0.993 (1)	1.98 (1.99)
MD	0.995 (1)	1.98 (1.99)
FD	0.947 (1)	1.83 (1.93)

Figure 6. Observed Virtual Speedup: Typical real-time speedup occurs in the range 1.6 to 1.8. Results shown in the above table are for FFT, molecular dynamics and fluid dynamics benchmarks.

7.0 References

In the following list, IBM Research Reports are identified by the ***RC*** designation.

[*1*] G. F. Pfister, W. C. Brantley, D. A. George, W. J. Kleinfelder, K. P. McAuliffe, E. A. Melton, V. A. Norton, J. Weiss, ***Proceedings of the 1985 International Conference on Parallel Processing***, IEEE Computer Society, and ***The IBM Research Parallel Processor Prototype (RP3): Introduction and Architecture*** (RC 11060)

[*2*] F. Darema-Rogers, D. A. George, V. A. Norton, G. F. Pfister, ***A VM Parallel Environment*** (RC 11225)

[*3*] E. A. Melton, G. F. Pfister, ***WSSOS - Writeable Shared Segment Operating System*** (RC 11371)

[*4*] F. Darema-Rogers, D. A. George, V. A. Norton, G. F. Pfister, ***Environment and System Interface for VM/EPEX*** (RC 11381)

[*5*] J. M. Stone, F. Darema-Rogers, V. A. Norton, G. F. Pfister, ***Intro to the VM/EPEX FORTRAN Preprocessor*** (RC 11407)

[*6*] J. M. Stone, F. Darema-Rogers, V. A. Norton, G. F. Pfister, ***The VM/EPEX Preprocessor Reference*** (RC 11408)

[*7*] F. Darema-Rogers, V. A. Norton, G. F. Pfister, ***Using a Single-Program-Multiple-Data Computational Model for Parallel Execution of Scientific Applications*** (RC 11552)

[*8*] K. So, F. Darema-Rogers, D. A. George, V. A. Norton, G. F. Pfister, ***PSIMUL- A System for Parallel Simulation of the Execution of Parallel Programs*** (RC 11674)

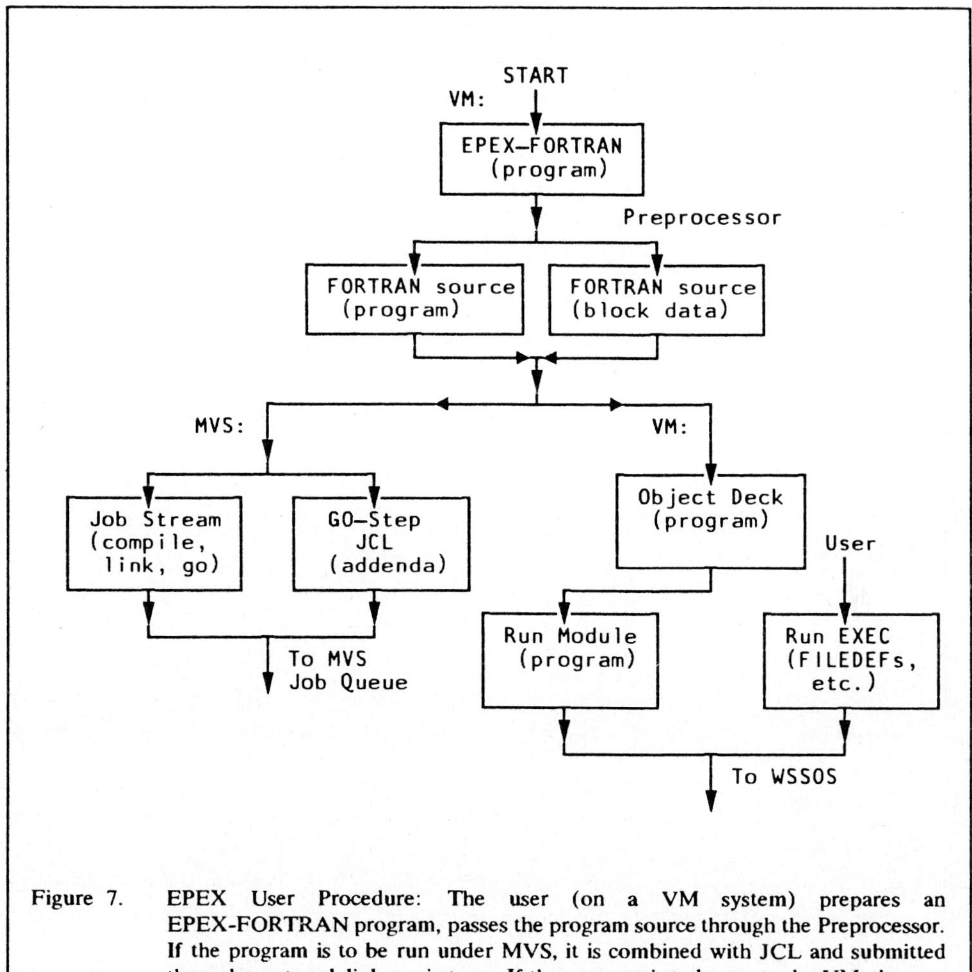

Figure 7. EPEX User Procedure: The user (on a VM system) prepares an EPEX-FORTRAN program, passes the program source through the Preprocessor. If the program is to be run under MVS, it is combined with JCL and submitted through a network link or via tape. If the program is to be run under VM, the user compiles it and submits it to WSSOS for execution on service machines.

Parallel Systems and Computation
G. Paul and G.S. Almasi (Editors)

Microtasking on IBM Multiprocessors

P. Carnevali, P. Sguazzero, V. Zecca

IBM European Center for Scientific and Engineering Computing, via Giorgione 159, 00147 Rome, Italy

Fine-grain parallelism in scientific applications can only be exploited if a low-overhead multitasking environment is available. Such a "microtasking" environment has been implemented, at a prototype level, for IBM multiprocessors and is described in this paper. Its applicability and potentials are discussed.

1. Introduction

In the past decade the use of vector processors has become a standard means of enhancing the performance of scientific and engineering programs. Vector processors have become very popular among end users because they require of the programmer little or no knowledge of the machine. In fact, thanks to the availability of good vectorizing compilers and vector libraries, significant performance enhancements can be obtained with these machines, even from standard programs written in FORTRAN by programmers who are basically unaware of the vector architecture. While vector processors have been available since the mid 70's, IBM announced in 1985 a Vector Facility that adds vector processing capabilities to the general purpose 3090 processor complex[(1)(2)].

In the past few years there has been increasing interest in introducing parallel computing as an additional possibility available to the scientific user. In the mid 80's multiple pipelined vector CPUs sharing a common memory and FORTRAN-accessible multitasking environments are available to the scientific users. On IBM machines, for example, a FORTRAN programmer can schedule the asynchronous execution of subroutines using a feature (FORTRAN Multitasking Facility, MTF) which is now part of the IBM FORTRAN run-time library[(3)]. This software uses MVS macros to execute the desired subroutines in parallel and to synchronize their execution. The operating system then schedules the subtasks on the available CPUs. In this way a FORTRAN programmer can introduce in his programs suitable calls to simple MTF primitives to specify the parts of his program to be executed in parallel. However, scheduling the execution of a parallel subroutine is relatively expensive ($\sim 75\ \mu s$ for an empty subroutine in a two-way 3090 processor with negligible system load). Consequently, the programmer must be careful that the parallel subroutines execute long enough to justify the asynchronous subroutine call. In practice it is not worthwhile to execute in parallel less than a few thousand floating-point operations. This implies that only calculations that exhibit parallelism at a quite high level ("coarse-grain parallelism") can be efficiently multitasked; attempting to exploit parallelism at a low level ("fine-grain parallelism") results in slowing down, rather than accelerating, the execution of the program. While coarse-grain parallelism is quite common in many scientific applications and the MTF approach is perfectly justified (see [(4)] for an example), there are many cases of algorithms that exhibit fine-grain parallelism only, and are thus excluded from parallel execution using MTF unless the algorithms are restructured so that they do exhibit coarse-grain parallelism.

"Parallelizing compilers" capable of automatically detecting and exploiting parallelism in FORTRAN programs could leave the programmer basically unaware of the parallel execution of his code and free to concentrate on the problems inherent in the program rather than on problems induced by the process of parallelization. However, due to above-mentioned high cost of executing parallel subroutines with MTF, such a parallelizing compiler would have to be smart enough to identify large pieces of code to be executed in parallel, and this usually implies and *interprocedural* program analysis in which several subroutines are analyzed at the same time. Work on interprocedural program analysis oriented to the automatic parallelization of FORTRAN programs is in progress within IBM(5)(6), while state-of-art techniques for automatic detection of parallelism, such as those found in the Parafrase package(7), only detect parallelism information at the single subroutine level.

We have recently proposed(8), and summarize here, another approach which could allow automatic parallelization with no need for interprocedural program analysis. The basic idea consists in providing an environment in which the overhead for scheduling parallel work and synchronization is drastically lower than with standard MTF. In such an environment it becomes efficient to exploit fine-grain parallelism ("microtasking"). This makes life easier for the programmer, because it does not require high-level rethinking of entire algorithms, and would also make it easier to implement a parallelizing compiler. A user would then get the benefits of a parallel architecture with basically no intervention on his part, much as with vectorizing compilers and vector architectures.

The very low overhead of the microtasking environment is obtained by using busy wait loops to schedule and synchronize subtasks, instead of standard MVS macros. That is to say, a number of CPUs are dedicated to the parallelized job for the duration of its execution. As a consequence, the use of microtasking implies wasting cycles when any of the CPUs is waiting for work in a busy wait loop. This is only justified if turnaround time of the "parallel" job is really the main concern. Otherwise, and if other jobs of the same priority are active on the same system, it does not really make sense to execute parallel jobs at all, and the best choice is to run, at the same time, various sequential jobs, with the operating system allocating them to the available CPUs.

While the microtasking approach is distinctly different from an approach based on the high-level parallel decomposition of programs through interprocedural analysis, it is however clear that the two approaches could usefully complement each other, and in combination exploit efficiently both coarse- and fine-grain parallelism automatically.

2. The microtasking environment and its user interface

In its simplest form, a tool for parallel programming must only include two simple primitives: "fork" and "join". Before the call to the fork primitive, program execution is sequential. The fork primitive is used to schedule parallel execution of some work, which could be either a subroutine or simply a fragment of code. The join primitive is used to synchronize the execution of the main sequential flow with all the parallel activities started by fork primitives, to make sure that execution of the sequential program continues only when all parallel activities are concluded. In the IBM FORTRAN Multitasking Facility (MTF) these primitives are implemented by creating subtasks at program initialization and putting them in a wait state using the MVS WAIT macro. The fork primitive then uses MVS POST to inform a waiting subtask that a parallel subroutine needs to be executed. The subtask initiates execution of the subroutine and, when terminating, uses POST to inform the main task of its termination. The subtask then re-enters the wait state. The join primitive simply needs to WAIT for all subtasks to signal the finish of execution of their parallel subroutines. In this description, a wait state means a state in which a main task or subtask is considered to be temporarily inactive by the operating system, and consequently does not use any processor time. However, switching from this "dormant" state to an active state is a costly process, and this is the main reason why scheduling subroutines with MTF is expensive.

With microtasking everything works similarly, except that the wait state just described is replaced with a different kind of wait state, namely, one in which the subtask (or main task) keeps checking a predetermined storage location to determine whether some work needs to be started. With this "busy wait" state it takes very little time to schedule some parallel work as a subtask. The main task simply alters a storage location, and the subtask starts execution of useful work immediately after the next cycle of its very short busy wait loop.

However, busy wait has two important shortcomings. First, it uses CPU cycles even when no useful work is being done in parallel. Nonetheless, it is reasonable to assume that, if the job is to be executed in parallel using the microtasking environment, it belongs to a very high priority class of jobs for which turn-around time is critical. For such jobs the required number of CPUs are allocated by preempting lower priority jobs if necessary, and the CPUs remain with the job until completion. Second, microtasking is useful only if the total number of tasks (main task plus subtasks) is at most equal to the number of CPUs actually available to the job being executed in parallel. If this is not the case, a lot of time is spent in busy waiting for subtasks for which CPU time has not been allocated. Thus, while with MTF one can specify any number of subtasks, with microtasking it is only reasonable to specify at most a total number of tasks equal to the number of available CPUs.

To summarize, microtasking works as follows. It there are n available CPUs, $n - 1$ subtasks (which we call Process 1 through Process $n - 1$) are started at initialization and enter a busy wait state. Each subtask keeps checking a separate storage location for a nonzero value indicating that work has to be done. The main task (which we call Process 0) initiates execution of the sequential part of the program. When Process 0 issues a fork primitive, it stores a nonzero value in the storage location checked by Process 1 in its busy wait loop. As a consequence, Process 1 starts executing a subroutine or a fragment of code whose initial address has been previously stored at some other predetermined storage location (one for each of the subtasks) by Process 0. Other work can be started on the other processes in the same way. Similarly, Process 0 enters a busy wait loop when it issues the join primitive, waiting for all the active processes to signal their termination through storage. The n Processes are constantly mapped onto the n available CPUs by the operating system (except for some sporadic system activity) provided that the job is given high priority or the system does not have any additional load. As a result of the busy waiting, the process of scheduling and synchronizing parallel work does not involve any operating system intervention and is very fast.

We have implemented two prototype versions of a microtasking environment for IBM Multiprocessors under MVS. They are oriented to Assembler and FORTRAN programming respectively[(9)].

The first prototype results in the lowest scheduling overhead. The piece of work executed in parallel is a fragment of code. This should be considered to be "native" microtasking, and in this form microtasking could, in the future, be introduced into a compiler, as discussed in the conclusion of this paper. The Assembler programmer is provided with various macros that can be used to implement microtasking fork and join constructs. The macros use very few registers: this allows the programmer to initialize the remaining registers of the parallel subtasks to useful values (base registers, etc.) once and for all, thus reducing the work to be done by the parallel subtasks after each fork.

The second prototype is more oriented to FORTRAN programming, and is organized as a compatible extension of MTF, with the advantage that the programmer can mix, in the same program, the usual MTF wait state and the microtasking busy wait state. One can, for example, use standard MTF in sections of the program that have coarse-grain parallelism, and activate microtasking only in parts requiring fine-grain parallelism. This reduces one of the shortcomings of microtasking, namely, the fact that it wastes CPU cycles in useless waiting loops. The FORTRAN programmer is provided with subroutine calls that can be used to switch between the standard MTF wait state and the busy wait state needed for microtasking and viceversa. In addition to the standard MTF calls, additional subroutines that implement fork and join constructs when microtasking is active are also provided. This FORTRAN-oriented microtasking environment is not as fast as the Assembler-oriented microtasking prototype. In addition, if the subroutines called are written in FORTRAN themselves, there is an additional overhead incurred in calling them. This overhead, which would appear even if the subroutines were called sequentially, is mainly due to the subroutines having to initialize pointers to the array arguments passed to them. It can be avoided by calling only Assembler coded routines, either user-written or belonging to the vector library(10).

3. Performance examples and conclusions

At the simplest level, the overhead of a multitasking environment can be characterized by the time needed to schedule an empty piece of work in a processor and to synchronize with it. We have measured this time (which we refer to as "basic synchronization overhead") on an IBM 3090 with two CPUs for the various parallel programming environments described in this paper. The results are summarized in Table 1.

Table 1 - Basic synchronization overheads

Environment	Basic Fork-Join overhead
FORTRAN Multitasking	75 μs
Assembler-oriented microtasking	2 μs
FORTRAN-oriented microtasking	5 μs

It is clear from these data that microtasking reduces overhead by more than an order of magnitude as compared to standard multitasking, and consequently makes much smaller the minimum size of a piece of work that can be efficiently executed in parallel.

In particular, the basic synchronization overhead obtained with the Assembler-oriented microtasking environment ($2\mu s$) equals the one reported for the Cray X-MP Processor(11), despite the fact that, unlike the Cray machines, the IBM 3090 has no special architectural features such as shared registers.

A more sophisticated measure of synchronization overhead has been introduced by Hockney(11)(12) by means of a parameter called $s_{1/2}$, which measures the synchronization overhead in equivalent floating-point operations. If s floating-point operations are to be executed in parallel, the execution time will be given by

$$T = T_{start-up} + r_{\infty}^{-1} s = r_{\infty}^{-1}(s_{1/2} + s). \qquad (1)$$

The meaning of the two parameters, r_{∞} and $s_{1/2}$, is easily explained: r_{∞} is the processing rate of the parallel system for very long sequences of floating-point operations, and $s_{1/2}$ is the number of floating-point operations that could be performed, at the asymptotic speed r_{∞}, during the time $T_{start-up}$ needed for synchronization. Alternatively but equivalently, $s_{1/2}$ can be defined as the number of floating-point operations that result in half the maximum speed r_{∞}. This parameterization is formally consistent with another parameterization, introduced by the same author, for the performance of vector processors:

$$T = T_{start-up} + r_\infty^{-1} n = r_\infty^{-1}(n_{1/2} + n), \quad (2)$$

which models the time needed by a vector processor to process a vector of length n. Here $n_{1/2}$ is the number of vector elements that could be processed, at the asymptotic speed r_∞, during the vector start-up time $T_{start-up}$, or, equivalently, the vector length needed to achieve half the peak speed. Depending on whether one considers single vector instructions or vector subroutines, $n_{1/2}$ will account for the start-up time of either a vector instruction or a vector subroutine.

It should be pointed out, however, that, if vector operations are executed in parallel, the $s_{1/2}$ parameter in formula (1) will account at the same time both for the synchronization overhead and for the vector start-up overhead associated with $n_{1/2}$. Thus, while $s_{1/2}$ is always a good measure of the overall start-up overhead as seen by the programmer, it is not true in general that $s_{1/2}$ is a direct measure of synchronization overhead alone. Such a direct measure of synchronization alone, which we will indicate as $s^*_{1/2}$, can instead be obtained by subtracting the start-up time related to vector processing, which can easily be measured using a sequential version of the parallel program.

We have measured[8] these parameters for three sample problems, chosen to be representative of three different operating modes of a vector processor: a scalar problem for which vector processing capabilities are not used; a typical vector problem; and a "supervector" problem, in which the highest processing speeds are achieved. The three problems are, respectively, the product of a sparse matrix by a vector, the vector multiply-and-add, and convolution. All tests and timings have been made using an IBM 3090 Model 200, with two CPUs and two vector features. Table 2 contains the measured values of the parameters r_∞, $s_{1/2}$ and $s^*_{1/2}$.

Table 2

Problem	r_∞(Mflop/s)	$s_{1/2}$	$s^*_{1/2}$
Sparse matrix-vector multiply	10	130	70
Vector multiply and add	26	150	100
Convolution	100-150	1000-2000	500-1000

The ranges indicated for the various parameters for the case of convolution refer to different lengths of the convolution kernels used.

The values obtained for $s_{1/2}$ and $s^*_{1/2}$ make it worthwhile to execute in parallel even very small pieces of work, of the order of ~ 100 floating point operations, with the exception of the super-vector case where grain sizes about ten times larger are needed to justify the overhead of working in parallel. In contrast, using a more standard multitasking environment such as MTF, only medium-grain and coarse-grain parallelism can be efficiently exploited, synchronization costs being typically larger by more than an order of magnitude. Of course, this is not a limitation for problems that exhibit intrinsic coarse-grain parallelism[4].

The values of the $s_{1/2}$ parameter measured here compare favorably with those measure for the Cray X-MP processors[11]. This has been achieved without without *ad hoc* architectural enhancements such as shared registers.

Thus, microtasks of one hundred floating-point operations or more can be efficiently parallelized using microtasking. The microtasking prototypes are available to the Assembler and FORTRAN programmers, with different degrees of flexibility, ease of use, and speed.

The possibility of imbedding microtasking in a FORTRAN compiler is also appealing. Using techniques already implemented in automatic vectorizers[13] a parallelizing compiler[7] could detect low-level loops or generic fragments of code that could be executed in parallel, without the need for a complex interprocedural analysis. The parallel execution would then be scheduled using microtasking as the parallel run-time environment. While this would make parallelism entirely invisible to the user, one could also allow the programmer to assist the parallelizing compiler with directives, similarly to what happens with vectorizing compilers. This approach could then be combined with an approach based on interprocedural analysis to realize an environment in which all kinds of parallelism, from coarse-grain to fine-grain, are automatically recognized and efficiently exploited by the compiler.

References

1. IBM Journal of Research and Development **30** (March 1986).

2. IBM Systems Journal **25** (January 1986).

3. VS Fortran Version 2 Programming Guide IBM publication SC26-4222.

4. J. Gazdag, G. Radicati, P. Sguazzero, and H. H. Wang,Seismic migration on the IBM 3090 Vector Facility, IBM Journal of Research and Development **30** (1986) pp. 172-183.

5. M. Burke,An Interval Analysis Approach Toward Interprocedural Data Flow, IBM Research Report RC 10640 (#47724) (Yorktown Heights, 1984).

6. M. Burke and R. Cytron,Interprocedural Dependence Analysis and Parallelization, Proceedings of the SIGPLAN 1986 Symposium on Compiler Construction, SIGPLAN Notices **7** (1986).

7. D. J. Kuck, R. H. Kuhn, B. Leasure, and M. Wolfe,The structure of an advanced vectorizer for pipelined processors, Proceedings of the IEEE Computer Society Fourth International Computer Software and Applications Conference (Chicago, 1980).

8. P. Carnevali, P. Sguazzero, and V. Zecca,Microtasking on IBM Multiprocessors, IBM Journal of Research and Development (to appear).

9. V. Zecca,Microtasking Facility on IBM Multiprocessors: Programming Guide, IBM ECSEC Technical Report (Rome, 1986).

10. Engineering and Scientific Subroutine Library Guide and Reference, IBM publication SC23-0184.

11. R. W. Hockney,$(r_\infty, n_{1/2}, s_{1/2})$ measurements on the 2-CPU CRAY X-MP, Parallel Computing **2** (1985) pp. 1-14.

12. R. W. Hockney,Performance characterization of the HEP, in J. S. Kowalik editor, MIMD Computation: HEP Supercomputer, MIT Press (Cambridge, Mass., 1985) pp. 59-90.

13. R. G. Scarborough and H. G. Kolsky,A vectorizing Fortran compiler, IBM Journal of Research and Development **30** (1986) pp. 163-171.

Parallel Systems and Computation
G. Paul and G.S. Almasi (Editors)

Automatic Detection of Parallelism in Scientific Programs with Application to Array-Processors

A.Lichnewsky, F.Thomasset, C.Eisenbeis

I.N.R.I.A., BP.105 Rocquencourt, 78153 Le Chesnay Cedex
and
Université de Paris-Sud, Bat425-Mathématique, 91405 ORSAY

ABSTRACT

Techniques for automatic detection of parallelism are described, in connection with a prototype vectorizer which has been implemented by the authors. Our aim has been to be able to specialize several versions of our software, pertinent to several computer architectures. In this paper, we describe the adaptation for a program generator aiming at an Array-Processor.

The first area in which the Array-Processor approach differs from the Vector machine counterpart, is the model of parallelism sought. The second obeys to very formal rules that define a vector operation, and that correspond to hardware or firmware-micro code "once for all" realizations. The first is capable of a variety of uses, ranging from sequential code ([1]), to highly chained pipeline operation of complex instruction groups. However, this has to be fully commanded by user code, and therefore leads to a complex compiler.

Our approach has been to implement an Array-Processor code generator as a backend for a more general vectorizer. The specific part deals with scalar (*non-loop mode*) micro-instruction scheduling, vector (*loop mode*) micro-instruction scheduling and makes global optimization aimed at a fast loop-mode execution during several resource allocation phases.

1. INTRODUCTION

During the last decade, parallel computers of several kinds have been introduced making it necessary to perform some form of parallelism detection, as well as program transformation in order to expose the parallel constructs that are suited to the target machine. This activity can be done by the user, who would then be provided with a parallel programming language (e.g. FORTRAN-8X [AN84], DAP-FORTRAN [F179], ACTUS [PCM82], ADA [AD81], OCCAM [MS85], CSP [Ho78]). Another approach is to have the compiler software handle this task, making it a "Vectorizer" or a "Parallelizer". Both approaches are not necessarily contradictory and can complement each other in many occasions ([2]).

The basic techniques of Automatic Parallelism Detection ([3]), now well known and widely used in commercial applications, are mainly due to D.J.Kuck [KK81], L.Lamport [La74] and K.Kennedy [Ke80]. Among the reason we had to implement them into a prototype vectoriser named "VATIL", is the fact that they have permitted us to construct both a unified theoretical frame and a software basis applicable to the systematic study of several parallel architectures. These architectures can be very different from one another, as our forthcoming treatment of Array-Processor specifics will show. In other occasions they exhibit only so subtle variations that a high-level parallel language is not likely to convey to the user, giving to its implementor no choice but applying "Automatic Parallelism Detection" techniques. An example of this is given by the "chaining" strategies of most recent Vector Processors when they deal with main store objects. (Cf. [CRA1], [CXMP], [FU84]) ([4])

Conceptually, our approach to Automatic Parallelism Detection involves several steps, the most important of which are:

- the definition of pertinent parallel constructs,
- the derivation of semantic criteria making them equivalent with one another and with some sequential program,
- the derivation of a performance model,
- criteria evaluation ([5]),
- sequential program transformation for parallelism improvement,
- final optimization and parallel form construction.

We shall therefore compare the requirement on these steps for the treatment of "Vector Computers" and "Array-Processors". First of all, when dealing with "Array-Processors", we cannot stay at the level of "vector counterparts" of the sequential operators, but have to explicitely schedule the parallel micro-operations, and arrange for their chaining during the loop executions. This implies handling a large set of micro-operations, indexed by the loop iteration count, in contrast with the situation for the vector model, were the criteria strongly suggest working on a *quotient graph* where the various iteration numbers are merged. (Cf.[LT85]). In order to reduce the complexity of this problem, we distinguish three phases, dealing respectively with single loop body scheduling, loop initiation frequency optimization, global optimization. Among the most striking aspects is the fact that some transformations that are imperative in the first case are merely performance improving heuristics when applied to the second.

We shall then discuss the performance of the "Array-Processor" optimiser, specifically targeted to the ST-100 [STAR] and show the relevance of some classical vectorization transformation to this context. This will also show the most important role of ressource allocation for some practical applications.

2.VECTOR EXECUTION OF LOOPS

2.1. Programs Models.

In order to simplify the exposition, and avoid several difficulties that are not essential to our argument ([6]), we restrict ourselves here to the case of simple non-nested loops. The programs thus follow the following abstract syntax, decorated with italicised keywords for easier reading:

```
<Program>        := <Declarations> <Bloc> <End>
<Declarations> := (<Type> <Var_Id> <Var_Bounds> )*
<Bloc>           := <Instructions>*
<Instructions> := <Assign> | <Do-Seq>
<Assign>         := <Var> = <Exp>
<Do-Seq>         := DO <Index_Var> = 1, <Niter>
                           <Assign>+
                    CONTINUE
```

In order to relate a program to a corresponding parallel version, it is convenient to distinguish:

- an *instance* of an abstract rule in the program.
- an *occurrence* of an instruction during the run of the program.These correspond to well defined state changes of the conceptual target machine, are instances indexed by the loop counters. They are partially ordered under the relation : A « B which means that A occurs before B. Of course, for a sequential program, we have a total order.
- an *action*, which is normally indexed by an instruction occurrence, a data index, and possibly an instance of a (low level) expression tree.

These distinctions are illustrated in the following example, although actions will be more useful in parallel constructs later:

```
(X) DO I = 1,1000
(Y)        A(I) = B(I)+C(I)
   CONTINUE

X           :: instance of <Do-Seq> with  <Niter> = 1000.
Y(12)       :: occurrence of Y where A(12) is computed.
                 Y(12)«Y(14).
Y(12).<+> :: action : computation of B(12)+C(12),
                 irrespective of its use.
```

The classical procedure of denotational semantics would be to attach semantic functions to the various instances. To introduce vector constructs and their meaning, our approach will be to introduce new constructs in the abstract syntax, to give *consistency conditions* under which their instances are well defined. We then specify how these can be translated to an equivalent sequential program fragment, to which classical semantic methods can be applied. *Occurrences* and *actions* are used in consistency conditions and proofs.

2.2. Sequential computation of Vectors

The easiest construct pertaining to vector execution is the <Do-Vect>, which corresponds to the sequential execution of vector instructions. Typical computers to which this model is readily applicable are the Cray-1, and the CDC-Cyber-205. To define it, we first give its abstract syntax:

```
<Do-Vect>          := DOVECT <Index_Var> = 1, <Niter>
                              <Assign>
                          CONTINUE
```

An occurrence X of this will be considered consistent if the *non-recurrence* condition is satisfied, namely:

(1) $1 \leq i < j \leq X.\text{<Niter>} \Longrightarrow out(X.\text{<Assign>}(i)) \cap in(X.\text{<Assign>}(j)) = \emptyset$

Its meaning will then be the same of the corresponding sequential <Do-Seq>.

NOTES:

• It should be noted that the previous model is satisfactory for vector computers which serialize their write accesses to memory, which is the case for most machines. Otherwise, we would have to add a condition resolving these output dependences:

(2) $1 \leq i < j \leq X.\text{<Niter>} \Longrightarrow out(X.\text{<Assign>}(i)) \cap out(X.\text{<Assign>}(j)) = \emptyset$

• Also this construct is quite different from the FORTRAN-8X vector assignment, where the non-recurrence condition is not required, since the vector operation is first evaluated and then stored. Excluding 0 stride in vectors also suppress the second condition. However, if a FORTRAN-8X implementor wants to restrict the use of intermediate storage to the necessary cases only, then the previous conditions apply.

• Finally, this model is also satisfactory for the Cray-1 chaining of vector operations, since the hardware provides for all the dependence checking at the register level, and serializes the memory operations.

• The performance model for such an execution mode involves the vector startup times and the rate of operations per machine cycle. It can also be characterized in term of asymptotic speed and half-speed vector length, as advocated by R.W.Hockney [HJ81].

2.3. The Vectorization procedure

Now, let us consider the case of an instance of a <Do-Seq> involving several <Assign>s in the inner loop:

```
Y.<Do-Seq>      := DO  I = 1, N
                        X1.<Assign>
                        X2.<Assign>
                        ...........
                        ...........
                        Xq.<Assign>
                   CONTINUE
```

Its transformation to vector form should be, to keep all actions, a sequence of vector loops such as:

```
TR_Y.<Bloc> :=  (Z1) DOVECT I = 1,N
                          X(p(1)).<Assign>
                      CONTINUE
                      .....................
                (Zq) DOVECT I = 1,N
                          X(p(q)).<Assign>
                      CONTINUE
```

where p(.) is a permutation of the indices 1,...,q. This is well defined if the q occurrences of <Do-Vect> satisfy the above stated *non-recurrence condition.* In this case, TR_Y would not be equivalent to the initial sequential program, but to the sequential program:

```
TR_Y_EQU.<Bloc>:=(ZE1) DO I = 1,N
                           X(p(1)).<Assign>
                       CONTINUE
                           .....................
                 (ZEq) DO I = 1,N
                           X(p(q)).<Assign>
                       CONTINUE
```

This implies that we have to impose further conditions on the instance of Y.<Do-Seq>, making TR_Y_EQU equivalent to Y. These simply state that the order of interacting actions should be kept the same as in the original program, and have been derived by D.J.Kuck[KK81]. Here they can be stated in the following way:

$$Xk(i) \ll Xl(j) \text{ and } ZE(p^{-1}(k)) \gg ZE(p^{-1}(l)) \text{ then:}$$

(3)
- $in(Xl(j)) \cap out(Xk(i)) = \emptyset$ *Data Dependences*
- $out(Xl(j)) \cap in(Xk(i)) = \emptyset$ *Anti Dependences*
- $out(Xl(j)) \cap out(Xk(i)) = \emptyset$ *Output Dependences*

These criteria can be more conveniently expressed in terms of Dependence Graphs and Quotient Dependence Graphs. (Cf. [KK81] [LT85]). The vectorization procedure consists then in a loop distribution pass, in order to obtain TR_V_EQU satisfying (3), and is followed by a check of (1) for each individual loop.

NOTES

•An actual realistic implementation has to perform a series of transformations in order to find vector indexing information, suppress unnecessary dependences, and can use several approximations for the computations of conditions (1-3). The reader will find a detailed exposition in Kuck [KK81], Kennedy[Ke80]. An example of VATIL output showing the effect of these preliminary steps is shown below.

•An easier way to formulate the preceding vectorizability criterion is to state that the quotient dependence graph is acyclic. The required permutation of instruction is then given by a topological sort.

```
<bloc nest>     — CODE —

        C$(avail (n . 100) (l . 0) (k . 0))

        C$
   >      DO 1 i = 1 ,n ,2
   >          k = 1+k
   >          j = k
   >          a(j) = 1+b(j)
   >          k = 1+k
   >          c(k) = a(j)+b(j)
   >          l = 3+l
   >          a(j) = c(l)
   >1         CONTINUE

   - Original loop -
```

```
<bloc nest>     — CODE —

   >    DOVEC 1 i_ = 1 ,50 ,1
   >        a(2*i_-1) = 1+b(2*i_-1)
   >1       CONTINUE
   >    DO 2 i_ = 1 ,50 ,1
   >        c(2*i_) = a(2*i_-1)+b(2*i_-1)
   >        a(2*i_-1) = c(3*i_)
   >2       CONTINUE
   >    i = 99
   >    l = 150
   >    j = 99
   >    k = 100

   - Vectorized form -
```

- DO-VECT Vectorization -

2.4. Concurrent Chains of Vector Operations.

Our previous vector execution model is far from being able to describe the form of parallelism present in the most recent Vector Processors, which are capable of concurrent vector activities. Usually this means that several functional units are capable of concurrent operation, that the hardware automatically keeps track of dependences in register storage, and that special serialization instructions are provided to deal with main memory data dependences. We have chosen to model this behaviour by the following construct:

```
<Do-CVect>          := DOCVECT <Index_Var> = 1, <Niter>
                       <Synch_List>
                           <Assign>+
                       CONTINUE
<Synch_List>        := SYNCH { <Var>+ }
```

Roughly speaking, this states that the series of vector operations corresponding to the <Do-CVect>.<Assign>$^+$ part will be executed concurrently. However, the dependences concerning the elements in the synchronized list <Do-CVect>. <Synch_List> are respected by adequate chaining of instructions. These dependences are defined relatively to the order of vector instructions in <Do-CVect>.<Assign>$^+$. We can now state the conditions under which <DO-CVect> is defined, and give it a meaning in terms of a sequential equivalent. The problem of finding the <Do-CVect> equivalent of some sequential program will then be solved much like in the previous case. It will be defined if the following set of conditions is satisfied:

(4) $\forall$ k, $1 \leq i < j \leq$ Niter ==> out(Xk.<Assign>(i)) $\cap$ in(Xk.<Assign>(j)) = $\emptyset$

(5) if Xk $\neq$ Xl then:

- $\left(\bigcup_{j=1,Niter} in(Xl(j))\right) \cap \left(\bigcup_{i=1,Niter} out(Xk(i))\right) \subset$ Synch-list — *Data & Anti Dependences*
- $\left(\bigcup_{j=1,Niter} out(Xl(j))\right) \cap \left(\bigcup_{i=1,Niter} out(Xk(i))\right) \subset$ Synch-list — *Output Dependences*

And then equivalent to the sequential program:

```
Y_EQU.<Bloc>:=       DO I = 1,N
                        X1.<Assign>
                     CONTINUE
                        .............
                     DO I = 1,N
                        Xq.<Assign>
                     CONTINUE
```

NOTES

• The mechanisms by which hardware perform dynamic dependence checking involve register reservations, result renaming and several vector chaining techniques. Moreover, for a practical application in existing Super-Computers, the variables in the <Synch-List> should satisfy further constraints which would make them eligible for register storage. If it becomes necessary to allocate a variable in <Synch-List> to memory because of register shortage, adequate synchronisation instructions should be issued together with the required loads ans stores.

• A performance model can be constructed for this type of execution, in addition to start_up times and operation rates, it will be necessary to take into account the number of "*chimes* " that model the concurrent execution of several chains. The effect of chaining can be very nicely expressed in terms of asymptotic speed and half-speed vector length.

As an illustration, we show an example of VATIL's handling of this feature below.

```
>      DO 1 i = 1 ,n ,1
>           cx4(i) = ar
>           ar = cx5(i)
>           br = ar-px5(i)
>           px5(i) = ar
>           cr = br-px6(i)
>           px6(i) = br
>           ar = br-px7(i)
>           px7(i) = br
>1          CONTINUE

   - Original loop -
```

```
>      DO-CVECT 1 i = 1 ,n ,1
 C$SYNCH-LIST :(ar_1_ px5 br_ ar_ px7)
>           ar_1_(i) = cx5(i)
>           br_(i) = ar_1_(i)-px5(i)
>           px5(i) = ar_1_(i)
>           ar_(i) = br_(i)-px7(i)
>           px7(i) = br_(i)
>           cx4(i) = ar_(i-1)
>1          CONTINUE
>      cr = br_(n)-px6(n)
>      DO-CVECT 2 i = 1 ,n ,1
>           px6(i) = br_(i)
>2          CONTINUE

   - Vectorized Form -
```

- DO-CVECT Vectorization -

3.ARRAY-PROCESSORS EXECUTION OF LOOPS

In the previous paragraphs, we have looked at computers capable of handling Vector Operations at the instruction set level, and even allow for concurrency and chaining between them. Here we will adress a much less sophisticated environment were the basic capability for chained and concurrent operations on vectors are possible, but not handled automatically by the hardware.

3.1. Micro-Instruction Execution.

The execution model can be easily described at a very low level, the *micro-program* level. This amounts to the definition of:

- the functional units : include every pipeline stage of every operator, or memory access pipeline. They possess part of the registers making the state of the machine in the form of *input registers* (inr1(U),inr2(U),...), a *result register* (outr(U)), and intermediate latches.

- the register storage: made of a set of registers.

- the memory banks: are seen as quite peripheral through memory access pipes (functional units), but are capable of storing, holding and retrieving any type of data.

- the *micro-instructions* : these are sets of simultaneous possible actions by the functional units, together with possible transfers of register data.

- the *micro-program:* a sequence of micro-instructions with non-nested iteration loops.Each occurrence of a micro-instruction can thus be labeled by an execution date.

In the case of the ST-100 Array-Processor, a global view at this level is shown in the following two figures.(Cf.[STAR], [Ei86], [EE85]). The execution time of some micro-program will be the product of the clock cycle time and the number of executed micro-instructions. The translation from our original source code to a micro-program thus involves:

- generation of micro-actions, and register assignment.

- compaction of these micro-actions into a scheduled set of legal micro-instructions.

- optimization at the local level (also called straight line micro-code compaction)

- global optimization. Here we will limit ourselves to the fast execution of loops in a chained fashion.

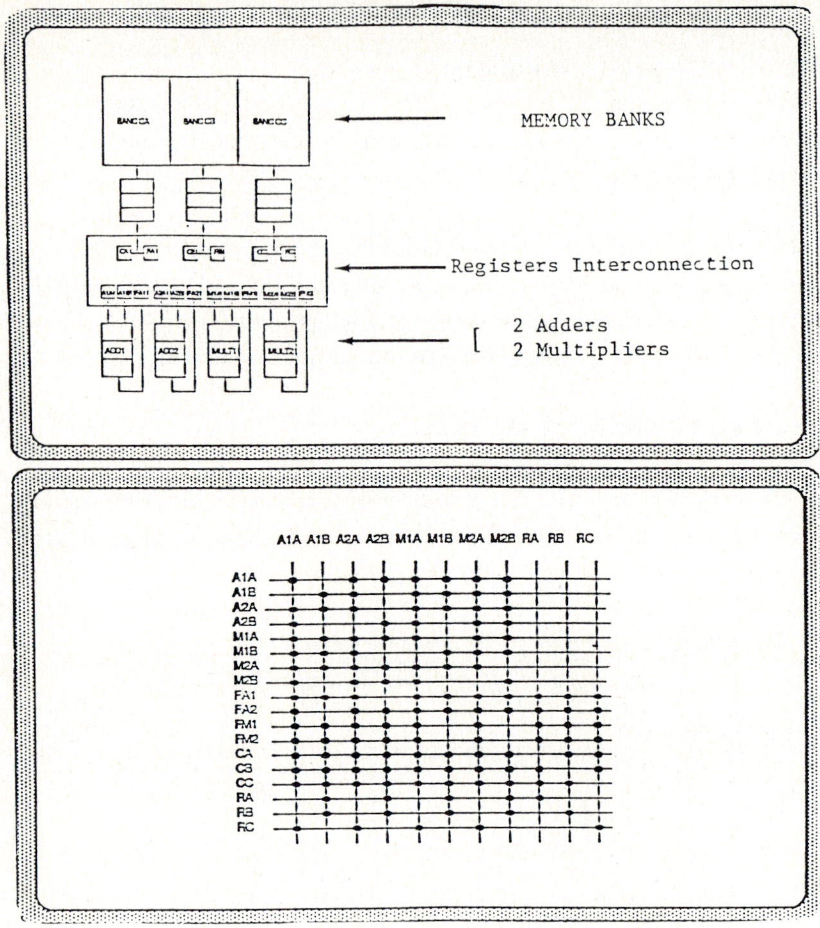

- Architecture and Register Interconnection of ST100 -

More precisely, a <Do-Seq> loop will be translated into a fragment of micro-program :

<Entry-M> <Loop-M> <Exit-M>

where the <Loop-M> bloc will be repeated. Each iteration through <Loop-M> may cover one or more iterations of the initial <Do-Seq>. After a start_up period spent executing <Entry-M>, we will be initiating iterations of <Do-Seq> periodically, the period corresponding to <Loop-M>. In order to cleanup the last actions we will then have to go through the <Exit-M> bloc. A performance model can then be derived, involving :

(6) start_up_time = |<Entry-M>| + |<Loop-M>| + |<Exit-M>|

$$\text{(7) mean\_latency} = \frac{|\text{<Loop-M>}|}{\text{Number of Equivalent <Do-Seq> Iterations}}$$

$$\text{(8) asymptotic rate} = \frac{|\text{Number of Operations in <Do-Seq>}|}{\text{mean\_latency}}$$

It should be noted than the start_up time we are referring to here is the number of micro-instruction cycles needed to reach the periodic behaviour, during this phase Min_Iter iterations of the original <Do_Seq> have been performed, and the formula for *half-speed vector length* thus reads:

$$\text{(9) } N_{1/2} = \frac{\text{start\_up\_time}}{\text{mean\_latency}} - \text{Min\_Iter}$$

In order to minimize start_up times, it is very interesting to look for constant <Loop-M> cycles each performing one <Do-Seq> iteration. This must not be done when it implies sacrificing asymptotic rate, since we are optimizing for potentially long vectors.This is in sharp contrast with the handling of loops by J.Fisher [Fi83], where the emphasis seems to be on rarely iterated loops. Our approach is quite similar of the one taken by R.Touzeau [To84], however we treat the loop-carried dependences much in the same fashion a vectorizer does.

3.2. Micro-code generation from the original program

In order to go from the original program to the optimized micro-code we are looking for, several steps are necessary, since it is not desirable to make any decision too early that would be found inadequate at a later stage in the process. In particular, register and redundant functional unit assignments should be done at a stage when the entire scheduling is visible. On the other hand, micro-actions are usually related to one another : for instance, a memory load will require several memory pipeline "advance" steps.

In our implementation, the first step uses a 3 adress code, the M-code, reminiscent of usual assembler programs, operating on a set of registers of arbitrary size. To summarize, we can give a flavour of its abstract syntax:

```
<M-Program>   := <M-Instruct>+
<M-Instruct> := <M-oper> | <M-Do-Seq>
<M-oper>       := <Reg> = <Reg> ("+" | "-" | "*" | "/" ) <Reg>
                 | <Reg>  LOAD <Var> |  <Var> STORE <Reg>
<M-Do-Seq>      := DO <Index_Var> = 1, <Niter>
                        <M-oper>+
                 CONTINUE
```

In the same fashion as previously, we can define dependences between these <M-instructions>, taking as a reference the original <M-Program>. This allows to work with parallel actions in very much the same way than we have been dealing with pipelines and concurrency in the above paragraphs.

The major difficulty comes here from the fact that we want to execute several iterations in a pipelined fashion: it is not sufficient to work simply with a quotient dependence graph where the iteration numbers have been factored out, on the other hand a completely unrolled graph is not a better candidate. It should be noted that the reason that made the quotient dependence graph totally satisfactory for the study of <Do-Vect> and <Do-CVect> was the special form of conditions (1-5).

To take into account this new difficulty, we will split the problem into a *straight line code generation,* and *a loop optimization.* The straight line code generation must handle <M-oper>$^+$ blocs outside of loops and loop bodies. Each of these are processed separately.

Considering an isolated straight line block, the dependences form a Directed Acyclic Graph. To go from the <M-code> to a micro-program, we associate with each instance of a <M-oper> a template that describes a series of corresponding micro-actions, together with their resource and timing constraints. Some templates can have variants that will be used in case of resource conflicts ([7]), the use of such a variant implying a change of the original <M-code> to an equivalent one . We can deduce from this a set of scheduling constraints on possibly parallel activities, a feasible scheduling of the block and the related set of register assignments. The feasibility of this step is assured by the acyclic nature of the dependence graph, and the fact that we can systematically use template variants using main memory to resolve any resource shortage. The scheduling algorithm we use at this step is a simple list scheduling, giving priority to the longuests paths.

Part of our very prudent attitude at this step can be explained by the fact that many choices made here will have to be modified in order to optimize loops , as we will explain below.

3.3. Loop optimization

At this stage, we can envision the loop execution as the repetition of the execution of loop bodies identical to the one we have already determined, at the fastest possible rate. It is indeed possible to use a collision vector technique, such as described by Davidson [Da71] and Shar [Sh72] to find an optimal (or only "good") periodic initiation rate. If iterations were independent, this would involve simply marking the future cycles where a loop iteration are possible in a linear cycle reservation vector. The technique can be extended to cope with inter -iteration dependences.The fact that the possible states of this vector are finite, since current machines activities will all be terminated after a finite amount of time (cycles), encourages the exploration of the finite but possibly large set of situations by several techniques.

It must be emphasized that the situation at hand is very different to the optimization of a pipeline subjected to a series of *fixed identical independent requests,* here described by the loop-body micro code. It that situation, the only optimization parameter, is to delay some operations in the pipeline to reduce the conflicts, and thus improve the asymptotic speed. (Cf. Kogge [Ko81]).Here, we could modify the micro-code scheduling, the expansion of templates and the resource allocation. Due to their complex interaction we shall have a heuristic based approach.

We can now discuss the similarity and difference of the problem at hand with those of vector execution of loops in the two modes we have shown previously. The most striking difference is that the vector loops had most precise *vectorization criteria,* and the Array-Processor execution seems to have none. It is indeed possible to run the loop slow enough and ignore all inter-iteration dependences. This will result to a global speed far from satisfactory, but shows that the very systematic vector approach,with criteria (1-5), due to hardware scheduling of the pipelines and a simple execution model, is not adequate here. The parallel between the two dissimilar situations will be made more precise by the following result:

LEMMA:

Let us consider the following micro-code loop:

```
(X)             DO I    = 1, Niter
                            Y0
                            Y1
                        ...........
                            Yp
                CONTINUE
```

where the loop has been scheduled : Yq executes at initiation time + q cycle.Then if there is a dependence :

Yk(i) « Yl(j) and one of the following is true:

(10)	• $in(Yl(j)) \cap out(Yk(i)) \neq \emptyset$	*Data Dependences*
	• $out(Yl(j)) \cap in(Yk(i)) \neq \emptyset$	*Anti Dependences*
	• $out(Yl(j)) \cap out(Yk(i)) \neq \emptyset$	*Output Dependences*

Yl(j) cannot be scheduled until Yk(i) has executed.

Applying this with j = i+1, we get the most stringent scheduling constraint between iterations. It bears strong similarity with the condition pertaining to vector execution where operations are indeed performed at 1 cycle intervals in the pipelines. Another way to exploit this is by remarking that if the loop X satisfies the vectorizability criterion of paragraph 2.3, then it is possible to schedule the micro-operations of its body in such a way that inter-iteration dependences will be satisfied whatever the loop initiation rate.

3.4 Global Optimization

We can present here a very brief sketch of the optimization strategy that has been implemented. The details can be found in C.Eisenbeis [Ei86]. To summarize, the first pass is to perform sequentially the above translation to M-code, a straight line code scheduling of the loop body, and finally to look for a suitably fast intiation rate for the iterations. While this is done, many choices are taken concerning scheduling strategies and ressource usage.

The second optimization pass tries to perform M-code to micro-code translation for a single iteration per <Loop-M> period at a prescribed initiation rate. All rates higher than the previously constructed result have to be tried. Here the initiation rate objective is used to test the adequation of many choices concerning template variants, register and functional unit usage.

The improvement optained by this procedure are shown in the illustrations below

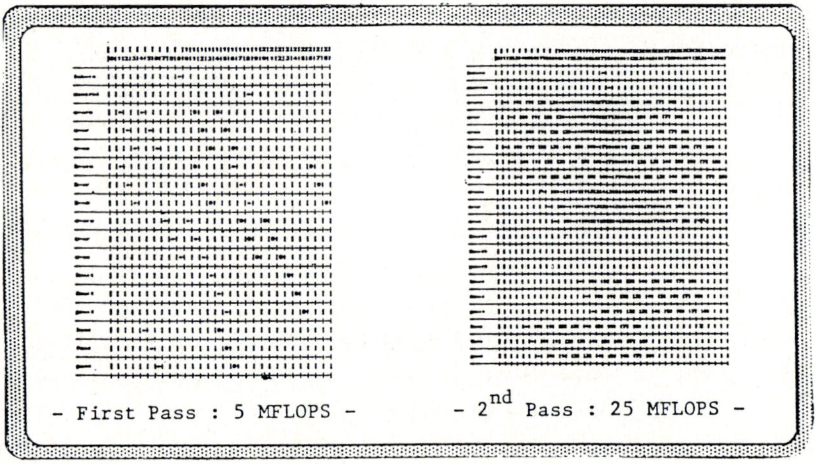

- Improvement after global optimization -

4.CONCLUSION

The way pipeline type of parallelism can be exploited in a Vectorizer and in a code generator for an Array-Processor have been compared. Most of the precise criteria permitting to distinguish highly optimisable (vectorisable) programs are common, even though they should be given quite different presentations. The discussed concepts and methods have been illustrated by the output of an implementation made by the authors, the vectorizer VATIL and a micro-code optimizer for the ST-100. With the introduction on the market of both new vector computers and VLSI chips making pipelined units more and more attractive, it is felt that the techniques we have illustrated will be more and more important for practical high-speed applications.

```
      DO 1 I = 1, 100, 1
         X1(I) = A1(I) + ( O1(I) * C1(I) -O2(I) * C2(I) )
         X2(I) = A2(I) + ( O2(I) * C1(I) +O1(I) * C2(I) )
         Y1(I) = A1(I) - ( O1(I) * C1(I) -O2(I) * C2(I) )
         Y2(I) = A2(I) - ( O2(I) * C1(I) +O1(I) * C2(I) )
1     CONTINUE

                        First Pass      2nd Pass
start_up_time     =     47 clocks       38 clocks
mean_latency      =     20 clocks       15 clocks
asymptotic speed  =     20 MFLOPS       27 MFLOPS
```

- Example of Performances -

NOTES

(1) Unoptimally obtained by pipeline flushing.

(2) For instance sequential FORTRAN transformation into FORTRAN-8X [PSRe], "micro-tasking" preprocessor transforming "loop- slices" into a parallel program using special constructs. [CRA1], [SCSI].

(3) We shall quite often refer to it as "Vectorization", when this does not lead to ambiguities, even if the form of parallelism involved is different.

(4) We have modelled these possibilities with the "DO-VECT" and "DO-CVECT" construct [LT85]

(5) Usually refered to as "*dependence testing* " or "*dependence analysis* "

(6) These have to be delt with for a production grade vectorizer, and include *aliasing*

phenomena , interference of *control structure,* semantics of intrinsics operator applicable to the language. The framework we are using here is far more restrictive than VATIL's capabilities, but is well suited to our present treatment of Array-Processors.

(7) e.g. a register assignment template can have a variant involving some spill to main memory

REFERENCES

[AD81] Reference Manual for the ADA Programming Language, Proposed Standard Document, Dep. of Def., Lect. Not. on Comp. Sc. 106, 1981.

[AN84] ANSI Inc., "Proposal approved for Fortran 8X", X3J3/S7/Vers 89 (Working Document), 1984.

[CRA1] Cray Research Inc., Cray 1 Computer Systems, Hardware Reference Manual,1980.

[CXMP] Cray Research Inc., Cray XMP Computer Systems, Mainframe Reference Manual,1980.

[Da71] Davidson E.S., "The Design and Control of Pipelined Function Generators", Proc 1971 Int. IEEE Conf. on Syst., Networks & Computers, 1971.

[EE85] Eisenbeis C., Erhel J. " Etude des performances du calculateur vectoriel ST-100", Rap. Tech. INRIA, n°51, 1985.

[Ei86] Eisenbeis C., "Optimisation automatique de programmes sur Array-Processors", Thèse de 3ème Cycle, Univ. Paris 6, 1986.

[Fi83] Fisher J.A., "Very Long Instruction Word Architectures and the ELI-512", 10th Ann. Int. Symp. on Comp. Archi., Stockholm, June 1983.

[Fl79] Flanders P.M., "FORTRAN extensions for a highly parallel processor", Infotech. State of the Art Report "Supercomputers", Infotech Int.Ltd, UK, Nov. 1979.

[Fu84] Fujitsu Ltd., "FACOM VP: General Description", 1984.

[HJ81] Hockney R.W. & Jesshope C.R., "Parallel Computers", Adam Hilger, Bristol, 1981.

[Ho78] Hoare C., "Communicating Sequential Processes", Comm. ACM 21, 8, Aug. 1978, pp 666-676.

[Ke80] Kennedy K., "Automatic Translation of Fortran Program to Vector Form", Rice U., Tech. Rep. 476-029-4, 1980.

[KK81] Kuck, D.J., Kuhn R., Padua D., Leasure B.,Wolfe M., "Dependence Graphs and Compiler Optimizations", Proc. 8th ACM Symp. POPL, Williamsburg, VA, 1981.

[Ko81] Kogge P.M., "The Architecture of Pipelined Processors", McGraw-Hill, New York 1981.

[La74] Lamport L., "The Parallel Execution of DO Loops", CACM, Vol 17, N°2, 1974.

[LT85] Lichnewsky A. & Thomasset F., "Techniques de base pour l'exploitation automatique du parallélisme dans les programmes", Rap. Rech. INRIA, N° 460, 1985.

[MS85] May D. & Shepherd R., "OCCAM and the Transputer", Conc. Lang. in Dist. Sys., Amsterdam, North Holland, 1985, pp 19-33.

[PC82] Perrott R., Crookes D., Milligan P., "The programming language ACTUS", Dep. Comp. Sci. , Queen's Univ. Belfast,1982.

[PSRe] Pacific-Sierra Research, "VAST 2"

[RL77] Ramamoorthy C.V. & Li H.F., "Pipeline Architectures", ACM Comp. Surveys, vol 9, n°1, pp 62-102, 1977.

[SCSI] Sequent Computer Systems Inc.

[Sh72] Shar L.E.," Design and Scheduling of Statically Configured Pipelines ", Stanford Univ., Tech. Rep. n°42, 1972.

[STAR] Star Technologies Inc., "St-100: The 100 Megaflops Array-Processor", Hardware & Software Reference Manuals.

[To84] Touzeau R.F., "A Fortran Compiler for the FPS-164 Scientific Computer", ACM 1984.

SECTION 2
PARALLEL ALGORITHMS

Parallel Systems and Computation
G. Paul and G.S. Almasi (Editors)

STRATEGIES FOR PARALLELISM IN ALGORITHMS

F. Hossfeld
Central Institute for Applied Mathematics
Nuclear Research Center (KFA) Jülich
D-5170 Jülich, Fed. Rep. Germany

1. PARALLEL VERSUS SEQUENTIAL PROCESSING

The increasing interest in parallel processing has enhanced the developments in the design, analysis, and implementation of parallel algorithms significantly [1-4]. While the practice of high-speed computation in scientific and technical applications is dominated by numerical methods exploiting the vectorization of - mainly Fortran - code [5], research in parallel algorithms is focussing on: (1) parallel numerical algorithms with a large granularity of the inherent parallelism which is suitable for computer systems with a relatively small number of relatively powerful processors (multiprocessors, MIMD systems); (2) highly parallel computational structures to benefit from elaborate parallelism in linear algebra and related fields by mapping the parallel algorithmic streams directly onto technology, thus yielding, in particular, the "systolic" algorithms and arrays; (3) parallel algorithms for non-numerical applications where progress has been made, especially, in parallel graph algorithms which may give impact on highly parallel computing structures as well.

The expectations concerning parallel processing are based, on the one hand, on the potentiality that a computer system consisting of p parallel processors, instead of one, might be able to solve a problem with p-fold speed, and, on the other hand, on the technological perspectives that the progress in VLSI will provide the means to build parallel computers with many thousands, if not millions, of processing elements which can be technically operated and economically justified.

A necessary prerequisite of these potential enhancements in computer power is the parallelization of the problems in question. While, for instance, the addition of two vectors in linear algebra can be easily transformed into parallel structure, since the additions of the vector components are independent with respect to the individual operands, there are computations which cannot be speeded up by any number of parallel processors; a wellknown example is the computation of a (high) power of x, say x^n with $n=2^k$. With a serial computer, k steps of successive squaring yield the result; since within one step only the power x^2, in two steps only x^4, and so on, can be computed, this computation principally cannot be speeded up on a parallel processor system.

Therefore, the central issue of parallel processing aims at the design of originally parallel algorithms whose performance can be related with optimal sequential algorithms. A parallel algorithm which solves a given problem of size n with P(n) parallel processors within the time T(n), yields a corresponding sequential algorithm which solves the same problem on an equivalent serial computer within the time $P(n)\cdot T(n)$. The product $P(n)\cdot T(n)$, therefore, has to be compared with the lower bound in the time complexity of the best sequential algorithm known to solve that problem. A reasonable objective in designing parallel algorithms is to reach this target.

Although the body of theoretical knowledge about parallel algorithms is still fragmentary, this research field has already achieved a plethora of important results. However, many of these results have been of only academic interest due to the idealistic computational models on which the design and analysis of these parallel algorithms have been built ignoring widely the characteristics and restrictions in real parallel computer structures and, in particular, the implications of parallel algorithms with respect to the intrinsic data-transfer requirements. While in the sequential case it is sufficient to treat the time (and space) complexity of an algorithm, the performance of parallel algorithms is, in addition, essentially determined by the novel phenomena involved with the data communication complexity which takes into account the interaction between the algorithmic dynamics and the intrinsic structure of the flow of data with respect to specific parallel processor architectures.

In this paper we review strategic concepts capable to exploit parallelism in algorithms and application problems. In chapter 2 we illustrate how conceptual and operational redundance may provide the potential of parallel computer arithmetic, for instance. Chapter 3 recollects some results from vectorization. In chapter 4 we deal with the paradigm of partitioning applied to the restructuring of numerical algorithms and to the design of non-numerical algorithms for MIMD systems, including the multitasking concept. Chapter 5, finally, is concerned with the communication issue in SIMD algorithms; the strategy of balancing computation and communication complexities involves systolic algorithms.

2. CONCEPTUAL AND OPERATIONAL REDUNDANCE: PARALLELIZING ARITHMETIC OPERATIONS

A traditional, effective strategy for problem solving is the expansion or the change of the representation space in order to overcome fundamental limitations involved with the representation of the problem rather than with the problem itself. Therefore, the introduction of conceptual redundance may also provide the means to extend the problem description framework to a space dimension where parallelism becomes obvious. In order to illustrate this paradigm, we have chosen the "lowest level" of algorithms: the problem of addition in computer arithmetic.

The performance of a digital arithmetic processor depends heavily on the speed of the adders used in the system. Extensive literature was published in the 1950s and 1960s on high-speed adder designs. During the last decade, the technological impact has pushed this field into highly integrated concepts [6]. Today's computer arithmetic is widely based on the conventional fixed-radix number representation systems of various kind: Given a positive integer number q, the "radix" of the number system, numbers x and y, for instance, are represented by the n-tuples of "digits"

$$x = (x_{n-1} \ldots\ldots x_0)_q \ ,$$
$$y = (y_{n-1} \ldots\ldots y_0)_q \ ,$$

where the digits x_i and y_i, $1 \leq i \leq n-2$, are elements of the set $B_q = (0,1,\ldots,q-1)$ and the digits x_{n-1} and y_{n-1} as the "sign digits" can be either 0 or (q-1). (The traditional decimal system would correspond to q=10; the well-known binary number representation system implies q=2.)

It is well known, that the operation of adding two numbers in fixed-radix number representation involves carry propagation throughout the n-digit chain which is fundamentally a strictly sequential process. (Here, we will not be able to discuss the many sophisticated approaches to partially circumvent this fundamental difficulty by designs like carry look-ahead and others.)

The conventional addition algorithm for n-digit fixed-radix number systems may be written as follows:

Algorithm:

(1) $c_0 = 0$; ("Carry-in")

(2) for i=0 step 1 until n-1 do
begin

$s_i = (x_i+y_i+c_i)$ modulo q ;

$c_{i+1} = \lfloor (x_i+y_i+c_i)/q \rfloor$;

end

(3) $s_n = c_n$; ("Carry-out")

This algorithm is strictly sequential with O(n) time complexity. Within the representation space of the fixed-radix number systems, the limitation to sequential processing cannot be resolved.

In 1961, Avizienis introduced "signed-digit" number representations into high-speed arithmetic [7]; later, this concept has been further elaborated [8]. These signed-digit number systems (SD-systems) are one class of so-called redundant number representations. In an SD-system, a number a is again represented by an n-tuple of digits a_i, $0 \leq i \leq n-1$, which are elements of a set $S_r(q)$ where q is the radix given by a positive integer and r is controlling the redundance of the number system:

$$a = (a_{n-1} \ldots\ldots a_0)_{SD(q)} ,$$

$$S_r(q) = (-r, \ldots., 0, \ldots., r) ,$$

$$\lceil (q+1)/2 \rceil \leq r \leq (q-1) .$$

(For simplicity, we only introduce the symmetric case determined by the single bound r rather than by a lower bound r_{min} and an upper bound r_{max}. If r takes the minimum value $\lceil (q+1)/2 \rceil$, the system is called "minimal redundant"; if r=q-1, it is called "maximal redundant".)

The fundamental difference of such SD-systems compared with conventional fixed-radix systems is given by the fact that every digit a_i has a sign. This freedom provides the potential of redundant representations of numbers; for example, in the case q=10 and r=6 the 5-digit representation of the integer decimal number -5954 can take, for instance, the following variants

$$a = \begin{matrix} (0\ \bar{6}\ 0\ 5\ \bar{4}) \\ (\bar{1}\ 4\ 0\ 5\ \bar{4}) \\ (0\ \bar{6}\ 0\ 4\ 6) \end{matrix} ,$$

when we define $\bar{a}_i = -a_i$, for convenience. (The special case $q=2: S_1(2)=(-1,0,1)$ as a binary SD-system does not satisfy the redundance condition for r; nevertheless, it is a valuable SD-system in parallel arithmetic.)

Based on such SD-systems, the problem of sequential carry propagation in the addition algorithm has been eliminated. Thus, a powerful parallel algorithm has been designed which has O(1) time complexity, i.e. the execution time does no longer depend on the length n of the number representation.

In order to perform addition within an SD-system, a further parameter has to be introduced:

$$w_{max} : (q-r) \leq w_{max} \leq (r-1) .$$

(Again, for simplicity, we consider the symmetric case only: $w_{min}=-w_{max}$.)

The algorithm for adding two SD-numbers a and b can then be structured in three stages:

Algorithm:

(1) Parallel computation of the "transfer digits" t_{i+1} for all $0 \leq i \leq n-1$:

$$t_{i+1} = \begin{cases} 0 \ , \text{ if } w_{min} \leq a_i+b_i \leq w_{max} \ ; \\ 1 \ , \text{ if } a_i+b_i > w_{max} \ ; \\ -1 \ , \text{ if } a_i+b_i < w_{min} \ . \end{cases}$$

(2) Parallel computation of the "interim sum digits" d_i for all $0 \leq i \leq n-1$:

$$d_i = (a_i+b_i) - q \cdot t_{i+1} \quad .$$

(3) Parallel computation of the "sum digits" s_i for all $0 \leq i \leq n-1$:

$$s_i = d_i + t_i \quad .$$

Since $|d_i+t_i| \leq r$ for all $0 \leq i \leq n-1$, the "carry" is absorbed in each position; hence, carry propagation does not arise in such redundant SD-systems by construction; thus, parallelism can be effectively exploited. (Of course, it has to be admitted that the effort of the implementation of this parallel add algorithm on the hardware level and of the SD-system as well will be much higher than for the conventional binary adders and number systems; however, technology may provide the necessary cost-efficiency ratios in the future.)

Besides such conceptual redundance parallelism can also benefit from operational redundance. Referring to computer-arithmetic add operation again, we would like to mention the design of the "conditional-sum adder" [6]: based on the conventional n-bit binary number representation, all possible alternatives - depending on the individual carry-in variants - of the sum digits (and, in recursive steps, of sum-digit groups doubled in size at every step) are computed prophylactically. These processes can be executed for all groups in parallel at every step. The recursive doubling of the length of the digit groups involves $\log_2 n$ steps; thus, a parallel algorithm with O(logn) time complexity results from this concept of operational redundance.

Beyond computer arithmetic, the introduction of conceptual or operational redundance as a strategy for parallelism can be considered a powerful paradigm; in a sense, the idea of self-similarity has introduced the conceptual redundance then providing the necessary problem space expansion for the development of renormalization group methods and other ideas enabling powerful problem solving and parallelism [9].

3. VECTORIZATION: PIPELINING, CHAINING, UNROLLING

The situation in supercomputing today is dominated by the vector-processor architecture [10] represented at the high end primarily by the supercomputers manufactured by Cray Research. Vector computers owe their power to the technology of high speed cicuits, on the one hand, and to the pipeline principle, on the other hand. Like in an assembly line, the work of arithmetic operations is divided into subtasks called segments; the successive segments mapped onto hardware represent "pipelines" or pipelined functional units. Pipelining yields valuable speedup, when many identical operations (e.g. additions) have to be executed with independent data. This prerequisite to feed continuously the pipeline with operands, is usually satisfied with numerical methods in linear algebra and its data structures, the vectors. (Hence, "vector computers" are synonymous with "pipeline computers".) The speedup against a conventional arithmetic processing unit is given, asymptotically, by the number of pipeline segments; the maximum is reached for "long vectors" when the startup time of the pipelines can be neglected.

Further gain can be achieved, if pipelined functional units can be concatenated to yield a "superpipeline"; this combination is called "chaining". It can be applied if computation consists of "triads": $z_i=x_i+r_i s_i$, with independent data x_i, r_i, s_i, $i=1,2,\dots,n$, representing the three vectors x,r,s yielding, finally, z_i. The result of a multiplication $r_i s_i$ is fed directly from the end of a multiplication pipeline into the first segment of an independent add pipeline and is added to x_i there. The computation therefore has not to wait until all multiplications have been executed before starting the additions; but the additions start as soon as the first product $r_1 s_1$ has left the multiplication pipeline. Hence, chaining represents an efficient combination of the pipeline principle with the independent operation of different functional units, although the computations to be executed are sequentially dependent with respect to the data.

In order to benefit from vectorization and chaining, the FORTRAN code for the multiplication of a matrix A with a vector x has to be written in the form

```
      DO   1   J = 1,N
      DO   1   I = 1,N
    1 Y(I) = Y(I) + X(J) * A(I,J)
```

rather than in the non-vectorizing form:

```
      DO   1   I = 1,N
      DO   1   J = 1,N
    1 Y(I) = Y(I) + X(J) * A(I,J)
```

For CRAY machines, for instance, the FORTRAN compiler translates this "scalar" code sequence into a vectorized mode with chaining.

Unfortunately, not all computations lend themselves directly to vector processing, although all modern supercomputers are based on the pipeline principle as a major architectural element for achieving high performance; in many cases, therefore, the computation incorporated in a computer program has to be restructured in a way to make it amenable to vectorization. The programming of today's supercomputers almost exclusively relies on FORTRAN. Therefore, vectors are rather implicit in loops that manipulate arrays; the vector length is defined by the number of passes through a loop. Strategies for vectorization are necessarily focussing on the analysis and transformation of loop structures [11]. The success of vector processing, however, is strongly limited by the amount of unvectorizable computation within a program; this scalar portion "contaminates" the optimization of code according to "Amdahl's law" which tells us that significant speedup can be obtained only for problems which can be vectorized beyond 90 %.

Besides the percentage of vectorization, due to the startup times of the pipelines the length of the associated vectors is also critical for the performance of vector computers [12,13].

Although progress has been made, the vectorizing compilers provided by the manufacturers today are still restricted to simple constructs; thus the task of program optimization is essentially left to the programmer [14]. Therefore, in order to "squeeze the most out of an algorithm" - at least in CRAY FORTRAN - one has to adapt the code to the architecture of the CRAY machines in a way which is far from any software technological paradigm, although very efficient with respect to performance enhancement.

The strategy of unrolling outer FORTRAN DO loops developed in [15] is capable to effectively utilize the vector registers and data-path structure of CRAY computers by expanding the scope of the vectorizing process to more than simple vector operations, thus achieving "supervector performance". In order to illustrate unrolling, let us consider again matrix-vector multiplication:

```
      DO 2 J = 1,N
        DO 1 I = 1,N
          Y(I) = Y(I) + X(J) * A(I,J)
1       CONTINUE
2     CONTINUE
```

The outer loop is unrolled to a certain depth (K1=K+1); by inserting parentheses the arithmetic operations are forced to be performed in the most efficient order by reducing the memory references compared with the vector floating-point operations:

```
      DO 2  J = JMIN,N,K1
         DO 1  I = 1,N
            Y(I) = ((...(Y(I)+X(J-K)*A(I,J-K))
                    + X(J-K+1)*A(I,J-K+1))
                    + ...................
                    + ...................
                    + X(J-1)*A(I,J-1))
                    + X(J)*A(I,J)
1        CONTINUE
2     CONTINUE
```

In [15] the unrolling strategy has been applied to matrix multiplication, Cholesky decomposition, and LU decomposition; by varying the depth of unrolling until K1=16, performance enhancements have been achieved ranging from about 1.7 to 2.8 (as compared with depth K1=1) for CRAY X-MP and CRAY-1 computers.

A detailed analysis of the state of the art of vector processing necessarily comes to the conclusion that the strategies and tools for vectorization, program optimization, and efficient restructuring are getting more and more understood by the experts in this field. Since the community of people using vector supercomputers is growing rapidly, especially since IBM has added vector features to its recent mainframe system thus broadening the interest in vectorization strategies to an even bigger user community, however, the need for a coherent body of tools and functions, in particular implemented in intelligent compilers, is urgent.

By the trends in vector computer architecture, we will certainly be faced with multiprocessor vector computers well beyond CRAY X-MP/4x and CRAY-2 with four processors. Therefore, vectorization versus "multitasking" will become an issue challenging vector processing into parallel (MIMD) processing.

4. PARTITIONING: MIMD ALGORITHMS AND MULTITASKING FOR NUMERICAL AND NON-NUMERICAL PROBLEMS

4.1 Structural Issues of Parallel Processors

Considering the principal structure of the parallel processor architecture which is illustrated in Figure 1, however, the data communication requirements inherent in the parallel algorithms turn out to be crucial for the performance of parallel computers and parallel algorithms if implemented in hardware and software.

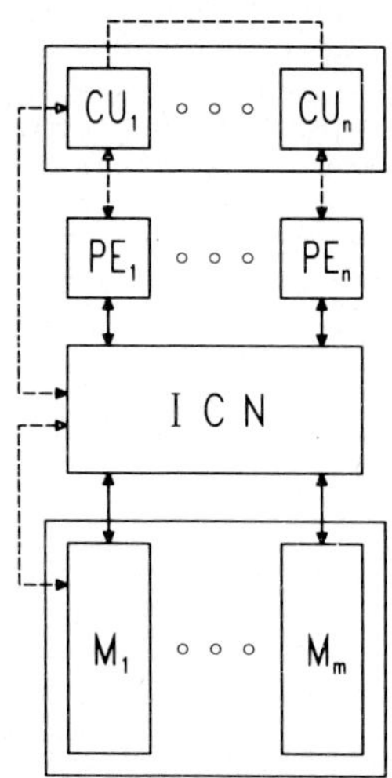

FIGURE 1
Parallel processor architecture
(CU_i=Control processor unit(s); PE_j=processor element;
ICN=interconnection network; M_k=parallel (shared or private) memory)

There are two main concepts of "genuine" parallel processors:

(1) parallel processor with shared memory,
(2) parallel processor with private memory;

in both concepts, the data communication requirements have to be satisfied by the novel architectural component of the so-called interconnection network which depends on the organizational structure of the main memory as far as its functionality is concerned.

In the shared-memory concept where all parallel processing elements utilize one common memory, the simultaneous access to this shared memory from different processors may lead to access conflicts which deteriorate the performance of the parallel computers and algorithms, since the orderly provision of the processor elements with the data cannot be guaranteed [16,17]. Thus, the access conflicts depend on the organizational structure of the shared memory, but also on the data structure utilized in the algorithm. The requirements of conflict-free access of parallel processors to memory has led to the theory - and practice - of skewing schemata which are based on the mapping of "d-ordered N-vectors modulo M" well-known in basic number theory (see [18] for a review of the present state of the art). The results can be implemented by structuring the shared main memory into parallel units where the number of units is determined by selection rules from skewing theory.

In order to avoid these access conflicts, the shared memory can be distributed over the parallel processor elements by providing them with "private" memories each, thus leading to an alternative parallel processor architecture. In this concepts, however, data communication is crucial, since the access by one processor to data produced by another processor and stored in its private memory has to be achieved by transmitting these data through the interconnection network which now is the only data transfer vehicle in the system.

From a technical point of view, the interconnection network has to be as simple as possible, since the number of processors is intended to be very large in this architecture in order to exploit the inherent parallelism. Since during execution of a parallel algorithm the necessary operands, which have to be available to a parallel processor element, are typically results of operations by other processors, they must be transferred to the processor requesting the operands according to a data-flow structure determined by the underlying algorithm; therefore, one cannot expect that any simple interconnection pattern between the parallel processor elements will satisfy the needs of an algorithm with respect to data communication and synchronization.

4.2 Partitioning of Numerical Algorithms in Linear Algebra

Although the technology as well as the state of the art in organizing parallel processor systems seem to favour SIMD architectures - an impression which is supported also by surveying the publications on parallel processing -, there is strong impact on the development of MIMD algorithms today. One of the reasons is the appearance of the multi-CPU vector computers on the market; but aiming at major applications in physics and engineering, important projects have been set up to design innovative architectures of MIMD type [19-21]. These developments have already lead to stronger emphasis on the MIMD-algorithm design [22-27]. A drawback for the development of MIMD algorithms is the lack of a general framework for the analysis of these algorithms [28]. Nevertheless, initiated by the early attempts of designing parallel algorithms by restructuring sequential numerical algorithms of linear algebra, the strategy of partitioning the algorithmic work into subtasks of rather coarse granularity proves to be more and more successful.

As an illustrative example of an MIMD algorithm, we will present the parallel LU decomposition as developed by Lord et al. [29]. The sequential LU algorithm can be written in the form:

```
        LU-ALGORITHM:
           for k = 1 to n - 1 do

             [  find l so that
             |     |C(l,k)| = max (|C(k,k)|, ..., |C(n,k)|)
             |  PIV(k) = l                                   pivot row
             |  C(PIV(k),k) = C(k,k)                         exchange
(T_k^k):     |  r = 1/C(k,k)
             |  for i = k+1  to n do
             L     C(i,k) = r * C(i,k)                       L-elements
                for j = k+1  to n do
             [     C(PIV(k),j) = C(k,j)                      exchange
(T_k^j):     |     for i = k+1  to n do
             L     C(i,j) = C(i,j) - C(i,k) * C(k,j)         U-elements
```

This algorithm which includes pivoting can be structured into the task sequence

$$(T_k^j\ ,\ 1 \leqq k \leqq j \leqq n),$$

which can be mapped onto a task dependency graph which illustrates that the tasks

$$(T_k^{k+1},\ T_k^{k+2},\ \ldots\ldots,\ T_k^n;\ 1 \leqq k < n)$$

are mutually independent.

Therefore, a parallel LU-algorithm can be designed which will efficiently run on an MIMD parallel computer. With $P = \lceil n/2 \rceil$ processors, the tasks can be distributed in a way that processor j will execute the task sequence

$$T_1^{2j-1},\ T_1^{2j},\ T_2^{2j},\ T_2^{2j+1},\ \ldots\ldots,\ T_{n-2(j-1)}^{n}\ ;$$

thus yielding the time complexity of this parallel algorithm from the longest path in the dependency graph (Fig. 2).

$$T_p(n;LU) = O(n^2).$$

The sequential algorithm has the well-known cubic complexity:

$$T_1(n;LU) = O(n^3).$$

For numerical stability reasons, usually, pivoting cannot be omitted in LU-decomposition. In order to avoid pivoting the Givens tranformation may be applied in order to reduce a matrix A to (upper) triangular form.

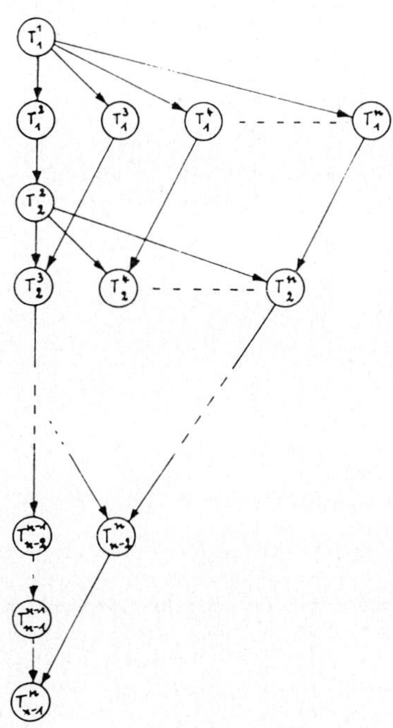

FIGURE 2
Task-Dependency Graph of MIMD LU-Decomposition
(after Lord et al. [29])

The Givens algorithm is based on the orthogonal factorization of the real, non-singular (nxn)-matrix $A=(a_{ij})$:

$$Q \cdot A = R,$$

where Q is an orthogonal matrix which is built as the product of elementary rotations; R is the resulting upper-triangular matrix.

From the task structure according to a maximum parallel dependency graph (Fig. 3), a parallel MIMD-algorithm has been designed for $P = \lceil (n-1)/2 \rceil$ parallel processors [29] yielding

$$T_p(n;\ \text{Givens}) = O(n^2),$$

compared to the sequential Givens transformation algorithm with

$$T_1(n;\ \text{Givens}) = O(n^3).$$

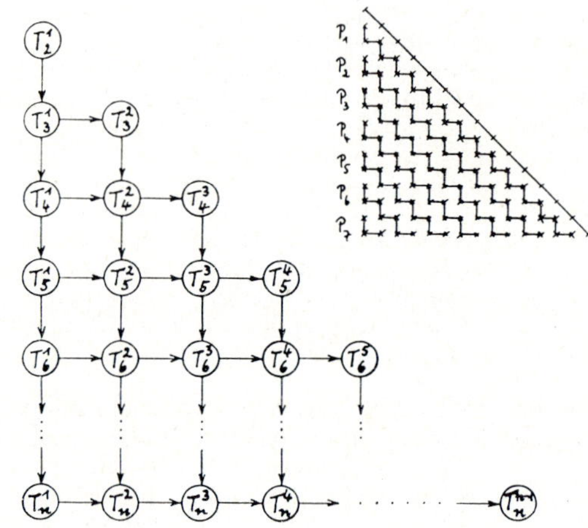

FIGURE 3
Task-Dependency Graph and "Zic-Zac"
Processor Schedule Scheme of MIMD Givens Transformation
(after Lord et al. [29])

Obviously, this partitioning strategy lends itself also to the design of algorithms for multiprocessor vector computers with multitasking like the CRAY X-MP/2x or X-MP/4x systems [30]. LU decomposition, Jacobi method, and Cholesky decomposition have been studied on CRAY X-MP utilizing the multitasking option to speed up the algorithms [31]. Also mathematical programming algorithms have been implemented on CRAY X-MP in multitasking mode yielding interesting results [32].

While these algorithms have been directly derived from the corresponding sequential algorithms, the design goals of MIMD algorithms, of course, target at genuine parallel algorithms.

The deep analysis of the LU and Givens algorithms performed by the designers [29] has hidden the serious problems involved with MIMD computers and algorithms. One of these problems is the lack of tools to analyze a computational problem in order to achieve an optimal or, at least, reasonable parallel task structure which will lead to an efficient schedule of the tasks with respect to the MIMD computer in mind. Although already good heuristics have been developed to schedule tasks on MIMD computers (see, for instance, [33]), there remain still the principal problems of designing algorithms of MIMD type. The lack of powerful paradigms and the incomplete theoretical body of knowledge concerning parallel processing leaves a challenging area of future research and development.

4.3 Non-Numerical Parallel Algorithms

While parallel algorithms were originally designed for linear algebra problems which have been dominating the field of scientific-technical applications, new areas are of growing interest.

Over the last decade, parallel sorting algorithms have been the focus of active research and development. A comprehensive survey has been published just recently [3]. The numerous parallel sorting algorithms can be broadly classified according to [3], into three categories: (1) network sorting algorithms, (2) shared memory sorting algorithms, and (3) parallel file sorting algorithms. In addition, there are several designs of hardware algorithms for sorting problems. In this field of parallel sort, typical algorithms have been designed for hypothetical computers with unlimited parallelism and memory space to solve the sorting problem in asymptotically minimal time. While the complexity of sorting today seems to be fairly understood, open questions on the complexity of parallel sorting refer to the so-called VLSI complexity combining chip area with time. After a decade of fundamental research in the theoretical complexity, in the future the technological feasibility of parallel sorting has to be investigated in a systematic way, especially with respect to limited parallelism and to the communication issue (see Chapter 5). Research is also focussing on parallel search [34].

An interesting class is represented by the asynchronous parallel algorithms where synchronizing communication between the individual processors is widely eliminated by introducing common variables, for instance, which can be accessed by all processors or, respectively, tasks. A main feature of asynchronous parallel algorithms is referred to the fact that the tasks have never to wait for the results of other tasks executed in the distributed processors. An asynchronous algorithm for the minimum-maximum search in a set of n real numbers has been implemented in multitasking mode on a two-processor CRAY X-MP yielding speedup factors up to 1.98 for large n values by Knecht [31]:

n	Execution Time without Multitasking T_1 (msec)	Execution Time with Multitasking T_2 (msec)	Speedup T_1/T_2
4000	1.74	1.55	1.12
8000	3.49	2.43	1.44
16000	6.99	4.29	1.63
32000	13.98	7.78	1.80
64000	28.27	14.77	1.91
128000	55.94	28.76	1.98
256000	112.77	56.73	1.98
512000	224.18	113.20	1.98

Increasing research activities are focussing on parallel graph algorithms (see [4] for a recent survey). Parallel graph algorithms have been developed for all models of parallel computation considered in the literature. The development of parallel graph algorithms, nevertheless, is still in its infancy, although graph theory is widely applied to problems in science and engineering where practical graph problems often require large amounts of computer time if treated on conventional serial computers. Few implementations of graph algorithms on parallel computers have been reported [35]. However, as parallel computers will become available in the future on a broader basis, the design, implementation, and application of parallel graph algorithms will experience great advances.

Whereas many parallel graph algorithms have been designed in analogy to parallel SIMD matrix algorithms by utilizing the incidence or adjacency matrices as a basis for solving graph problems [36], the strategy of partitioning is used more and more as a design principle for MIMD algorithms. An important paradigm in this respect is found in the generalized recursive doubling principle which corresponds to the divide-and-conquer strategy in sequential algorithm design and analysis and which holds for general associative operators. The paradigm is tightly related with the parallel "prefix" computation; just recently an important design of a parallel algorithm has been developed for the parallel prefix problem with data dependency (where the data addresses are given by a linked list) [37]. Therefore, the potential of the partitioning strategy will be exploited for rather complex problems.

Recently, in addition to the work on the design and analysis of algorithms and data structures for the efficient solution of graph theoretic problems on MIMD computers by Quinn [38], graph algorithms for MIMD computers have been studied and implemented in multitasking mode on CRAY X-MP by Gurke [39] including the shortest-path problem, the minimal spanning tree problem as well as the traveling salesman problem realizing Karp's partitioning algorithm.

These research areas will expand further also due to the impact of artificial intelligence and the computer projects of the next generations, where the issue of parallel processors and parallel algorithms will become crucial.

5. OPTIMIZING VERSUS COMPROMIZING: BALANCING COMPUTATION AND COMMUNICATION COMPLEXITIES OF SIMD ALGORITHMS

The design and investigation of interconnection networks for SIMD systems has become a broad field of research (for a recent survey see G. Broomell and J.R. Heath [40]. According to the types of interconnection patterns we can classify the parallel processor structures which have been extensively analyzed with respect to parallel algorithms for SIMD-type parallel processors. Certainly one of the most interesting interconnection networks is found in the Omega network [41] consisting of $n=\log P$ successive perfect-shuffle stages with (2x2)-switching units ($P=2^n$); the Omega network presents a powerful system to provide $O(\log P)$ communication complexity for a wide class of applications. In addition, it has been proved to map classes of skewing schemata utilized for conflict-free access to data structures in parallel linear algebra algorithms. The Omega network has been recently extended to redundant fault-tolerant systems by exploiting generalized shuffle operations [42].

Obviously, the models of parallel computing must include the costs of synchronization and data transfers in addition to the operation counts for the computational steps of a parallel algorithm. It is necessary to define, in addition to the time (and space) complexity, a measure which takes into account these data communication costs: the communication complexity $C_p(n)$, which is counting the number of data transfer steps necessary for a parallel processor system. Thus, $C_p(n)$ depends on the algorithm, the problem size n and the interconnect structure of the parallel computer as well; hence, the design and analysis of parallel algorithms is getting even more complicated and is requesting for new paradigms [43].

Hence, we have two options in order to design and implement parallel algorithms effectively: (1) We have to look for more powerful interconnections yielding "sub-linear" communication complexity; (2) We have to search for parallel algorithms which balance the computation time and the communication effort by the same complexity order.

5.1 Optimal Matching: FFT

An extraordinary example of adapting the interconnection network to the computational and data-flow structure of an algorithm (and vice versa) is represented by the parallel Fast Fourier Transform (FFT).

Cooley and Tukey have outlined already in 1965 in their original paper on the sequential FFT algorithm that it can be translated into a parallel algorithm [44].

This sequential FFT yields the time complexity

$$T_1(N;\ FFT) = O(N\log N).$$

This recursive algorithm is easily translated into a parallel algorithm. Introducing the binary representation

$$r = (r_{n-1}, \ldots, r_0)$$

$$f(r, k) = (r_{n-1}, \ldots, 0, r_{n-k-1}, \ldots, r_0)$$

$$h(r, k) = (r_{n-1}, \ldots, 1, r_{n-k-1}, \ldots, r_0)$$

$$g(r, k) = (r_{n-k}, \ldots, r_{n-1}, 0, \ldots, 0)$$

$$\mathrm{rev}(r) = (r_0, \ldots\ldots\ldots\ldots, r_{n-1}) = g(r, n)$$

and defining the operations as to be executed in parallel for the set of indices in brackets, the parallel FFT for the case $N=2^n$ can be written in the following form (where w is the N-th root of unity and the $c_0(j)$ are the Fourier coefficients):

$$z_j = w^j, \quad (0 \leqq j \leqq N-1);$$

$$c_j = c_0(j), \quad (0 \leqq j \leqq N-1);$$

for k=1 step 1 until n do

$$c_j = c_{f(j,k)} + z_{g(j,k)} \cdot c_{h(j,k)}, \quad (0 \leqq j \leqq N-1);$$

$$q_j = c_{\mathrm{rev}(j)}, \quad (0 \leqq j \leqq N-1).$$

This parallel algorithm yields the time complexity

$$T_p(N;FFT) = O(\log N)$$

utilizing P=N processor elements.

If we consider the data-flow graph corresponding to the sequential Cooley-Tukey algorithm which in each recursive step s brings together pairs of operands (according to the "butterfly" operation) which are initially separated by a displacement 2^{n-s}, we can map this data-flow graph into an isomorphous data-flow graph which consists of n successive perfect-shuffle stages with N/2 "butterfly" processors on each stage which perform the complex multiplication of one operand with the adequate power of w as well as the addition and, respectively, subtraction of this product to or, respectively, from the other operand fed into the processor element.

In this parallel FFT utilizing the perfect-shuffle interconnection, the structure of the parallel computations and the parallel flow of data are optimally balanced yielding O(logN) each. Therefore, this parallel procedure can easily be mapped onto an integrated parallel FFT computer.

5.2 Suboptimal Balance: Matrix Multiplication

5.2.1 Optimal Parallel Matrix Multiplication

Utilizing binary tree structures, the effective design principle for parallel algorithms can be illustrated: the recursive doubling, which is a special case of tree-height reduction as a general design method: A computation is recursively divided in two independent subtasks of identical complexity; but contrary to the sequential algorithm, the operations on each level of recursive decomposition are executed in parallel on individual processing elements, where parallel processing is starting on the lowest level of independent (elementary) operations after feeding the input operands into the leaves of the equivalent binary tree. If we consider the ordinary sequential multiplication of matrices,

$$C = A \cdot B,$$

where A, B, and C are (n x n) square matrices, just for simplicity, the computation of each element c_{ij} requires n multiplications and (n-1) additions, thus leading to the cubic time complexity $n^2(2n-1)$:

$$T_1(n) = O(n^3) .$$

For the optimal parallel algorithm we need n^3 parallel processors in order to execute the n multiplications in one time step for all inner products

$$c_{ij} = \sum_{k=1}^{n} a_{ik} b_{kj}, \quad 1 \leq i,j \leq n,$$

simultaneously; based on the recursive-doubling principle, the n^2 summations of the individual products can be performed with $n^2 \cdot n/2$ processors by adding them pairwise in parallel continuing with the parallel pairwise addition of the intermediate sums recursively, thus yielding each inner product in $\lceil \log n \rceil$ time steps. The time complexity of this parallel algorithm is therefore

$$T_p(n) = \lceil \log n \rceil + 1 = O(\log n)$$

where, in total, $P=n^3$ parallel processor elements are required. Comparing this result with the sequential algorithm of the ordinary type outlined above (or even with Strassen's algorithm), the speedup by the parallel algorithm is tremendous:

$$S_p(n) = O(n^3/\log n).$$

Similar results hold true for many other computational problems thus leading to very optimistic views on parallel computing, if the high number of processors and the communication requirements are ignored.

5.2.2 Linear-Time Array Matrix Multiplication

The dilemma between computation and communication has been ignored for a long time in parallel algorithm design and analysis. This can be seen from the fact that the first significant contribution to treat this problem has been published by Gentleman in 1978 [45]. As a model of computation he considers a very large number of independent processors, each with its own (private) memory. Data paths are provided to move data between processors, but data from one processor are available directly only to a limited number of other processors; in general, the transfer of data from one processor to another requires several transfer steps moving the data via the links between adequate intermediate nodes which are directly connected.

Gentleman has shown within more general results, that on a computer structure which is classified as an (nxn)-mesh-connected parallel computer, any computational problem depending on n^2 input data (like matrix multiplication and matrix inversion) is characterized by a linear order of the communication complexity:

$$C_p(n) = O(n).$$

If we refer to the optimal parallel algorithm for matrix multiplication with $T_p(n)=O(\log n)$, we recognize that this algorithm cannot be mapped onto such a mesh-connected parallel processor in any efficient way, since the performance of the algorithm will be dominated by the communication complexity which is linear while the computational complexity is logarithmic.

A parallel multiplication algorithm for (nxn)-square matrices $C=A\cdot B$ on a two-dimensional (nxn)-mesh-connected computer which, compared with the optimal algorithm yielding $O(\log n)$ time complexity, shows a linear dependency on the matrix size n. This algorithm, thus, provides a comfortable compromise: $T_p(n)=O(n)$ with $P=n^2$ processors.

If we consider again the inner-product form of matrix multiplication and if we introduce the modulo function, we can substitute $k=(i+j-s) \bmod n$ yielding

$$c_{ij} = \sum_{s=0}^{n-1} a_{i,(i+j-s)\bmod n} \cdot b_{(i+j-s)\bmod n,j}$$

$$= \sum_{r=0}^{n-1} a^*_{i,(j-r)\bmod n} \cdot b^*_{(i-r)\bmod n,j} .$$

We store the elements of the square matrices A and B into the registers of the n^2 processor elements of such nearest-neighbours interconnected array in such a skewed way that row i of A is shifted to the left by i columns, column j of B is shifted upward by j rows, while simultaneously closing rows and columns cyclicly; the multiplication algorithm proceeds rhythmically by multiplying first the element of A stored in register AREG(i,j) with the element of B stored in register BREG(i,j) of processor PE(i,j) and adding the product to the accumulated intermediate result in register CREG(i,j), simultaneously in all PE(i,j), $0\le i,j\le n-1$, and then shifting the elements of A to their neighbours on the right-hand side and the elements of B to their lower neighbours and repeating the arithmetic operations of multiplication and addition.

After n rhythmic steps alternating data shifts and arithmetic operation, the product matrix C is obtained, c_{ij} being stored in PE(i,j), $0\le i,j\le n-1$; thus $T_p(n)=O(n)$, balancing computation and communication.

5.2.3 Systolic Algorithms

Due to the alternating processes of arithmetic operations and synchronous data transfers, in analogy to the rhythm of heart function and blood flow through the veins, algorithms like the FFT on a shuffle-connected parallel processor and the linear-time matrix multiplication on an (nxn)-array are called "systolic" algorithms [46].

Since the initiating paper of Kung and Leiserson, an important alternative which is strongly supported by the progress in VLSI technology is seen in the development of linear-complexity systolic algorithms which can be mapped onto regular "systolic arrays" thus harmonizing, in their architectural concept for special applications or application classes, the arithmetic computational steps, the data transfers as well as the control functions. This leads to an interesting category of parallel hardware algorithms with already wide-spread applications.

Modifying the (nxn)-processor array to a hexagonal structure, the multiplication of banded matrices can be mapped into a systolic algorithm [46]; by a minor change of the connection paths this hexagonal array can be utilized for the LU-decomposition of the matrix C if C is shifted through the processor array.

This systolic LU-decomposition of an (nxn)-matrix C is based on the assumption that pivoting is not required; in this case, the LU-process can be written in the recurrent way:

$$c_{ij}^{(1)} = c_{ij}, \qquad 1 \leqq i, j \leqq n;$$

$$c_{ij}^{(k+1)} = c_{ij}^{(k)} - l_{ik}u_{kj}, \qquad 1 \leqq i,j \leqq n, \quad 1 \leqq k \leqq n;$$

$$l_{ik} = \begin{cases} 0 & \text{if } i < k, \\ 1 & \text{if } i = k, \\ c_{ik}^{(k)} u_{kk}^{-1} & \text{if } i > k, \end{cases}$$

$$u_{kj} = \begin{cases} 0 & \text{if } j < k, \\ c_{kj}^{(k)} & \text{if } j \geqq k, \end{cases} \qquad 1 \leqq i,j,k \leqq n.$$

The recurrence system can be derived from the sequential algorithm, which has been presented in Chapter 4. As has been mentioned there, numerical stability requires pivoting, in general, which cannot be realized by this systolic LU algorithm.

On the other hand, the Givens transformation had been developed just in order to avoid this disadvantage of the LU-decomposition with respect to parallel processing, as has been outlined also in Chapter 4.

From a detailed analysis of the Givens transformation and the data flow structure involved, a nearest-neighbour connected triangular systolic array of processing elements PE(j,k), $1 \leqq k < i \leqq n$, has been constructed for a systolic algorithm. Although it realizes the Givens rotations and the data communication streams in linear time, it yields a numerically stable solution of dense systems of linear equations [47].

There is strong scientific and technological emphasis on the development of systolic systems. These efforts have resulted in systolic algorithms and arrays for several frequent applications, for instance:

- matrix multiplication of dense and banded matrices,
- LU-decomposition of dense and banded matrices,
- inversion of triangular and symmetric matrices,
- (triangular) systems of linear equations,
- Toeplitz systems of equations,
- eigenvalues of symmetric matrices,
- least squares problems,
- convolution, filtering; DFT,
- geometric problems (convex hull),
- greatest common divisor of polynomials and binary numbers; polynomial multiplication and division,
- interpolation,
- dynamic programming,
- graph problems.

In a sense, the systolic arrays and algorithms balancing the parallel flow of computation and communication on a lattice of processing elements are in structural accordance with the traditional strategy which builds the models of natural systems on the discretization of time and space in order to analyze the dynamics and evolution of these systems; the space-time discretization in the numerical treatment of differential equations which form the mathematical basis for most current models of natural systems, is the most prominent category.

On the other hand, systolic structures are quite similar to a category of mathematical models which just recently seems to gain new scientific interest in the investigation of physical systems, showing complex, self-organizing and "chaotic" behaviour: the cellular automata [48].

The study of these parallel processes may influence the design of future parallel processing computers far beyond the concept of systolic arrays; the progress in the high-integration technologies may, on the one hand, provide necessary prerequisites, while, on the other hand, theoretical equivalences between certain cellular automata and universal computers may contribute the appropriate conceptual basis for this purpose.

Whereas most parallel computer concepts which have been pursued so far involve a relatively small number of high-level processors, the cellular automata, as well as the systolic arrays, suggest the design of parallel computer systems with very large numbers of relatively primitive processing elements. Such parallel processing systems seem to have better capabilities to map natural systems and their parallel space and time evolution into computer architecture. However, while the algorithmic analysis has initiated the design of systolic structures, the programming and control of parallel processing systems which may imitate cellular automata will be a significant challenge.

REFERENCES:

[1] Ortega, J.M. and Voigt, R.G., SIAM Review 27 (1985) 149

[2] Rodrigue, G. (ed.), Parallel Computations (Academic Press, New York, 1982)

[3] Bitton, D., De Witt, D.J., Hsiao, D.K. and Menon, J., ACM Computing Surveys 16 (1984) 287

[4] Quinn, M.J. and Deo, N., ACM Computing Surveys 16 (1984) 319

[5] Hossfeld, F., Parallele Algorithmen, Informatik-Fachberichte Vol. 64 (Springer, Heidelberg, 1983)

[6] Hwang, K., Computer Arithmetic - Principles, Architecture, and Design (Wiley, New York, 1979)

[7] Avizienis, A., IRE Trans. Electr. Computers EC-10 (1961) 389

[8] Avizienis, A., Proc. Symp. on Computers and Automata (Polytech. Inst. Brooklyn, New York, 1971) pp. 504-525

[9] Wilson, K.G., Scientific American, August 1979, 140
[10] Hwang, K. and Briggs, F.A., Computer Architecture and Parallel Processing (McGraw-Hill, New York, 1984)
[11] Buzbee, B.L., Parallel Computing 3 (1986) 187
[12] Hockney, R.W. and Jesshope, C.R., Parallel Computers (Hilger, Bristol, 1981)
[13] Dongarra, J.J. and Hinds, A., Report ANL-85-19 (Argonne National Laboratory, Argonne, 1985)
[14] Petersen, W.P., Comm. ACM 26 (1983) 1008
[15] Dongarra, J.J. and Eisenstat, S.C., ACM TOMS 10 (1984) 219
[16] Oed, W. and Lange, O., IEEE Trans. Computers C-34 (1985) 949
[17] Shapiro, H.D., IEEE Trans. Computers C-27 (1978) 421
[18] Wijshoff, H.A.G. and van Leeuwen, J., IEEE Trans. Computers C-34 (1985) 501
[19] Schwartz, J.T., ACM TOPLAS 2 (1980) 484
[20] Seitz, C.L., Comm. ACM 28 (1985) 22
[21] Giloi, W.K. and Mühlenbein, H., Rationale and Concepts for the SUPRENUM Supercomputer Architecture (Preprint, GMD, Birlinghoven, 1985)
[22] Kowalik, J. (ed.), Parallel MIMD Computation: The HEP Supercomputer and its Applications (MIT Press, Cambridge, 1985)
[23] Chen, S.C., Dongarra, J.J. and Hsiung, C.C., J. Parallel and Distributed Computing 1 (1984) 22
[24] Dongarra, J.J. and Sameh, A.H., Parallel Computing 1 (1984), 223
[25] Meier, U., Parallel Computing 3 (1986) 205
[26] Seitz, C.L., J. VLSI and Computer Systems 1 (1986) 311
[27] Chauvet, Y., Comp. Phys. Comm. 37 (1985) 281
[28] Weidner, P., MIMD Algorithms and Their Implementation, Proc. WOPPLOT 1986 (preprint)
[29] Lord, R.E., Kowalik, J.S. and Kumar, S.P., J. ACM 30 (1983) 103
[30] Larsen, J.L., IEEE Computer 17 (1984) 62
[31] Knecht, S., Jül-Spez-361 (Kernforschungsanlage Jülich, Juli 1986)
[32] Phillips, A.T. and Rosen, J.B., UMSI 86/28 (University of Minnesota Supercomputer Institute, Minneapolis, June 1986)
[33] Sahni, E., IEEE Trans. Computers C-33 (1984) 637
[34] Snir, M., SIAM J. Comput. 14 (1985) 688
[35] Ribeiro, C., Parallel Computing 1 (1984) 287
[36] Dekel, E., Nassimi, D. and Sahni, S., SIAM J. Comput. 10 (1981) 657
[37] Kruskal, C.P., Rudolph, L. and Snir, M., IEEE Trans. Computers C-34 (1985) 965
[38] Quinn, M.J., The Design and Analysis of Algorithms and Data Structures for the Efficient Solution of Graph Theoretic Problems on MIMD Computers, Ph.D. Dissertation (Washington State University, Pullman, 1983)
[39] Gurke, R., Jül-Spez-355 (Kernforschungsanlage Jülich, Juni 1986)
[40] Broomell, G. and Heath, J.R., ACM Computing Surveys 15 (1983) 95
[41] Lawrie, D.H., IEEE Trans. Computers C-24 (1975) 1145
[42] Padmanabhan, K. and Lawrie, D.H., IEEE Trans. Computers C-32 (1983) 1099
[43] Hossfeld, F., Parallel Algorithms: The Impact of Communication Complexity, Colloquia Mathematica Societatis János Bolyai 44, Theory of Algorithms (Pécs, Hungary 1984) pp. 207
[44] Cooley, J.W. and Tukey, J.W., Math. Comp. 19 (1965) 297
[45] Gentleman, W.M., J. ACM 25 (1978) 112
[46] Kung, H.T. and Leiserson, C.E., Systolic Arrays (for VLSI), Sparse Matrix Proceedings 1978 (SIAM, 1979) pp. 256
[47] Bojanczyk, A., Brent, R.P. and Kung, H.T., SIAM J. Sci. Stat. Comput. 5 (1984) 95
[48] Farmer, D., Toffoli, T. and Wolfram, S. (eds.), Cellular Automata, Proc. Interdisciplinary Workshop, Los Alamos, Special Issue of Physica 10D (North-Holland, Amsterdam, 1984)

Parallel Systems and Computation
G. Paul and G.S. Almasi (Editors)

Algorithm Design for High-Performance Computers*

J. J. Dongarra and D. C. Sorensen

Mathematics and Computer Science Division
Argonne National Laboratory
9700 South Cass Avenue
Argonne, Illinois 60439-4844

Introduction

In this paper we look at two ways of constructing algorithms for parallel architectures. The first is based on taking well-understood algorithms and restructuring them to isolate simple, computationally intense modules. We then parallelize the well-defined modules for the specific architecture. In the second approach we develop new algorithms for parallel architectures.

Our main emphasis is on algorithms for solving linear algebra problems where the software we develop would reside in a library on high-performance computers.

We also discuss a software environment for developing parallel algorithms in Fortran. This environment provides for ease of program development, debugging, and algorithm understanding.

A Look at EISPACK and LINPACK

Both EISPACK [16, 13] and LINPACK [5] are based on the *decompositional* approach to numerical linear algebra. The general idea is the following. Given a problem involving a matrix A, one factors or decompose A into a product of simpler matrices, from which the problem can easily be solved. This divides the computational problem into two parts: first compute an appropriate decomposition; then use it to solve the problem at hand.

EISPACK is a collection of routines that compute the eigenvalues and eigenvectors of matrices and matrix systems. The algorithms in EISPACK are primarily based on Algol procedures developed in the 1960's by nineteen different authors and published in the journal *Numerische Mathematik*. J.H. Wilkinson and C. Reinsch collected a number of these procedures, together with some background material, in a volume entitled *Linear Algebra* in the *Handbook for Automatic Computation* series[18] .

In early 1970 a group of researchers from Argonne National Laboratory, the University of Texas, and Stanford University proposed to the National Science

* Work supported in part by the Applied Mathematical Sciences subprogram of the Office of Energy Research, U.S. Department of Energy, under Contracts W-31-109-Eng-38, DE-AC05-840R21400, and DE-FG02-85ER25001.

Foundation a project to "explore the methodology, costs, and resources required to produce, test and disseminate high-quality mathematical software and to test, certify, disseminate, and support packages of mathematical software". The project was to take the algorithms dealing with the eigenvalue problem from the Wilkinson - Reinsch *Handbook;* translate them to Fortran; and produce a portable, robust, accurate, uniform, and well-documented package. At the time, little thought was given to high-performance computers; the state of the art in supercomputers was a CDC 7600. By May of 1972 the collection of Fortran routines called EISPACK was ready for public use.

A few years later there was a general feeling in the community that a unified package dealing with the solution of linear equations was needed. LINPACK is a package of routines for solving various kinds of linear systems of equations. The subroutines in the package are not the result of a translation but of a rewrite of many of the algorithms to conform to a certain style.

LINPACK uses column-oriented algorithms to preserve locality of reference. Column orientation means that the LINPACK codes always reference arrays down columns, not across rows. This approach works because Fortran stores arrays in column order. Thus, as one proceeds down a column of an array, references proceed sequentially in memory. On the other hand, as one proceeds across a row references jump across memory, the length of the jump being proportional to the length of a column. The effects of column orientation are dramatic; on systems with virtual or cache memories, the LINPACK codes will significantly outperform codes that are not column oriented.

An important factor affecting the efficiency of LINPACK is the use of the Basic Linear Algebra Subprograms (BLAS)[15]. This set of subprograms performs basic operations from linear algebra, such as computing an inner product or adding a multiple of one vector to another. In LINPACK the great majority of floating-point calculations are done within the BLAS.

One difficulty with using the BLAS, however, is that they operate only on vectors. However, the algorithms as implemented tend to do more data movement than is necessary. As a result, the performance of the routines in LINPACK suffers on high-performance computers where data movement is as costly as floating-point operations. To illustrate the point, we examine in Table 1 the peak theoretical performance of various high-performance computers available today.

Table 1
Theoretical Peak Performance

Machine	Cycle time, nsec	Number Procs,	Peak Perf, MFLOPS
CONVEX C-1	100	1	20
SCS-40	45	1	44
Alliant FX/8	170	8	94
FPS 264	38	1	54
Amdahl 500	7.5	1	133
CRAY-1	12.5	1	160
CRAY X-MP-1	9.5	1	210
IBM 3090/VF-200	18.5	2	216
Amdahl 1100	7.5	1	267
NEC SX-1E	7	1	325
CDC CYBER 205	20	1	400
CRAY X-MP-2	9.5	2	420
IBM 3090/VF-400	18.5	4	432
Amdahl 1200	7.5	1	533
NEC SX-1	7	1	650
CRAY X-MP-4	9.5	4	840
Hitachi S-810/20	14	1	840
NEC SX-2	6	1	1300
CRAY-2	4.1	4	2000

By peak theoretical performance we mean that the manufactures guarantees that programs will not exceed these rates, sort of a *speed of light* for a given computer.

In practice, with LINPACK routines SGEFA and SGESL (used to solve dense systems of equations) we observe the following:[4].

Table 2
LINPACK Benchmark

Machine	Peak Performance MFLOPS	Actual Performance MFLOPS	System Efficiency
CONVEX C-1	20	3.0	.15
SCS-40	44	5.5	.18
Alliant FX/8	94	7.6 (8 proc)	.08
FPS 264	54	5.6	.10
Amdahl 500	133	14	.11
CRAY-1	160	12	.075
CRAY X-MP-1	210	24	.11
IBM 3090/VF-200	216	12 (1 proc)	.11(.056)
Amdahl 1100	267	16	.060
NEC SX-1E	325	35	.11
CDC CYBER 205	400	17	.043
CRAY X-MP-2	420	24 (1 proc)	.11(.057)
IBM 3090/VF-400	432	12 (1 proc)	.11(.028)
Amdahl 1200	533	18	.034
NEC SX-1	650	39	.06
CRAY X-MP-4	840	24 (1 proc)	.11(.029)
Hitachi S-810/20	840	17	.020
NEC SX-2	1300	46	.035
CRAY-2	2000	15 (1 proc)	.030(.0075)

At one time, a programmer had to go out of his way to code a matrix routine that would not run at nearly top efficiency on any system with an optimizing compiler. Owing to the proliferation of exotic computer architectures, this situation is no longer true. However, by using one of the new features of many modern computers namely, hierarchical memory organization one can gain high performance by some algorithmic ingenuity.

Restructuring Algorithms

Typically a hierarchical memory structure involves a sequence of computer memories ranging from a small, but very fast memory at the bottom to a capacious, but slow memory at the top. Since a particular memory in the hierarchy (call it M) is not as big as the memory at the next level (M'), only part of the information in M'

will be contained in M. If a reference is made to information that is in M, then it is retrieved as usual. However, if the information is not in M, then it must be retrieved from M', with a loss of time. To avoid repeated retrieval, information is transferred from M' to M in blocks, the supposition being that if a program references an item in a particular block, the next reference is likely to be in the same block. Programs having this property are said to have *locality of reference.*

If we examine the algorithm used in LINPACK and look at how the data are referenced, we see that at each step of the factorization process there are vector operations that modify a full submatrix of data. This update causes a block of data to be read, updated, and written back to central memory. The number of floating point operations is $\frac{2}{3}n^3$ and the number of data references, both loads and stores, is $\frac{2}{3}n^3$. Thus, for every *add/multiply* pair we must perform a load and store of the elements, unfortunately obtaining no reuse of data. Even though the operations are fully vectorized, there is a significant bottleneck in data movement, resulting in poor performance (see Table 2). On vector computers this translates into 2 vector operations and 3 vector-memory references. To achieve high-performance rates, this *operation to memory reference rate* must be higher.

It is possible to express the algorithms in terms of matrix-vector operations. These operations have the benefit that they can reuse data and achieve a higher rate of execution than the vector counterpart. In fact, the number of floating-point operations remains the same; only the data reference pattern is changed. This change results in a operation to memory reference rate on vector computers of effectively 2 vector operations and 1 vector-memory reference.

When the algorithm is recast to minimize memory traffic, the results can be impressive. In [7] the algorithm for solving dense systems of linear equations was recast in terms of a matrix-vector multiply, which has the desired effect (see Table 3).

Table 3
Comparison with Matrix-Vector Operations

Machine	Performance Before MFLOPS	Performance After MFLOPS	System Efficiency
CONVEX C-1	3.0	9.6	.48
SCS-40	5.5	13	.30
Alliant FX/8	7.6 (8 procs)	10	.11
FPS 264	5.6	24	.44
CRAY-1	12	38	.24
CRAY X-MP-1	24	48	.23
IBM 3090/VF-200	12	24(1 proc)	.22
Amdahl 1100	16	48	.18
NEC SX-1E	35	71	.22
CDC CYBER 205	17	24	.06
CRAY X-MP-2	24 (1 proc)	37 (2 procs)	.088
IBM 3090/VF-400	12	24(1 proc)	.22
Amdahl 1200	18	52	.098
NEC SX-1	39	74	.11
CRAY X-MP-4	24 (1 proc)	74 (4 procs)	.088
Hitachi S-810/20	17	48	.057
NEC SX-2	46	100	.076
CRAY-2	14	28 (1 proc)	.056

The same behavior can be seen for many of the algorithms in linear algebra[9].

Table 4 shows the comparison between the original EISPACK formulation and the restructured matrix-vector algorithms.

Table 4
Speedup of Matrix-Vector Versions over the EISPACK Routines

Routine	order 50	100	Machine
ELMHES	1.5	2.2	CRAY 1
ORTHES	2.0	1.9	CRAY 1
ELMBAK	2.2	2.6	CRAY 1
ORTBAK	2.8	2.5	CRAY 1
TRED1	1.5	1.5	CRAY X-MP-1
TRBAK1	4.2	3.7	CRAY X-MP-1
TRED2	1.6	1.6	CRAY X-MP-1
SVD no/v	1.7	2.0	Hitachi S-810/20
SVD w/v	1.6	1.7	Hitachi S-810/20
REDUC	1.8	2.2	Fujitsu VP-200
REBAK	4.4	5.8	Fujitsu VP-200

The data represent a Fortran implementations; no attempt was make to explicitly exploit the vector hardware through assembly language.

These algorithms can be thought of as having n major steps. At each of these major steps we reduce one column of the matrix by an application of a matrix-vector operation. To get more reuse of data, we can think of performing multiple column reductions at a each major step, so instead of performing n matrix-vector operations, we can apply, say, $n/2$ major steps, were each step applies two matrix-vector operations or a *matrix-matrix* operation. The computation can be organized to reuse the matrix, so the operation is in fact a matrix-matrix multiplication, where one of the matrices has 2 columns. Thus by doing more than one major step of the algorithm at a time we get reuse of data and a reduction in the memory traffic.

As an example of this we have taken the computation involved with reducing a matrix to Hessenberg form, this is performed during the computation of the eigenvalues of a general matrix.

Table 5
Speedup of over Vector-Vector Version
CRAY 1

Routine	order 50	order 100
ORTHES (one column reduced per step)	2.0	1.9
ORTHES (two columns reduced per step)	2.5	2.5
ORTBAK (one column reduced per step)	2.8	2.5
ORTBAK (two columns reduced per step)	3.6	3.3

If we look at the current generation of high-performance computers on the market, we see even more emphasis on memory hierarchies. Machines such as the CRAY-2, FPS 164/w MAX boards, Alliant FX/8, NAS AS/XL 60, Sperry 1100/90 w/ISP, Star Technology's ST-100, and IBM 3090/VF all have an additional level of memory between the main memory and the vector registers of the processor. This memory, referred to as *cache* or *local memory* is relatively small (on the order of 16K words in some cases) and may not be under the control of the programmer.

Nevertheless, the issues are the same: to come close to gaining peak performance, one must optimize the use of this level of memory (i.e. retain information as long as possible before the next access to main memory) obtaining as much reuse as possible. In the case of matrix factorization this means that instead of *matrix-vector* operations, one must perform *matrix-matrix* operations[10, 8]. Here we can achieve a high operation to memory reference rate. In the case of matrix-matrix operations we get a *surface to volume* effect, $O(mn^2)$ operations to $O(mn)$ memory references. An effort is currently under way to recast the algorithms from linear algebra in terms of these Level 3 BLAS, matrix-matrix operations. This involves modifying the algorithm to perform more than one step of the decomposition process at a given loop iteration.

In an attempt to easily transport algorithms to a wide variety of architectures and to achieve high performance, we are isolating the computationally intense parts in high-level modules. When the architecture changes, we deal with the modules separately, rewriting them in terms of machine-specific operations; however, the basic algorithm remains the same. By doing so we can achieve the goal of a high operation to memory reference ratio.

This technique will work will with a computer system that has a modest number of processors, say less than 100. We can think of spreading the matrix-matrix operation over the available processors. However, when the number of available processors to exceeds 100, we must rethink the algorithms to gain the potential benefits.

1. Developing New Algorithms

The ideas presented in the previous section are fine for low-level parallelism, something on the order of 1 to 100 processors. As the number of processors grow, however, we are required to rethink the algorithms. Amdahl's law shows us that with 16 processors, if 95 percent of the computation can be parallelized, then we can expect only a speedup of around 9; and with an unlimited number of processors, and 95 percent of the computation in parallel, the speedup can be at most 20.

As an example of the kind of rethinking that must occur to use a large number of processors effectively, we look at the problem of computing the eigenvalue and eigenvectors of a symmetric tridiagonal matrix. The classical method of solution, the QR algorithm, is an iterative procedure based on [12].

The process is sequential and is not amenable to parallization. We can, however implement an algorithm, based on a divide-and-conquer scheme proposed by Cuppen[3], that does not suffer from loss of parallelism associated with typical divide-and-conquer approaches[11]. This new parallel algorithm retains throughout the computation a number of active parallel processes greater than or equal to the initial number.

The crux of the algorithm is to divide a given problem into two smaller subproblems. To do this, we consider the symmetric tridiagonal matrix

$$T = \begin{bmatrix} T_1 & \beta e_k e_1^T \\ \beta e_1 e_k^T & T_2 \end{bmatrix}$$

$$= \begin{bmatrix} \hat{T}_1 & 0 \\ 0 & \hat{T}_2 \end{bmatrix} + \theta\beta \begin{bmatrix} e_k \\ \theta^{-1} e_1 \end{bmatrix} (e_k^T , \theta^{-1} e_1^T)$$

where $1 \leq k \leq n$ and e_j represents the $j-th$ unit vector of appropriate dimension. The $k-th$ diagonal element of T_1 has been modified to give $\hat{T}_1$, and the first diagonal element of T_2 has been modified to give $\hat{T}_2$. Potential numerical difficulties associated with cancellation may be avoided through the appropriate choice of θ. If the diagonal entries to be modified are of the same sign, then $\theta = \pm\ 1$ is chosen so that $-\theta\beta$ has this sign and cancellation is avoided. If the two diagonal entries are of opposite sign, then the sign of θ is chosen so that $-\theta\beta$ has the same sign as one of the elements, and the magnitude of θ is chosen to avoid severe loss of significant digits when $\theta^{-1}\beta$ is subtracted from the other. This is perhaps a minor detail, but it does allow the partitioning to be selected solely on the basis of position and without regard to numerical considerations.

We now have two smaller tridiagonal eigenvalue problems to solve. According to the equation above we compute the two eigensystems

$$\hat{T}_1 = Q_1 D_1 Q_1^T , \quad \hat{T}_2 = Q_2 D_2 Q_2^T .$$

This gives

$$T = \begin{bmatrix} Q_1 D_1 Q_1^T & 0 \\ 0 & Q_2 D_2 Q_2^T \end{bmatrix} + \theta\beta \begin{bmatrix} e_k \\ \theta^{-1} e_1 \end{bmatrix} (e_k^T , \theta^{-1} e_1^T)$$

$$= \begin{bmatrix} Q_1 & 0 \\ 0 & Q_2 \end{bmatrix} \left[\begin{bmatrix} D_1 & 0 \\ 0 & D_2 \end{bmatrix} + \theta\beta \begin{bmatrix} q_1 \\ \theta^{-1} q_2 \end{bmatrix} (q_1^T , \theta^{-1} q_2^T) \right] \begin{bmatrix} Q_1^T & 0 \\ 0 & Q_2^T \end{bmatrix}$$

where $q_1 = Q_1^T e_k$ and $q_2 = Q_2^T e_1$. The problem at hand is to compute the eigensystem of the interior matrix in the equation above. A numerical method for solving this problem has been provided in [3] and a full description can be found in [11].

A perhaps surprising result for the performance of the parallel algorithm is that, even when run in serial mode, the parallel algorithm is significantly faster than the previously best sequential algorithm on large problems, and is effective on moderate size (order $\geq$ 30) problems when run in serial mode.

n	Ratio of time TQL2/SESUPD	TQL2 $\|\|Ax - \lambda x\|\|$	SESUPD $\|\|Ax - \lambda x\|\|$	TQL2 $\|\|X^T X - I\|\|$	SESUPD $\|\|X^T X - I\|\|$
50	.78	1.6×10^{-12}	4.8×10^{-13}	1.9×10^{-12}	1.2×10^{-13}
100	1.26	2.6×10^{-12}	7.6×10^{-13}	3.9×10^{-12}	2.5×10^{-12}
200	1.93	6.1×10^{-12}	1.8×10^{-12}	7.0×10^{-12}	5.8×10^{-11}
300	3.62	1.1×10^{-11}	3.3×10^{-12}	1.1×10^{-11}	2.8×10^{-12}
400	4.70	1.2×10^{-11}	3.8×10^{-12}	1.4×10^{-11}	3.8×10^{-12}

A comparison on the CRAY X-MP for TQL2 vs the parallel algorithm run sequentially

As can be seen in the table above, the performance of the parallel algorithm as implemented to run on a sequential machine is impressive. The surprising result here is the observed speed up even in serial mode of execution. This is unusual in a parallel algorithm. Often more work is associated with synchronization and computational overhead required to split the problem into parallel parts.

Tools for Developing and Analyzing Parallel Fortran Programs

Many new parallel computers are now emerging as commercial products[6]. Exploitation of the parallel capabilities requires either extensions to an existing language such as Fortran or development of an entirely new language. A number of activities[17, 19] are under way to develop new languages that promise to provide the ability to exploit parallelism without the considerable effort that may be required in using an inherently serial language that has been extended for parallelism. We applaud such activities and expect they will offer a true solution to the software dilemma in the future. However, in the short term we feel there is a need to confront some of the software issues, with particular emphasis placed on transportability and use of existing software.

Our interests lie mainly with mathematical software typically associated with scientific computations. Therefore, we concentrate here on using the Fortran language. Each vendor of a parallel machine designed primarily for numerical calculations has provided its own parallel extensions to Fortran. These extensions have taken many forms already and are usually dictated by the underlying hardware and by the capabilities that the vendor wishes to supply the user. This has led to widely different extensions ranging from the ability to synchronize on every assignment of a variable with a full empty property[14] to attempts at automatically detecting loop-based parallelism with a preprocessing compiler aided by user directives[2]. The act of getting a parallel process executing on a physical processor ranges from a simple "create" statement[14] which imposes the overhead of a subroutine call, to "tskstart" [1] which imposes an overhead on the order of 10^6 machine cycles, to no formal mechanism whatsoever[2]. These different approaches reflect characteristics of underlying hardware and operating systems and to a large extent are dictated by the vendors view of which aspects of parallelism are marketable. It is too early to impose a standard on these vendors, yet it is disconcerting that there is no agreement among any of them on which extensions should be included. There is not even an agreed-upon naming convention for extensions that have identical functionality. Program developers interested in producing implementations of parallel algorithms that will run on a number of different parallel machines are therefore faced with an overwhelming task. The process of developing portable parallel packages is complicated by additional factors that lie beyond each computer manufacturer supplying its own, very different mechanism for parallel processing. A given implementation may require several different communicating parallel processes, perhaps with different levels of granularity. An efficient implementation may require the ability to dynamically start processes, perhaps many more than the number of physical processors in the system. This feature is either lacking or prohibitively expensive on most commercially available parallel computers. Instead, many of the manufacturers have limited themselves to providing one-level loop-based parallelism.

We have developed an environment for the transportable implementation of parallel algorithms in a Fortran setting. By this we mean that a user's code is virtually identical for each machine. The main tool in this environment is a package called SCHEDULE which has been designed to aid a programmer familiar with a Fortran programming environment to implement a parallel algorithm in a manner that will lend itself to transporting the resulting program across a wide variety of parallel machines. The package is designed to allow existing Fortran subroutines to be called through SCHEDULE, without modification, thereby permitting users access to a wide body of existing library software in a parallel setting. Machine intrinsics are invoked within the SCHEDULE package, and considerable effort may be required on our part to move SCHEDULE from one machine to another. On the other hand, the user of SCHEDULE is relieved of the burden of modifying each code he disires to transport from one machine to another.

When designing a parallel algorithm one is required to describe the data dependencies, parallel structures, and shared variables involved in the solution. Typically, such algorithms are first designed at a conceptual level and later implemented in Fortran and its extensions. Each manufacturer provides a different set of extensions and targets these extensions at different implementation levels. For example, some manufacturers allow only test-and-set along with spawn-a-process, while others allow concurrent execution of different loop iterations.

Our attempt here is to allow the user to define the data dependencies, parallel structures, and shared variables in his application and then to implement these ideas in a Fortran program written in terms of subroutine calls to SCHEDULE. Each set of subroutine calls specifies a unit of computation or process which consists of a subroutine name along with the calling parameters and the data dependencies necessary to coordinate the parallel execution.

The basic philosophy here is that Fortran programs are naturally broken into subroutines that identify self-contained units of computation which operate on shared data structures. This allows one to call on existing library subroutines in a parallel setting without modification, and without having to write an envelope around the library subroutine call in order to conform to some unusual data-passing conventions imposed by a given parallel programming environment.

A parallel(izable) program is written in terms of calls to subroutines which, in principle, may be performed either independently or according to data dependency requirements that the user is responsible for defining. The result is a serial program that can run in parallel given a way to schedule the units of computation on a system of parallel processors while obeying the data dependencies.

There are three basic operations in SCHEDULE other than the lowest level synchronization provided through locks. They are **call sched**, **call putq**, and **call spawn**. Various additional calls must be made in association with these three basic operations to enforce data dependencies, and orchestrate the correct execution of the parallel program.

The statement

call sched(nprocs,paralg,< parms>)

is used to initiate the execution of a parallel program *paralg* and will devote *nprocs* physical processors to the computation. The symbol < *parms*> stands for a set of parameters that would normally be supplied to the Fortran subroutine *paralg* through a Fortran call in a sequential program. One should think of the memory associated with the parameter list represented by < parms> as shared memory throughout the execution of *paralg*. Another way to share memory is through the use of *named common*.

Table 6
User Calls

```
CALL SCHED ( nprocs, subname, <parms> )
CALL DEP   ( jobtag, icango, ncheks, mychkn )
CALL PUTQ  ( jobtag, subname, <parms> )
CALL PRTSPN( myid )
CALL SPAWN ( myid, jdummy, subname, <parms> )
CALL WAIT  ( myid )
CALL LCKASN( ilock )
CALL LOCKON( ilock )
CALL UNLOCK( ilock )
```

```
nprocs   - Number of virtual processors to be used on subname.
subname  - Subroutine to be executed.
<parms>  - list of parameters for subname.
jobtag   - A unique user supplied identifier.
icango   - The number of processes that must complete before
           this process starts.
ncheks   - Specifies the number of processes that depend on
           this process.
mychkn   - An integer array whose first ncheks entries
           contain the identifiers of the processes that
           depend on this process.
myid     - An alias process id assigned by SCHEDULE to record
           completion of the spawned processes.
jdummy   - A dummy integer parameter.
ilock    - A globally shared variable used as a lock.
```

The pair of statements

call dep(jobtag,icango,ncheks,mychkn)

call putq(jobtag,subname,< parms>)

are used to place a process in the large grained data dependency graph with *dep* used to record the data dependencies and *putq* to record the unit of computation. In this case the unit of computation will be a call to the subroutine *subname* with the calling sequence < *parms*> . When the data dependencies for this process have been satisfied the *icango* counter will have been decremented to zero and this process will be placed upon the ready queue. At some point in time a physical processor executing a *work* program will be free and will pick this process off of the ready queue and execute a *call subname*(< *parms*>). It is the user's responsibility to assure that the addresses passed in < *parms*> are addresses in shared memory. That is to say that these addresses must reference shared memory that has been declared in the program that made the call to *sched*. Hence these addresses must come from named common declared in that program and referenced by the subroutine *subname* or which have been passed as parameters in the call to *sched*.

Conclusions

We have presented two approaches in constructing algorithms for parallel architecture. The first is based on taking existing algorithms and modify them to run in the parallel environment. The second is to design entirely new algorithm for parallel architectures. The current state of programming existing parallel computers has forced us into implementing a Fortran software environment for which allows for the portable development, debugging, understanding of our parallel numerical algorithms.

References

References

1. *CRAY 2 Multitasking Users Guide,* Cray Research Inc, Minn, MN, 1986.
2. Alliant Computer Systems Corp, *Alliant FX/Fortran Programmer's Handbook*, Acton Mass., 1985.
3. J.J.M. Cuppen, "A Divide and Conquer Method for the Symmetric Tridiagonal Eigenproblem," *Numerische Mathematik*, vol. 36, pp. 177-195, 1981.
4. J.J. Dongarra, "Performance of Various Computers Using Standard Linear Equations Software in a Fortran Environment," Argonne National Laboratory MCS-TM-23, April, 1987.
5. J.J. Dongarra, J. Bunch, C. Moler, and G. Stewart, *LINPACK Users' Guide,* SIAM Pub., Philadelphia, 1979.
6. J.J. Dongarra and I.S. Duff, "Advanced Architecture Computers," Argonne National Laboratory Report, ANL-MCS-TM-57 (Revision 1), January, 1987.
7. J.J. Dongarra and S. C. Eisenstat, "Squeezing the Most out of an Algorithm in Cray Fortran," *ACM Trans. Math. Software*, vol. 10, 3, pp. 221-230, 1984.

8. J.J. Dongarra and T. Hewitt, "Implementing Dense Linear Algebra Algorithms Using Multitasking on the CRAY X-MP-4," *SIAM J. Sci. Stat. Comp.*, vol. 7, 1, pp. 347-350, January, 1986.

9. J.J. Dongarra, L. Kaufman, and S. Hammarling, "Squeezing the Most Out of High Performance Computers for Finding the Eigenvalues," *Linear Algebra and Its Applications*, vol. 77, pp. 113-136, 1986.

10. J.J. Dongarra and D.C. Sorensen, "Linear Algebra on High-Performance Computers," in *Proceedings Parallel Computing 85*, ed. U. Schendel, pp. 3-32, North Holland, 1986.

11. J.J. Dongarra and D.C. Sorensen, "A Fully Parallel Algorithm for the Symmetric Eigenvalue Problem," *SIAM SISSC*, vol. 8, 2, March, 1987.

12. J. Francis, "The QR Transformation, Parts I and II," *Computer Journal*, vol. 4, pp. 265-271, 332-345.

13. B.S. Garbow, J.M. Boyle, J.J. Dongarra, and C.B. Moler, *Matrix Eigensystem Routines - EISPACK Guide Extension*, 51, pp. Springer-Verlag, Lecture Notes in Computer Science, 1977.

14. H. Jordan, "HEP Architecture, Programming and Performance," in *Parallel MIMD Compuation: HEP Supercomputer and Its Applications*, ed. Ed. J. Kowalik, MIT Press, 1985.

15. C. Lawson, R. Hanson, D. Kincaid, and F. Krogh, "Basic Linear Algebra Subprograms for Fortran Usage," *ACM Transactions on Mathematical Software*, vol. 5, pp. 308-323, 1979.

16. B.T. Smith, J.M. Boyle, J.J. Dongarra, B.S. Garbow, Y. Ikebe, V. Klema, and C. Moler, *Matrix Eigensystem Routines - EISPACK Guide, Second Edition,*, 6, pp. Springer-Verlag, Lecture Notes in Computer Science, 1976.

17. John VanRosendale and Piyush Mehrotra, "The BLAZE Language: A Parallel Language for Scientific Programming," ICASE Report # 85-29, 1985.

18. J. Wilkinson and C. Reinsch, *Handbook for Automatic Computation: Volume II - Linear Algebra,* Springer-Verlag, New York, 1971.

19. J.R. McGraw, et al.,, "SISAL: Streams and Iteration in a Single Assignment Language," Language Reference Manual, Ver. 1.2, Lawerence Livermore National Laboratory M-146.

Parallel Systems and Computation
G. Paul and G.S. Almasi (Editors)
Elsevier Science Publishers B.V. (North-Holland), 1988

PARALLELISM IN SPARSE MATRICES

Iain S. Duff

Computer Science and Systems Division, Harwell Laboratory,
Didcot, Oxon OX11 0RA, England.

We discuss the solution of large sparse systems using Gaussian elimination on both local and shared memory parallel computers.
There is a natural parallelism to Gaussian elimination that has been frequently exploited. We can take advantage of this parallelism in addition to that provided by the sparsity itself. We discuss this latter parallelism in some detail.
We discuss an approach that exploits the parallelism due to the sparsity and that can automatically benefit also from the parallelism of Gaussian elimination. This approach, which is applicable to quite general systems, is based on a multifrontal technique.
We look at the implementation of the multifrontal approach on shared memory machines and discuss its implementation on a hypercube.

1. INTRODUCTION

A system of linear equations is called **sparse** if most of the entries of its coefficient matrix are zero. The solution of large sparse systems of linear equations is one of the major calculations in large-scale computation in science and engineering. It is thus of great importance to study the performance of existing and new solution techniques on the range of parallel processors which are currently being marketed.

In this paper, we consider direct methods for the solution of sparse systems. We see that these techniques, based on Gaussian elimination, exhibit a very natural small granularity parallelism even when used in the solution of **full** systems (that is systems where all entries of the coefficient matrix are treated as nonzero). Further parallelism can be obtained from the sparsity, and it is primarily the exploitation of this that we will discuss. We examine Gaussian elimination parallelism in Section 2 and illustrate the phenomenon of parallelism due to sparsity in Section 3. We discuss a general technique for automatically using both forms of parallelism in Section 4 and consider its implementation on both shared and local memory machines in Sections 5 and 6 respectively. We draw some conclusions in Section 7.

In this presentation, we have assumed that our readership has a background in computer science but not necessarily in numerical analysis. We have therefore defined the principal numerical analysis terms when they are first used.

2. PARALLELISM IN GAUSSIAN ELIMINATION

Gaussian elimination involves factorizing a matrix **A** into the product **A**=**LU** of a lower triangular matrix **L** and an upper triangular matrix **U** so that the solution to the set of linear equations **Ax**=**b** can be easily effected by solving the triangular system **Ly**=**b** followed by the triangular system **Ux**=**y**. In the case of full matrices **A**, the work for the factorization is $O(n^3)$ for a matrix of order n, while the solution of the triangular factors only involves $O(n^2)$ work. Although the factorization of a sparse matrix has a much lower operation count and is dependent on the number and distribution of nonzeros (the **sparsity pattern**), it is still true that the factorization step is much more costly than the solution phase. We therefore concentrate on the factorization step in this paper.

Assume that the coefficient matrix **A** has entries a_{ij}, $1 \leq i,j \leq n$. Gaussian elimination on a system of order n consists of $n-1$ major steps. Major step k, $1 \leq k \leq n-1$, involves the selection of a **pivot** a_{kk}. This process of selection, called **pivoting**, is used to ensure good numerical performance and is followed by the elimination of the entries $a_{k+1,k}, .., a_{nk}$ by adding appropriate multiples of row k to rows $k+1, ... n$ producing the updating operations

$$a_{ij} = a_{ij} - a_{ik}[a_{kk}]^{-1}a_{kj} \quad k < i,j \leq n \qquad (2.1)$$

on rows and columns $k+1$ to n of the matrix (the **reduced matrix**). The important feature is that each update to an entry a_{ij} is independent so that they can all be performed in parallel.

If each single update operation is considered separately then the amount of parallelism is large ($(n-1)^2$ processes at the first stage) but the communication costs are high since each process must have the entries necessary for forming its triple product (2.1). Indeed, the biggest problem in Gaussian elimination on a local memory machine is that the pivot row ($a_{k\bullet}$) and the pivot column ($a_{\bullet k}$) or the multipliers ($a_{\bullet k}[a_{kk}]^{-1}$) must be communicated to all other rows or columns of the matrix. The most common way to overcome this is to treat all the operations updating a submatrix or a column or row as a single unit, thus increasing the granularity although decreasing the number of parallel processes. Many authors have suggested doing this for the Cholesky factorization (Gaussian elimination on a symmetric **A** to produce the factorization $\mathbf{A}=\mathbf{LL}^T$) on a hypercube both by subdividing **A** into submatrices and assigning a submatrix to each processor (Saad 1986) or by splitting the matrix into columns and assigning columns to processors either in a wrap around fashion or by contiguous blocks (Geist and Heath 1985). It is fairly easy to incorporate pivoting with this approach, advantage being taken of its lower order of complexity relative to the (2.1) update (Geist 1985). It is also possible to design a sparse version of the Cholesky factorization although present experience with it is disappointing (George *et al.* 1986a, 1986b). In Section 4 we consider a more general technique for sparse systems.

For surveys of parallel algorithms for full systems we refer the reader to Heller (1978) or Sameh (1983).

3. PARALLELISM DUE TO SPARSITY

In Gaussian elimination on full systems, the major steps must be done sequentially. Although it is not necessary to wait until the completion of the first step before commencing the second, the second pivot must be updated before it can be used. Similarly, the third pivot must have been updated by both first and second steps before it can be used. The wavefront approach to Cholesky decomposition (Kung *et al.* 1981, O'Leary and Stewart 1985) uses pivots as soon as they are updated but must still process the pivots in order. However, if sparsity is present, this constraint of sequential pivoting does not necessarily hold.

The easiest way to see the influence of sparsity in removing the sequential pivot restriction is to consider the simple example of a tridiagonal matrix, arguably the most common sparse matrix.

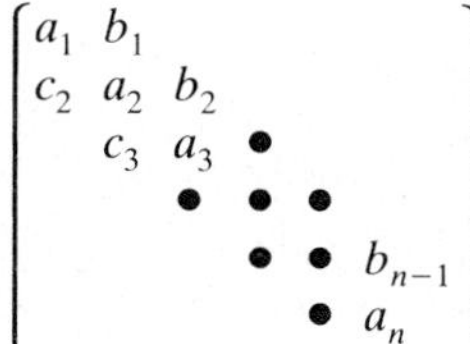

Figure 3.1. A tridiagonal matrix.

From the example of a tridiagonal matrix shown in Figure 3.1, it is clear that selecting pivots in order down the diagonal imposes a sequential restriction. However, without increasing the number of arithmetic operations, we can simultaneously choose the first and last diagonal entries as pivot. Continuing in this way on the reduced matrix, we get the burn at both ends (BABE) algorithm with a parallelism of two throughout most of the calculation. If we allow an increase in the number of arithmetic operations then far greater parallelism can be obtained. Indeed, we can choose as pivots diagonal entries a_1, a_3, a_5, ... and obtain a parallelism of $[n/2]$ at the first stage. Although this ordering causes some zero entries in **A** to become nonzero in the factors (that is it causes **fill-in**) and more work than the sequential or BABE algorithms, if it is applied successively to subsequent reduced matrices, the number of major steps is $[log_2 n]$ rather than the $n-1$ of the sequential algorithm. Indeed, this is just the pivotal ordering that the nested dissection ordering of George (1973) would give us. Duff and Johnsson (1986) have looked at the effect of this ordering and others on general systems, but we defer further comments until we describe our approach for general systems in the following section.

4. MULTIFRONTAL TECHNIQUES

Multifrontal methods are described in some detail by Duff, Erisman, and Reid (1986) and their potential for parallelism by Duff (1986). We do not intend to describe this class of methods in detail here but we will work through a small example shown in Figure 4.1 to give the reader a flavour for the important points and to introduce the notion of an elimination tree (discussed in detail by Duff 1986 and Liu 1986). In Figure 4.1, × denotes a nonzero entry and zeros are left blank.

$$\begin{array}{cccc} \times & & \times & \times \\ & \times & \times & \times \\ \times & \times & \times & \\ \times & \times & & \times \end{array}$$

Figure 4.1. Matrix used to illustrate multifrontal scheme.

We assume the matrix in Figure 4.1 is ordered so that pivots will be chosen down the diagonal in order. At the first step we can perform the elimination step corresponding to row and column 1 by first **assembling** row and column 1 to get the submatrix

$$\begin{array}{ccc} \times & \times & \times \\ \times & & \\ \times & & \end{array} ,$$

Figure 4.2. Assembly of first pivot row and column.

which is termed a **frontal matrix**. By 'assembling', we mean placing (or summing) the nonzeros of row and column 1 into an array of dimension the number of nonzeros in row and column 1. Thus the zero entries a_{12} and a_{21} have been omitted in Figure 4.2 and an index vector is required to identify the rows and columns in the frontal matrix. Column 1 is then eliminated using pivot (1,1) to give a reduced matrix of order two with associated row (and column) indices 3 and 4. Note that, at this stage, no reference has been made to any of the other entries of the original matrix. The updating operations corresponding to the entries of the reduced matrix are not performed immediately and the reduced matrix can be stored until these updates are necessary. Row (and column) 2 is now assembled, the (2,2) entry is used as pivot to eliminate column 2, and the reduced matrix of order two, with associated row (and column) indices of 3 and 4, is stored. Before we perform the pivot operations using entry (3,3), the updating operations from the first two eliminations (the two stored submatrices of order two) must be performed on the original row and column 3. This is effected by summing or 'assembling' the reduced matrices with the original row and column, using the index list to control the summation. Note that this gives rise to a fill-in in positions a_{34} and a_{43}. The pivot operation which eliminates column 3 using pivot (3,3) leaves a reduced matrix of order one with row (and column) index 4. The final step sums this matrix with the (4,4) entry of the original matrix. The sequence of major steps in the elimination can be represented by the tree shown in Figure 4.3.

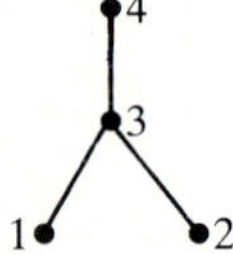

Figure 4.3. Elimination tree for the matrix of Figure 4.1.

The same storage and arithmetic is needed if the (4,4) entry is assembled at the same time

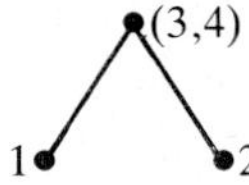

Figure 4.4. Elimination tree for the matrix of Figure 4.3 after node amalgamation.

as the (3,3) entry, and in this case the two pivotal steps can be performed on the same submatrix. This corresponds to collapsing or amalgamating nodes 3 and 4 in the tree of Figure 4.3 to yield the tree of Figure 4.4. On typical problems, node amalgamation produces a tree with about half as many nodes as the order of the matrix. Duff and Reid (1983) employ node amalgamation to enhance the vectorization of a multifrontal approach. In the present context, node amalgamation creates a larger granularity at each node which can assist in realizing the parallelism of this technique.

The computation at a node of the tree is simply the assembly of information concerning the node together with the assembly of the reduced matrices from its sons followed by some steps of Gaussian elimination. We can represent this by the system

$$\begin{pmatrix} \mathbf{A}_1 & \mathbf{A}_2 \\ \mathbf{A}_3 & \mathbf{A}_4 \end{pmatrix} \tag{4.1}$$

where eliminations are performed corresponding to pivots from $\mathbf{A}_1$ and the Schur complement $\mathbf{A}_4 - \mathbf{A}_3\mathbf{A}_1^{-1}\mathbf{A}_2$ is passed on for assembly at the father node.

The main feature of general elimination trees is that computation at any leaf node can proceed immediately and simultaneously and computations at nodes not on the same path from the root are independent. All that is required for computations to proceed at a node is that the calculations at its sons have been completed. A full discussion of this is given by Duff (1986).

5. IMPLEMENTATION ON SHARED MEMORY MACHINES

When implementing multifrontal techniques on shared memory machines we are concerned to reduce contention for shared data. In particular, we wish to design our data structures to avoid updating information used by more than one process. Duff (1986) studies these issues in some detail. Here we will sketch the data structures employed and report on some work that has been done since that paper.

Clearly, information on tree nodes available for computation must be kept so that, when a processor is free, it can easily find work to do. We do this by keeping a list of available nodes in a queue. Free processors take the next item on the queue, and when calculations on the last son node are complete, its father node is added to the back of the queue. Thus we need only protect two sets of pointers to prevent simultaneous updating or simultaneous accessing of the queue by different processors. Additionally, for each non-leaf node a count must be kept of the number of its sons whose calculations have not completed. Again this information must be protected against simultaneous access and a node is added to the queue when its count reaches zero.

Reading the data from the sons presents no problems since only one processor at a time can be accessing a particular item and we do not update the information anyway. Furthermore, since it is possible to tell in advance how much storage is required for the assembled frontal matrix, this space can be reserved before starting the actual assembly and so only a pointer to the first location of free space need be protected.

At some point when we advance up the tree towards the root there cannot be sufficient nodes available to satisfy the parallelism of our machine. However, as was observed by Duff and Johnsson (1986), the frontal matrices grow in size as we near the root, so it is natural to take advantage of parallelism within each node. That is, we utilize the inherent parallelism of Gaussian elimination that we discussed in Section 2. In our current implementation, we do this by identifying two types of work package, the selection of pivots and the elimination operations on a row. We hold both types of work in the same pool using flags to identify what type of work each entry in the pool represents. When a processor accesses the pool for more work, it interprets the flag and does the appropriate work. We have found this a good method for increasing the parallelism although at the cost of decreasing the granularity. We can, however, control things by making each unit correspond to elimination operations on a block of rows and are currently experimenting to find the best compromise between granularity and parallelism. Clearly the optimal parameters will depend on the architecture but our approach allows them to be set as input parameters to the code and so it should not be hard to adjust them for any shared memory machine. The issues involved when using local memory machines are, however, quite different and we discuss them in the following section.

6. IMPLEMENTATION ON LOCAL MEMORY MACHINES

The elimination tree view of multifrontal Gaussian elimination lends itself fairly naturally to local memory machines. After the computations corresponding to a node of the graph have been completed on a processor, the resulting frontal matrix is passed to the processor at which the computations for the father node will be performed. Since that target processor may at that time be doing work on some other node, there can be much overlap between communication and computation. If we wish to achieve good processor utilization and keep communication between processors to a minimum, two major issues are the balanced assignment of tree nodes to processors and the change of parallelism as we advance to the root of the elimination tree.

The first constraint that we wish to impose on the elimination tree is that it is a binary tree and indeed most nodes, except the leaves, have exactly two sons. Furthermore, we wish the tree to be reasonably balanced, that is we wish the lengths of the paths between leaf nodes and the root node to be about the same. The reason for these restrictions is that it is really not possible to map a balanced assignment of the nodes of a general tree onto the processors of a multiprocessor system, but much work has been done on mapping binary trees (for example, see Bhatt and Ipsen 1985). Duff and Johnsson (1986) examined the structure of the trees produced by various ordering strategies and found that although the most popular ordering for sparse systems, the minimum degree ordering (Tinney and Walker 1967), gave a very irregular tree, the nested dissection ordering could be organized to give exactly the sort of tree we desire.

With a tree that is binary and nearly-balanced, we then look at the number of nodes at each level of the tree. At the first level going away from the root at which the number of nodes exceeds the number of processors, level k say, we allocate the subtrees rooted at that level to different processors, allowing some processors to have two subtrees with the same father so that all of the tree below level k is allocated to processors. Each processor can then perform elimination and updating operations independently on its subtree without any interprocessor communication. When two subtrees on different processors but with the same father complete, then several processors must co-operate in one elimination or updating operation and we must subdivide further computations using the parallelism of Gaussian elimination. We assume that each computation is of the form shown in (4.1) and that submatrices of the kind $\mathbf{A}_4 - \mathbf{A}_3\mathbf{A}_1^{-1}\mathbf{A}_2$ will be assembled at the common father node. However, the calculations at this father node will be spread over the two processors originally holding the two subtrees. Following earlier work on full systems (for example, see Geist and Heath 1985), we assemble columns 1, 3, 5, ... in one processor and columns 2, 4, ... in the other. At the next level in the tree, the frontal matrix will be distributed among four processors and so on. As the sparse parallelism reduces, we must subdivide the frontal matrices further to maintain a sufficient level of parallelism. On a hypercube, the natural way to distribute these increasing number of subdivisions is to use hypercubes of increasing dimension. The submatrix corresponding to the root is factorized on the whole cube.

7. CONCLUDING REMARKS

The important feature about the work discussed in this paper is that we have developed a general approach for the direct solution of sparse systems of linear equations which can automatically take advantage of both parallelism in Gaussian elimination and parallelism due to sparsity. Furthermore, the approach can be implemented on both shared and local memory machines. Additionally, there are many parameters which can be varied both in the original generation of the tree and in the implementation of the factorization given the tree structure. It is still too early to pass judgement on the best method to adopt but we can say with some certainty that it will be strongly dependent on the computer architecture involved.

ACKNOWLEDGEMENT

I would like to thank Ilse Ipsen for her most helpful comments.

REFERENCES

Bhatt, S. N. and Ipsen, I. C. F. (1985). How to embed trees in hypercubes. Report YALEU/DCS/RR-443, Department of Computer Science, Yale University, Connecticut.

Duff, I. S. (1986). Parallel implementation of multifrontal schemes. *Parallel Computing* **3**, 193–204.

Duff, I. S. and Johnsson, S. L. (1986). Node orderings and concurrency in sparse problems: an experimental investigation. Proceedings International Conference on Vector and Parallel Computing, Loen, Norway, June 2–6, 1986. (To appear).

Duff, I. S. and Reid, J. K. (1983). The multifrontal solution of indefinite sparse symmetric linear systems. *ACM Trans. Math. Softw.* **9**, 302–325.

Duff, I. S., Erisman, A. M., and Reid, J. K. (1986). Direct methods for sparse matrices. Oxford University Press, London.

Geist, G. A. (1985). Efficient parallel LU factorization with pivoting on a hypercube processor. Report ORNL–6211, Engineering Physics and Mathematics Division, Oak Ridge National Laboratory, Tennessee.

Geist, G. A. and Heath, M. T. (1985). Parallel Cholesky factorization on a hypercube multiprocessor. Report ORNL–6190, Engineering Physics and Mathematics Division, Oak Ridge National Laboratory, Tennessee.

George, A. (1973). Nested dissection of a regular finite-element mesh. *SIAM J. Numer. Anal.* **10**, 345–363.

George, A., Heath, M., Liu, J., and Ng, E. (1986a). Sparse Cholesky factorization on a local-memory multiprocessor. Report CS–86–01. Department of Computer Science, York University, Ontario, Canada.

George, A., Heath, M., Ng, E., and Liu, J. (1986b). Symbolic Cholesky factorization on a local-memory multiprocessor. Proceedings International Conference on Vector and Parallel Computing, Loen, Norway, June 2–6, 1986. *Parallel Computing* (To appear).

Heller, D. (1978). A survey of parallel algorithms in numerical linear algebra. *SIAM Review* **20**, 740–777.

Kung, H., Sproull, R., and Steele, G. (Eds.) (1981). *VLSI systems and computations.* Computer Science Press, Rockville, Maryland.

Kung, S.–Y., Arun, K., Bhuskerio, D., and Ho, Y. (1981). A matrix data flow language/architecture for parallel matrix operations based on computational wave concept. In *VLSI Systems and Computations,* H.T. Kung, R. Sproull, and G. Steele (eds.), Computer Science Press, Rockville, Maryland.

Liu, J. W. H. (1986). Computational models and task scheduling for parallel sparse Cholesky factorization. *Parallel Computing* **3**, 327–342.

O'Leary, D. P. and Stewart, G. W. (1985). Data-flow algorithms for parallel matrix computations. *Communications ACM* **28**, 620–632.

Saad, Y. (1986). Gaussian elimination on hypercubes. Report YALEU/DCS/RR–462, Department of Computer Science, Yale University, Connecticut.

Sameh, A. H. (1983). An overview of parallel algorithms in numerical linear algebra. Bulletin de la Direction des Etudes et Recherches, EDF, France. Serie C., 129–134.

Tinney, W. F. and Walker, J. W. (1967). Direct solutions of sparse network equations by optimally ordered triangular factorization. *Proc. IEEE* **55**, 1801–1809.

Parallel Systems and Computation
G. Paul and G.S. Almasi (Editors)

Some New Parallel Methods for Solving the Heat Equation

Garry Rodrigue

University of California, Davis
Lawrence Livermore National Laboratory
Livermore, California

Abstract

Three ideas for solving the heat equation are presented. Each idea is developed with the goal of exploited parallelism and exposes parallelism at different levels of granularity.

I. Heat Equation

One of the most troublesome equations to deal with in scientific computing is the heat equation

$$\frac{\partial u}{\partial t} = \Delta u = \sum_{j=1}^{n} \frac{\partial^2 u}{\partial x_j^2}. \tag{1.1}$$

The heat equation is rarely solved by itself but instead is solved amongst a myriad of other partial differential equations where its presence in these equations is to introduce heat, viscosity, resistivity, or transport phenomenon into the physical problem being modeled. A typical scenario for the solution of these equations is to introduce a grid of spatial points and to solve for the dependent variables of the equations at successive time intervals $t_n = t_{n-1} + \Delta t_n$. The time step Δt_n is specified through some means and each equation is solved in succession.

From a physical standpoint, the heat equation causes trouble because its presence tends to "smear" out fronts of the numerical solution that were once clearly discernible in an adiabatic situation. This makes it difficult to determine maximal time steps Δt_n so as to avoid numerical instability. From a computational standpoint, the heat equation causes trouble because solving it using any type of explicit time differencing methods requires a stable time step that would be much smaller than the stable time steps necessary for the other more hyperbolic equations. Since the stable time step for an explicit numerical solution of the heat equation can be so severe so as to render the problem computationally impractical, a time step Δt is chosen so as to provide a stable explicit calculation of the other equations and the heat equation is solved using implicit time differencing methods.

II Predictor-Corrector-Iterative Methods

As a model problem , we consider the numerical solution of the equation

$$(2.1) \qquad \frac{\partial u}{\partial t} = \frac{\partial^2 u}{\partial x^2} + \frac{\partial^2 u}{\partial y^2} = \Delta u$$

$$(x,y) \in \Omega = [0,1] \times [0,1]$$

$$u(x,y,t) = 0 \ , \ (x,y) \in \beta(\Omega) = \text{boundary } (\Omega)$$

where f(x,y) has a convergent Fourier series.

If a spatial discretization on a uniform grid is applied to the right hand side of (2.1), then a system of ordinary differential equations

$$\frac{d\bar{u}}{dt} = A\bar{u}$$

is generated where

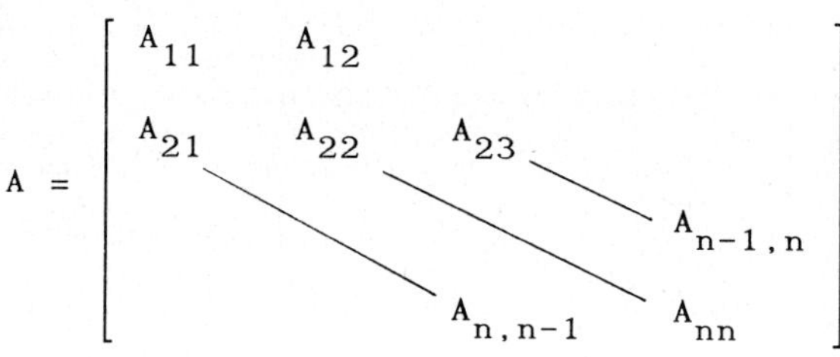

Numerical methods for solving (2.1) have the general form

$$\bar{u}_{t+\Delta t} = E(\Delta t)\bar{u}_t$$

where $\bar{u}_t$ is the numerical approximation to $\bar{u}(t)$ and $E(\Delta t)$ is a matrix operator. For simplicity, we concern ourselves only with the following operators

1) Forward Euler: $E(\Delta t) = I + \Delta t A$,

2) Backward Euler: $E(\Delta t) = (I - \Delta t A)^{-1}$,

3) A.D.I. : $E(\Delta t) = (I - \Delta t A_x)^{-1} \ (I - \Delta t A_y)^{-1}$.

In the A.D.I. scheme, $A = A_x + A_y$ where A_x and A_y have a simpler sparsity structure than A, e.g., they can be tridiagonal matrices.

The above methods (1), (2), and (3) are representative of methods typically classified as explicit, implicit, and locally one-dimensional methods respectively.

Desirable methods are those that possess the following three properties:

1) Consistency:

$$\lim_{\Delta t \to 0} \| \bar{u}(t + \Delta t) - \bar{u}_{t+\Delta t} \| = 0$$

2) Stability:

$$\| \bar{u}_{t+\Delta t} \| \leq \| \bar{u}_t \|$$

3) Asymptotic Stability

$$\lim_{\Delta t \to \infty} \| \bar{u}_{t+\Delta t} \| = 0$$

Explicit methods such as the Forward Euler are attractive for multiprocessors since their implementation requires only matrix-vector multiplicationss. Thus, on a system of n processors, one can achieve a speed-up of n over a uniprocessor. Explicit methods have the undesirable property that a severe constraint on the magnitude of the time step must be placed for otherwise the calculations become unstable. That is, explicit methods such as the Forward Euler method are consistent, stable for small range of values Δt, and not asymptotically stable. But, asymptotically stable explicit methods can be constructed in the following manner. Using the Forward Euler method as an example, let

$$E(\Delta t) = \prod_{i=1}^{k} (I + \delta t E)$$

where $k\delta t = \Delta t$ and δt is such that $I + \delta t E$ is a stable operator. The asymptotically stable numerical method is then

$$\text{(2.2)} \qquad \bar{u}_{t+\Delta t} = \left[\prod_{i=1}^{k} (I + \delta t E) \right] \bar{u}_t$$

This new method is again quite suitable for multiprocessors provided the integer k is not too large so as to require an impractical number of matrix-vector multiplications. However, as one might expect, it is not difficult to construct a problem where the integer k is too large for practical use, see [1]. On the other hand, this does raise the question as to whether one can construct different explicit methods with a larger stability range so that practical asymptotically stable numerical schemes can be constructed. One such way is by combining explicit and implicit methods with matrix iterative methods. To see how this is done,

one uses the important Fourier property of explicit methods that the error $\bar{u}_{t+\Delta t} - \bar{u}(t + \Delta t)$ has a Fourier series whose largest coefficients occur in the high-end of the series, i.e., high frequencies.

Implicit methods such as the Backward Euler methods have the disagreeable property that a linear system must be solved but, on the other hand, they have the desirable property of being stable and asymptotically stable. The linear system of an implicit method is generally solved by an iterative method. Using the Backward Euler as an example, iterative methods have the form

$$(I - \Delta tE) = M - N$$

$$Mx^{n+1} = Nx^{n} + \bar{u}_{t}$$

$$x^{0} = \text{arbitrary}$$

where M and N are chosen so that $x^{n} \to \bar{u}_{t+\Delta t}$.

Iterative methods have the useful Fourier property that the error $\bar{u}(t + \Delta t) - x^{n}$ has a Fourier series whose coefficients are largest at the low end of the series, i.e., low frequency errors, when n is large. That is, high frequency errors are eliminated after the first few iterations. Thus, the strategy behind predictor-corrector-iterative methods is to take the initial guess of the iterative method to be $x^{0} = (I + \Delta tE)\bar{u}_{t}$. Then $\bar{u}(t + \Delta t) - x^{0}$ will have high frequency errors and only a few iterations are required to reduce these errors.

As an example, suppose a relaxed-point-Jacobi method is the underlying iterative method. Specifically,

$$I - \Delta tE = M - N$$

where $M = \frac{8}{5}$ diagonal $(I - \Delta tE)$. Then the corresponding predictor-corrector-iterative method (taking only a single iteration) is

$$x^{0} = (I + \Delta tE)\bar{u}_{t}$$

$$\bar{u}_{t+\Delta t} = M^{-1}Bx^{0} \equiv Q(\Delta t)\bar{u}_{t} \quad . \tag{2.3}$$

It has been shown in [3] that if $\Delta t \leq \Delta x^{2}$, where Δx is the spatial mesh size, then the method (2.3) is stable and consistent. On the other hand, the Forward Euler method is stable if $\Delta t \leq \Delta x^{2}/4$. Since (2.3) is an explicit method, an asymptotically stable method can be constructed in the same way as was done in (2.2). That is,

$$\bar{u}_{t+\Delta t} = \left[\prod_{i=1}^{m} Q(\delta t) \right] \bar{u}_t \tag{2.4}$$

where $\delta t \leq \Delta x^2$. Comparing to (2.2), we see that (2.4) is twice as fast. Furthermore, (2.4) is easily implementable on a multiprocessor.

III Domain Decomposition

For computational efficiency in multiprocessing environments, it is necessary to use numerical methods that decompose into reasonably sized tasks that have as little numerical communication as possible between them. Numerical methods based around the ideas of domain decomposition have been shown to possess such properties, [2], [5]. The basic idea behind domain decomposition is to first decompose the spatial domain of (1.1) into a finite, union (not necessarily disjoint) of subdomains

$$\Omega = \bigcup_{j=1}^{k} \Omega_j .$$

A related equation is then solved on each subdomain and numerical information is communicated through the artificial internal boundaries, see Figure 1.

As an example, consider the problem given by (2.2) . For numerical calculations, partitioning of the domain is best performed around a superimposed quadulateral grid on Ω. To illustrate this, for a given integar n, define the grid

$$G = \{ (i\Delta x, j\Delta x) : i,j = 0,1,\ldots, n\} ,$$

$$\Delta x = 1/n$$

Now define

$$D = \left\{ \{r_i\}_{i=1}^{p} , \{\ell_i\}_{i=1}^{p} \right\}$$

such that

$$0 < \ell_1 < \ell_2 < r_1 < \ell_3 < \ldots < r_{p-1} < r_p = n$$

These integers delimit the right and left boundaries on the abscissa of the subdomains

$$\Omega_i = [x_{\ell_i}, x_{r_i}] \times [0,1] , \ 1 \leq i \leq p ,$$

see Figure 2.

Suppose an approximation to the solution is given on the artificial internal boundaries. We then define

$$(3.1) \qquad \frac{\partial u_i}{\partial \tau} = \Delta u_i \ , \quad t \leq \tau \leq t + \Delta t$$

$$u_i(t,x) \in \Omega_i$$

with boundary conditions given by the original problem (1.1) or an approximation on the internal boundaries, the α's and β's respectively in Figure 2.

In the same way as before, we then solve (3.1) by an appropriate numerical scheme to yield an approximation $\bar{u}_{i,t+\Delta t}$ to $\bar{u}_i(x, t + \Delta t)$. The solution of $\bar{u}_{t+\Delta t}$ is obtained through some connection process of the $\bar{u}_{i,t+\Delta t}$.

Questions as to how to choose the subdomains, the approximation on the artificial boundaries, and the numerical integration scheme in (3.1) are interesting research questions and have been explored at a very cursory level in [2], [5]. Once the above questions have been answered, one must then ask questions of consistency, accuracy, and stability.

One idea is to use an explicit method such as the forward Euler method on the global problem to obtain internal boundary conditions and initial conditions for the subdomains. Then an implicit on local 1-D method such as the backward Euler or ADI scheme is used to obtain $\bar{u}_{i,t+\Delta t}$ on each of the subdomains. The solution $\bar{u}_{t+\Delta t}$ is then obtained by an averaging of the subsolutions $\bar{u}_{i,t+\Delta t}$ in the overlapped areas.

IV. Cellular Automata

The heat equation, like other equations in mathematical physics, is pervaded by the notion of a "continuum". The great advantage of differential equations is that we have three centuries' experience with methods for their symbolic interpretation. One could argue that they were developed because all computation had to be done by hand and it paid to "stylize" the physics in this manner so as to be able to handle the resulting mathematics. In fact, if symbolic manipulation is the major motive for using differential equations, one starts asking whether one should still keep them as the starting point for numerical modeling. They lead to numerical computations that are at least three levels removed from the physical world. First (a) we stylize physics into differential equations, then (b) we force these equations into the mold of discrete space and time so as to arrive at finite-difference equations, and finally, in order to commit the latter to algorithms, (c) we project real-valued variables onto finite computer words ("round-off"). At the end of the chain we find the computer which is again a physical system. This leads to questions as to whether there might exist a less roundabout method to make nature model itself.

A partial differential equation whose independent variables

are space and time is translated into a finite-difference equation by the following process: (a) continuous apace and time are replaced by a discrete grid, (b) the system's state at each point remains a continuous variable of the same kind as in the original equation, and (c) derivatives are replaced by differences between state-variables that are contiguous in space and time. When one translates the finite-difference equation into a computer algorithm, all one does is discretize the real variables and restrict them to a finite range. State variables are then represented by finite sets. The dynamics of the system is expressed by essentially the same difference rules, with the proviso that overflow or underflow will abort the computation; if the state of the set is made too small (i.e. not enough precision) this aborting will happen so often as to make this method useless, see [6].

A computational scheme, called "cellular automata" is essentially like that described in the previous paragraph with the exception that the variables at each point of the grid are only allowed to range over a very small set - say, two states.

For example, suppose we have k cells arranged at locations x_i, i = 1, 2, ..., k in the line and m colliding particles moving between the cells. In a unit time Δt, the particles will advect to the neighboring cell on the right or left. Cells with one particle will have that particle directed to the right with probability 1/2 and to the left with probability 1/2. We assume that no two particles occuping the same cell may be moving in the same direction. Hence, if two particles enter a cell in opposite directions they leave in opposite directions.

Now, at the specific $t^n = n\Delta t$ amd cell $x_i = i\Delta x$, let

$f_0(x_i, t^n)$ = number of particles moving to right at cell x_i and time t^n

$f_1(x_i, t^n)$ = number of particles moving to left at cell x_i and time t^n

Note that f_0 and f_1 take values 0 or 1. In fact,

$$f_0(x_{i+1}, t^{n+1}) = \frac{1}{2}\left[f_0(x_i, t^n) + f_1(x_i, t^n)\right]$$

$$f_1(x_{i-1}, t^{n+1}) = \frac{1}{2}\left[f_0(x_i, t^n) + f_1(x_i, t^n)\right]$$

Given a large number M of initial distributions, define

$$\hat{f}_0(x_i, t^n) = \underset{M}{\text{Average}}\,(f_0(x_i, t^n))$$

$$\hat{f}_1(x_i, t^n) = \underset{M}{\text{Average}}\,(f_1(x_i, t^n))$$

If $\hat{f}_0$ and $\hat{f}_1$ are smooth functions of x and t, then it has been shown [4] that

$$\partial_t \rho - \partial_{xx} \rho = O(\Delta x^2)$$

where $\rho(x,t) = \hat{f}_0(x,t) + \hat{f}_1(x,t)$

That is, the quantity $\hat{f}_0(x_i, t^n) + \hat{f}_1(x_i, t^n)$ yields the solution to the heat equation at the point (x_i, t^n) with an accuracy of $O(\Delta x^2)$.

Computationally, two bit vectors are initialized to an initial distribution. One vector represents the right moving particles and the other represents the left moving particles. For example, a possible scenario would be

$$\begin{array}{ccc} R & \underline{\text{cell position}} & L \\ \left[\begin{array}{c} 1 \\ 0 \\ 1 \\ 1 \\ 0 \end{array}\right] & \begin{array}{c} \text{-- } c_1 \text{ --} \\ \text{-- } c_2 \text{ --} \\ \text{-- } c_3 \text{ --} \\ \text{-- } c_4 \text{ --} \\ \text{-- } c_5 \text{ --} \end{array} & \left[\begin{array}{c} 1 \\ 1 \\ 0 \\ 1 \\ 1 \end{array}\right] \\ \text{right moving particles} & & \text{left moving particles} \end{array}$$

A "1" bit indicates the existence of a particle, and a "0" indicates the absence. The particles are then advected to yield

$$\begin{array}{ccc} \left[\begin{array}{c} 0 \\ 1 \\ 0 \\ 1 \\ 1 \end{array}\right] & \begin{array}{c} \text{-- } c_1 \text{ --} \\ \text{-- } c_2 \text{ --} \\ \text{-- } c_3 \text{ --} \\ \text{-- } c_4 \text{ --} \\ \text{-- } c_5 \text{ --} \end{array} & \left[\begin{array}{c} 1 \\ 0 \\ 1 \\ 1 \\ 1 \end{array}\right] \end{array}$$

This amounts to a right shift (end around) on R and a left shift (end around) on L when periodic boundary conditions are used. We then exclusive OR the vectors R and L to determine the cells containing only one particle. This results in

$$\begin{bmatrix} 1 \\ 1 \\ 1 \\ 0 \\ 0 \end{bmatrix}$$

A random vector $v = [v_i]$ is generated and if $0 \leq v_i \leq 1/2$ then the particle in cell i moves to left and if $1/2 \leq v_i \leq 1$ then the particle in cell i moves to right. The game is then repeated.

The potential for parallelism and immense gains in speed are obvious.

Acknowledgements

This work was supported (in part) by the Applied Mathematical Sciences subprogram of the Office of Energy Research, U.S. Department of Energy, by Lawrence Livermore National Laboratory under contract No. W-7405-Eng-48

References:

[1] Rodrigue, G. "A Parallel First-Order Method for Parabolic Partial Differential Equations", NATO-ASI Series, Vol. F7, High Speed Computation, J.S. Kowalik (ed.), Springer-Verlag, 1984

[2] Rodrigue, G. "Inner/outer iterative methods and numerical Schwarz algorithm", Parallel Computing 2 (1985), pp 205-218

[3] Rodrigue G., and Wolitzer D., "A New Class of Explicit Methods for the Heat Equation", submitted for publication.

[4] Levermore D., personal communication

[5] Tang, N., Ph.D. Dissertation, Computer Science Department, Stanford University.

[6] Wolfram, S., "Cellular Automaton Fluids 1: Basic Theory", Institute for Advanced Study, Princeton, NJ, Report.

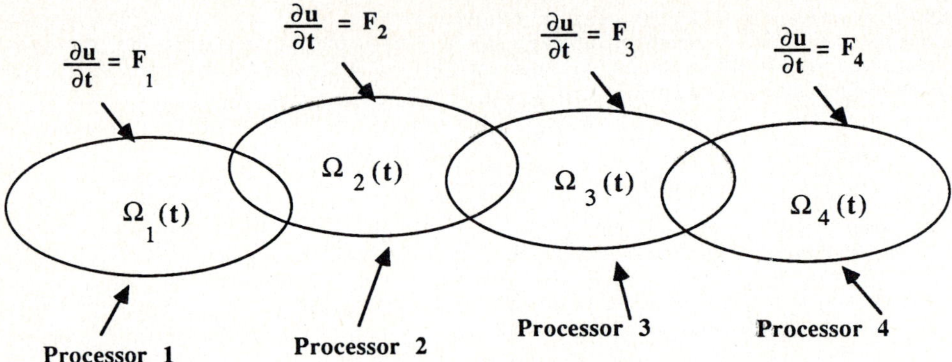

Figure 1

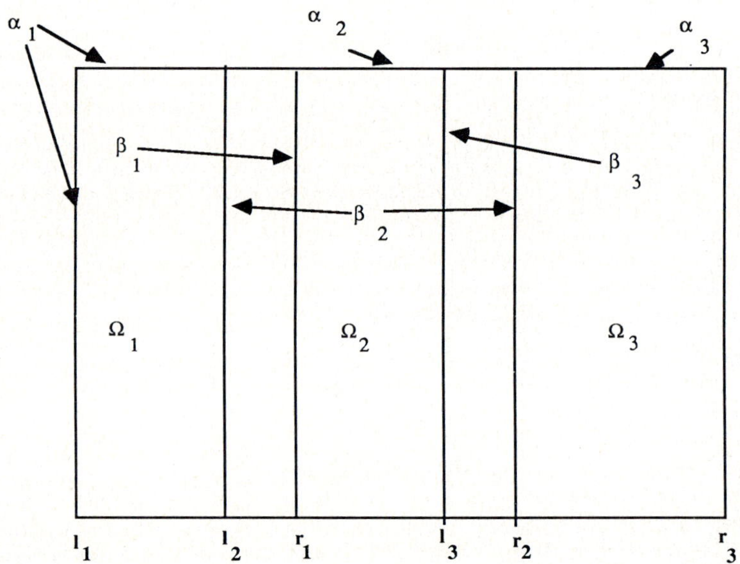

Figure 2

Parallel Systems and Computation
G. Paul and G.S. Almasi (Editors)

The Design of Parallel Algorithms Principles and Problems

Ernst W. Mayr
Stanford University
Stanford, California 94305

Abstract

We present a uniform method for obtaining efficient parallel algorithms for a rather large class of problems. The method is based on a logic programming model, and it derives its efficiency from fast parallel routines for the evaluation of expression trees.

1 Introduction

Computational complexity theory tries to classify problems according to the amount of computational resources needed for their solution. In this sense, the goal of complexity theory is a refinement of the basic distinction between *decidable* (solvable, recursive) and *undecidable* (unsolvable, non-recursive) problems. There are basically three types of results: (i) algorithms or upper bounds showing that a certain problem can indeed be solved using a certain amount of resources; (ii) lower bounds establishing that some specified number of resources is insufficient for the problem to be solved; and (iii) reductions of one problem to another, showing that the first problem is essentially no harder than the second. Complexity classes are collections of all those problems solvable within a specific bound, and complete problems in a complexity class are distinguished problems such that every other problem in the class is efficiently reducible to them. In this sense, they are hardest problems in the class.

A very important goal of computational complexity theory is to characterize which problems are *feasible*, i.e. solvable efficiently in an intuitive sense. For (standard) sequential computation, the class $\mathcal{P}$ of those problems solvable in polynomial time has become accepted as the "right" class to represent feasibility. For parallel computation, on a wide number of machine models (idealized and realistic), the class $\mathcal{NC}$ is considered to play the same role. It is the class of problems solvable (in the PRAM model, discussed below) in time polylogarithmic in the size of the input while using a number of processing elements polynomial in the input size.

In this paper, we show an interesting relationship between efficient parallel computation and the existence of reasonably sized *proof trees*. While the reader may feel reminded of the well-known characterization of the class $\mathcal{NP}$ as those problems permitting short (polynomial length) proofs of solutions, proof trees are considerably more restricted in the sense that if some intermediate fact is reused the size of its (sub) proof tree is counted with the appropriate multiplicity. Drawing on, and generalizing, work reported in [14], [18], and [21], we give a very general scheme to obtain efficient parallel algorithms for many different

---

This work was supported in part by a grant from the AT&T Foundation, ONR contract N00014-85-C-0731, and NSF grant DCR-8351757.

problems in a way that abstracts from details of the underlying parallel architecture and the necessary synchronization and scheduling.

The remainder of the paper is organized as follows. In the next section, we discuss a few techniques for parallel algorithm design appearing in the literature. Then we introduce our new technique, the *dynamic tree expression problem* or *DTEP*, and present some of its applications and extensions. In particular, we show an adaptation of the basic DTEP paradigm to the evaluation of straightline programs computing polynomials. The final section summarizes our results and mentions some open problems.

2 Techniques for Parallel Algorithm Design

General techniques for the design of efficient parallel algorithms are hard to come by. To a large degree, this is due to the fact that there are so many vastly different parallel machine architectures around, and no compilers between the programmers and the machines that could provide a uniform interface to the former. Obviously, this is a situation quite different from sequential computation. We may even ask ourselves why we should be looking for such a compiler, or whether parallel algorithms shouldn't be developped for specific architectures in the first place. Even more so, we might ask whether parallelism is any good for solving problems in general, or whether there are just a few selected, and highly tuned, applications that could benefit from heavy parallelism. We believe that there is a large number of problems and applications out there which should be parallelized individually, designing architectures permitting the highest speedup for these applications. There is also a large class of applications whose data structures and flow of control are extremely regular and can easily be mapped onto appropriate parallel machine architectures, like systolic arrays or n-dimensional hypercubes. It is our impression, however, that many other problems, particularly in Artificial Intelligence, exhibit the same specifications (with respect to parallelization) as we would expect from general purpose parallel computation. It is the interest in these, and other, applications that makes us convinced that general purpose parallelism is relevant, and that in fact it carries immense potential for areas of general importance.

The design of parallel algorithms may be guided by several, sometimes conflicting, goals. The first, and maybe most obvious, goal in using parallel machines may be to obtain fast, or even the fastest possible, response times. Such an objective will be particularly important in security sensitive applications, like warning or monitoring systems; weather forecasters also seem to be interested in this particular aspect of parallel computation. Another option seems to worry about the marginal cost factor: how much real computational power do we gain by adding one (or k) additional processors to the system? While optimal speedup can be achieved over a certain range of execution times (depending on the problem), fastest execution times may be obtained, for certain problems, only by using a very large number of parallel processors, thus decreasing, in effect, the actual speed-up.

Another consideration is what could be termed the *Law of Small Numbers*. Many of the very fast parallel algorithms have running times which are some power of the logarithm of the input size n, like $O(\log^2 n)$. If we compare this running time with one given by, say, $O(\sqrt{n})$, and assume that the constant factor is 1 in both cases for simplicity, we get that the *polylogarithmic* algorithm is actually slower than the *polynomial* algorithm for n greater than 2 and less than $65,536$.

2.1 Parallel Machine Models

We shall base most of our discussions onto a theoretical machine model for parallel computation called the *Parallel Random Access Machine*, or *PRAM* [4]. This machine model has the following features. There is an unbounded number of identical *Random Access Machines* (or *RAM*'s), and an unbounded number of global memory cells, each capable of holding an arbitrarily big integer. The processors work synchronously, controlled by a global clock. Different processors can execute different instructions. Each processor can access (read or write) any memory cell in one step. Our model also allows that more than one processor read the same memory cell in one step (*concurrent read*), but it disallows *concurrent writes* to the same memory cell. For definiteness, we assume that all reads of global memory cells in a step take place before all writes (resolving *read/write conflicts*).

Most of our algorithms actually do not use concurrent reads, and can be run on a somewhat weaker machine model in which concurrent reads are forbidden. In any case, algorithms in our model can always be simulated on this weaker model with a very small slowdown.

The shared memory feature of the PRAM model, allowing unbounded access to memory in a single step, is somewhat idealistic. A more realistic machine model consists of a *network* of (identical) processors with *memory modules* attached to them. The processors are connected via point-to-point communication channels. Each processor can directly access only cells in its own memory module, and it has to send messages to other processors in order to access data in their modules. To respect technological constraints, the number of channels per processor is usually bounded or a very slowly growing function of the number of processors. Examples for such networks of processors are the Hypercube [20], the Cube-Connected-Cycles network [17], or the Ultracomputer (RP3) [15], [19].

2.2 Parallel Complexity Measures

The two most important parameters determining the computational complexity of algorithms in the PRAM model are the time requirements and the number of processors used by the algorithm. Both are usually expressed as functions of the input size n. Note that another factor determining the practical efficiency of a parallel algorithm — its communication overhead — is of no importance in the PRAM model. As in sequential computation, and its associated complexity theory, complexity classes are defined based on bounds of the available resources, like time or number of processors. One such class has become particularly important in the theoretical study of parallel algorithms and the inherent limits of parallelism. This class is called $\mathcal{NC}$ and is defined as the class of problems solvable on a PRAM in time *polylogarithmic* (polylog for short) in the size of the input while using a number of processors *polynomial* in the input size. Thus, a problem is in $\mathcal{NC}$ if there is a PRAM algorithm and some constant $c > 0$ such that the algorithm runs in time $O(\log^c n)$ and uses $O(n^c)$ processors on instances of size n.

The resource constraints for $\mathcal{NC}$ reflect two goals to be achieved by parallelism: a (poly)logarithmic running time represents an "exponential" speedup over sequential computation (requiring at least linear time); and the restriction on the number of processors limits the required hardware to be "reasonable". Of course, both these considerations have to be taken in the asymptotic sense, and are thus of a rather theoretical nature (see the Law of Small Numbers above).

However, the class $\mathcal{NC}$ is *robust* in the sense that it does not change with small modifications in the underlying machine model. In fact, it is the same for the PRAM model(s) outlined above as well as the Hypercube or Ultracomputer architecture. It was originally defined for boolean circuits in [16]. Membership in $\mathcal{NC}$ has become (almost) synonymous with "efficiently parallelizable".

Real parallel machines have, of course, a fixed number of processors. Even though some parallel algorithm may have been designed for a (theoretical) parallel machine with a number of processors depending on the input size, the following theorem states that it is always possible to reduce, without undue penalty, the number of processors:

Simulation Theorem: An algorithm running in time $T(n)$ on a p-processor PRAM, can be simulated on a p'-processor PRAM, $p' \leq p$, in time $O(\lceil p/p' \rceil\, T(n))$. □

If an algorithm runs in time $T(n)$ on a sequential architecture, and we port it to a parallel architecture with p processors we cannot expect a parallel running time better than $\Omega(T(n)/p)$ — unless our machine models exhibit some strange quirks which are of no concern here. Conversely, we say that a problem of sequential time complexity $T(n)$ exhibits *optimal speedup* if its parallel time complexity on a PRAM using p processors is in fact $O(T(n)/p)$, for p in an appropriate range.

2.3 Parallel Programming Techniques

Only relatively few parallel programming schemes and/or techniques can be found in the literature. This is due in part to the fact that there is universal parallel architecture, and no commonly accepted way of hiding architectural details from parallel programs. Nonetheless, the PRAM model can, to a certain degree, play this role. Certain operations have been identified to be fundamental or important for a large number of parallel applications, and efficient algorithms have been developed for them. Examples are the parallel prefix computation [10], census functions [11], (funnelled) pipelines [7], parallel tree evaluation [13], [14], and sorting [2]. As an illustration, we state a procedural implementation of an algorithm for the parallel prefix problem, in a PASCAL like notation. Given an array $s_1, \ldots, s_n$ of elements from some arbitrary domain, and a binary operator $\circ$ over that domain, this procedure computes all partial "sums" $s_1 \circ \cdots s_i$, for $i = 1, \ldots, n$.

```
procedure census_function(n, s, result, ∘);
int n; gmemptr s, result; binop ∘;
co n is the number of elements in the input array starting at position s in global memory; result is
the index of the global memory cell receiving the result; ∘ is an associative binary operator oc
begin
  local type_of_S: save, int: mask, myindex
  if PID < n then
    mask := 1; myindex := s + PID; save := M_myindex;
    while mask < n do
      if (PID & (2 * mask − 1) = 0) and PID + mask < n then
        M_myindex := M_myindex ∘ M_myindex+mask
      fi;
      mask := 2 * mask
    od;
    if PID = 0 then M_result := M_s fi;
    if myindex ≠ result then M_myindex := save fi
  fi;
  return
end census_function.
```

This algorithm takes, on a PRAM, $O(\log n)$ steps and uses n processors. As such, its speedup is suboptimal since the straightforward sequential algorithm runs in linear time. However, by grouping the input elements into contiguous groups of size $\lceil \log n \rceil$ (the last group may be smaller), we can solve the parallel prefix problem using just $\lceil n/\log n \rceil$ processors. Using one processor for every group, we first compute the prefix "sums" within every group. Then we run the above algorithm with the group prefix "sums" as input, and finally we extend the partial sums over the groups inside the groups, again using one processor per group. The time for this modified algorithm is still $O(\log n)$ (with a somewhat larger constant).

The parallel prefix problem has many applications. It occurs as a subproblem in algorithms for *ranking*, *linearization of lists*, *graph traversals*, *processor scheduling*, and others.

In the next section, we discuss another fundamental algorithm for parallel computation.

3 The Dynamic Tree Expression Problem

In [18], Alternating Turing machines using logarithmic space and a polynomial size computation tree are studied. These machines can be thought of as solving a recognition problem by guessing a proof tree and recursively verifying it. Each internal node in the proof tree is replaced, in a universal step, by its children in the tree while leave nodes correspond to axioms which can be verified directly. In every step, the machine is allowed to use only logarithmic storage (at every node) to record the intermediate derivation step.

We in effect turn the top-down computation of ATM's as discussed in [18] around into computations proceeding basically bottom-up, similar to the approach taken in [13], [14], and [21]. We present a uniform method containing and extending the latter results.

3.1 The Generic Problem

For the general discussion of the Dynamic Tree Expression Problem, we assume that we are given

i. a set P of N boolean *variables*, $p_1, \ldots, p_N$;

ii. a set I of *inference rules* of the form

$$p_i :- p_j p_k \quad \text{or} \quad p_i :- p_j.$$

Here, juxtaposition of boolean variables is to be interpreted as logical AND, and ":−" is to be read as "if". In fact, the two types above are Horn clauses with one or two hypotheses, written in a PROLOG style notation: $(p_j \wedge p_k) \Rightarrow p_i$ and $p_j \Rightarrow p_i$, respectively. We note that the total length of I is polynomial in N.

iii. a distinguished subset $Z \subseteq P$ of *axioms*.

Definition 3.1 *Let (P, I, Z) be a system as above. The* minimal model *for (P, I, Z) is the* minimal *subset $M \subseteq P$ satisfying the following properties:*

(i) *the set of axioms, Z, is contained in M;*

(ii) *whenever the righthand side of an inference rule is satisfied by variables in M, then the variable on the lefthand side is an element of M:*

$$\left.\begin{array}{l} p_j, p_k \in M,\ p_i :- p_j p_k \in I \\ p_j \in M,\ p_i :- p_j \in I \end{array}\right\} \Rightarrow p_i \in M.$$

We say that (P, I, Z) *implies* some fact p if the boolean variable p is in the minimal model M for (P, I, Z). For each such p, there is a *derivation* or *proof tree*: This is a (rooted) tree whose internal vertices have one or two children, and whose vertices are labelled with elements in P such that these four properties are satisfied:

1. the labels of the leaves are in Z;
2. if a vertex labelled p_i has one child, with label p_j, then $p_i :- p_j$ is a rule in I;
3. if a vertex labelled p_i has two children, with labels p_j and p_k, then $p_i :- p_j p_k$ is a rule in I;
4. the label of the root vertex is p.

The *Dynamic Tree Expression Problem* consists in computing the minimal model for a given system (P, I, Z), or, formulated as a decision problem, in deciding whether, given (P, I, Z) and some $p \in P$, whether p is in the minimal model for (P, I, Z). The algorithm below can be used to solve DTEP on a PRAM.

algorithm $DTEP(N, P, I, Z)$;
int N; set of boolean P, Z; set of inference rules I;
co N is the number of boolean variables in P; Z is the subset of P distinguished as axioms; I is a set of Horn clauses with at most two variables on the righthand side; P is implemented as an array of boolean variables; the algorithm sets to **true** exactly those elements of the array P corresponding to elements in the minimal model **oc**
begin
  array $DI[1..N, 1..N]$;
  co initialization **oc**
  $P[i] :=$ **true** for all $p_i \in Z$, else **false**;
  $DI[j, i] :=$ **true** for $i = j$ and all $p_i :- p_j \in I$, else **false**;

  do l times **co** l will be specified below **oc**
    for $i \in \{1, \ldots, N\}$ with $P[i] =$ **false do in parallel**
      if $((P[j] = P[k] = \textbf{true}) \wedge (p_i :- p_j p_k \in I)) \vee ((P[j] = \textbf{true}) \wedge (DI[j, i] = \textbf{true}))$
      then $P[i] :=$ **true**
      fi;
      if $(P[k] = \textbf{true}) \wedge (p_i :- p_j p_k \in I)$ **then** $DI[j, i] :=$ **true fi**
    od;
    $DI := DI \cdot DI$
  od
end $DTEP$.

We first remark about the intuition behind the array DI used in the DTEP algorithm. If entry (i, j) of this array is **true** then it is known that p_i implies p_j. This is certainly true at the beginning of the algorithm, by way of the initialization of DI. Whenever for an inference rule $p_i :- p_j p_k$ with two antecedents, one of them, say p_k, is known to be **true**, the rule can be simplified to $p_i :- p_j$. But this means that p_j implies p_i, as recorded in the assignment to $DI[j, i]$. Also, the net effect of squaring the matrix DI in the last step of the outer loop is that chains of implications are shortened. Note that entry (i, j) of the matrix becomes **true** through the squaring of the matrix only if there was a chain of implications from p_i to p_j before the squaring.

Lemma 3.1 *If p_i is in the minimal model M, and if there is a derivation tree for p_i in (P, I, Z) of size m then $P[i] =$ **true** after at most $l = 2.41 \log m$ iterations of the outer loop of the DTEP algorithm. $P[i]$ never becomes* **true** *for $p_i \notin M$.*

Proof: The proof is by induction on the number of iterations of the main loop. We use the following induction hypothesis:

> At the end of each iteration of the main loop, there is a derivation tree for p_i of size at most 3/4 of the size at the end of the previous iteration, allowing as inference rules the rules in I and the "direct implications" as given by the current values of the elements of DI, and as axioms the p_j with $P[j]$ currently **true**.

This induction hypothesis is trivially satisfied before the first iteration of the loop. For the r-th iteration, let $m = |T|$ be the size of a derivation tree T for p_i, using the current axioms and derivation rules. We distinguish two cases:

1. T has at least $m/4$ leaves: since the parallel loop in the DTEP algorithm set $P[k] =$ **true** if the children of a vertex labelled p_k are all leaves, this case is trivial.

2. Let r_k be the number of maximal chains in T with k internal vertices, and let b be the number of leaves of T, both at the start of the loop. A chain in T is part of a branch with all internal vertices having degree exactly 2. Then we have:

$$\begin{aligned} m &= 2b - 1 + \sum_{k \geq 1} k \cdot r_k; \\ m' &\leq b - 1 + \sum_{k \geq 1} \lceil k/2 \rceil \, r_k \\ &\leq b - 1 + \frac{1}{2}\Big(\sum_{k \geq 1} k r_k + \sum_{k \geq 1} r_k\Big) \\ &\leq b - 1 + \frac{1}{2}(m + 1 - 2b) + \frac{1}{2} \cdot 2b \\ &< \frac{3}{4} m \,. \end{aligned}$$

Here, m' is the size of the derivation tree after execution of the loop, using the current set of axioms and inferences. The first inequality follows since squaring of the matrix DI halves the length of all chains. The third inequality stems from the observation that in a tree with b leaves, the number of (maximal) chains can be at most $2b - 1$ as can be seen by assigning each such chain to its lower endpoint.

There is a trivial derivation tree for p_i after at most $\log_{4/3} m \leq 2.41 \log m$ (note that all logarithms whose base is not mentioned explicitly, are base 2). □

Theorem 1 *Let (P, I, Z) be a derivation system with the property that each p in the minimal model M has a derivation tree of size*

$$\leq 2^{\log^c N}.$$

Then there is an $\mathcal{NC}$-algorithm to compute M.

Proof: It follows immediately from the above Lemma that under the stated conditions the DTEP algorithm runs in polylogarithmic time. More precisely, for the bound on the size of derivation trees given in the Theorem, the running time of the algorithm is

$$O(\log^{c+1} N),$$

and it uses N^3 processors. □

3.2 Applications of DTEP

Longest Common Substrings

As a very simple example of a DTEP application we consider the *longest common substring* problem: given two strings $a_1 \cdots a_n$ and $b_1 \cdots b_m$ over some alphabet Σ, we are supposed to find a longest common substring $a_i \cdots a_{i+r} = b_j \cdots b_{j+r}$.

To obtain a DTEP formulation of this problem, we introduce variables $p_{i,j,l}$ whose intended meaning is:

$$p_{i,j,l} \text{ is true if } a_i \cdots a_{i+l-1} = b_j \cdots b_{j+l-1}.$$

Thus, we have the following axioms:

$$p_{i,j,1} \text{ iff } a_i = b_j;$$

and these inference rules:

$$p_{i,j,l} \;:-\; p_{i,j,\lceil l/2 \rceil} p_{i+\lceil l/2 \rceil, j+\lceil l/2 \rceil, \lfloor l/2 \rfloor}.$$

An easy induction on the length l of a common substring shows that $p_{i,j,l}$ is true in the minimal model for the above derivation system if and only if the substring of length l starting at position i in the first string is equal to the substring of the same length at position j in the second string. A similar induction can be used to show that for every common substring of length l, there is a derivation tree of size linear in l in the above derivation system. These two observations together establish the longest common substring problem as an instance of DTEP.

Other Applications

It is possible to rephrase a number of other problems as instances of the *Dynamic Tree Expression Problem*. A few examples are contained in the following list:

- transitive closure in graphs and digraphs
- the non-uniform word problem for context-free languages
- the circuit value problem for planar monotone circuits
- DATALOG programs with the *polynomial fringe property*
- the complexity class ALT($\log n$, expolylog n); these are the problems recognizable by log-space bounded Alternating Turing machines with a bound of $2^{\log^c n}$ for the size of their computation tree, for some constant $c > 0$.

For the DATALOG example, we refer the interested reader to [21]. We briefly discuss the third and the last example in the above list.

The Planar Monotone Circuit Value Problem

A *circuit* is a directed acyclic graph (dag). Its vertices are called *gates*, and the arcs correspond to *wires* going from outputs of gates to inputs. The gates are either input/output gates connecting the circuit to its environment, or they are combinational mapping the values on the input wires of the gate to values on the output wires, according to the function represented by the gate. In a *monotone* circuit, all combinational gates are AND or OR gates. Therefore, the output of the circuit, as a function of the inputs, is a monotone function. A *planar* circuit is a circuit whose dag can be laid out in the plane without any wires crossing one another, and with the inputs and output(s) of the circuit on the outer face.

We assume that circuits are given as follows. The description of a circuit with n gates is a sequence $\beta_0, \ldots, \beta_{n-1}$. Each gate β_i is

1. 0-INPUT or 1-INPUT (also abbreviated as 0 and 1, respectively); or
2. AND(β_j, β_k), OR(β_j, β_k), or NOT(β_j), where $j, k < i$; in this case, the gate computes the logical function indicated by its name, with the values on the input wires to the gate as arguments, and puts this function value on all of the gate's output wires.
3. The output wire of β_{n-1} carries the output of the circuit.

The *circuit value problem* (CVP) consists in computing the output of a circuit, given its description. It is well known that CVP is complete for $\mathcal{P}$ under log-space reductions, and hence is a "hardest" problem for the class of polynomial time algorithms [9]. Even if we restrict ourselves to monotone circuits (allowing only AND and OR gates), or to planar circuits, the corresponding restricted CVP remains $\mathcal{P}$-complete [5]. However, the circuit value problem can be solved efficiently in parallel for circuits which are monotone *and* planar [3], [6]. While the original solutions were indirect and technically quite involved, the DTEP paradigm gives us a relatively simple approach.

For ease of presentation, we assume that the description $\beta_0, \ldots, \beta(n-1)$ of a planar monotone circuit satisfies the following additional properties:

- The circuit is arranged in *layers*; the first layer is constituted by the inputs to the circuit; the last layer consists of the output of the circuit; for every wire in the circuit, there is a (directed) path from an input to the output of the circuit, containing that wire.
- All wires run between adjacent layers, without crossing one another.
- All gates on even layers are AND gates with at least one input.
- All gates on odd layers (except the first) are OR gates.

These restrictions are not essential. Given a general type description of a circuit, there are well-known $\mathcal{NC}$-algorithms to test whether it represents a monotone and planar circuit, and to transform it into a description of a functionally equivalent circuit satisfying the restrictions listed above.

To obtain a DTEP formulation, it is helpful to look at *intervals* of gates. Formally, let the triple (l, i, j) denote the interval from the ith through the jth gate (in the order in which they appear in the circuit description) on the lth layer of the circuit. We shall introduce boolean variables $p(l, i, j)$ with the intended meaning

$$p_{l,i,j} \text{ is } \mathbf{true} \text{ iff the output of every gate in } (l, i, j) \text{ is } \mathbf{true}.$$

We simply observe that an interval of AND-gates has outputs all **true** if and only if all inputs to this interval of gates are **true**, and that these inputs come from an interval of gates on the next lower layer. For intervals of OR-gates, the situation is a bit more complicated since in order to obtain a **true** output from an OR-gate, only one of its inputs needs to be **true**. We must therefore be able to break intervals of **true** OR-gates down into smaller intervals which are **true** because a contiguous interval of gates on the next lower layer is **true**. Because wires don't cross in a planar layout, such a partition is always possible.

More formally, the inference rules for a given instance of the planar monotone circuit value problem are:

1. $p_{l,i,j} :- p_{l-1,i',j'}$ for every (nonempty) interval of AND-gates; here, i' denotes the first input of the first gate, and j' the last input of the last gate in the interval;

2. $p_{l,i,j} :- p_{l,i,k}p_{l,k+1,j}$, for all $i \leq k < j$; and

3. $p_{l,i,j} :- p_{l-1,i',j'}$, for all layers l of OR-gates and all pairs (i',j') where $i' \leq j'$ and $\beta_{i'}$ is an input of β_i, and $\beta_{j'}$ is an input of β_j.

The axioms are given by all intervals of **true** inputs to the circuit.

It is easy to see that the total length of the representation for the axioms and for all inference rules is polynomial in n. A straightforward induction, using the planarity of the circuit as outlined above, also shows that $p_{l,i,i}$ is **true** in the minimal model if and only if the ith gate on layer l has output **true** in the circuit.

Suppose $p_{l,i,j}$ is in the minimal model. To see that there is a linear size derivation tree for $p_{l,i,j}$ we consider the sub-circuit consisting of all gates from which a gate in (l,i,j) is reachable. Whenever we use an inference rule of type 1 or of type 3 in a derivation tree for $p_{l,i,j}$ we charge the vertex in the derivation tree (corresponding to the left-hand side of the rule) to the interval (l,i,j). We observe that we need to use an inference rule of type 2 for an OR-gate on some layer l' only if the interval of gates on layer $l'-1$ feeding into this interval contains more than one maximal sub-interval of **true** gates. In this case, we can split the interval (l',i,j) into sub-intervals (l',i,k) and $(l',k+1,j)$ in such a way that one of the inputs to gate k on layer l' is **false**. We charge the left-hand side of the type 2 inference rule to the interval of **false** gates on layer $l'-1$ containing this input. Because of the planarity of the circuit, rules used to derive $p_{l',i,k}$ and $p_{l',k+1,j}$ are charged to disjoint sets of intervals. Therefore, the number of maximal intervals of gates with the same output value is an upper bound on the size of a smallest derivation tree for any element in the minimal model. We conclude

Theorem 2 *There is an $\mathcal{NC}$ algorithm for the planar monotone circuit value problem.*

□

Tree Size Bounded Alternating Turing Machines

Alternating Turing Machines are a generalization of standard (nondeterministic) Turing Machines [8], [1]. They are interesting because their time complexity classes closely correspond to (standard) space complexity classes, and because their computations directly correspond to first order formulas in prenex form with alternating quantifiers.

For an informal description of Alternating Turing Machines (ATM's), we assume that the reader is familiar with the concept of standard (nondeterministic) Turing machines [8]. An ATM consists of a (read-only) input tape and some number of work or scratch tapes, as in the standard model, as well as a finite control. The states of the finite control, however, are partitioned into *normal*, *existential*, and *universal* states. Existential and universal states each have two successor states. Normal states can be *accepting*, *rejecting*, or *non-final*. An *instantaneous description* or *id* of an ATM consists of a string giving the state of the finite control of the ATM, the position of the read head on its input tape, and head positions on and contents of the work tapes. It should be clear that, given the input to the machine, an id completely determines the state of the machine.

A computation of an ATM can be viewed as follows. In any state, the machine performs whatever action is prescribed by the state it is in. If the state is a normal non-final state, the finite control then simply goes to its unique successor state. Accepting or rejecting states have no successors. If the state is existential or universal, the machine clones itself into as many copies as there are successor states, with each clone starting with an id identical to that of the cloning id, except that the state of the cloning id is replaced by that of the successor state. The cloning machine disappears. It is best to view the computation of an ATM as a tree, whose nodes correspond to id's of the computation, in such a way that children of a node in the tree represent successor id's.

Given this interpretation, each computation of an ATM can be mapped into a (binary) tree. This tree need not necessarily be finite, since there can be non-terminating branches of the computation. To define whether an ATM *accepts*, or, dually, *rejects* some input, we look at the corresponding computation tree as defined above. A *leaf* in this tree is called *accepting* iff the state in its id is accepting. An internal node whose id contains a normal state is accepting iff its (unique) descendent in the tree is accepting. An internal node with an existential state is accepting iff at least one of its immediate descendents is accepting, and a node with a universal state iff all of its immediate descendents are accepting. An id of the ATM is called *accepting* if it is attached to an accepting node in the computation tree. An ATM is said to accept its input if and only if the root of the corresponding computation tree is accepting by the above definition, or, equivalently, if the initial configuration of the machine is accepting.

To cast ATM computations into the DTEP framework we note that if the space used by the ATM on its worktapes is bounded by $O(\log n)$ then the number of distinct id's for the machine is bounded by some polynomial in n. Assume that $id_0, \ldots, id_r$ is an (efficient) enumeration of these id's. Our instance of DTEP will have boolean variables p_i, for $i = 0, \ldots, m$, with the intended meaning

$$p_i \text{ is } \mathbf{true} \text{ iff } id_i \text{ is accepting.}$$

The axioms are given by those id's containing accepting states, and we will have inference rules

- $p_i :- p_j p_k$ iff p_i contains a universal state with two successor states, and id_j and id_k are the two immediate successor id's of id_i; and

- $p_i :- p_j$ in all other cases where id_j is a (the) immediate successor id of id_i.

A straightforward induction shows that there is an exact correspondence between derivation trees for the p_i corresponding to the initial id of the ATM, and certain subtrees of the ATM's computation tree. These subtrees are obtained by removing, for each node whose id contains an existential state, all but one of the children of that node, together with their subtrees. Also, the leftover child has to be an accepting node.

Since the computation tree of the ATM is of polynomial size, so is any derivation tree obtained by the above construction. This concludes the (informal) proof for

Theorem 3 *Problems in the complexity class ALT(*$\log n$, expolylog n*) are instances of the Dynamic Tree Expression Problem. In particular, they are members of* $\mathcal{NC}$.

□

$$\begin{aligned} x_4 &= x_1 + x_2 & x_5 &= x_4 \times x_4 \\ x_6 &= x_5 \times x_4 & x_7 &= x_1 \times x_1 \\ x_8 &= x_3 \times x_7 & x_9 &= x_6 \times x_8 \\ x_{10} &= x_4 \times x_9 \end{aligned}$$

Figure 1: Straightline program for polynomial $((x_1 + x_2)^3 + x_1^2 x_3)(x_1 + x_2)$

4 Application to Algebraic Straightline Programs

Straightline programs consist of a sequence of assignment statements executed in order. Each variable referenced in a statement is either an input variable, or it has been assigned a value in an earlier assignment. In *algebraic straightline programs*, the expressions on the righthand side of the assignment are basic unary or binary expressions involving the arithmetic operators $+$, $-$, $\times$, and $/$, as well as constants and input or computed variables. Each non-input variable is assigned a value in exactly one statement in the straightline program. In what follows, we are only concerned with straightline programs containing the operators $+$, $-$, and $\times$. Any such straightline program computes some (multivariate) polynomial of the input variables. Conversely, every multivariate polynomial can be expressed as an algebraic straightline program.

A straightline program corresponds, in a natural way, to a *directed acyclic graph* or *dag*. In this dag, the vertices correspond to the assignment statements, the *sources* of the dag (*i.e.*, vertices of indegree zero) correspond to the input variables of the program, and arcs signify the use of variables defined in one statement by some other statement. We define the *size* of a straightline program to be its number of assignment statements. Figure 1 shows a straightline program for the polynomial $((x_1 + x_2)^3 + x_1^2 x_3)(x_1 + x_2)$ with indeterminates x_1, x_2, and x_3, and Figure 2 gives the corresponding computation dag. In Figure 2, all edges represent arcs directed upward.

We assume without loss of generality that the operation in the last assignment in a straightline program is a multiplication.

To make straightline programs more uniform and easier to deal with, we first wish to transform them into an (algebraically equivalent) sequence of *bilinear forms* of the form

$$y_i = (\sum_{j<i} c_{ij}^{(l)} y_j) \cdot (\sum_{j<i} c_{ij}^{(r)} y_j).$$

Again, the y_j are either input variables or assigned a value in an earlier assignment. In fact, each non-input variable y_i is in exact correspondence with some x_{k_i} in the original straightline program which is the result of a multiplication operation. Assuming that $i = k_i$ for the input variables, the coefficients $c_{ij}^{(l)}$ (resp., $c_{ij}^{(r)}$) give the number of distinct paths from x_{k_j} to the left (resp., right) multiplicand of x_{k_i} in the dag belonging to the original straightline program. These coefficients can be obtained in a straightforward way by repeatedly squaring a matrix A obtained as follows. We first construct, from the computation dag for the straightline program, an auxiliary dag by splitting every multiplication node v into three nodes, v^1, v^2, and v^3: v^1 receives the arc from the left multiplicand, v^2 the arc from the right multiplicand. All arcs originally leaving v are reattached to v^3. In the resulting digraph, the original input nodes and the type 3 nodes are sources, the type 1 and type 2 nodes are the sinks. The matrix A mentioned above is the adjacency matrix of this digraph, after we attach a loop (directed cycle of length one)

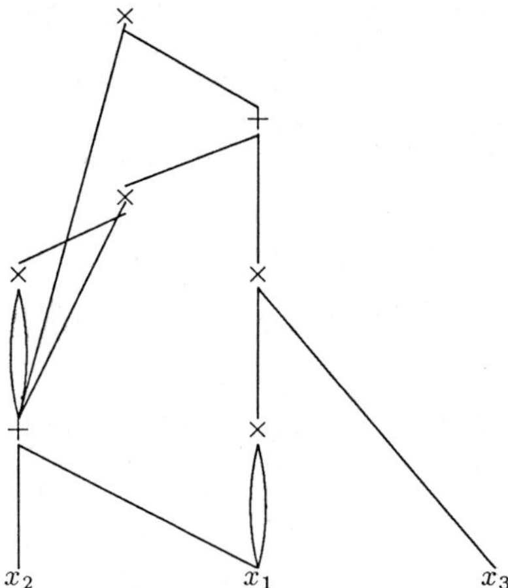

Figure 2: Computation dag for straightline program in Figure 1

to every sink. Further details are left to the reader. The coefficients in the bilinear forms can be computed on a PRAM in time $O(\log^2 n)$, using $M(n)$ processors. Here, n is the size of the original straightline program, and $M(n) \leq n^3$ is the number of processors required to perform matrix multiplication in time $O(\log n)$.

Figure 3 shows a graphical representation of the transformed "bilinear straightline program" for the straightline program resp. computation dag given in Figures 1 and 2. Each bilinear form is represented by a flat 'V', with the terms in the first (second) factor given by the arcs ending in the left (right) arm of the 'V'. The coefficient belonging to a term is attached to the arc unless it is one or zero. In the latter case, no arc is drawn at all.

For the digraph B of a bilinear straightline program, we can define operations analogous to the DTEP operations. The boolean variables are replaced by pairs (c_i, v_i) for every node i in B. The first element, c_i, is a boolean indicating whether the value of the polynomial corresponding to vertex i has been computed; if c_i is **true** then v_i holds this value. Initially, the values of all the input variables are known. We call a node of B a *1-node* iff it is not a sink (*i.e.* a node of outdegree zero) and the value of exactly one of its factors is known (*i.e.* the values of all nodes with arcs to the corresponding "leg" have been computed). All other nodes whose value is still unknown are called *2-nodes*.

We also have several matrices describing the arcs in the graph, and the coefficients attached to them. The set of arcs and coefficients, and consequently the entries in these matrices, change during the course of the algorithm.

- the (i,j)th entry of $C^{(l)}$ contains the coefficient of the arc from the ith node of B to the *left leg* of the jth node, for all nodes i and j such that j is a 2-node; the other entries are zero;
- $C^{(r)}$ is defined correspondingly for the righthand factors;
- the (i,j) entry of the matrix D, for j a 1-node, is the coefficient of the arc from node

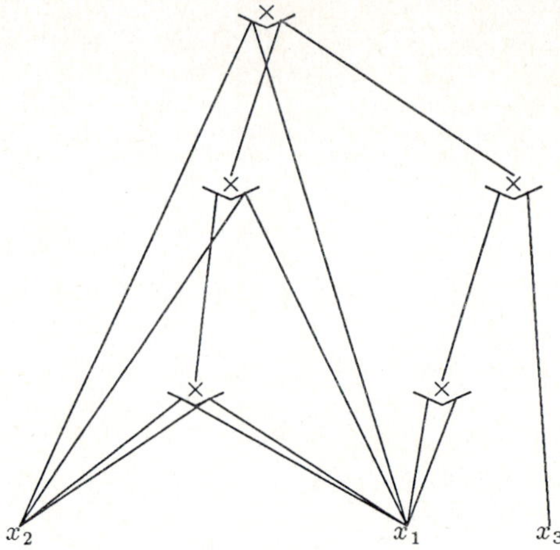

Figure 3: Graph of bilinear straightline program

i to node j;

- the matrix $\bar{C}$ is a projection matrix; all its entries are zero except for those on the diagonal positions corresponding to 2-nodes.

Each phase of the adapted DTEP algorithm consists of the following steps:

co one phase of adapted DTEP **oc**
for all i with $c_i =$ **false** and both factors known **do in parallel**
  compute v_i and set $c_i =$ **true**;
for all nodes i which just became new 1-nodes **do in parallel**
  multiply the coefficients of all arcs entering the unknown "leg" by the other, known factor;
update all matrices so as to reflect the changes in the sets of 1-nodes and 2-nodes;
$C^{(l)} := (\bar{C} + D) \cdot C^{(l)}$; $C^{(r)} := (\bar{C} + D) \cdot C^{(r)}$;
$D := (\bar{C} + D) \cdot D$;
update B to correspond to the newly computed matrices;
co end of phase **oc**

It is straightforward to verify that the bilinear program given by the modified graph after execution of one phase computes the same values as the original bilinear program. Also, one phase can be executed on a PRAM in time $O(\log n)$ employing $M(n)$ processors, where $M(n) \leq n^3$ is the number of processors required to multiply two $n \times n$ matrices in $O(\log n)$ parallel steps.

To obtain a bound on the required number of phases, it is not sufficient to unfold the dag B into a tree and then use our general results about DTEP since there are easy examples where the unfolded tree is of exponential size. However, the following *worst-term* argument works.

Define, for each node in the graph of a bilinear straightline program, its *formal degree* inductively as follows: The original input variables have formal degree 1, and each other variable has a formal degree equal to the sum of the formal degrees of its two factors. Here, the formal degree of a factor is defined to be the maximum of the formal degrees of all its terms.

For every factor of a non-input variable y_i in a bilinear straightline program, we define a *worst term*, derived from the execution of the above algorithm: determine, for the corresponding "leg" of the node i in the sequence of graphs generated by the algorithm, which other node j with an arc to that leg is the latest to have its value computed. If j has an arc to i in the first graph of the sequence, y_j becomes the worst term for the factor of y_i under consideration, and we distinguish the arc from j to i. Otherwise, distinguish any path from j to the appropriate leg of i in the first graph of the sequence. Every node on this path corresponds to the worst term of the appropriate factor of the next node on the path.

Consider the subgraph B' induced by the distinguished arcs. Assume without loss of generality that B' has only one sink. Clearly, B' computes some monomial. If we unfold B' into a tree T then T's size is exactly twice the formal degree of this monomial, minus one. The reason is that all non-leaf nodes in T are multiplication nodes, with exactly one term per factor.

A simple induction shows that the adapted DTEP algorithm computes the values of nodes in T in exactly the same phases as it computes them when run on B, the full graph. The analysis of the general DTEP algorithm applies to the adapted algorithm, executed on T. We obtain that the adapted DTEP algorithm computes the value of each y_i in a number of phases proportional to the logarithm of the formal degree of y_i. Since the initial transformation to a bilinear straightline program is basically a transitive closure computation, we obtain the

Theorem 4 *Suppose S is a straightline program containing n variables and computing a polynomial of formal degree d. The adapted DTEP algorithms computes the value of the polynomial given by S, at a specified point, in time $O(\log n(\log n + \log d))$ using $M(n)$ processors on a unit cost PRAM.*

□

Thus, polynomials given by straightline programs can be evaluated by an $\mathcal{NC}$ algorithm as long as their formal degree is expolylog in n. This result was originally obtained in [13]. Our presentation is intended to give evidence for the wide applicability of the DTEP paradigm, and maybe to supply a somewhat simpler, less technical proof.

5 Conclusion

The DTEP paradigm establishes an interesting connection between fast parallel computation and small proof or derivation trees. In more technical terms, the instances of DTEP in $\mathcal{NC}$ are characterized as ALT($\log n$, expolylog$n$) or the set of problems recognizable by log space bounded alternating Turing machines with "expolylogarithmically" bounded computation trees. DTEP is not necessarily intended to provide optimal parallel algorithms for a given problem. Instead, its primary function is to provide a convenient, high level way for the specification of an efficient and highly portable parallel algorithm. The input to DTEP is in a format very similar to logic programs, rather declarative than procedural, and thus allows to abstract away many peculiarities of any underlying parallel architecture.

The DTEP algorithm can be efficiently implemented on various "real world" parallel architectures, like binary hypercubes, butterfly networks, shuffle-exchange based networks, and multi-dimensional meshes of trees [12]. The algorithm can also be tailored and made more efficient (both in terms of time and number of processors) for more restricted instances of the dynamic tree expression problem. Some of these optimizations are also discussed in [12].

We have also shown how to extend the basic DTEP paradigm to problems over algebraic domains, in particular the parallel evaluation of algebraic computation dags, or straightline programs. Further interesting extensions include the possibility of handling non Horn clauses in the basic formulation of DTEP, along the lines discussed in [21].

Another interesting line of research is the characterization of more classes of problems for DTEP in independent terms, in particular the derivation of conditions for the existence of small proof trees.

References

[1] A. Chandra, D. Kozen, and L. Stockmeyer. Alternation. *J.ACM*, 28(1):114–133, 1981.

[2] R. Cole. Parallel merge sort. In *Proceedings of the 27th Ann. IEEE Symposium on Foundations of Computer Science (Toronto, Canada)*, pages 511–516, 1986.

[3] P. Dymond. *Simultaneous resource bounds and parallel computation.* Ph.D. Thesis, Department of Computer Science, University of Toronto, 1980.

[4] S. Fortune and J. Wyllie. Parallelism in random access machines. In *Proceedings of the 10th Ann. ACM Symposium on Theory of Computing (San Diego, CA)*, pages 114–118, 1978.

[5] L. Goldschlager. The monotone and planar circuit value problems are log-space complete for $\mathcal{P}$. *SIGACT News*, 9(2):25–29, 1977.

[6] L. Goldschlager. A space efficient algorithm for the monotone planar circuit value problem. *Information Processing Letters*, 10(1):25–27, 1980.

[7] P. Hochschild, E. Mayr, and A. Siegel. Techniques for solving graph problems in parallel environments. In *Proceedings of the 24th Ann. IEEE Symposium on Foundations of Computer Science (Tucson, AZ)*, pages 351–359, 1983.

[8] J. Hopcroft and J. Ullman. *Introduction to Automata Theory, Languages, and Computation.* Addison-Wesley, 1979.

[9] R. Ladner. The circuit value problem is log-space complete for $\mathcal{P}$. *SIGACT News*, 7(1):583–590, 1975.

[10] R. Ladner and M. Fischer. Parallel prefix computation. *J.ACM*, 27(4):831–838, 1980.

[11] R. Lipton and J. Valdes. Census functions: An approach to VLSI upper bounds (preliminary version). In *Proceedings of the 22nd Ann. IEEE Symposium on Foundations of Computer Science (Nashville, TN)*, pages 13–22, 1981.

[12] E. Mayr and G. Plaxton. *Network Implementations of the DTEP Algorithm.* Technical Report, Department of Computer Science, Stanford University, 1987.

[13] G. Miller, V. Ramachandran, and E. Kaltofen. *Efficient parallel evaluation of straight-line code and arithmetic circuits.* Technical Report TR-86-211, Computer Science Dept., USC, 1986.

[14] G. Miller and J. Reif. Parallel tree contraction and its application. In *Proceedings of the 26th Ann. IEEE Symposium on Foundations of Computer Science (Portland, OR)*, pages 478–489, 1985.

[15] G. Pfister. *The architecture of the IBM research parallel processor prototype (RP3).* Technical Report RC 11210 Computer Science, IBM Yorktown Heights, 1985.

[16] N. Pippenger. On simultaneous resource bounds. In *Proceedings of the 20th Ann. IEEE Symposium on Foundations of Computer Science (San Juan, PR)*, pages 307–311, 1979.

[17] F. Preparata and J. Vuillemin. The cube-connected-cycles: A versatile network for parallel computation. In *Proceedings of the 20th Ann. IEEE Symposium on Foundations of Computer Science (San Juan, PR)*, pages 140–147, 1979.

[18] W. Ruzzo. Tree-size bounded alternation. In *Proceedings of the 11th Ann. ACM Symposium on Theory of Computing (Atlanta, GA)*, pages 352–359, 1979.

[19] J. Schwartz. Ultracomputers. *ACM Transactions on Programming Languages and Systems*, 2(4):484–521, 1980.

[20] C. Seitz. The cosmic cube. *CACM*, 28(1):22–33, 1985.

[21] J. Ullman and A. van Gelder. Parallel complexity of logical query programs. In *Proceedings of the 27th Ann. IEEE Symposium on Foundations of Computer Science (Toronto, Canada)*, pages 438–454, 1986.

SECTION 3
SURVEY OF PARALLEL PROCESSOR ARCHITECTURE

Parallel Systems and Computation
G. Paul and G.S. Almasi (Editors)

ARCHITECTURE OF THE CEDAR PARALLEL SUPERCOMPUTER

Pen–Chung YEW

Center for Supercomputing Research and Development
University of Illinois at Urbana–Champaign
104 South Wright Street
Urbana, Illinois 61801

Limitations in vector processing and in device speed have led to the development of parallel supercomputer systems. The Cedar parallel supercomputer system currently being designed and developed at the University of Illinois at Urbana–Champaign is an effort to provide high system performance through parallel processing. Its system organization and key architectural features are briefly described here.

1. INTRODUCTION

Computer designers have to make tradeoffs among desirable system features, system cost and the actual hardware needed to build a system. In supercomputer design, these tradeoffs have to be considered even more carefully because of the high costs and the high hardware complexity that can be easily incurred when we are trying to push for higher computing speed. Supercomputer systems built today can perform at peak speeds of more than one billion arithmetic operations per second and may cost well over 10 million dollars. However, these supercomputers have delivered only a small portion of their peak performance for most applications. Achieving good efficiency over a wide range of applications is a goal that has not been delivered in today's supercomputer systems.

Several limitations found in uniprocessor supercomputers in the first half of this decade have led to the development of multiprocessor supercomputers. Uniprocessor supercomputers usually feature special *vector instructions* to capitalize on the occurrence of substantial amounts of vector data in scientific calculations. These processors depend on pipelining arithmetic operations to achieve a high degree of concurrency among operations on successive vector elements.

Vector processing has the constraint that it is useful only when the same operation can be applied to an entire vector of data, and this requires that the programmer express

---

This work was supported in part by the *National Science Foundation* under Grants No. US NSF DRC84-06916 and US NSF DCR84-10110, the *US Department of Energy* under Grant No. US DOE DE FG02-85ER25001, and by the Center for Supercomputing Research and Development of the University of Illinois at Urbana-Champaign.

algorithms in vector form, or that a restructuring compiler create vector operations by rewriting programs expressed in a traditional scalar language. Furthermore, the speedup of a pipeline machine is limited by the number of pipeline segments inherent in a particular operation. If the particular operation can not be further divided into smaller sub–operations, then no further speedup can be achieved through pipelining. Another problem with vector processing is the overhead incurred in setting up the vector instructions and filling the pipeline with data before results emerge. This frequently leads to performances that grow slowly, not reaching half of their peak speeds until vector lengths exceed 100 elements.

In recent years the rate of increase in switching speeds of silicon semiconductor devices has been dropping off, and much effort is being devoted to new semiconductor materials, e.g. III–V compounds such as gallium arsenide.

While new semiconductors promise more speed, gallium arsenide devices are not expected to increase clock speeds by more than a factor of 5 in the next 5 to 10 years. With these limitations, parallel processing seems to be a promising way of extending the growth of computing speed beyond these limitations. It clearly has the potential that by increasing the number of processors in the system, we can increase the peak system speed.

However, parallel processing requires very special hardware and software support. There has been a good deal of research on parallel processing in recent times. This work has included the study of parallel memory systems, parallel networks for communication of control and data between multiple processors and memories, special synchronization requirements, and software to restructure programs and schedule them for parallel processing. The Cedar System [1] is being developed in the Center for Supercomputing Research and Development to demonstrate this approach.

2. SYSTEM ORGANIZATION

It is important to realize that parallel processing is not in fundamental competition with vector processing; both can be combined into one system as has been done in the new Cray products and in the Alliant FX/8. These machines can execute a multiplicity of vector and scalar operations concurrently. This is the main advantage of such systems over vector machines which have to execute one vector operation at a time.

For any parallel processor to be successful in the market place, it must be cost–effective. It also should be scalable to larger number of processors if the architecture is to enjoy a growth in speed over time that goes beyond that obtainable from new circuit technology alone. However, there is an interesting and unresolved cost–effectiveness question about how many processors of what type should be used in parallel machines.

Processors in the Cedar supercomputer are organized into clusters, which are then interconnected to form a larger system with a globally shared memory (Fig. 1). There are several motivations for using clusters. First, the manufacturing of a parallel machine necessitates packaging some fixed size system in one cabinet. Large machines can then be built from cabinet–sized components, which can be defined as clusters. It is relatively easier to design an optimal system configuration for a smaller system than for a larger one. We can first design a small optimal system as a building block, and consider the scalibility and other global issues on a higher system level. Cost–effectiveness can be achieved by matching the application requirements with the number of clusters needed for the application. Second, an n–processor interconnection network of the highest performance level has a cost that grows more rapidly than n. Thus a more powerful network can be chosen for a small (8–16 processor) system than for a larger one, making cluster–wide communication economical, yet highly effective. Third, scheduling of tasks can be done so that cluster–sized amounts of work are assigned to individual clusters for nearly autonomous processing with relatively little inter–cluster communication.

At present, each cluster in the Cedar supercomputer is a slightly modified Alliant FX/8 with eight processors. Each processor in Alliant FX/8 has a set of vector registers and an instruction cache. It uses the Motorola 68020 instruction set with enhanced vector instructions executed in Weitek and Alliant–designed Fujitsu floating–point chip sets. There is a set of registers that can store vector length, vector increment, and vector mask to facilitate vector instructions. Vector instructions include "gather" and "scatter" operations for sparse arrays, and may have up to three operands (provided that one of the three is a scalar stored in one of the floating–point registers) to perform operations similar to Cray's "chaining", i.e. two floating–point operations per clock.

A separate concurrency control bus for fast synchronization is shared by all of the processors. With some special instructions, this bus allows processors to do self–scheduling on parallel loops by dynamically assigning loop iterations to available processors at run time. It also provides a fast mechanism to enforce data dependences between loop iterations, so loop structures like *doacross* [2] can be executed like parallel loops.

There is a 4–way interleaved, 128kbyte, hardware–managed cache shared by the eight processors in a cluster. The shared cache uses a write–back scheme to the cluster memory. The cluster memory and the shared cache are connected through a high speed bus with a bus protocol that supports cache miss operations and provides for cache coherence.

Each floating–point processor is connected to a private port of the global interconnection network that provides access to the shared global memory. A crossbar switch is used as a cluster interconnection network to connect each processor to the shared 4–way interleaved cache and to its private port of the global interconnection network. There is a data prefetching facility at the interface between a processor and its global network port in the Cedar system, so array data can be prefetched into a data buffer for vector operations. This interface buffer allows global array data to be prefetched as early as possible.

The global interconnection network consists of two unidirectional multiple–stage shuffle–exchange networks: one for connecting processors to the global memory; the other for connecting the global memory back to processors. They are packet–switching networks with buffers at each input port of each 8x8 crossbar switch element.

The global memory contains one module per floating–point processor in the system with an on–board synchronization processor in each memory module. A set of elaborate synchronization operations can be performed on these synchronization processors. The indivisibility of these synchronization operations is enforced by each synchronization processor. The global memory is used to store globally shared data for clusters; it can also be used as a fast backup memory for cluster memories and for high rate vector and page streaming through the prefetch buffer. There is a single–error–correction–double–error–detection (SECDED) code on each memory word to enhance its reliability. Using the synchronization processors, it can also perform intercluster synchronizations.

Each cluster has its own I/O complex with I/O processors and caches, high transfer rate I/O port, disks and other I/O devices. Hence, as the number of clusters increases, the number of I/O complexes will also increase proportionately to satify the increased I/O demand.

Cross–processor interrupts are supported even between processors in different clusters. A cross–processor interrupt between clusters can be issued from a processor in one cluster, and be routed through the global interconnection networks to a processor in another cluster. A direct path is provided in each global memory module so an interrupt request can be routed directly from the forward network to the return network.

3. MEMORY HIERARCHIES

Performance of supercomputers is usually limited by memory accessing. With problem size growing larger with faster supercomputers, we need larger and faster memories. However, it is extremely expensive to construct such a massive memory using memory chips with an access time comparable to processor clock speed. A well designed memory hierarchy can be used to achieve high bandwidth and fast access time with reasonable cost. This is done by using a smaller memory with fast and expensive memory chips near the processor, and larger, slower, cheaper memory chips for memories farther from the processor. Program locality will allow these faster local memories to be accessed more often than those slower shared memories that are farther away.

In the Cedar supercomputer, the memory hierarchy includes an I/O system, a large shared global memory using larger and slower memory chips, a smaller and faster cluster memory with shared cache in each cluster, and very fast local storage including vector and scalar registers and instruction caches in each processor.

There are multiple memory modules in the shared global memory. Array data are stored across all memory modules to avoid possible memory conflicts and to allow data to be accessed in parallel. The global memory provides very high memory bandwidth when many processors are accessing array data at the same time.

These memory modules are connected through the global interconnection network to the processors. Long memory access delay to the global memory is unavoidable in such systems. There are serveral reasons for this:

(1) Due to physical pin limitations in packaging, it is extremely expensive to have a very wide data path in the global interconnection network. This prohibits large amounts of data from being transfered in parallel between processors and the global memory.

(2) Various skewing schemes have been designed to store array data so that memory conflicts can be avoided when a certain block of array data is accessed in parallel by processors. It has been proved impossible to have a storage scheme that can avoid memory conflicts totally for all array access patterns.

(3) No interconnection networks, other than crossbar switches, have complete connections among all of the memory modules and the processors. Hence, there will be network conflicts when a request is being routed through the interconnection network.

(4) Due to cost effectiveness, we use larger and slower memory chips in the large shared global memory.

This problem has to be dealt with effectively to keep global memory from becoming a bottleneck. In Cedar, the long global memory access delay can be offset in two ways:

(1) For programs with good locality, faster and smaller local memories in each cluster and also in each processor can be used to minimize the number of global memory accesses. For example, an instruction cache in each processor will provide fast instruction fetches for each processor. Using compiler techniques, programs can be restructured to enhance program locality for data, e.g. by blocking and merging loops, etc. [3]. This improvement of program locality will reduce the traffic in the network, which in turn will reduce the network and memory conflicts and improve global memory access delay.

(2) Data are prefetched into local memories before they are needed, so long memory access delay can be overlapped with other useful operations. In Cedar, specific data prefetching instructions are provided to allow data prefetching to be done as early as possible. Futhermore, the global interconnection network allows requests to be pipelined through each stage of the network. So after a startup time, data can stream into local memories at a rate that closely matches that of a processor.

Fast local memory (e.g. cache) has been used in high performance uniprocessor systems for a long time [4]. In a parallel system, multiple copies of the same data in different caches will create coherence problems if the data are updated at different instants of time in those caches. Hardware can be built to maintain coherence by updating automatically all of the copies in different caches with appropriate sequence control with respect to local reads and writes. In the Alliant cluster, those caches for floating–point processors and for I/O processors are managed by hardware to maintain coherence through the cluster memory bus. However, it is extremly costly and slow to maintain coherence among all clusters when a system becomes large.

Notice that read–only data and the private data that are not shared among processors can be brought into local stores without causing data coherence problems. This will include program code and those variables that store temporary results during program execution. Only those shared data that will be updated at one time or another by different processors will have data coherence problems.

Futhermore, in a multiprocessor system, when processors are assigned to work on the same program, e.g. loop iterations scheduled on many processors, it is very rare that a shared variable will be fetched and stored in a random order among processors (except for some functions in the operating system). It usually requires synchronization to maintain a correct read/write sequence among those processors sharing the same variable. A processor has to wait if the shared data it needs has not yet been produced (or stored) by another processor.

There is a synchronization processor in each global memory module that can handle this kind of synchronization very efficiently. Hence, those shared data that can cause coherence problems will be designated as "nonlocal" either by the user or by the compiler, and these will remain in the global memory. Those data that are "partially shared", i.e. by processors within a single cluster, can be stored in the corresponding cluster memory.

Virtual memory is another complex issue in supercomputers. Some supercomputers, like Cray, do not have virtual memory because of poor locality in numerical applications. They require users to manage overlays of data in main memory explicitly in their application codes. However, the Cyber 205 has implemented virtual memory to shield users from the complexity of managing memory hierarchies. It allows the system to provide a large monolithic address space so a user need not manage complicated memory hierarchies himself. Virtual memory requires software and hardware support to translate virtual addresses into physical addresses efficiently to minimize possible overheads. Blocks of needed data can then be moved among the levels of memory hierarchies when demanded. Currently, virtual memory is supported on Cedar and compiler techniques have been developed to enhance data locality. These techniques are very similar to locality enhancement schemes for local storage, only at different levels in the memory hierarchy.

4. INTERCONNECTION NETWORKS

Interconnection networks for large numbers of units—processors, memories, I/O ports—are a very important aspect of parallel processors and one of the hardest to design properly. The simplest implementation is a *bus* —a network that can transmit one word at a time between any pair of ports and which has modest hardware requirements, proportional to the number of ports on the bus. Busses are used in most of the superminicomputers as the main interconnection network, but a single bus is not scalable to many ports since designers must provide a very fast bus relative to the microprocessors used. Thus as microprocessor speeds increase, either the bus will be a bottleneck, or fewer processors can be used.

On the other hand, a crossbar switch can provide complete connections between any set of pairs of distinct input and output ports. The hardware in a crossbar switch is proportional to n^2 for n input and output ports. The cost of the switch grows very quickly while system size increases only moderately. Also, its implementation suffers from the *pin-limitations* of integrated circuit chips, which are typically on the order of a few hundreds now, at best. Nevertheless, crossbars can be very effective for 8 to 16 ports.

Hence, several factors have to be considered when we choose an interconnection network:

(1) Hardware complexity should be reasonable because it will dictate the cost and the manufacturability of the network when system size becomes large.

(2) Network bandwidth should be adequate, otherwise, it will create a serious bottleneck if it can not satisfy a large number of processors working at very high rate.

(3) Network propagation delay should be as short as possible. Delay will directly affect the speed when serial code is being executed. We should minimize the unnecessary overhead being built into the network and try to make network design as simple as possible.

(4) The network control scheme should be very simple. It will directly affect the network delay for a request being routed through the network.

(5) It should be very reliable. There is an inherent redundancy among the processors and the memories in a multiprocessor system. If a processor fails, there are others that can be used to backup the failed processor and keep system functioning. An interconnection network is too expensive to have a duplicated backup, and if it fails, the whole system could stop functioning unless some amount of reconfigurability or redundancy is built into the interconnection network.

For larger systems, an attractive idea that meets most of the above objectives is a decomposed crossbar switch consisting of a shuffle-based interconnection of smaller crossbars (Fig. 2). Using smaller crossbars as building blocks, larger systems can be built with a hardware complexity proportional to **nlogn**. Requests can be decomposed into packets and pipelined through each stage of the network with a minimum delay proportional to **logn**. Routing these packets through the network can be done locally inside each small crossbar using a destination tag associated with the packet. There are also several simple schemes to enhance its reliability by providing redundant paths in the network. Currently, the basic building block for the Cedar interconnection network is an 8 by 8 crossbar switch with an input buffer at each input port of the switch. Input buffers allow conflicting requests to be stored to improve both network bandwidth and delay [5].

There are a number of other possibilities for memory and switch design. For example, it is not necessary to have shared memory at all. Data can be distributed among memories that are associated with processors. Then to access certain data items, a particular processor must communicate with other processors until the processor whose memory has the data is reached. The Caltech Cosmic Cube, Intel's iPSC, and others have processor–memory pairs associated with vertices of a hypercube to implement this approach. The hypercube connection affords a logarithmic growth in the number of steps needed to access other nodes, but it requires one additional interconnection port per node each time the system size doubles.

5. SYNCHRONIZATION

How to exploit a multiprocessor to speed up a single job is currently a serious question in machine design as well as software design. We can describe three levels of potential parallelism that one could attempt to exploit. The highest level is that of separate subroutines, separate loops within a subroutine, etc. Most programmers can easily find some independent tasks at this level in their programs. However, most evidence indicates that only a small constant speedup is possible in most programs, using such high–level parallelism.

The next level down is that of parallelism between individual loop iterations. Here, the discovery of parallelism is sometimes rather intricate. For example, in a weather code, it is easy to see that the northern and southern hemispheres can be computed simultaneously, but exactly how to break a program up so that all the mesh points can be computed at once may be trickier, because there are many dependences between different variables. Nevertheless, the potential for parallelism here is enormous, because of the large number of mesh points involved. In general, the potential speedup is proportional to the loop limit, or the product of nested loop limits. Experimentally, we have observed that this level of parallelism is by far the most important in program speedup.

Finally, one can look at the lowest levels of parallelism, namely arithmetic expressions or blocks of assignment statements. Methods of speedup are well understood at this level, but the potential speedups are relatively small due to the limited nature of the complexity of individual statements, or even blocks of statements. Factors of 2 or 3 at most are possible here, and this is based on extensive measurement of real Fortran programs.

To exploit loop level parallelism, some low level synchronizations are needed to enforce data dependences among loop iterations. Cray X–MP has the test–and–set type of primitives on a set of shared one–bit semaphore registers. HEP computer has a full–empty bit on each memory word. Hardware will enforce the rule that if the full–empty bit indicates "full" the memory word cannot be written, and if the bit indicates "empty" it cannot be read. Ultracomputer and IBM RP3 have a set of higher level synchronization primitves which allow arithmetic or logical operations to be performed on a memory word. The operations of these synchronization primitves can be combined through the interconnection network if they are intended for the same memory word.

Cedar uses a general and flexible synchronization mechanism [6]. A shared variable (either a scalar or an array) can be declared as a synchronization variable. Each element of a synchronization variable will have an integer key associated with the data word.

Both data and key are stored in the same global memory module.

Each global memory module has a simple synchronizaton processor that performs an indivisible sequence of synchronization operations in response to a synchronization instruction issued from a processor. A regular global memory read or write operation will bypass this hardware so overhead will not be incurred on these most frequent operations.

In each synchronization operation, a transmitted key is compared with a stored key, and one of several tests is performed. If the test is successful, an arithmetic or logical operation can be performed on the stored key and trasmitted data can be stored. A return packet to the processor contains the test result and (if the test is successful) key or data values (or both) as requested.

This synchronization mechanism allows execution–sequencing information to be stored in the key, so it can be compared, updated, fetched or stored indivisibly thorough one global memory access. For synchronizations among loop iterations, especially when they are scheduled on several clusters, operations like loop self–scheduling [7], barrier synchronization and data dependence enforcement [6] can be done very efficiently using this scheme.

6. SOFTWARE AND APPLICATION

A Unix–based operating system, called Xylem [8], supports multiprocessing within individual programs. System calls which allow tasks to be created, deleted, started, ended, etc. from a process are provided in the operating system. Xylem also provides facilities to allow tasks to control their own memory environments. Thus a task can allocate or deallocate memory pages, share pages with other tasks, unmap pages from any task, etc. A page in the address space of a task will have global/local and shared/private attributes to reflect the memory hierarchies in the Cedar system. There is also a scheduler to schedule tasks on available clusters and processors. To increase the efficiency of the system, the operating system supports multiprogramming in a way that multiple programs are allowed to be executed in disjoint subsets of clusters.

The Cedar optimizing compiler [9] which can analyze a user's source program, detect inherent parallelism in the program, and restructure the program so that the architecture features in the Cedar system can be fully exploited. This process can be iterated as many times as needed. A user can participate in the process by providing additional information that is useful to the compiler.

Since our goal is to use parallelism to provide high performance over a wide range of applications, we should also develop and implement new algorithms that can take full advantage of the features in system architecture, operating system, compiler, etc. Given a multicluster system with vector processors, algorithms must take advantage of the available three–level parallelism (decomposing the problem among the clusters, dividing tasks among the processors, and finally taking advantage of the vector capability of each processor), so larger granularity parallelism can be exploited among the clusters and smaller granularity parallelism within each cluster.

In the next few years, many efforts will be made to expand parallel processors to provide higher performance. The Cedar system growth plans call for an average doubling of the number of processors annually for the next five years. This rate of growth would lead to a factor of one thousand in a decade. Each new system will give us the opportunity to understand the limitation of various algorithms as the number of clusters increases, and will help us develop algorithms that are increasingly suitable for multiprocessing.

ACKNOWLEDGEMENTS

The author would like to thank David Kuck, Ed Davidson, Duncan Lawrie and Ahmed Sameh for their help in preparing this paper.

REFERENCES

[1] Kuck, D.J., et al., Parallel Supercomputing Today and the Cedar Approach, Science Vol. 231, February 1986, pp. 967–974.

[2] Padua, D.A., et al., High–Speed Multiprocessor and Compilation Techniques, IEEE Trans. Computers, Vol. C–29, No. 9, Sept. 1980, pp. 763–776.

[3] Abu–Sufah, W., et al., On the Performance Enhancement of Paging Systems Through Program Analysis and Transformations, IEEE Trans. Computers, Vol. C–30, No. 5, May 1981, pp. 341–356.

[4] Simth, A.J., Cache Memories, Computing Surveys, Vol. 14, No. 3, Sept. 1982, pp. 473–530.

[5] Chen, P.Y., Multiprocessor Systems: Interconnection Networks, Memory Hierarchy, Modeling and Simulation, Ph.D. Thesis, Univ. of Illionis at Urbana–Champaign, Rept. No. UIUCDCS–R–82–1083, Jan. 1982.

[6] Zhu, C.Q., Yew, P.C., A Synchronization Scheme and Its Applications for Large Multiprocessor Systems, 4th Int'l Conf. Distributed Computing Systems, May, 1984, pp. 486–491.

[7] Tang, P., Yew, P.C., Processor Self–Scheduling for Multiply–Nested Parallel Loops, Proc. of Int'l Conf. Parallel Processing, Aug. 1986.

[8] Emrath, P., Xylem: An Operating System for the Cedar Multiprocessor, IEEE Software, July 1985, pp. 30–37.

[9] Wolfe, M.J., Optimizing Supercompilers for Supercompuers, Ph.D. Thesis, Univ. of Illinois at Urbana–Champaign, Rept. No. UIUCDCS–R–82–1105, Oct. 1982.

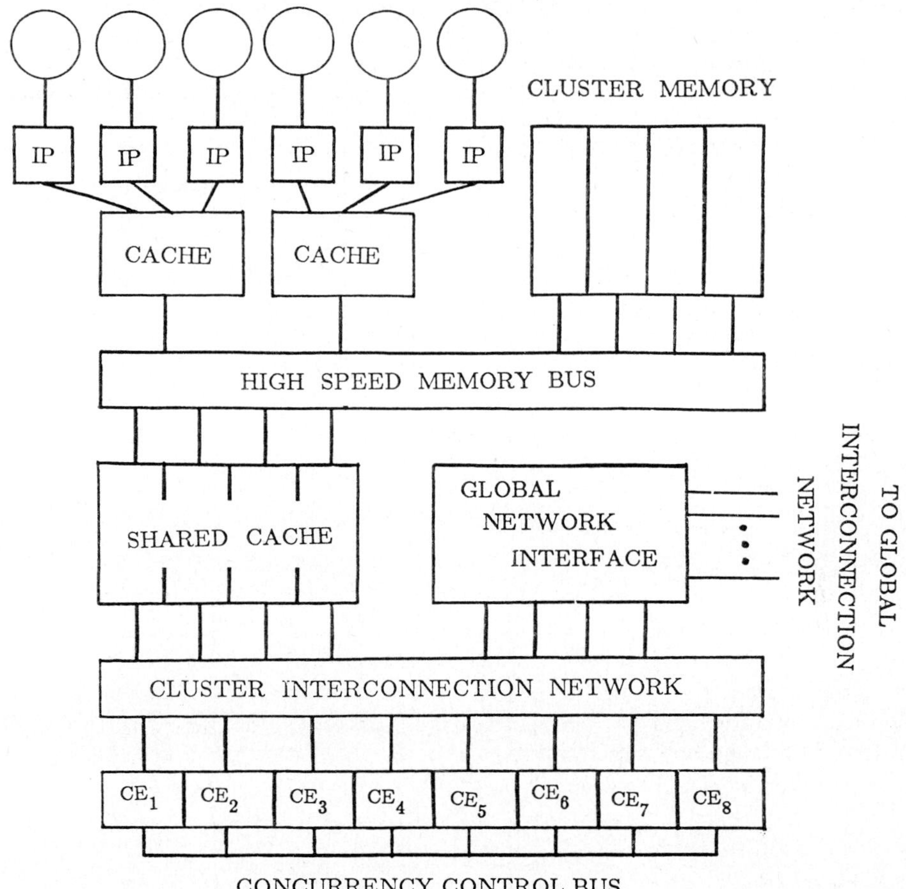

Fig. 1.a One Cluster

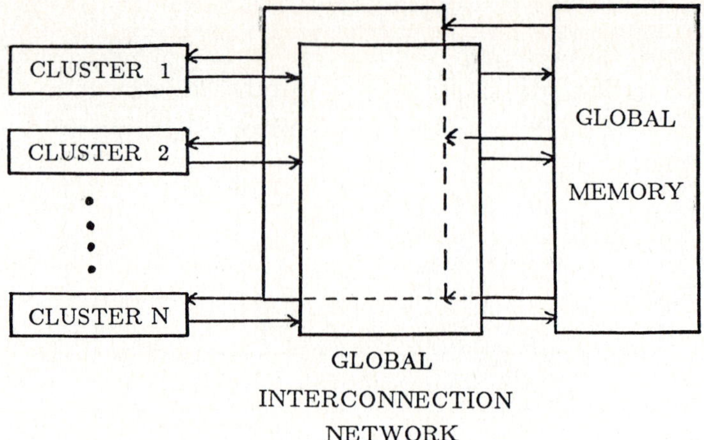

Fig. 1.b A Multi–cluster Cedar System

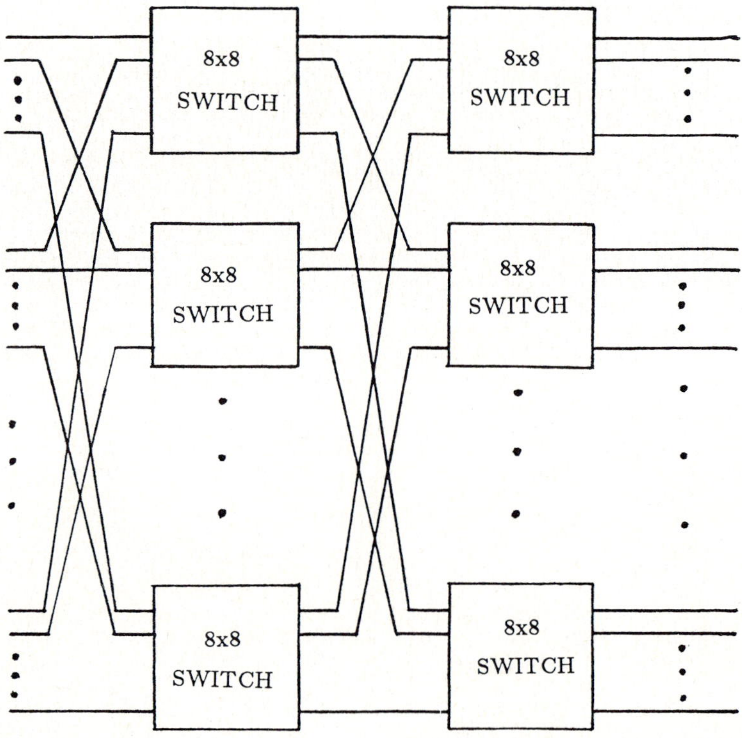

Fig. 2 A 64x64 Global Interconnection Network with 8x8 Crossbar Switch as its building blocks.

Parallel Systems and Computation
G. Paul and G.S. Almasi (Editors)
Elsevier Science Publishers B.V. (North-Holland), 1988

MULTIPROCESSOR TESTBED DIRMU 25: EFFICIENCY AND FAULT TOLERANCE

Erik Maehle

Department of Computer Science (IMMD)
University of Erlangen-Nuremberg
Martensstr. 3, D-8520 Erlangen
Federal Republic of Germany

DIRMU 25 is a multiprocessor testbed with 25 processors which is in operation at the University of Erlangen-Nuremberg. First the testbed itself (hardware architecture and system software) is introduced with special emphasis on interprocessor communication. Efficiency of user programs from different fields of applications which have been implemented on DIRMU 25 is discussed next. Finally a concept for fault-tolerant operation of the system (self-diagnosis, reconfiguration and recovery) is presented.

1. INTRODUCTION

As there is an increasing demand for high-performance computing systems MIMD multiprocessor architectures are becoming more and more important [1]. On the one hand, they have the potential for high computational performance by making use of parallel processing on a large number of processors in a very flexible way. On the other hand, reliability and availability can be improved by incorporating fault tolerance which is facilitated by their modular structure and their 'natural' redundancy. Another advantage is modular growth by adding more processing elements if performance requirements increase.

An important problem is the design of suitable parallel algorithms and their mapping on a multiprocessor architecture such that high efficiency and fault-tolerant operation is achieved. In principle simulation can be used for these investigations. However, because of the complexity of the problem real prototypes or testbeds will give more realistic results and insights. At our university several multiprocessor systems have already been built (e.g. EGPA [2] or MUPSI [3]). In this paper we will describe the testbed DIRMU 25 (DIstributed Reconfigurable MUltiprocessor kit). First an 8-processor version has been put into operation [4]. In summer 1985 the system has been expanded to 25 processors (plus one spare).

A special characteristic of DIRMU 25 is that it does not have a fixed interconnection structure. It is a multiprocessor kit based on an universal microcomputer building block. The DIRMU building block consists of a processor module (P-module) and a multiport memory module (M-module). By pluggable cables several building blocks can be combined to a multiprocessor configuration. As the number of memory ports (M-ports) and corresponding processor ports (P-ports) is limited (currently to 8), DIRMU configurations usually have a restricted neighbourhood interconnection structure with a distributed shared memory, i.e. there is no central global memory shared by all processors. A wide variety of such configurations can easily be set up simply by replugging the cables (rings, nearest-neighbour arrays, hypercubes, pyramids etc.). The interprocessor communication to the neighbours can be made very fast because of the tight coupling by shared multiport memories (which of course also means fast routing between not directly connected building blocks).

2. MULTIPROCESSOR TESTBED DIRMU 25

2.1. Hardware Architecture

A photograph of the DIRMU system is shown in Fig. 1. A building block is housed in a 3/4 19" rack with its own front panel and power supply. Though based on microprocessor technology the building block is not very small. The reason is that the design started about 1979, when the density of VLSI chips was still rather modest. Today the whole building block would fit on a single board.

Fig. 1b shows a look inside the tower with the rear side of the building blocks. As can be seen there are two columns of 8 connectors for the P-ports and M-ports respectively. P-port 0 is always connected to M-port 0 for accessing the own M-module (the connection is made externally for testing purposes only). The remaining P-ports can be connected with 37-wire cables to the M-ports of other building blocks according to the desired configuration.

A block diagram of a DIRMU building block is shown in Fig. 2. The P-module contains the 16-bit microprocessor 8086 with arithmetic coprocessor 8087, private ROM (16 K bytes), private RAM (320 K bytes) and some standard I/O interfaces (for terminals, disks etc.). A P-port control allows the microprocessor to access not only the private memory but also its own multiport memory (64 K bytes) as well as neighbouring ones if a cable is plugged, i.e. all M-modules a processor can access become part of its address space. The M-port control has the task to resolve access conflicts which can occur if two or more processors try to access the same M-module at exactly the same time. In this case the processors are granted access one after the other. Note that this arbitration is done completely in hardware and is invisible to software.

Though it can happen that some processors are delayed for a few clock cycles, measurements and experiments have shown that the performance degradation of user programs on DIRMU due to memory access conflicts is negligible in practice. One of the reasons is that only shared data is stored in the M-modules. Program code and private data are always stored in private memory, i.e. only a small percentage of the total memory cycles are accesses to M-modules. Furthermore, most parallel user programs tend to access different M-modules at the same time.

The access time to private memory is 800 nsec and that to multiport memory (own one or one of the neighbouring ones) is about 1.2 μsec (16 bit data path, no access conflicts). In case of access conflicts the delay is 1 μsec for each waiting cycle. The M-module also contains some status registers which can be accessed like memory words from all attached P-modules. One status register shows the fault status of a building block for neighbourhood diagnosis (see section on self-diagnosis). Another two registers allow to send interprocessor interrupts to support interprocessor communication. Once two building blocks are connected by a cable they can interrupt each other.

2.2. Operating System and Programming Environment

Parallel programs for DIRMU 25 consist of a set of cooperating concurrent processes with at least one process per processor. Our preferred programming language is Modula-2 [5]. We use this high-level language for user programs as well as for system programming.

The development of parallel programs for DIRMU 25 is done on a single building block (MASTER) in monoprocessor operation. We use Concurrent CP/M-86 as our development operating system. After a program has been edited, compiled and linked, it can be executed under control of our multiprocessor operating system DIRMOS written in Modula-2. First a distributed loader allows to load the parallel program from the MASTER's disk into a number of SLAVE building blocks specified by the user in a configuration dialogue, as well as into the MASTER

(a) Front view with building blocks and peripherals.

(b) Pluggable cables between building blocks inside the tower.

FIGURE 1
Multiprocessor testbed DIRMU 25.

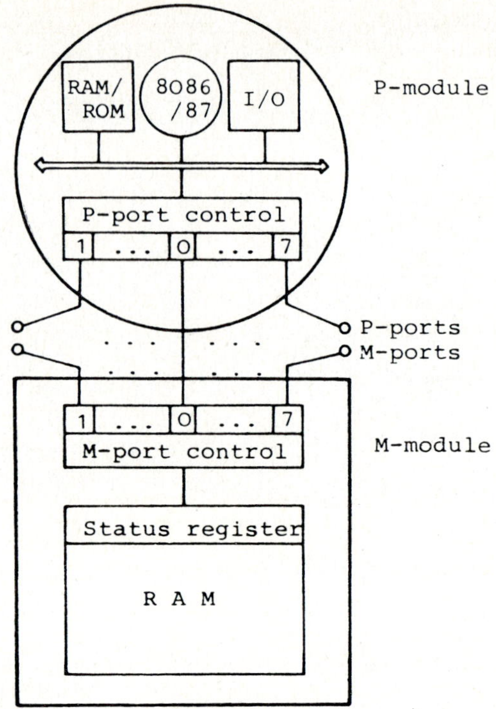

FIGURE 2
Block diagram of a DIRMU building block.

itself. The program is then executed in parallel on MASTER and SLAVES with the MASTER being also responsible for I/O.

For multi-user operation we use a space-sharing concept. If there is more than one MASTER they compete for free SLAVE building blocks. There is no time-sharing. Once a SLAVE has been allocated by a MASTER it cannot serve another MASTER at the same time. After a parallel user program has finished, MASTER and SLAVES are returned into free SLAVES again.

For the runtime support of a parallel program a copy of a resident operating system kernel is provided within all building blocks. It contains synchronization and communication primitives, a memory manager for the M-modules as well as runtime support to implement a fault-tolerant mapping of the processes onto the net of intact processor (see section on reconfiguration).

2.3. Interprocessor Communication

As DIRMU is mainly a testbed we offer several different communication and synchronization primitives [6] and leave it to the user to select the ones that he thinks to be most appropriate for his application.

One possible choice is message passing (Fig. 3). In this case all processes have their own separate address space. By SEND and RECEIVE primitives messages can be exchanged via mailboxes. If the processes reside in the same building block the

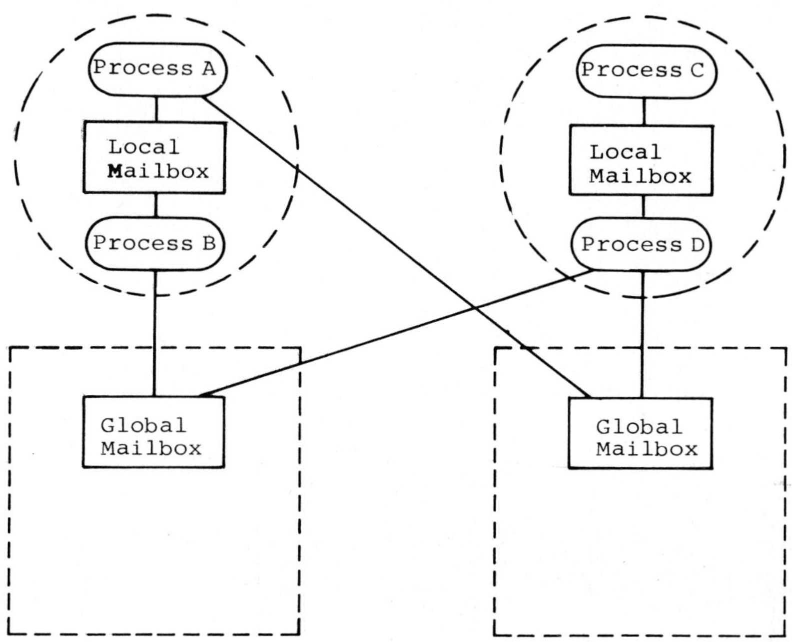

FIGURE 3
Message passing via local mailboxes within building blocks and via global mailboxes between neighbouring building blocks.

mailbox is placed in the private memory within the P-module. Communication between processes in neighbouring building blocks is established by a global mailbox in a common M-module. If building blocks are not directly connected the message has to be forwarded by a routing process.

The SEND is non-blocking (no-wait send). This means that messages have to be buffered in the mailboxes (FIFO). A RECEIVE primitive allows to retrieve the first message. If the mailbox is empty the process is blocked until a message arrives (notified by an interprocessor interrupt). As it is in some cases desirable to avoid blocking at a RECEIVE primitive, there is also a routine MAILFOR which tells the calling process whether there is a message deposited in a mailbox. Fig. 4 shows interprocessor communication time measurements for this message system which has been implemented in Modula-2 [7]. It was assumed that the receiving process has already called the RECEIVE primitive and is blocked when the message arrives. The time measurement starts, when SEND is called in the sending process, and ends after the receiving process in the other processor leaves the RECEIVE routine.

As can be seen there is a fixed communication time of about 8 msec for short messages (1 - 10 bytes). For longer messages the communication time goes up to 12 msec and then increases with the message length. The reason is that short messages of up to 10 bytes are passed directly over the mailbox. For longer messages the memory manager for the M-module is called and the message is placed in some free shared memory space. The mailbox now only holds a pointer to the message. In both cases the message is copied twice: from the address space of the sending process (private memory) into the shared memory and back into the private address space of the receiver.

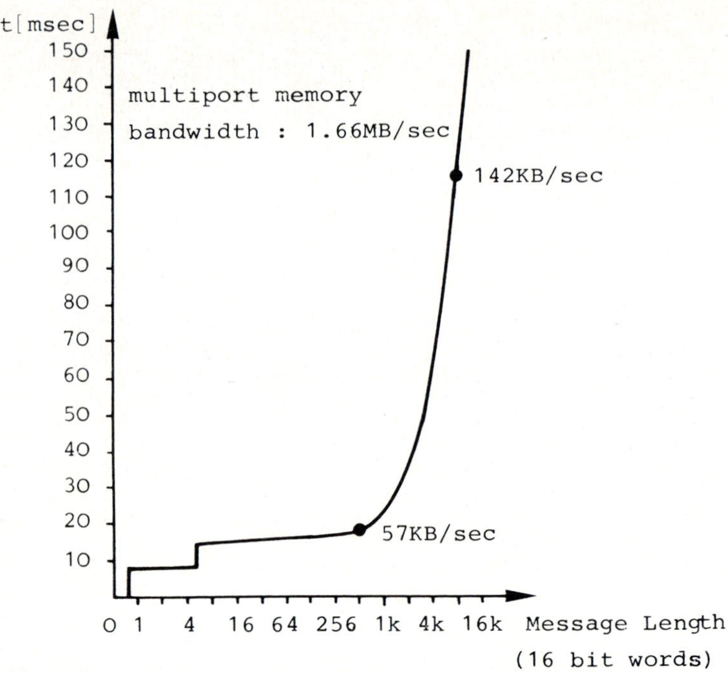

FIGURE 4
Communication time measurements for message passing between neighbouring building blocks.

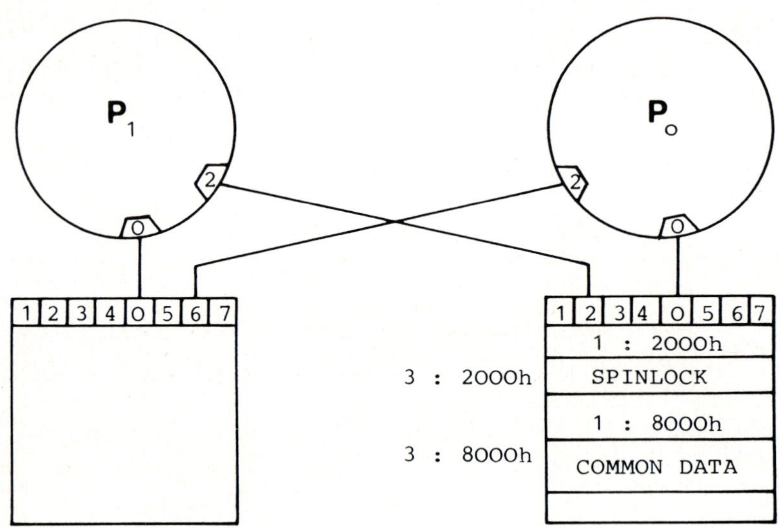

FIGURE 5
Communication by common data objects and synchronization by spinlock variables. Addresses within shared memory have the same offset, the segment part is determined by the P-ports (P-port number + 1).

Though our message system implementation is surely not the most efficient one, it shows a typical property of all such systems: there is a non-negligible start-up time due to a certain protocol overhead and then an increasing communication time with increasing message length because of the copying of data. This overhead makes message systems only recommendable for applications where communication is rather infrequent and not time-critical.

Another possibility which makes use of the distributed shared memory in DIRMU 25 more directly is shown in Fig. 5. Here, common data objects are placed directly in the M-modules. This can be done by an ALLOCATE primitive we provide in our Modula-2 library. Now the data can be accessed with the same speed (usually under different addresses as shown in Fig. 5) from all attached processors via pointers in Modula-2. Synchronization can be done by semaphores or spinlocks with WAIT and SIGNAL primitives. Our experience is that for many applications synchronization by spinlocks is very efficient though the WAIT primitive executes a polling loop (active waiting) on the synchronization variable and thus evidently wastes processor time and consumes memory cycles. The reason is that often the waiting times are short and the waiting processor does not have anything else to do anyway. As the program code for the polling loop is stored in private memory there is also only a moderate memory load. The benefit of spinlocks is that if a SIGNAL primitive by another processor is executed the reaction time for the waiting one is only one loop cycle (about 20 µsec for DIRMU) in the worst case. For all applications to be described in the next section we have therefore used this scheme of communication directly over shared data and synchronization by spinlocks.

3. PARALLEL APPLICATION PROGRAMS ON DIRMU 25

Several parallel application programs have already been implemented on DIRMU ring configurations (Fig. 6), nearest neighbour arrays (Fig. 7) or hypercubes Fig. 8). Many parallel programs are from the fields of numerical mathemathics (e.g. PDE-solvers based on multi grid algorithms [10], which are part of the investigations in connection with the German supercomputer project SUPRENUM) or pattern recognition. Further applications also from other fields like artificial intelligence or robotics are currently under study. As many of the programs from Fig. 6 - 8 have been already described in detail elsewhere (e.g. [8,9,10]) we will here only concentrate on some general aspects concerning efficiency.

Often the performance of parallel programs on multiprocessors is measured in terms of speedup $S = T1/Tp$, where Tp is the execution time on p processors and T1 the execution time of the corresponding sequential program on one processor of the same type. Given speedup S efficiency E can be defined as $E = S/p$. Clearly $S = p$ is the maximum obtainable speedup corresponding to an efficiency $E = 1$. (There are some special cases of superlinear speedups discussed in the literature [11] which however do not apply here.)

From Fig. 6 - 8 it can be seen that for many important applications high speedups (efficiencies) have been measured on DIRMU 25 (e.g. $S = 23.3$ for 25 processors, i.e. $E = 0.93$, for the asynchronous iterative solution of the Laplace PDE with fixed boundary conditions). There are other applications (e.g. parallel sorting by QuickSort and pipelined MergeSort with $E = 0.57$ for 15 processors) where the efficiency is considerably lower.

The main reasons for losses in efficiency are the following:

(1) Not ideally parallelizable algorithms
(e.g. smaller degree of parallelism than available processors)

(2) Non-balanced processor utilization
(e.g. not equally balanced workload or data dependent execution times)

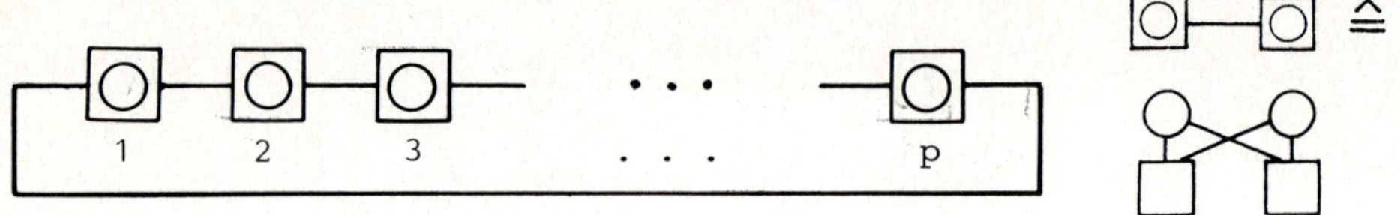

* Laplace PDE (Dirichlet's Problem)

- asynchronous method
  S = 23.3 (25 processors, 100 x 100 grid)

- wavefront Gauss-Seidel method
  S = 22.8 (25 processors, 100 x 100 grid)

- Jacobi's method
  S = 23.6 (25 processors, 100 x 100 grid)

* Median Filtering of Digital Images
  S = 22.8 (26 processors, 128 x 128 image, 3 x 3 window)

* Edge Detection in a Sequence of Medical Images
  S = 6.3 (7 processors, 12+1 images)
  S = 12.5 (13 processors, estimated)

* Parallel Sorting (QuickSort + Pipelined MergeSort)
  S = 8.5 (15 processors)

FIGURE 6
Speedup S for some applications on DIRMU ring configurations. A single line between building blocks corresponds to two 'crossed' cables between P- and M-modules.

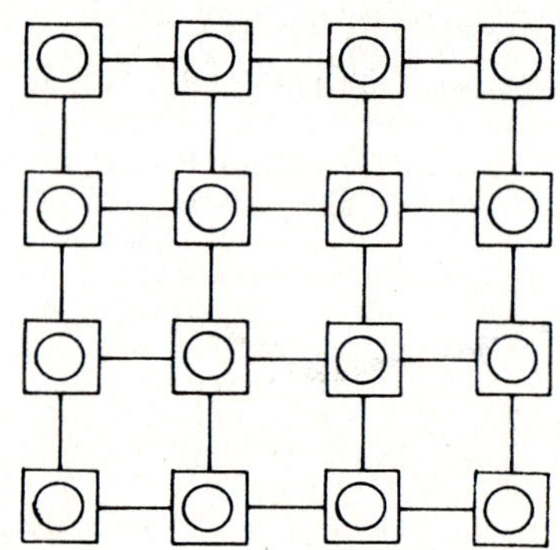

* Multi Grid Programs

- Steady-Stokes equations
  S = 7.8 (8 processors, 2 x 4 nearest-neighbour array)

- Poisson equation with Dirichlet conditions (MGOOD)
  S = 15.3 (16 processors, 4 x 4 nearest-neighbour array)

FIGURE 7
Parallel multi grid programs on DIRMU [10].

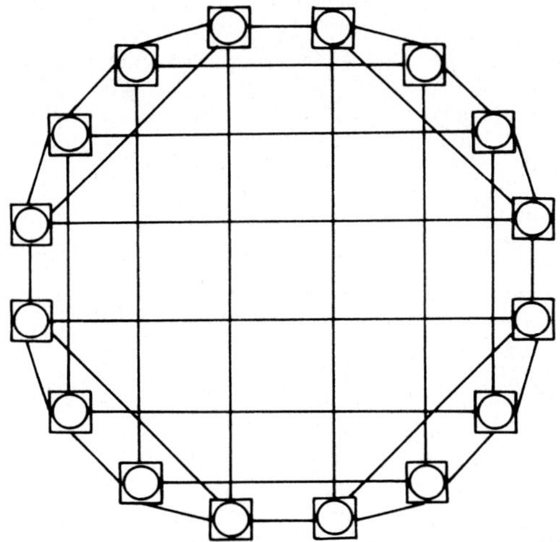

* Fast Fourier Transform (FFT)

S = 14.3 (16 processors, 4-cube, 4096 points)

FIGURE 8
DIRMU hypercube configuration.

(3) Synchronization and communication overhead
(e.g. execution times of synchronization primitives like WAIT/SIGNAL or SEND/RECEIVE)

(4) Contention for common resources
(e.g. bus contention or memory interference)

The first point refers to the algorithm itself. If it contains for example sequential parts (as for example in our parallel sorting program) the speedup clearly is restricted even on a perfect parallel machine. Non-balanced processor utilization is a matter of scheduling. Finding a balanced schedule can become very difficult if the execution times of the processes are not known from the beginning (e.g. because of data-dependent execution times). Sometimes so-called neighbourhood help can improve the situation: if a processor has already completed its processes it can take over some work from its neighbours in order to rebalance the workload. This concept has already been developed and successfully tested in the Erlangen EGPA project on a 5-processor pyramid system [12].

While the first two points are rather machine-independent, (3) and (4) are mainly influenced by the particular multiprocessor system itself. Fast synchronization and communication primitives are always desirable for high efficiency though their influence decreases with increasing computation/communication ratio. Contention for common resources can be avoided by suitable architectures. If a multiprocessor is for example based on a single common bus, this bottleneck always will get saturated if the number of processors is increased beyond a certain point. However, in other architectures, like DIRMU, the total memory bandwidth increases linearly with the number of processors and, as already mentioned before, the influence of memory contention at the multiport memories is insignificant.

Our experience with DIRMU so far has shown that point (1) clearly dominates the efficiency of parallel programs. Also (2) can have a considerable influence for some problems depending on the scheduling strategy used. As can be seen from the PDE-program which is nearly ideal in respect to (1) and (2), the influence of the other two points is only in the range of a few percent of efficiency.

4. FAULT-TOLERANT DIRMU CONFIGURATIONS

4.1. Basic Concepts

Although VLSI components are very reliable by themselves, large multiprocessors easily reach an overall hardware complexity which makes fault tolerance a necessity. A brute force approach would be to use massive redundancy (e.g. TMR - Triple Modular Redundancy [13]). However, because of the large number of processors involved this approach is far too expensive. Furthermore, the reliability and availability requirements of large high-performance multiprocessors for scientific computing are not so stringent that massive redundancy is justified.

So, for DIRMU 25 we have taken a dynamic redundancy approach which allows both, standby sparing as well as graceful degradation. The following basic steps have to be executed:

- Distributed self-diagnosis
  (detection and localization of defective building blocks and links)

- Reconfiguration
  (redistribution of the affected processes on the remaining intact processors)

- Restart
  (continuation of the parallel program with consistent data)

Self-diagnosis and reconfiguration have been designed systematically based on a formal graph model described in [14]. Here, we will only give an informal discussion of the basic concepts.

4.2. Distributed Self-Diagnosis

Self-diagnosis in DIRMU is based on a three-level approach:

- Self-diagnosis within a building block

- Neighbourhood diagnosis

- Distributed sytem-level self-diagnosis

Step (1) is implemented by standard error-detection techiques for monoprocessor systems like self-test programs, hardware checkers, watchdog timers etc. The result of this self-diagnosis is stored in the fault-status register located in the M-modules (Fig. 2). If a fault is indicated an interrupt is sent to all neighbouring processors which have direct access to the corresponding M-module. In addition these processors periodically check the status register and a special mailbox to be able to tolerate a faulty interrupt mechanism as well.

Usually it is not sufficient that only the immediate neighbours know about the fault situation, because the other processors in a configuration which have to cooperate with the processes in the failed building block are affected as well, and have to be informed. Therefore, the neighbours of a faulty building block send messages about the fault situation to their intact neighbours, those relay it to their intact neighbours etc., until all fault-free processors are informed (if this is still possible). This concept is known as distributed system-level

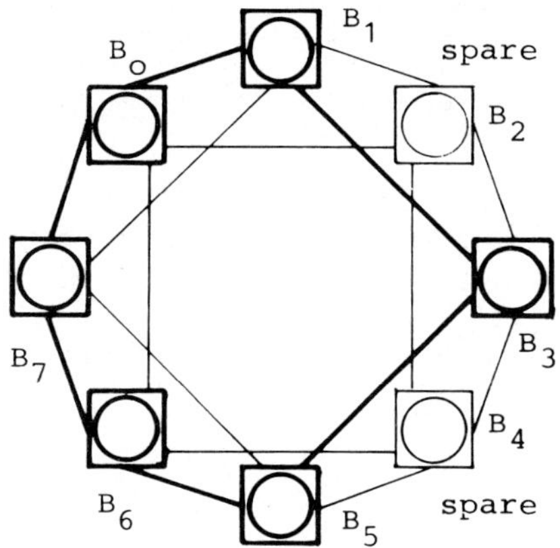

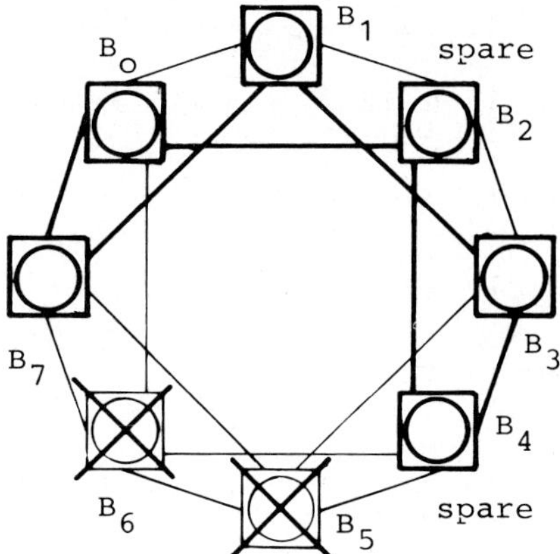

FIGURE 9
Reconfiguration by mapping application graph AK onto a machine graph MK with spares.

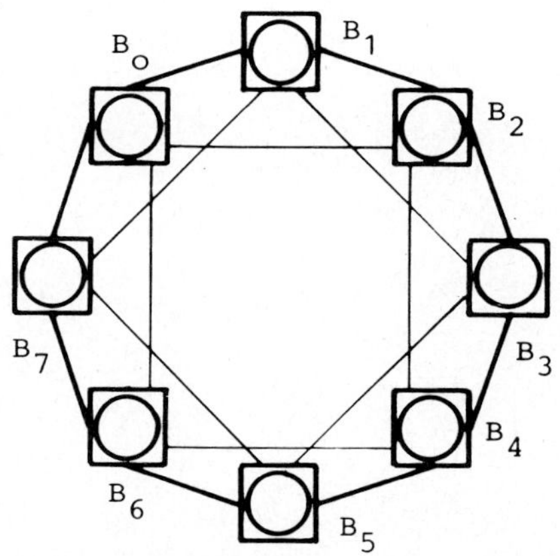

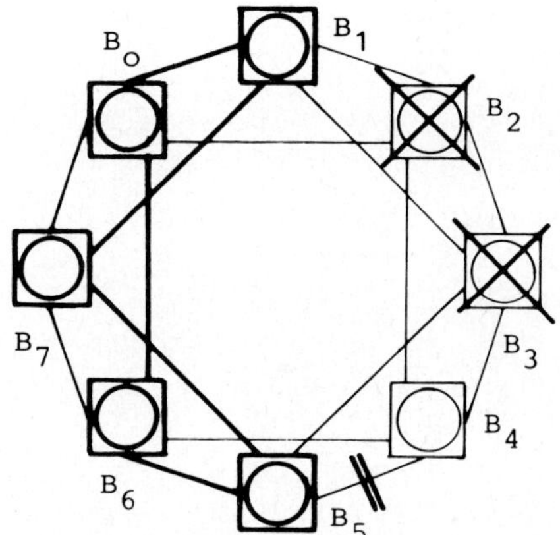

FIGURE 10
Reconfiguration by mapping AK onto MK with graceful degradation.

fault diagnosis [15]. The distributed diagnosis algorithm we have developed and implemented is rather sophisticated (see [16] for a detailed description). It can handle the failure of building blocks and links as well as their repair.

4.3. Reconfiguration and Restart

After successful fault diagnosis a new intact configuration must be established. For DIRMU we have adopted a concept based on subgraph isomorphism (similar to an approach introduced by Hayes [17]). Application programs are assumed to run on a configuration modeled by an application graph AK (e.g rings, arrays or hypercubes in Fig. 6 - 8). The machine configuration which usually has more building

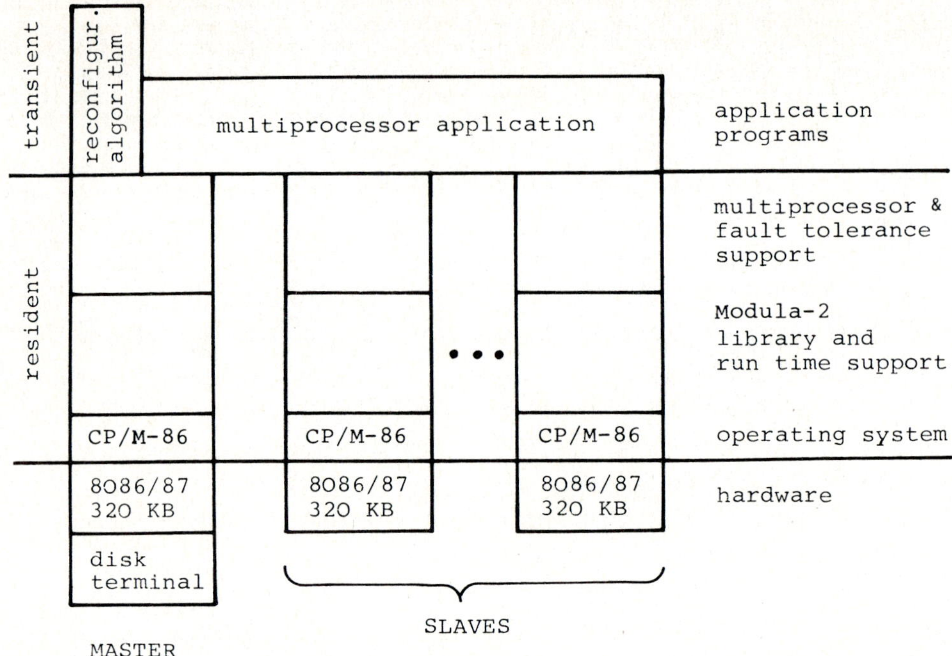

FIGURE 11
DIRMOS multiprocessor operating system.

blocks and links is described by a machine graph MK. In order to execute a parallel program , the AK has to be mapped onto a subgraph of MK consisting only of intact nodes and edges.

Two situations can be distinguished. Firstly, some building blocks can be declared to be spares (e.g. B2 and B4 in Fig. 9). If AK (a ring with 6 building blocks in Fig. 9) is mapped onto a completely intact MK (a meshed ring with 8 building blocks in Fig. 9), the spares remain idle. In case of a failure a new mapping of AK onto MK is searched for now including the spares. By graph theoretical analysis the diagnosability and reconfigurability of a given MK and AK can be computed [17,18]. For the example in Fig. 9 MK is optimal 3-diagnosable and optimal 2-reconfigurable in respect to AK, i.e. all 1-, 2- and 3-faults (building blocks or links) can be diagnosed, and in presence of any 1- or 2-fault AK can still successfully be embedded. Optimality means that there exists no MK with fewer nodes and edges that has the same properties.

If the parallel program is written such that it can be executed not only on a fixed AK but on a class of AKs, fail-soft operation (graceful degradation) is possible. For example, all programs mentioned in Fig. 6 can run on rings of length 2,3,...,p depending on the number of processors available. In this case we can search for the maximum AK still possible on a given MK. In the example of Fig. 10 we start with a ring of 8 building blocks if MK is intact and degrade to a ring of length 5 for the 3-fault shown. It must be mentioned that finding an embedding of AK in MK can in general become very hard because subgraph isomorphism is an NP-complete problem [19]. However, for many cases of practical interest we could find sufficiently efficient reconfiguration algorithms [20].

After a successful reconfiguration the affected parallel program must be restarted. Here, we use a simple rollback scheme. Short programs are simply restarted from the beginning. For longer programs checkpoints are set under user control on the MASTER's and at least one SLAVE's disk. In case of SLAVE failure the MASTER reconfigures the system according to the result of the distributed self diagnosis and restarts the user program on the new configuration (if at all possible). If the MASTER itself fails, a SLAVE with a disk becomes the new MASTER and executes the same steps, now restarting the user program from the checkpoint on its own disk. Note that with this concept no critical central facility exists.

Diagnosis and reconfiguration as described above are part of the DIRMOS multiprocessor operating system which is built on top of Concurrent CP/M-86 and the Modula-2 runtime system (Fig. 11). A resident layer within all building blocks (fault-tolerance and multiprocessor support) contains the distributed self-diagnosis routines as well as the runtime support for reconfiguration (distributed loader, manager for shared memory, synchronization primitives etc.). It supplies an interface for the virtual intact configuration described by AK to the parallel application program sitting on top. As the current MASTER requires the reconfiguration algorithm itself only if a new configuration has to be established (either before the first execution of a user program or after a failure), it is a transient program loaded from disk.

5. CONCLUDING REMARKS

In this paper we have given an overview of the multiprocessor testbed DIRMU 25 concerning parallel processing and fault tolerance. Our experiments so far have shown that with the DIRMU architecture which is based on restricted neighbourhood interconnection structures and distributed shared memory (multiport memories) high efficiences can be achieved for a wide range of applications. Also fault-tolerant operation in case of failed building blocks and/or links is possible.

Further work will continue these investigations with other applications including more complex ones. Also the programming environment will be further improved (e.g. by a distributed debugger). The absolute performance of our testbed is of course limited by the rather slow 8086/87 microprocessors. Also memory space is not large enough for all applications of interest. So, we are thinking of a follow-on system based on the experience with DIRMU, which will contain a 32-bit microprocessor, a fast arithmetic coprocessor, much larger memory and a higher number of processing elements.

ACKNOWLEDGEMENTS

The author wishes to thank the head of the DIRMU project Prof. Dr. W. Handler who also developed the basic concept of the DIRMU kit. Thanks are also due to all members of the DIRMU group, especially to K. Moritzen and K. Wirl, as well as to the many students who contributed in the project.

The project DIRMU has been supported by DFG (Deutsche Forschungsgemeinschaft), the German ministry of research and technology (SUPRENUM project) and Siemens AG, Munich.

REFERENCES

[1] Patton, P.C., Multiprocessors: Architecture and Applications, IEEE Computer 6 (1985) pp. 29-40.

[2] Handler, W., Hofmann, F., Schneider, H.J., A General Purpose Array with a Broad Spectrum of Applications, in: Handler, W. (ed.), Computer Architecture, Informatik Fachberichte, vol. 4 (Springer, Berlin Heidelberg New York, 1976) pp. 311-335.

[3] Bolch, G. et al., A Multiprocessor System for Simulating Data Transmission Systems (MUPSI), Microprocessing and Microprogramming 12 (North Holland, 1983) pp. 267-277.

[4] Handler, W., Maehle, E., Wirl, K., The DIRMU Testbed for High-Performance Multiprocessor Configurations, Proc. 1st Int. Conf. on Supercomputing Systems, St. Petersburg, FL. (1985) pp. 468-475.

[5] Wirth, N., Programming in Modula-2, (Springer, Berlin Heidelberg New York, 1982).

[6] Andrews, G.R., Schneider, F.B., Concepts and Notations for Concurrent Programming, ACM Computing Surveys, vol. 15, no. 1 (March 1983) pp. 3-43.

[7] Haider, L., Entwurf und Implementierung einer Interprozessorkommunikation fuer das DIRMU Multiprozessorsystem in der Programmiersprache Modula-2, Diploma Thesis, University of Erlangen-Nuremberg (1984).

[8] Handler, W., Maehle, E., Wirl, K., DIRMU Multiprocessor Configurations, Proc. 1985 Int. Conf. on Parallel Processing, St. Charles (1985) pp. 652-656.

[9] Maehle, E., Wirl, K., Japel, D., Experiments with Parallel Programs on the DIRMU Multiprocessor Kit, Proc. Parallel Computing 85, Berlin (North Holland, 1986) pp. 515-520.

[10] Volkert, J., Henning, W., Multi Grid Algorithms Implemented on EGPA Multiprocessor, Proc. 1986 Int. Conf. on Parallel Processing, St. Charles (1986) pp. 799-805.

[11] Mehrotra, R., Gehringer, E.F., Superlinear Speedup Through Randomized Algorithms, Proc. 1985 Int. Conf on Parallel Processing, St. Charles (1985) pp. 291-300.

[12] Henning, W., private communication, University of Erlangen-Nuremberg.

[13] Siewiorek, D.P., Swarz, R.S., The Theory and Practice of Reliable System Design (Digital Press, 1982).

[14] Maehle, E., Moritzen, K., Wirl, K., A Graph Model for Diagnosis and Reconfiguration and Its Application to a Fault-Tolerant Multiprocessor System, Proc. 16th Int. Symp. on Fault-Tolerant Computing FTCS-16, Vienna (1986) pp. 292-297.

[15] Kuhl, J.G., Reddy, S., Distributed Fault Tolerance for Large Multiprocessor Systems, Proc. 7th Int. Symp. on Computer Architecture , La Baule (1980) pp. 23-30.

[16] Moritzen, K., System-Level Fault Diagnosis in Distributed Systems, 2nd Conf. 'Fault-Tolerant Computing Systems', Bonn, Informatik Fachberichte 84 (Springer, Berlin Heidelberg New York Tokyo, 1984) pp. 301-312.

[17] Hayes, J.P., A Graph Model for Fault-Tolerant Computing Systems, IEEE Trans. on Computers, vol. C-25, no. 9, (Sept. 1976) pp. 875-884.

[18] Maehle, E., Fehlertolerantes Verhalten in Multiprozessoren - Untersuchungen zur Diagnose und Rekonfiguration, Ph.D. Thesis, University of Erlangen-Nuremberg (1982).

[19] Cook, S.A., The Complexity of Theorem Proving Procedures, Proc. 3rd Annual Symp. on Theory of Computing (1971) pp. 151-158.

[20] Moritzen, K., Softwarehilfsmittel zur Programmierung von Multiprozessoren mit begrenzten Nachbarschaften - ein Beitrag zur Konfigurationsverwaltung, Ph.D. Thesis, University of Erlangen-Nuremberg (1986).

Parallel Systems and Computation
G. Paul and G.S. Almasi (Editors)

SUPRENUM - A MIMD/SIMD SUPERCOMPUTER FOR NUMERICAL APPLICATIONS

Wolfgang K. Giloi

GMD-TUB Research Center for Innovative Computer Systems and Technology
Hardenbergplatz 2
1000 Berlin 12, Germany (West)

Supercomputer architectures for numerical applications can be based on either of two major principles, SIMD vector machines or MIMD multicomputer systems. In the paper both solutions are compared in terms of performance, cost-effectiveness, and software problems involved, thus providing the rationale for the decision to develop a MIMD/SIMD multiprocessor supercomputer, configurable to up to 256 nodes, where each node contains a floating-point vector processor. The crucial issues of such an architecture are the need for a bottleneck-free interconnection structure on the hardware side and for the appropriate program development environment on the software side. The architecture of the SUPRENUM MIMD/SIMD supercomputer, whose design is based upon the considerations discussed in the paper, is presented.

1. THE CHOICE OF SUPERCOMPUTER ARCHITECTURE

In this paper the term 'supercomputer' refers to very high performance machines for numerical applications; though our considerations to some extent hold true also for non-numerical supercomputers (should they evolve). Supercomputers obtain their performance from two contributing factors. Firstly, they operate at the highest possible speed technology can provide. Secondly, additional performance is gained through a large amount by parallel processing.

There exist various forms of parallel processing architectures differing in the nature of the **machine data types**, i.e. the data types the hardware recognizes and manipulates, the **control strategies** for execution control and data control, and the **hardware structure** by which these concepts are realized. The design decisions the computer architect has to make are to some extent predetermined by the manner in which the parallelism inherent in the algorithms of the application programs shall be exploited.

An algorithm may be generally defined as a partial order of operations, the partial order being determined by the data dependencies between the operations. We call the parallelism of an algorithm **explicit** if the data dependencies are a priori known from the nature of the data types to be processed. We call the parallelism **implicit** if it is not known a priori but must first be determined through data dependence analysis before the program can be executed. Figure 1 presents a taxonomy relating the nature of parallelism to the corresponding nature of machine data types, control structure, processor structure, and communication structure.

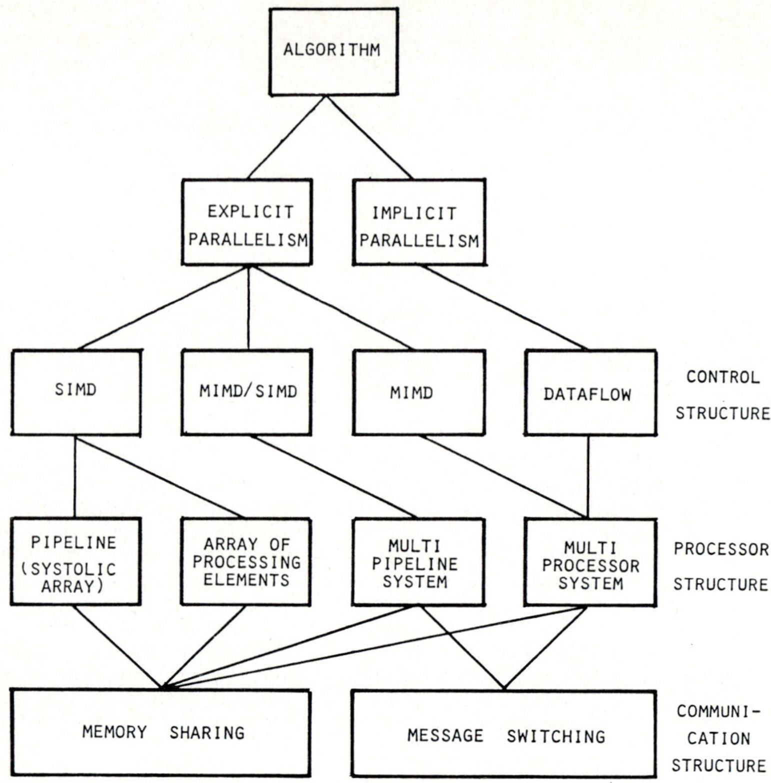

FIGURE 1
Taxonomy of parallel computer architectures

In principle, the data dependency analysis required in the case of implicit parallelism can be performed by either of three instances:

- the programmer
- the compiler
- the (hardware) machine.

The most promising approach is the third one, as provided by the **dataflow** principle. The attractiveness of this approach lies in the fact that it enables the machine to perform the data dependence analysis at run time and, thus, to determine at any instance of program execution the operations that can be executed at this point. Since implicit parallelism includes explicit parallelism, dataflow is the most general operational principle for parallel processing. However, the forte of the dataflow solution comes at the price of considerable overhead and, therefore, is not cost-effective in parallel processing applications where most of the parallel processing gain can be obtained already by exploiting the explicit parallelism in the program. In the latter case, the much simpler and more efficient SIMD or MIMD control schemes offer the more cost-effective solution.

In supercomputers for numerical applications the parallelism to deal with is predominantly explicit, the most important case being array processing.

Consequently, the question is which of the two control strategies for explicit parallelism to apply, SIMD or MIMD. Figure 2 lists some of the major trade-offs between SIMD pipeline architecture and MIMD multiprocessor architecture.

SIMD PIPELINE ARCHITECTURE	MIMD MULTIPROCESSOR ARCHITECTURE
PROCESSOR PERFORMANCE:	PROCESSOR PERFORMANCE:
- SIMD GAIN	- NO SIMD GAIN
- PARALLEL PROCESSING GAIN OF MULTI-STAGE PIPELINE FOR LARGE, ORDERED SETS OF DATA	- NO OR LITTLE PARALLEL OPERATION
- "SCALAR GAP"	- NO "SCALAR GAP"
PERFORMANCE LIMITATION DETERMINED BY:	PERFORMANCE LIMITATION DETERMINED BY:
- EFFECTIVE DATA MEMORY BANDWIDTH	- NODE INTERCONNECTION BANDWIDTH
POTENTIAL FOR PARALLEL PROCESSING:	POTENTIAL FOR PARALLEL PROCESSING:
- LOW TO MEDIUM	- HIGH TO VERY HIGH
COST-EFFECTIVENESS:	COST-EFFECTIVENESS:
- HIGHER	- LOWER
PROGRAMMING STYLE:	PROGRAMMING STYLE:
- PREDOMINANTLY OBJECT ORIENTED	- COOPERATING PROCESSES OR SINGLE ASSIGNMENT
CONFIGURABILITY AND FLEXIBILITY OF APPLICATION:	CONFIGURABILITY AND FLEXIBILITY OF APPLICATION:
- LOW	- HIGH

FIGURE 2
Trade-offs between SIMD and MIMD architecture

So far, only the SIMD pipeline machines have found a larger market penetration in the supercomputer domain. However, two decades of research in innovative ("non von Neumann") computer architecture have produced sufficient insight into all four forms of parallel architectures listed in Figure 1 to render is safe venturing the following conclusions:

1. A pipelined floating point (FP) processor costs about the same as a scalar FP-processor of comparable speed yet provides the additional pipeline gain. Therefore, in numerical applications SIMD pipeline processing is by far more cost-effective than both SIMD processing performed by an array of 'processing elements' or MIMD processing performed by an array of scalar processors. Consequently, the MIMD architecture with pipelined node processors, denoted 'MIMD/SIMD architecture', maximizes the cost-effectiveness.

2. In the realm of numerical supercomputers, we cannot envision at this point pure dataflow machines as a competitive solution; the reason being twofold.

Firstly, since the parallelism in large array processing tasks is predominantly explicit and, thus, can be handled by the extremely efficient SIMD control scheme, the ability of the dataflow machine to handle explicit parallelism does not pay. Secondly, the pure dataflow scheme is based upon the notion that the firing of an operation consumes the tokens that are the "carriers" of the operands. Consequently, a value can be used as operand only once. This causes copying overhead in numerical algorithms in which a value occurs as operand of several operations. Both the high control overhead and the inability of the pure dataflow scheme to handle data structure types result in an unfavourable MIPS/FLOPS rate. By special measures such as the introduction of the 'structure memory' by Gurd et al. /1/, this rate can be much improved; however, not yet to the point at which a dataflow machine would become a competitive array processing machine.

As conclusion of the discussion above we dare stating the following

CONVERGENCE THEOREM: Future supercomputers for numerical applications will be MIMD/SIMD architectures.

Proof: by exhaustion — all numerical supercomputers recently announced or already introduced into the market are of the SIMD/MIMD variety.

The trend towards the MIMD/SIMD solution happens from two ends, "bottom-up" and "top-down": Vector machines come now with several pipeline processors (e.g., CRAY-X MP and successors) and MIMD machines come now with "vectorized" nodes (e.g., INTEL iSPC, FPS T-series).

There is another trend to be observed, namely the trend towards a hierarchical structure of large, multi-node MIMD/SIMD machines, meaning that such a system consists of a number of clusters; each cluster consisting of a number of nodes. There are two decisive reasons for such a clustering. Firstly, a large MIMD/SIMD requires a number of local resources such as diagnosis nodes, back-up disks for data overflow in the nodes and recovery point storage for backward recovery after faults, etc. Providing these resources at the granularity of clusters rather than nodes is the more cost-effective solution. Secondly, as discussed below, the very high interconnection bandwidth necessary for large MIMD/SIMD architectures is obtainable only by a hierarchical interconnection structure.

2. THE CHOICE OF TECHNOLOGY

For the sake of discussion two main technologies shall be considered, denoted "microcomputer technology" (MCT) and mainframe technology" (MFT), respectively, and characterized as follows.

Microcomputer Technology (MCT):

- TTL or MOS, highly integrated, low-power logic and memory (some 10^4 to 10^5 transistor per chip);
- combination of highly integrated standard components ("stock hardware") with (few) semi-custom (gate array) chips, therefore lower design cost and risk;
- low cost of packaging and cooling (forced air suffices);
- lower operating speed than MFT.

Mainframe Technology (MFT):

- ECL, less highly integrated, high-power logic (some 10^3 transistor per chip), in combination with ECL or CMOS memory;
- large number of different gate array devices, therefore higher design cost;
- higher cost of packaging and cooling (liquid coolant may be required!);
- higher operating speed (up to a 10 times higher clock frequency).

Generally, a supercomputer development based on MCT is less costly and risky; however, if one wants to reach the same performance range as with MFT, a higher degree of parallel processing is needed to make up for the lower operating speed of MTC. Consequently, for reasons given above the MCT solution is more cost-effective than the MFT solution, at the price of a much higher program complexity.

3. THE PERFORMANCE OF SIMD PIPELINE MACHINES

Presently, the epitomy of an ultra high-speed, MFT vector machine is the CRAY-X MP with 8.5 nanoseconds clock cycle, leading to a peak performance of 235 MFLOPS per pipeline for the vector dot product. The paradigm of a highly integrated MCT pipeline processor is the Weitek chip set 2264/2265, which allows a peak performance of 25 MFLOPS for the vector dot product (IEEE double precision).

Ultimately, the performance of a pipeline machine, however, is not limited by the highest possible processing speed but the highest memory bandwidth obtainable. The vector dot product is a most favorable case since two operations are performed with only one fetch of an operand pair and since no result vector must be stored back in memory. The fastest presently available dynamic CMOS memory (DRAM), when operated in the 'static column mode', allows for a memory word access every 40 nanoseconds. Static CMOS memory (SRAM) has become available with an access time of down to 15 nanoseconds. That is, the fastest CMOS SRAM is almost as fast as ECL memory. Consequently, in the MCT case we find a better match between processor speed and memory speed than in the MFT case (for this reason, the CRAY machines reach their peak performance only in the case of register-to-register operation, while a memory-to-memory operation results in a considerable performance decrease). In order to fill up the vector registers at about the same rate at which their content can be processed, special measures must be taken, e.g., memory interleaving, to match the effective memory bandwidth to that of the vector registers. Memory interleaving causes a problem in cases where the memory content is read in an order different from the order in which the memory was written.

The same phenomenum occurs in the vectorized MCT nodes of MIMD/SIMD computers, if static column memory is used for reasons of economy, since the static column access requires consecutive addressing. Therefore, even in MCT pipeline machines it is advantageous to have a faster vector buffer memory that allows the components of a vector to be read in any arbitrary order at the same maximum speed. With the highly integrated, fast static memory available, one can afford to make such a vector buffer much larger than the vector registers in an MFT machine.

Summarizing this discussion, one can state that the peak performance obtained by a single pipeline processor, including memory bandwidth considerations, is by a factor of 5 to 10 higher for an MFT pipeline than for an MCT pipeline processor. On the other hand, we can readily have 1 to 2 orders of magnitude more nodes in an MCT computer than in the MFT vector machine — if we learn how to cope with the increased software complexity.

4. THE CHOICE OF THE INTERCONNECTION STRUCTURE

Interconnection networks (IN) that are capable of connecting a number of source nodes with a number of destination nodes are considered by many as the solution to the interconnection problem in large scale SIMD multiprocessor systems. Many papers have been published dealing with such structures, their complexity, and their interconnection properties. Hardly any of these many papers is addressing the topic of the technical feasibility and the interconnection bandwidth obtainable in view of such mundane parameters as pin limitation, packaging problems, driving power limitation, cost, etc.

INs come in two major categories: single-stage (permutation) and multi-stage networks. In single-stage networks, a data packet may have to travel through the network several times in order to reach a given destination from a given source. In contrast, in a multi-stage network the data can flow directly from the source to the destination. Another distinction is that between circuit switching, where a physical connection is provided from source to destination, and packet switching, where a logical connection is provided for a packet travelling through the network. Furthermore, control may be centralized or decentralized.

If one takes a closer look, the seemingly large variety of INs proposed can be identified as variants of one of the 4 basic classes listed in the following table /2/.

CLASS	NETWORK TYPE	COMPLEXITY
A	CROSSBAR SWITCH	$O(n^2)$
B	BENES NETWORK	$O(n \cdot \log n + n/2)$
C	N-CUBE, BASELINE, BANYARD, OMEGA, FLIP, DELTA	$O((n/2) \log n)$
D	DATA MANIPULATOR, INVERSE DATA MANIPULATOR	$O(n + n \log n)$

Networks with $(N \cdot \log N)$-complexity are not suitable for circuit switching, since they exhibit at any time a large incidence of mutual blockages of data paths. This leaves the crossbar switch, which provides total point-to-point connectivity, as the only viable solution for a circuit switching network. Packet switching networks, on the other hand, can readily deal with blockages, since the nodes have the capability of storing and keeping a packet for the duration of a blockage.

The switching elements of a circuit switching crossbar network are extremely simple (simple bus connection by tri-state logic). In addition, some hardware is needed to arbitrate the access to the crossbar busses. The switching elements of packet switching networks, on the other hand, must be intelligent **communication processors** that are orders of magnitude more complex than the simple switching elements of a circuit switching network. By the same token, they are also much slower, as they have to execute a complex microprogram to handle a packet. Therefore, if one compares only the switching complexity of different networks, one may be comparing apples with oranges.

A more detailed feasibility study conducted by Ermel /2/ has shown that the size of a crossbar network should not exceed that of a 32 x 32 switching matrix in order to be packagable in a reasonable manner; and 64 x 64 would absolutely be the technical limit. This means that the direct interconnection of, say, 256 or more nodes through a crossbar switching network is technically not feasible. Packet switching networks for the interconnection of an equally large number of nodes, even if still feasible in terms of pin limitation and packaging constraints, would be too slow for supercomputers.

The way out of this dilemma is a two-stage approach by forming **clusters** of nodes and connecting these clusters either via a crossbar network or an equally fast packet switching network. The most economical form of intra cluster communication is via one or several parallel busses. This restricts the number of printed circuit boards per cluster to a maximum of about 20, because in order to be fast such a parallel bus must not extend over more than one 19" rack at most. When designed right, such a system of parallel busses can satisfy any bandwidth requirement the MCT nodes of a cluster of an MIMD/SIMD machine may impose. It was mentioned above that clustering, in addition, leads to a most economical solution for local resource sharing.

5. MEMORY SHARING VERSUS MESSAGE PASSING

In the architecture of massively parallel computers there exist two competing concepts of inter node communication: **Memory sharing** and **message passing.** Both concepts have their true believers, forming two camps that vehemently disagree with each other.

The proponents of memory sharing claim that this is not only the more "natural" but also the more efficient solution. While the latter claim is backed by negative experience with some existing high-overhead message passing systems, the question of what is "natural" is in the eyes of the beholder. For designers who still subscribe to the von Neumann principle, memory sharing of course is natural.

In our view, however, unlike pure MIMD architectures large MIMD/SIMD systems should n o t be viewed just as a collection of cooperating von Neumann machines, lest one may get caught in the "conceptual von Neumann bottleneck" /3 /. An architectural principle that ensures a sufficiently abstract view of the MIMD/SIMD machine to the user as well as efficient parallel processing and internode communication is the principle of **object-oriented architecture** (alias 'datatype architecture') /4 /, /5 /.

The difference between object-oriented architectures and the conventional von Neumann architecture can readily be explained by introducing the notion of **machine datatypes**, i.e., the datatypes the hardware can recognize and manipulate, as the triple

$$(I,V,A),$$

where I denotes a set of object identifiers, V denotes a set of object values, and A denotes a set of object attributes. In the classical von Neumann machine, the members of I are memory addresses, the members of V are memory location contents (which can be anything as far as the hardware is concerned), and the set A is empty (there are neither data attributes nor access attributes specified at the hardware level). Conversely, in object-oriented architectures complex machine datatypes may exist with structured objects and operations defined on the data structure objects (DSO). A DSO is accessed by its (symbolic) identifier and transformed as an entity. Access to substructures or single elements happens through the application of appropriate selection functions. Consequently, the notion of addresses does not exist at the machine language level / 5 /; rather, what is visible are only the objects and functions of the machine datatypes. An object can be accessed only through the application of a function of its type (data encapsulation), and a type is defined solely by the effect the function applications have on the objects (information hiding). We recognize the definition of abstract datatypes.

It hardly need be emphasized that SIMD vector machines may be the typical example of an object-oriented architecture in which vectors together with vector operations form a type whose functions are performed directly by hardware, i.e., the pipeline processor. Addresses are not referred to in the machine language instructions but are generated by hardware address generators, that is, exist only deeper inside the hardware.

The irony is that the "high-level" programming language commonly used in numerical applications, FORTRAN, is a "von Neumann language" / 3 / that has a lower level of abstraction than the executing machine. To execute conventional FORTRAN programs, the lower level FORTRAN types must be mapped onto the higher level machine datatypes by an appropriate 'vectorizing compiler'. Since such mappings are feasible only under certain constraints and may be accompanied by a loss of efficiency, the user is given tools that allow him to perform such mappings by hand in an optimal way (by "hand-coding" in the machine language or by using a 'vector FORTRAN', e.g., FORTRAN 8X). However, these tools are still embedded into the FORTRAN world. Moreover, existing vector machine languages still render portions of the hardware visible (e.g., registers) in order to allow for optimizations; consequently, the presently existing vector machines do not exhibit the level of abstraction as offered in principle by object-oriented architectures. Overcoming these problems will remain to be a challenge for years to come.

The definition of data structure types in object-oriented architectures render such architectures by nature a message based system. This does not rule out that one may still have an underlying memory sharing architecture; the question being, however, whether such an approach is not a detour that unnecessarily causes problems and inefficiencies.

Memory sharing systems require elaborate mechanisms for data access synchronization (e.g., semaphores and the like), while the only synchronization needed in message based systems is the synchronization of cooperating processes. The question is whether the overhead caused by message passing is not worse than the overhead of data synchronization in memory sharing systems. The latter may well be the case if message passing is performed as an operating system task, whose execution will at least cost several hundred microseconds or even some milliseconds in the worst case. To avoid such high overhead, message passing must be made a machine instruction rather than an operating system task, e.g., by providing a special communication coprocessor solely for the purpose of handling the 'send' and 'receive' constructs that are now primitives of the machine language.

Last but not least, the interconnection structure of a high-performance MIMD/SIMD system with a large number of nodes must be blocking-free in order to avoid the considerable performance degradation that blocking may cause (the designers of interconnection networks based on permutation structures often go to great length stressing the point that their network is deadlock-free, while the problems caused by blockings are seldom addressed). Of course, the requirement of a blocking-free interconnection structure is valid for both message passing and memory sharing. Generally, the overhead encountered in packet switching interconnection networks (including the one caused by blockings) is more critical in memory sharing systems (which tend to have small packet sizes) than in message passing systems (which tend to have much larger packet sizes).

6. PROGRAMMING LARGE MIMD/SIMD MACHINES

The nature of MIMD/SIMD machines causes a dichotomy of programming as given by the need for SIMD vector processing within the node and MIMD multi-processing among the nodes.

The "MIMD part" can be structured in the form of cooperating processes, each process being a separately compiled module performing a certain service or executing a numerical algorithm. In each node there may be one or several processes. If application programs are to be written independently of the size of a particular installation, then the nodes must have multi-processing capabilities.

An application program written for an MIMD/SIMD machine must be partitioned into at least as many tasks (processes) as there are nodes, a task being a part of the program that can run in parallel with some other parts of the program (some other tasks). Three kinds of programming tools for multitasking must exist, namely tools for task creation, access control of shared objects, and synchronization. In the existing "multi-pipeline" vector machines, where "multi" means 2 or 4, the simple "task attraction" scheme is employed: The system maintains a task queue to which an unoccupied pipeline processor can go in order to find a task to execute. However, this simple scheme requires the sharing of (logical) memory. The simple task attraction approach is not acceptable when the number of pipelines becomes large, since the low-level multitasking tools provided for the existing multi-pipeline vector machines are too error prone for problems of higher complexity.

The tasks of an application program must be "vectorized" in order to be run on the vector processing nodes. The "vectorization" may be performed by either

- a "vectorizing compiler" or
- the programmer.

In the first case the programmer writes his or her program in a common, sequential high-level language, e.g., ANSI 77 FORTRAN. In the second case the programmer must be provided with a language that encompasses array types, e.g., FORTRAN 8X. In either case a 'superstructure' must be added to the FORTRAN to enable the programmer to define processes (modules) and to implement inter process communication and synchronization, e.g., through the use of SEND - RECEIVE constructs. The usual way of adding such a superstructure is to have a preprocessor that recognizes the additional constructs (which are not part of FORTRAN proper) and convert them into appropriate subroutine calls.

In principle there are four different ways of writing application software / 6 /:

1. Extend existing languages with new operations that allow users to express parallelism and synchronization (existing language extension approach).
2. Extend existing compilers to identify parallel operations wherever they can be recognized and replace them by the appropriate parallel operations of the machine, including synchronization (automatic parallelization approach).
3. Add a new language layer on top of an existing language that describes multiprocessing, while allowing the basic application programs to remain largely unaltered (meta language approach).

4. Employ a new, object-oriented, very high level language which incorporates all the required concepts of parallelism and synchronization at the highest possible level of abstraction, e.g., given in the form of a process-oriented procedural language or a functional language (new high-level language approach).

From a computer science point of view, of course, the 'new high-level language approach' is the most appealing one; alas, for reasons of user acceptance this path cannot be pursued at present in a product-oriented design.

As was mentioned above, employing message passing rather than memory sharing as the vehicle for inter node communication greatly facilitates the task of building application programs with a large number of cooperating processes, since there is no need for explicit access control of shared objects by the programmer. In addition to the "hot spot" contention problem encountered in large MIMD systems with memory sharing, this is a second reason why we feel that the message passing principle will prevail in large MIMD/SIMD machines.

As of yet not much experience has been gained in the realm of programming large MIMD/SIMD machines, as only a small number of experimental systems with rather rudimental software have so far become available. However, it has already become recognized that tracking down a bug in a parallel program of high complexity can be very difficult for reasons of logical complexity, non-repeatable behavior, and the lack of proper tools. The low level of existing programming systems, in particular, causes the programmer to lack the necessary insight into the logical structure of a complex application program.

On the other hand, it has been shown that the use of a sufficiently abstract, object-oriented programming environment for highly parallel MIMD systems (large number of cooperating processes) may result in an efficient and largely error-free manner of programming, especially if the appropriate program development and debugging tools are provided /7/. However, this approach by necessity causes considerable additional overhead; a price which one may not be willing to pay in numerical supercomputers.

7. RATIONALE FOR THE SUPRENUM SUPERCOMPUTER

SUPRENUM is a MIMD/SIMD supercomputer development project funded by the Ministry of Research and Technology (BMFT) of the German Federal Government. The project is being carried out by a task force consisting of several research institutions and companies. Specifically the Gesellschaft für Mathematik und Datenverarbeitung (GMD) is involved in the following tasks:

- development of a first prototype hardware and system software in close cooperation with the participating industry;
- development of specific program development environments;
- development of application software packages, e.g., multigrid partial differential equation solvers /8/.

The architectural concepts were developed by W.K. Giloi and his team at GMD-TUB FIRST; they reflect the discussion presented above.

The SUPRENUM project is product-oriented; that is, in contrast to pure research, additional market-oriented requirements must be satisfied such as:

- the desired absolute performance must be obtained at competitive cost-effectiveness;
- program development environments must be provided that will find user acceptance;

- the machine must be manufacturable, testable, maintainable, and sufficiently reliable;
- the computer system must be in production and marketable within a given time window determined by marketing considerations.

To meet the time window requirement, the architectural design of SUPRENUM is based on already proven yet highly innovative concepts and solutions obtained at GMD-TUB FIRST as result of preceding R&D projects, e.g., STARLET / 5 / and UPPER / 7 /. Specifically the UPPER project led to profound experience with message-based, object-oriented, distributed multi-node system architecture, its efficient implementation in hardware and software, and the appropriate program development environment. Both STARLET (the realization of an object-oriented data structure architecture / 4 /) and UPPER also provided a wealth of innovative hardware solutions that is exploited in SUPRENUM.

The packaging of the SUPRENUM MIMD/SIMD machine is based upon the following principles:

- VLSI "stock hardware" is used wherever available with the functionality and performance required;
- most of the additional, proprietary circuitry is packaged into a number of CMOS gate array devices;
- memory and bus drivers are packaged in surface mounted technology (SMT).

The use of (predominantly) CMOS and TTL circuits results in a low-power design that allows for high-density packaging without cooling problems (forced air only).

8. THE SUPRENUM HARDWARE ARCHITECTURE

For reasons discussed above the 'SUPRENUM CORE', i.e., the MIMD/SIMD machine proper, is hierarchically structured into 'nodes' and 'clusters' of nodes. There are general processing nodes (GPN) and specialized nodes in a cluster. Each node is a single-board computer, running under its own operation system and communication with other nodes. A global operating system for the entire SUPRENUM CORE exists only in virtual form, its functions being performed jointly by the collective of node operating systems.

As depicted in Figure 3 the GPN consists of CPU (MC68020), paged memory management unit (MC68581), private memory (1 million 64-bit words of DRAM), operand cache (8K 64-bit words of SRAM), and four coprocessors specialized to perform the following functions:

- floating-point scalar operations ('scalar coprocessor')
- floating-point array operations (pipelined 'vector coprocessor')
- DMA address generation ('array access coprocessor')
- inter node communication ('communication coprocessor').

All four coprocessors utilize the same unique coprocessor interface of the MC68020. The access bandwidth of the private memory will be 160M-bytes per second; the access bandwidth of the operand cache will be twice as high. The pipelined vector coprocessor is targeted to have a peak performance of 20 MFLOPS for the vector dot product, IEEE double precision.

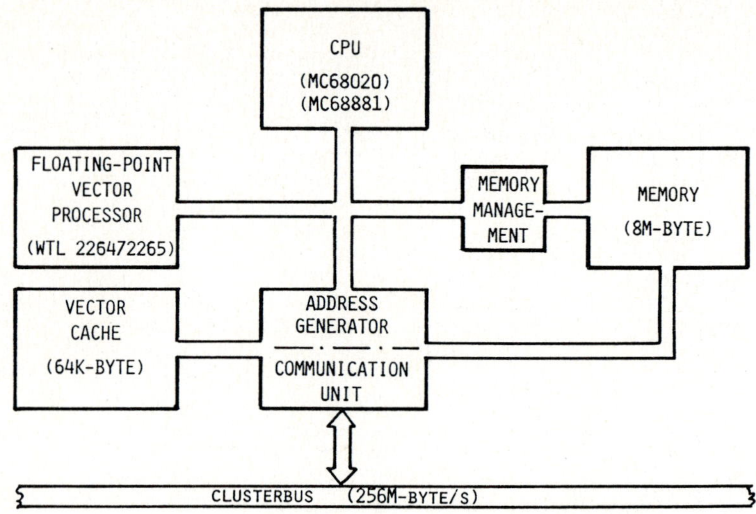

FIGURE 3
Structure of a node

As the block diagram figure 4 shows, a **cluster** consists of 20 nodes, accommodated in one 19" rack. 16 + 1 nodes are GPNs (16 working nodes, 1 "hot standby" for fault tolerance reasons). Specialized nodes are: the cluster disk controller, the inter cluster communication node, and the cluster diagnosis node. The nodes of a cluster communicate via the **cluster bus system**, which consists of 2 message switching parallel busses. Doubling the cluster bus including its controller logic renders the cluster bus system fault tolerant and, by the same token, doubles the interconnection bandwidth in the cluster to a total of 256M-bytes per second (arbitrated). Several nodes can communicate simultaneously via the cluster bus system.

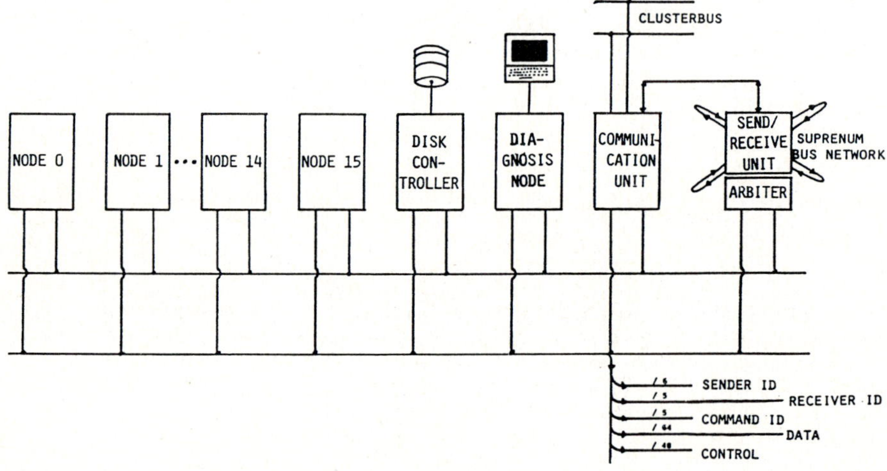

FIGURE 4
Structure of a cluster

The clusters of the SUPRENUM CORE communicate via a very unique interconnection structure, consisting of a matrix of bit-serial ring busses as indicated in figure 5.

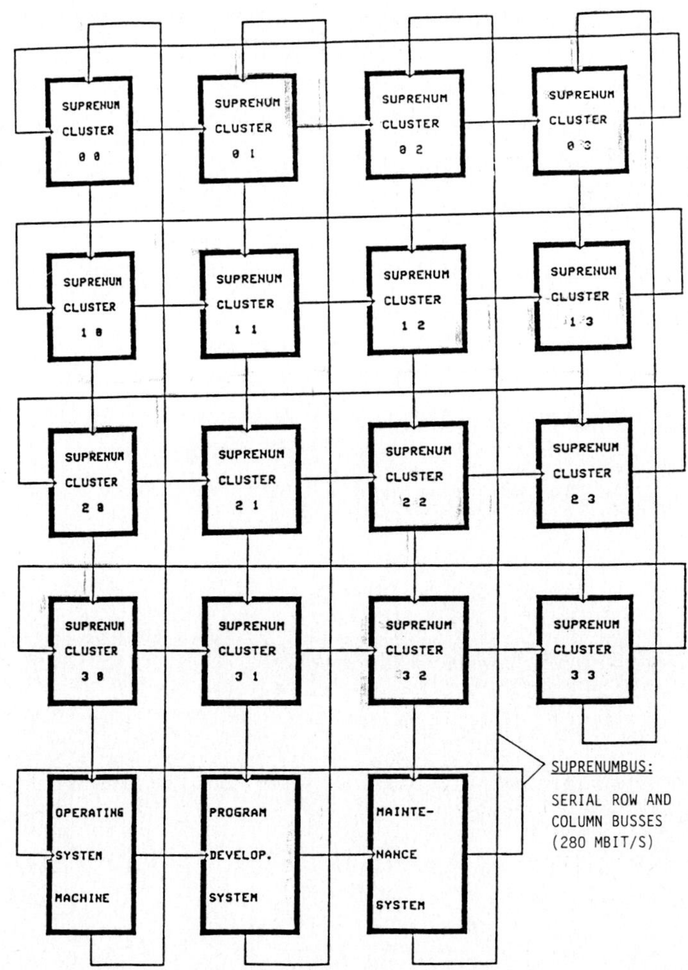

FIGURE 5
SUPRENUM System With 16 Clusters (256 Nodes)

Each such ring bus has a gross data transmission rate of 280M-bytes per second, resulting in a net data rate of 25M-bytes per second (arbitrated). The protocol employed on the ring busses is an optimized version of the slotted ring protocol / 9 /. Each cluster can be reached via two such busses, a 'row bus' and a 'column bus'. This measures not only doubles the interconnection bandwidth; it also renders the interconnection structure fault tolerant. Should a ring break down, there will still be alternate data paths in the bus matrix via which the clusters involved can be reached. The inter cluster communication node is intelligent enough to perform such alternate routing automatically in the case of a permanent bus fault (transient faults are detected and masked through retransmission by the slotted ring protocol). Furthermore, the inter cluster communication node is capable of handling the entire protocol hierarchy that regulates the exchange of packets or larger logical entities consisting of a number of packets, i.e., objects. The inter cluster communication node consists of a microprogrammable 'flow control unit', to handle the higher levels of the inter node communication protocol, some fast buffer memory, and a set of proprietary ECL gate array chips, to handle the lower levels of the slotted ring protocol /9 /.

The SUPRENUM system encompasses a separate 'operating system machine' whose task is to manage the global system resource such as global disk storage and take care of the workload distribution and system initialization tasks. The operating system machine, however, is not involved in the actual program execution. Moreover, the system includes a dedicated 'maintenance machine' which, in turn, communicates with all the 'diagnosis nodes' of the clusters via a separate, dedicated communication link. Additional peripheral computers may be inserted into the system such as one or more program development workstations or graphical workstations for the representation of results. The user interface on the operating system machine as well as all the other peripheral computers is the one provided by UNIX.

The unique inter cluster communication structure of the SUPRENUM system makes it a highly configurable system, ranging from one single cluster (320 MFLOPS peak performance) to 16 clusters accommodated in 8 cabinets (5 GFLOPS peak performance). To enhance the reliability and availability of the system, elaborate fault tolerance measures are incorporated.

REFERENCES

/1/ Kawakami K., Gurd J.R.: "A Scalable Dataflow Structure Store", Proc. International Symposium on Computer Architecture 1986, pp. 243-250

/2/ Ermel W.: "Untersuchungen zur technischen Realisierbarkeit von Verbindungsnetzwerken für Multicomputer-Architekturen", Ph.D. Thesis, Technical University of Berlin, FB Informatik 1986

/3/ Backus J.: "Can Programming be Liberated From the von Neumann Style? A Functional Programming Style and Its Algebra of Programs, CACM 21,8 (1978), pp. 613-641

/4/ Giloi W.K., Berg H.K.: "Introducing the Concept of Data Structure Architecture", Proc. 1977 International Conference on Parallel Processing, IEEE Catalog No. 77CH1284-9C, pp. 44-51

/5/ Giloi W.K., Gueth R.: "Concepts and Realization of a High-Performance Data Type Architecture", International Journal of Computer and Information Sciences 11,1 (1982), pp. 25-54

/6/ McGraw J., Axelrod T.S.: "Exploiting Multiprocessors — Issues and Options", Lawrence Livermoore Preprint UCRL-91734, 1984

/7/ Giloi W.K., Behr P.M.: "Obtaining a Secure, Fault-tolerant, Distributed System With Maximized Performance", in Reijns G. (ed.): Hardware Supported Implementation of Concurrent Languages in Distributed Systems, North-Holland, Amsterdam 1984

/8/ Trottenberg U. (ed.): "Rechnerarchitekturen für numerische Simulation auf der Basis superschneller Lösungsverfahren", GMD Studien Nr. 88, Sept. 1984

/9/ Giloi W.K., Zuber G.: "UPPERBUS: A High-Speed Backbone for Metropolitan Area Networks", Proc. The 4th Annual European Fibre Optic Communications and Local Area Networks Exposition (EFOC/LAN 1986), Information Gatekeepers, Inc., Boston, pp. 286-289

Parallel Systems and Computation
G. Paul and G.S. Almasi (Editors)

IMPLICIT PARALLEL PROCESSING: SISAL on the Manchester Dataflow Computer

John Gurd, Wim Böhm

Department of Computer Science, University of Manchester
Oxford Road, Manchester M13 9PL, England

In many current multiprocessor systems, explicit control of software parallelism by the programmer is proving expensive and error-prone. The incentive to develop implicit parallel programming styles is therefore great. One such style that has received recent attention is based on the notion of single-assignment languages. An example of such a language is SISAL, designed by a research partnership between Lawrence Livermore National Laboratory, Digital Equipment Corporation, Colorado State University and the University of Manchester. This paper describes SISAL together with its implementation on the Manchester Dataflow Machine. Dataflow is an asynchronous concurrent notation based on fine-grain message-passing in graphical programs. The Manchester Dataflow Machine implements a tagged-token model of computation using a multi-ring hardware structure. Techniques for code generation are discussed and some performance results are presented.

1. INTRODUCTION

1.1. Parallel Computing Systems

A parallel computing system comprises a *hardware architecture*, based on a model of computation with inherent parallelism, together with a *programming environment* that may or may not make the programmer aware of the hardware-level parallelism. Where the programmer must specify and control parallelism we call the resulting system *explicit*, otherwise it is *implicit*. In many practical parallel systems the use of explicit programming techniques is proving to be expensive and error-prone, and one reason for the recent growth of interest in functional and logic programming is the hope that such languages can form a basis for implicitly parallel systems. Recent advances in implementation of *single-assignment* programming languages on various multiprocessor architectures support this view. This paper describes the experiences of the dataflow research group at the University of Manchester when implementing the single-assignment language SISAL [15] on the prototype Manchester Dataflow Computer [12,13]. The SISAL language is introduced, including a complete example program that is subsequently used to illustrate the process of generating object-code for the prototype Manchester Dataflow Computer.

1.2. Implicit Parallel Programming

It is important that applications programs are written in high-level programming languages that allow the programmer to abstract away from details of the machine structure. There is clear evidence that the programming task becomes significantly more complex and error-prone when the programmer is required to take account of machine-level features, such as vectorisation, overlays, *etc.* This situation is exacerbated by the introduction of parallelism. It is therefore desirable that a parallel programming style be developed to retain the power of current programming languages and yet remove the necessity for explicit expression of parallelism, thus requiring no knowledge of the machine structure. This mirrors trends in conventional high-level programming languages, which hide details of complex architectural features (instruction pipelines, virtual memory, *etc.*) whilst reflecting the sequential nature of the machines that execute the compiled code. In implicit parallel programming, it is intended that compilers should extract parallelism from programs automatically, and that the run-time environment should handle all workload distribution and resource management [8]. Languages should be chosen so as to simplify implementation of these difficult tasks.

One option is to generate parallel code from a *conventional* high-level programming language (without any extensions to support parallelism). However, suitable analysis algorithms are highly complex because of the potential side-effects of program statements, due to explicit use of storage locations (accessed by the programmer as *variables*). Compile-time data dependence analysis is often impossible (e.g. when obscure array index expressions are used) unless assistance is available from the programmer (e.g. to indicate how the arrays will be accessed). However, the worst problem is that of *aliasing* via the use of unbounded arrays and arithmetic operations on pointers [7]. No amount of compile-time analysis can help unravel devious or undisciplined use of such language features.

Single-assignment languages (SALs) have no concept of sequential execution and no direct control statements such as the GOTO [10]. To combat the ambiguities that might arise from reassigning values to variables, the languages allow each variable to be assigned just once in a program. Constructs that permit controlled reassignment in special cases (such as loops) are provided. SALs tend to use simple data structures, such as *arrays* and *streams*, that can be readily implemented. There are often strict type and scope rules. In particular, it is common to prohibit all forms of side-effect in re-entrant constructs. The net results are languages that provide ideal textual syntax for the description of dependence graphs.

SALs are similar to *functional* languages which are based on the mathematics of functional algebra and have no concepts of storage state and assignment. When assignment is restricted to occur only once for each variable in a program, the effect is as if assignment statements are *definitions* of the variables. In this sense SALs and functional languages are identical, and the absence of GOTOs and side-effects are common to them both. However, functional algebra allows more powerful programming constructs than are used in SALs because it permits construction of higher order functions and abstract data structures. Consequently, the two groups are not directly equivalent. Nevertheless they have enough in common to make it attractive to implement full functional languages on parallel systems. There is similar interest in parallel implementations of *logic* programming languages.

1.3. Dataflow Computation

Dataflow notation expresses program parallelism in the form of *directed graphs* in which nodes describe operations to be performed and arcs describe paths along which data is routed from operation to operation. Although such graphs can be constructed at many different software levels, it is usual to consider nodes as machine *instructions*, rather than as *subroutines* or *procedures*. Some people use the term dataflow to cover all software levels, but this paper uses the term in the restricted sense of instruction-level dataflow. Execution of the directed graphs is *data-driven*, in that it proceeds according to the availability of data at the inputs to each node. Whenever a node has data available at all of its inputs, it executes, consuming the input data values from the input arcs, and subsequently producing its result, placing the output data value(s) on the output arc(s). Since the decision whether or not to execute is made locally at each node, and on the basis of information available only at that node, no communication other than that of data values is needed between nodes. The execution of nodes is thus entirely asynchronous, and it may be as parallel as desired within the constraints of the program.

Amongst the currently active dataflow research groups there is some degree of consensus on the general approach to adopt. Three components are agreed to be involved: (i) a *fine-grain graphical model of computation*, normally based on *tagged message-passing*; (ii) a *multiprocessor dataflow machine*, comprising (a) a number of *processing elements*, (b) some form of specialised, distributed *data structure storage*, and (c) a *network* to interconnect these units; and (iii) a *high-level programming language*, normally based on the principle of *single-assignment*. Models of computation have been investigated by Arvind and Gostelow [4]. Styles of hardware architecture have been surveyed by Treleaven *et al.* [21] and Watson [23], and suitable languages have been surveyed by Ackerman [1] and Glauert [11].

2. THE SINGLE-ASSIGNMENT PROGRAMMING LANGUAGE SISAL

2.1. Basic Concepts

SISAL is an expression oriented, single-assignment language [15]. It was designed as a result of a research partnership involving Lawrence Livermore National Laboratory, Digital Equipment Corporation and Colorado State University in the USA, and the Universities of Manchester and East Anglia in the UK. The language is weakly typed (types with the same structure are equal) and allows only explicit type conversion. A SISAL program is concerned with the definition and use of *values*. A value may be a *constant value* (such as '*2.71828*'), or a *value name* (such as '*time_step*') which is associated with the result of an *expression* evaluation. No value name may be redefined, and so all uses of a given value name in other expressions will always refer to the same value. If an expression uses a value name which has not yet been defined, evaluation of that expression cannot be completed until that value name is available for use. The *order of execution* of a SISAL program is thus determined solely by the availability of values for use in the computation of expressions, and will not affect the computed results.

An expression may yield more than one result. The number of results produced by an expression is referred to as its *arity*. In common with procedural expression oriented languages, SISAL's control constructs are *structured expressions*. Any expression may be freely nested within any other expression, provided that its arity and the types of its results are correct for the context in which it is used. Expressions are entirely free from side-effects. A *function call* may occur as part of any expression. A function definition simply encapsulates an expression within a parameter-passing mechanism. Functions have access only to their arguments and to other functions.

2.2. Types, Values and Associated Operations

2.2.1. Scalar Types

SISAL provides the following scalar types together with the usual operations on and between them: *boolean*, *integer*, *real*, *double_real* and *character*. Although SISAL provides for the declaration of value names, the typing system enables the type of any value name to be directly deducible from its defining expression, so declarations are only used when their inclusion improves program clarity. A number of predefined functions, such as modulus (*mod*), magnitude (*abs*), maximum (*max*), minimum (*min*), and real and mixed exponentiation (*exp*) are provided, together with explicit type conversion operations. No implicit type coercions are performed.

2.2.2. Arrays

An *array* has components of arbitrary (but uniform) type and an (implicit) integer index type. Each array has dynamic bounds, its size being determined by evaluation of the expression defining the array value. Multi-dimensional arrays are represented as arrays of arrays. A *creation operation* creates an array from component values. A *create empty* operation creates an empty array of given type; *create by elements* creates an array by listing all its elements; and *create by fill* creates an array of specified size with all elements equal to a given value. For example:

```
A := array aa_real [];                          % create empty
B := array a_real [low: 1.0, 10.0, 100.0];     % create by elements
C := array_fill (low, high, 0.0);               % create by fill
```

An *access operation* obtains a component part of an array value. *Array select* accesses an array element; *array_liml*, *array_limh* and *array_size* obtain the lower bound, upper bound and size of an array respectively. For example:

```
A := array [0: array a_real [] , array [1: 1.0, 2.0, 3.0] ];
B := A [1];                                  %  array [1: 1.0, 2.0, 3.0]
x := A [1, 2];                               %  2.0
i := array_size (A);                         %  2
j := array_liml (B);                         %  1
k := array_limh (A[0]);                      %  0
```

A *transformation operation* creates a new array from an existing array value. For example, *replace* replaces a specified element in an array with a new value, and *concatenate* (||) joins two arrays of the same type:

```
S := array [1: 2, 5, 7 ]                     % 2 5 7
V := S [2: 4; 3: 8 ];                        % 2 4 8
X := array [1: 1 ]
Y := X || V;                                 % 1 2 4 8
```

Finally, the *adjust* operation selects a subrange from an array, and *add* and *remove* allow an array to be extended by one element or reduced by one element at either end of its range.

2.2.3. Streams

A *stream* is an ordered sequence or list of values of some arbitrary but uniform type. Components of a stream cannot be accessed randomly; they must be accessed in order, using operations such as *first* and *rest*. Stream type definitions and operations are syntactically similar to those for arrays. A *creation operation* creates a stream from component values. The *create empty* operation creates an empty stream of specified type; and *create by elements* creates a non-empty stream by listing all its elements. An *access operation* obtains a component part of a stream value. *Select first* accesses the first element of a stream; *stream size* gives the number of elements in a stream; and *test for empty* returns a boolean value indicating whether the stream is empty. The *transformation operations* create a new stream from an existing stream value. *Stream_rest* discards the first element of a stream; *stream_append* adds a new value to the end of a stream; and *concatenate* (||) joins two streams of the same type.

2.2.4. Records

A *record* consists of one or more component fields of arbitrary types, each field being identified by a field name. There are three record operations: *create* a record value, *select* a field from a record, and *replace* a field in a record with a new value, giving a new record value. The type name for a record create is optional, since its type can be deduced from the types of the fields and the language is weakly typed. More than one field can be changed by a single replace operation. For example:

```
type dest = record [ Segment, Node : integer;
                     Input : character; MatchFn : array [character] ]

D        := record dest [ Segment : 2; Node : 2064;         % create
                          Input : 'L'; MatchFn : "EW" ];

in_point := D.Input;                                        % select
F        := D replace [ Segment: 1; Node: 1405 ];           % replace
```

2.2.5. Unions

A *union* consists of a set of alternative constituent types, each type being associated with a tag. The value of a union consists of a *tag value* and a *constituent value*, of type corresponding to the tag value name. For instance, in the following example, a value of type arith_op will have a tag value of int_op, real_op or dble_op and a corresponding constituent value of type *integer*, *real* or *double_real*, respectively:

```
type arith_op = union [ int_op:  integer;
                        real_op: real;
                        dble_op: double_real ]
```

Unions may be used to construct an enumerated scalar type, each tag name being used to represent one of the scalar values. A special constituent type *null* is provided for use with the tag, but it may be omitted to give a more natural style for enumerated scalars. For example, the following definitions are equivalent:

```
type move = union [Lft: null; Rght: null; Up: null; Down: null]
```

```
type move = union [Lft; Rght; Up; Down]
```

Recursive unions are permitted, as shown in the following example, which defines a binary tree with elements of type *data*:

```
type TreeTp = union [ Empty;
                      Full: record [ Element: data; Lft, Rght: TreeTp ]
                    ]
```

The mechanism for accessing constituent values from union values is the *tagcase* construct, introduced in section 2.3.4. There are two other union operations: *create* a union value (similar to array/stream create) and *test tag* (*is*), which tests whether a union value was created with a specified tag.

2.2.6. Error Values

Exceptions are handled in SISAL by generating *error values*. A special value *error* is a proper value of every type in SISAL. The production of an error value from an expression indicates that some exceptional condition prevented the normal evaluation of that expression. When an error value is generated for a component of a structured object, values for those components known to be correct are wherever possible preserved.

2.3. Control Structures

2.3.1. The *let* Block

The purpose of the *let block* is to define one or more value names, which are then used in the evaluation of an expression. The results of this expression are the results of the block. Value names defined in a block are not available for use outside that block. For example, the following block calculates the two roots of a quadratic equation:

```
x_1, x_2 := let  disc  := b * b - 4.0 * a * c;
                 root := sqrt (disc);
                 two_a := 2.0 * a
            in
                 (-b + root) / two_a ,
                 (-b - root) / two_a
            end let
```

2.3.2. The Conditional Construct

The *conditional construct* is used to select one of two *alternative* expressions for evaluation, depending on the result of a boolean test. The selected expression is evaluated, and its results are returned as the results of the whole construct. The *else* branch must always be present to define the results of the conditional when the test yields *false*. Similarly, the expressions given in the two branches must *conform* in the number and types of results produced. A single conditional construct can be used (without nesting) to select one of several expressions for evaluation using one or more *elseif* branches. For example:

```
result :=  if op_ch = '+'        then arg1 + arg2
              elseif op_ch = '-' then arg1 - arg2
              elseif op_ch = '*' then arg1 * arg2
              else                    arg1 / arg2
           end if
```

2.3.3. Iterative Constructs

Programming languages usually provide iterative constructs that repeatedly apply an operation to multiple data elements. Such constructs normally imply that executions of the operation occur in a serial order. In SISAL there is no such timing requirement; the only constraint on parallelism is that of data dependence. In the *for all construct*, there are no data dependencies between cycles, and so it is possible to execute all cycles of the iteration concurrently. The *for init construct* is used where there are data dependencies from one cycle to the next.

A *for all construct* comprises a *generator* which specifies the range of values for which the body will be executed, the loop *body*, and a *returns section* which specifies the value(s) to be returned. More than one result may be yielded by specifying a *list* of return values. The *greatest* or *least* value over all cycles may be returned or the values from each cycle may be reduced to a single value using a *sum* or *product* operation. Alternatively, the returns section may *collect* all definitions of some value name and return them as an *array* or *stream*. This is particularly convenient for generating and manipulating array and stream values. The generator may cause elements of an array to be available inside a loop without explicit subscripting. Also, multiple ranges may be specified and combined using either *dot* or *cross* products. In a dot product, the ranges must have the same size and the *i-th* element of each range is used to drive the *i-th* body. The cross product is short-hand for a nested *for all*. The following example performs matrix multiplication on two arrays *M1* and *M2* of type *array[array[real]]* and of size *(a x b)* and *(c x b)*, respectively (the second matrix is in transposed form). The size of the array *M3* produced by the loop is *(a x c)*, as determined by the cross product used in the generator.

```
M3 :=  for  Row in M1  cross Col in M2
         M3_El := for R_El in Row dot C_El in Col
                      P := R_El * C_EL
                  returns value of sum P
                  end for
       returns array of M3_El
       end for
```

A *for init construct* comprises an *initial section*, the loop *body*, a *termination test* and a *returns section*. The *initial section* defines initial values of *loop names* in order to start the iteration. Execution of this section is considered to be the first pass through the loop. The *body* is executed once for each subsequent pass, and defines new values for the loop names. The value of a loop name from the immediately preceding cycle may be used by prefixing the required loop name with the keyword *old*. The *termination test* determines the conditions under which iteration should finish. The keywords *until* and *while* are used to define the termination condition in the usual way. An iteration that executes the body *zero or more* times is constructed by placing the termination test before the body. The *returns section* specifies the result(s) to be returned in the same way as the *for all* construct. The keyword *value of* indicates that the last value of the given value name should be returned. The following example calculates the square root of a value x using the Newton-Raphson method:

```
sqrt_x :=  for initial est := 0.5 * x
           repeat est := 0.5 * (old est + x / old est);
                  diff := abs (est * est - x)
           until diff < tolerance
           returns value of est
           end for
```

2.3.4. The *tagcase* Construct

The *tagcase* construct is used to select one of a number of expressions for evaluation, depending on the tag of a union value. The following example updates a position in an <x,y> plane based on the direction of a given move:

```
type move = union [Lft; Rght; Up; Down]
this_move := Get_Move (Player); % yields a value of type move
new_x, new_y := tagcase this_move
                   tag Lft:  x-1, y
                   tag Rght: x+1, y
                   tag Up:   x  , y+1
                   tag Down: x  , y-1
                end tagcase
```

The *tagcase* construct is also the mechanism for accessing constituent values of a union value. A new value name is introduced as part of the tagcase header, which may then be used within any arm of the tagcase to refer to the constituent value. This value name may only be used in the tag arms, and will have a type and value according to the tag value of the arm.

2.4. Modules and Programs

A SISAL program consists of a collection of type and function definitions. A program may be written as a number of distinct *modules*. Each module will contain a number of type and function definitions, together with a *defines list* of functions defined in the module (at the outermost level) which are to be made available to other modules, and a *globals list* of functions which are used in the module, but (possibly) not defined there. If a function in the globals list is not defined in the module, it is assumed that some other module will provide a definition of that function via a defines list.

2.5. Examples

The following complete SISAL program (in a single module) will be used to illustrate the remainder of the paper. The basic program comprises a single function *Smooth_conditional* that performs a one-dimensional array "smoothing" operation using a *for all* construct embedded in a *for initial* loop.

```
define Smooth_conditional
type Vector = array[real]
function Smooth_conditional( Cycles: integer; In_Vec: Vector returns Vector )
for initial
 V := In_Vec;
 N := 0
repeat
 N := old N + 1;
 V :=
  for I in 1, array_limh( old V )
  Element := if (I = 1 | I = array_limh( old V ))          % | is logical OR
             then old V[I]
             else ( old V[I-1] + old V[I] + old V[I+1] ) / 3.0
             end if
  returns array of Element
  end for
until N=Cycles
returns value of V
end for
end function
```

The inner loop of *Smooth_conditional* contains a conditional construct which is known to produce highly inefficient code. The degree of inefficiency involved is assessed in subsequent sections by comparing the code generated from the above program with that generated for the following version (*Smooth_concatenate*) in which the conditional has been eliminated by using the concatenate (||) function to place the static end elements of the array around inner elements that are produced by a *for all* construct:

```
define Smooth_concatenate

type Vector = array[real]

function Smooth_concatenate( Cycles: integer; In_Vec: Vector returns Vector )

for initial
 V := In_Vec;
 N := 0
repeat
 N := old N + 1;
 V :=
   array Vector [1:old V[1]]
   ||
   for I in 2, array_limh( old V ) - 1
   Element := ( old V[I-1] + old V[I] + old V[I+1] ) / 3.0
   returns array of Element
   end for
   ||
   array Vector [1:old V[ array_limh( old V ) ]]
until N=Cycles
returns value of V
end for
end function
```

The input data defines the number of iterations to be performed and an initial value for the array to be smoothed. The size of the input array is implicit in its initial value. For the sample executions of the program described in sections 4 and 5, an array of 100 elements with the following initial values is processed for 100 cycles:

```
In_Vec[1] ... In_Vec[10]  = 1.0 2.0 3.0 4.0 5.0 6.0 7.0 8.0 9.0 10.0
In_Vec[11] .. In_Vec[20]  = 1.0 2.0 3.0 4.0 5.0 6.0 7.0 8.0 9.0 10.0
In_Vec[21] .. In_Vec[30]  = 1.0 2.0 3.0 4.0 5.0 6.0 7.0 8.0 9.0 10.0
In_Vec[31] .. In_Vec[40]  = 1.0 2.0 3.0 4.0 5.0 6.0 7.0 8.0 9.0 10.0
In_Vec[41] .. In_Vec[50]  = 1.0 2.0 3.0 4.0 5.0 6.0 7.0 8.0 9.0 10.0
In_Vec[51] .. In_Vec[60]  = 1.0 2.0 3.0 4.0 5.0 6.0 7.0 8.0 9.0 10.0
In_Vec[61] .. In_Vec[70]  = 1.0 2.0 3.0 4.0 5.0 6.0 7.0 8.0 9.0 10.0
In_Vec[71] .. In_Vec[80]  = 1.0 2.0 3.0 4.0 5.0 6.0 7.0 8.0 9.0 10.0
In_Vec[81] .. In_Vec[90]  = 1.0 2.0 3.0 4.0 5.0 6.0 7.0 8.0 9.0 10.0
In_Vec[91] .. In_Vec[100] = 1.0 2.0 3.0 4.0 5.0 6.0 7.0 8.0 9.0 10.0
```

3. DATA DEPENDENCE GRAPH REPRESENTATION OF PROGRAMS

3.1. Introduction

Although it is feasible to generate data dependence graphs from any programming language [2,14,16,22], the single-assignment and functional properties of SISAL make it particularly suited to translation into data dependence graph format (DDGF). This is essentially the first step taken in the SISAL compiler. A machine-independent DDGF known as IF1 (Intermediate Format - version 1) has been defined specifically for this purpose [19]. Interestingly, there are signs that IF1 may be adopted for use by research groups studying the translation of more conventional programming languages (such as Fortran) into DDGF. IF1 is introduced below.

3.2. IF1 - An Intermediate Format for SISAL

An IF1 program is a set of *graphs*, one for each SISAL function. Graphs consist of *nodes* and *edges*. Edges represent values travelling from node to node and are *typed* (the type descriptor being a tree of type records). Nodes represent operations and are of three main types. Firstly, there are *primitive nodes*, such as Plus, Minus, NoOp and AEL (Array ELement). The latter yields an array element given the array and an index. Secondly, there are nodes that deal with *multiple values*, such as RGN (Range GeNerate) ASC (Array SCatter) and AGA (Array GAther). RGN yields a sequence of integers between a given lower and upper bound. ASC yields selected elements from an array, given a lower bound, an upper bound and an offset by which indices are to be shifted. AGA takes an integer lower bound together with a multiple value and creates the corresponding array. Finally, there are *compound nodes*, such as SELECT, UNTIL and FORALL, which recursively contain subgraphs. A SELECT node contains a TEST subgraph and two BRANCH subgraphs. The TEST subgraph yields a boolean that selects the appropriate BRANCH subgraph. This is used to implement a SISAL conditional construct. An UNTIL node contains four subgraphs: INIT, TEST, BODY and RETURNS. These correspond to the parts of a SISAL *for initial* construct with the test after the body. A FORALL node contains GENERATE, BODY and RETURNS subgraphs and is used to implement the SISAL *for all* construct. There are no explicit edges between the subgraphs of a compound node since a standard configuration of links is implied for each type of compound node.

The following figure shows the IF1 version of the SISAL program *Smooth_conditional*, presented in section 2.5. Nodes are shown as dashed boxes, and explicit edges are shown as solid lines. The implicit links are indicated using the abbreviations E for Element and C for Cycles.

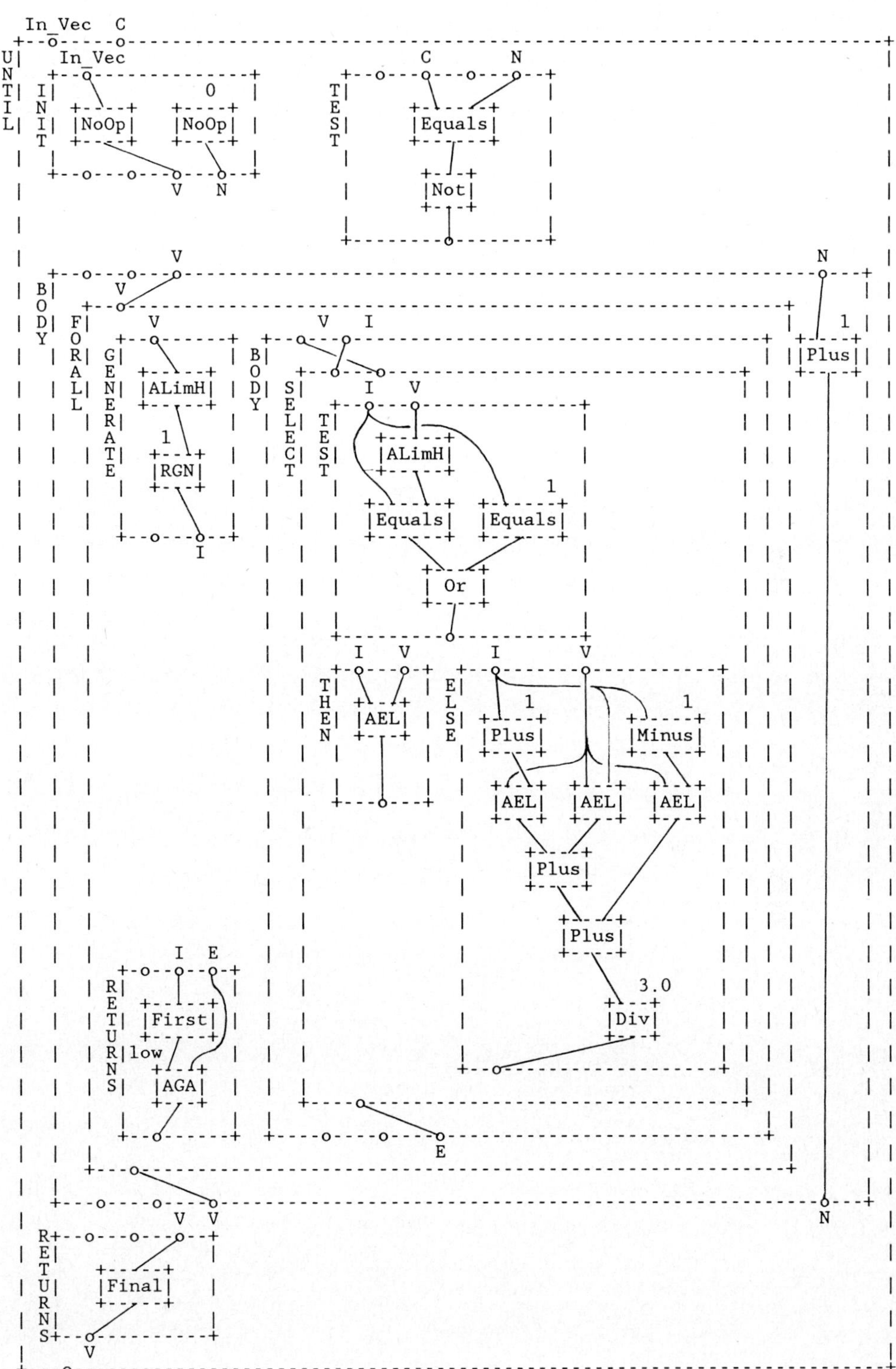

In_Vec
C
UNTIL
INIT
In_Vec
0
NoOp
NoOp
V
N
TEST
C
N
Equals
Not
V
N
BODY
V
FORALL
V
GENERATE
ALimH
1
RGN
I
BODY
V
I
1
Plus
SELECT
I
V
TEST
ALimH
1
Equals
Equals
Or
I
V
THEN
AEL
I
V
ELSE
1
Plus
1
Minus
AEL
AEL
AEL
Plus
Plus
3.0
Div
I
E
RETURNS
First
low
AGA
E
V
V
N
RETURNS
Final
V

The next figure shows how the inner loop changes when the conditional is removed, as in the SISAL program *Smooth_concatenate*, presented in section 2.5. Together with the appropriate concatenation nodes, the following subgraph would be substituted for the FORALL subgraph in the preceding figure.

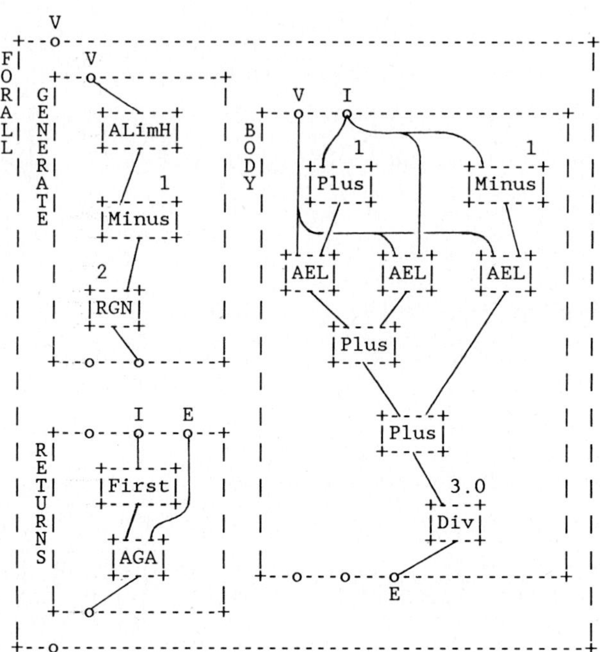

3.3. Optimisations

A number of machine-independent optimisations can be performed by IF1-to-IF1 transformations, the implementation of which is greatly simplified by the functional semantics of SISAL and IF1. Of these optimisations, common subexpression elimination and code motion (moving constant code out of loop bodies) have been implemented at Lawrence Livermore National Laboratory [20]. Function in-lining (replacing a function call by its definition) and vectorisation (moving array indexing from the BODY to the GENERATE subgraph) have been implemented at the University of Manchester [9]. Vectorisation exploits the ability of the Manchester Dataflow Machine to extract complete structures from storage in one operation (see below).

As an example, the following figure illustrates the effect of vectorising the inner loop of the *Smooth_concatenate* program. Compared with the previous figure, it will be seen that the BODY has been considerably simplified, at the expense of complicating the GENERATE subgraph.

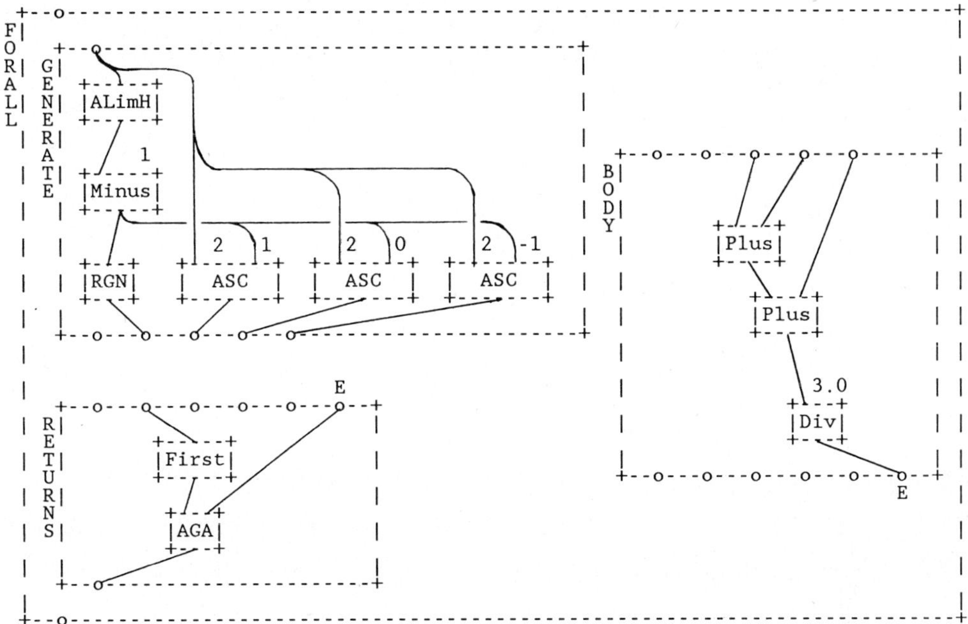

4. DATAFLOW CODE GENERATION

4.1. Dataflow Models of Computation

The use of data dependence graphs as an intermediate-level representation of SISAL programs naturally leads to the idea of generating object-code for a dataflow computer, since dataflow programs are well-known to be low-level dependence graphs. In general, a machine-level dataflow program is a directed graph in which *nodes* represent machine *instructions* and *arcs* represent paths along which data values travel from instruction to instruction at run-time. Simple program graphs, such as that shown in the figure below (which calculates the square root of $b^2 - 4ac$, given a, b and c), are *acyclic*. Such graphs are equivalent to the *expression evaluation trees* that are commonly constructed by compilers for high-level languages. Where a value is required in more than one part of the expression evaluation, the instruction marked *DUP* (for duplicate) in the figure is used to copy the input value to all the output arcs. The essence of the dataflow computational model is that it defines a direct means for concurrent execution of these graph programs. Carriers for data values, known as *tokens*, are fired into the graph, and each instruction determines individually whether or not to execute on the basis of the availability of its required input data. Since this decision is made locally at each instruction, the overall pattern of execution is entirely asynchronous.

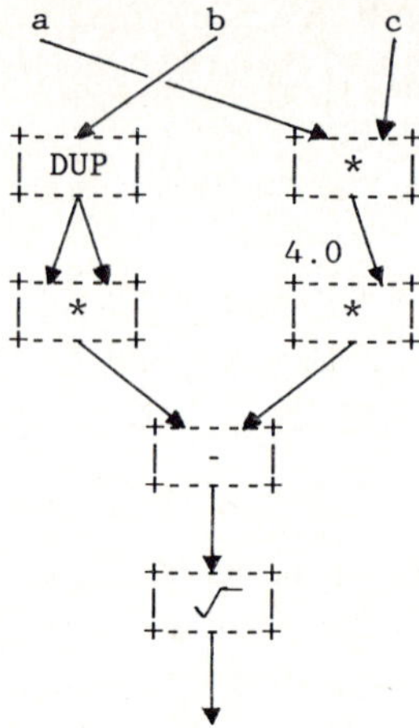

In order to measure the parallelism in a dataflow graph program, it is common to record the total number of instructions in the graph, known as *S1*, and the length of the critical path, known as *Sinf*. These values are derived from an abstract view of the execution of program graphs in which all instructions take the same period of time to execute and there is no delay between a *generating* instruction producing its result token and the corresponding *consuming* instruction receiving that token. Execution with *p* processors thus proceeds in *lockstep* fashion, with a maximum of *p* instructions being executed in each time-step, depending on the availability of input tokens. The number of time-steps required to execute the whole program is known as *Sp*. Hence, *S1* is equivalent to the number of time-steps required by a uniprocessor, and *Sinf* is the number of time-steps required by an *infinite* multiprocessor. The ratio *S1/Sinf* is a crude measure of the *average program parallelism* inherent in the graph. When the total number of floating point operations, *F1*, is also recorded, the value of *S1/F1* is known as the *MIPS/MFLOPS ratio* (MMR) which is a convenient measure of the overall efficiency of a numerical program. In the above example, S1 = 6, Sinf = 4, F1 = 5 and MMR = 1.2.

Graphs representing higher level constructs, such as conditionals, loops or functions, contain *conditional* instructions and may be *cyclic*. The introduction of cycles into such graphs poses certain implementation problems that have received much attention in the dataflow literature and have led to the distinct *static* and *dynamic* approaches to dataflow computation. The major problem is that the asynchronous nature of dataflow program execution can cause *race* conditions in cyclic graphs. For example, in a *for initial* loop, the cycle defining the next value of one loop value might race ahead of cycles calculating other loop values and cause confusion between tokens belonging to successive cycles of the loop. Either this situation must be prevented from arising (the *static* approach, which allows only one cycle to be active at a time), or there must be some means for distinguishing between such tokens (the *dynamic* approach). Note also that, for maximally parallel execution, multiple calls to a function should be performed concurrently. For example, successive cycles of a loop containing a function call can increase the level of concurrency by overlapping calls to the function in *pipelined* fashion. If such functions are implemented as the graphical equivalent of *subroutines*, with a single body of machine-code being shared amongst all calls to the function, then it must be feasible for several activations of the body to occur simultaneously.

The major dataflow research projects [3,5,12,18] resolve these problems using a dynamic scheme known as *tagging*. Each token carries an extra field, called the *tag*, that is guaranteed to be unique in this area of the graph, and which therefore distinguishes between all possible activations of a particular piece of code. By separating tokens with different tags from one another, the asynchronous execution rules can be followed without confusion due to race conditions. A discussion of the relative merits of these and other schemes for implementing cyclic dataflow graphs is given elsewhere [4].

4.2. Representation of Data Structures

The key dataflow research groups have been predominantly concerned with numerical scientific computation, and they have naturally concentrated on array-like data structures rather than lists. Arrays can be represented as *sequences* of tokens travelling on arcs, ordered either in time (as in a static scheme), or in space (as in a tagged scheme). However, the large number of tagging operations required (for example, when arrays are passed across function boundaries) has led to more efficient proposals. The most popular scheme is to hold each structure in a special-purpose *structure store*, and represent it by a *descriptor* which can be passed across a function boundary with a single tagging operation. Elements of a structure can be put into or obtained from the store using the descriptor together with an index to construct the appropriate *write* or *read* token. Where arrays have simple structure (e.g. a constant lower bound of 1), the descriptor can be a single (pointer) token. Otherwise it is necessary to use several tokens. Other simple structures, such as records and unions, can be implemented in a similar way, although there are circumstances where it is more effective to represent them by multiple tokens travelling on separate arcs. Where data structures are represented by descriptors and held in a structure store, the number of accesses made to the structure store during each program run (*SSA*) is an important factor determining performance.

4.3. Sample Dataflow Machine-Code

In order to illustrate real dataflow object code, the following figures present parts of the Manchester machine-code for the SISAL programs introduced in section 2.4. This code is derived from the IF1 graphs presented in sections 3.2 and 3.3. Arrays are stored in a special-purpose *structure store* (see section 5.2) and represented in the graph by simple pointer tokens containing a *size* and a structure store *base address* for the array.

The first figure shows how the conditional construct used in *Smooth_conditional* is implemented. This corresponds to the IF1 SELECT subgraph shown in the first figure of section 3.2. Conditional execution is achieved principally by the instructions marked BRR (for branch), which accept a boolean value on their right-hand input arc and route the incoming left-hand token to their left or right output arc according to the value of the boolean (left for *true*, right for *false*). Other instructions used in this example are: Extract Size from Pointer (ESP), Compare Equal Integers (CEI), OR Booleans (ORB), ADd Integers (ADI), SuBtract Integers (SBI), ADd Reals (ADR), DiVide Reals (DVR) and Single Vector Access (SVA). The operation of most of these instructions is self-evident. For example, ADI takes two integer input values and computes their sum. CEI takes two integer values and produces a boolean value that is *true* if and only if the two input values are equal. ESP takes a single pointer input value and yields the integer size of the array represented by it. Because the size is contained within the pointer (see above) this requires no access to the structure store. SVA causes a value to be read from the structure store address defined by the base address of its left-hand pointer input added to its right-hand integer (index) value.

For simplicity, duplicate (DUP) instructions are sometimes shown with three or more output arcs. This is not true Manchester machine-code since instructions are limited to two or less outputs. A simple transformation generates the proper code. Note also that an instruction may generate two copies of one of its outputs under certain circumstances. The rules defining legal machine-code are beyond the scope of this paper.

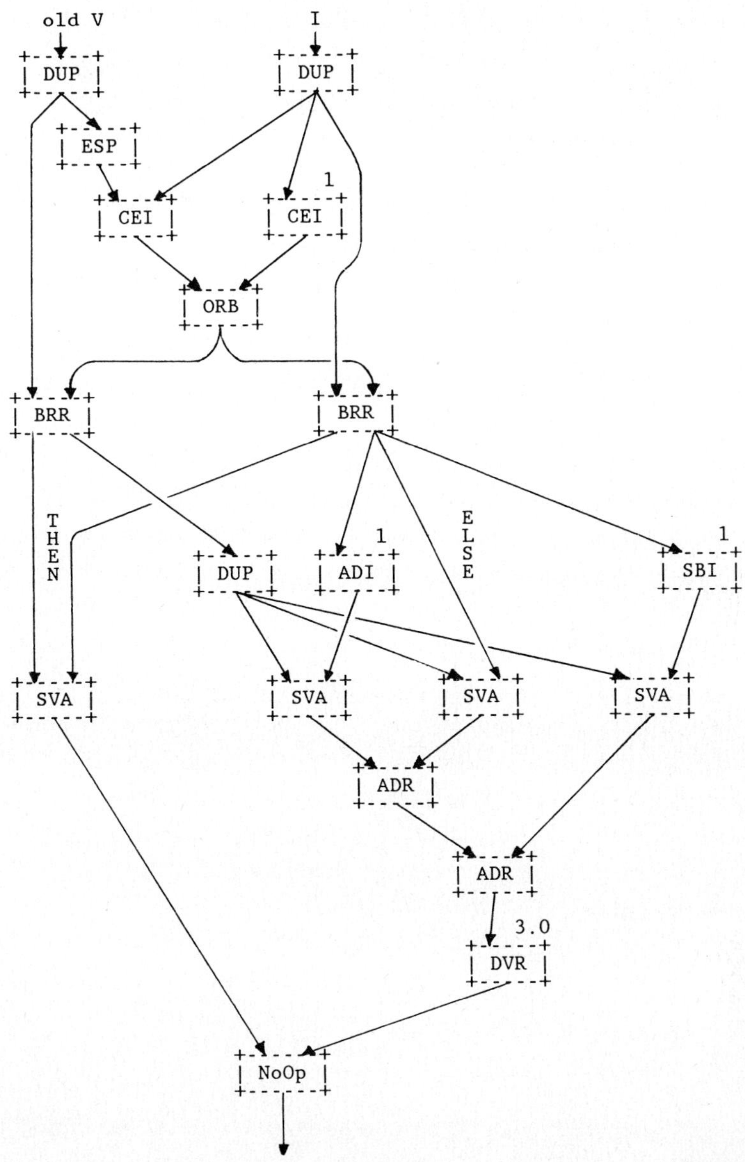

The second figure illustrates implementation of the IF1 node RGN (Range GeNerate), as used to implement the SISAL *for all* construct. The following instructions are used in addition to those introduced above: SOrt Integers (SOI), which places its two integer input values in order on the left-hand (lowest value) and right-hand (highest value) output arcs, and Proliferate with OFfset (POF), which generates a stream of integers with values L to L+R-1 and index tag values 0 to R-1, respectively, where L and R are the left and right integer input values.

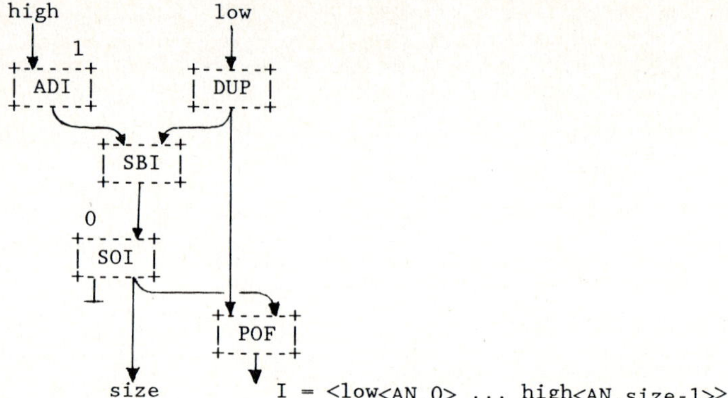

The final figure shows the implementation of the IF1 node ASC (Array SCatter), used for vectorisation. The following new instructions are used: CReate J-value (CRJ), which packs two integers into a single token, and Fetch SubRange (FSR), which fetches (a subset of) an array from the structure store.

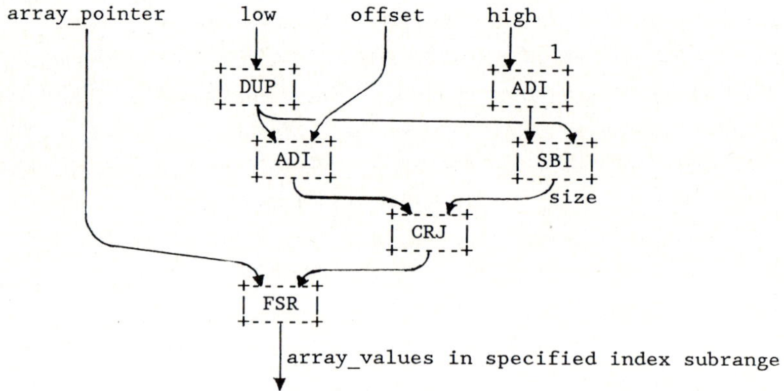

4.4. Machine-Code Characteristics

Following the guidelines, introduced in section 4.1, for measuring the degree of parallelism in dataflow programs, the table below indicates the execution characteristics of the three versions of the *Smooth* program described earlier. *Smooth_vectorised* is created using the IF1 vectorising optimisation on *Smooth_concatenate*.

Program name	**S1**	**Sinf**	**S1/Sinf**	**MMR**	**SSA**
Smooth_conditional	335157	3720	90.1	11.40	40101
Smooth_concatenate	237457	4620	51.4	8.08	60401
Smooth_vectorised	129446	4020	32.2	4.40	60401

5. DATAFLOW COMPUTERS

5.1. General Design Principles

With few exceptions, the present consensus is that a dataflow machine should implement the *tagged-token* model of computation with some form of separate data structure storage. The fundamentally asynchronous nature of the model leads to the expectation that multiple instruction processors and data structure memory modules should be capable of being coupled together to form high-performance parallel computer systems. There are thus three logical components in a dataflow machine, namely the *processing element*, the *structure store*, and the *interconnection network* (or *switch*).

The processing element is responsible for implementing the basic asynchronous tagged token dataflow model of computation. There are three tasks involved. Firstly, the processing element must recognise when all the input tokens to a particular instruction have arrived there. This is achieved by the *matching* process, executed in a special-purpose *token matching unit*. As each token arrives here, it is compared with resident tokens to see whether its *partner* tokens (if any) are already available, and, if so, all the relevant tokens are extracted from the local store and sent off for further processing. Otherwise the incoming token is added to the set of resident tokens in such a way that the subsequent arrival of all its partners will cause the above action. Secondly, the processing element must decide the operation to be performed on the data values produced by the matching process. This is achieved by fetching an instruction from the *instruction store*, which holds a complete copy of the graphical program. A program is normally expressed as a set of *nodes*, each defining the *operation* to be performed and the *destination* node for each of the required output arcs. Finally, the processing element must be capable of performing the required operation on the data and generating the appropriate output token(s). This is achieved in a *processing unit* which contains the necessary functional capabilities to support the machine instruction-set.

The structure store is responsible for servicing access requests to data structures. The store is usually responsible for management functions, such as space allocation and garbage collection, as well as read and write accesses. All communication between structure store modules and processing elements is achieved by sending messages in the form of tokens.

The interconnection network is responsible for sending messages from one physical unit to another. These messages are always sent in *packet-switched* fashion. The network comprises a number of individual *mxm* switch elements, each of which contains buffers at its input to hold incoming data. Routing information within the data packet indicates which of the network outputs it is directed towards. The overall structure is effectively a set of parallel pipelines. An N-input, N-output network requires $N/m(\log_m N)$ switch elements, and any route through the network is a pipeline of length $\log_m N$. Assuming random contention for switching resources, it can be shown that such a structure achieves a throughput approaching its maximum theoretical bandwidth although it has low complexity in terms of the number of switching elements required for a practical implementation. Since the communication is unidirectional, the only price paid is the pipeline delay between processors. As long as the processors are kept active and the pipeline is kept full by parallelism in the program, no performance degradation should result.

A key factor in the design of a dataflow system is the ability to expand its power by adding extra processors via an extended interconnection network. This desire to expand power by adding hardware (without changing software) is common to all dataflow system designs. The term "scalability" has been used to describe this requirement [7]. There is keen debate about the maximum size of network that can be constructed (or that will be feasible in the forseeable future) and there is an obvious relationship between the power of individual processors, the total power, and the size of the network. However, the key factor determining the scalability of an architecture is the way in which the computational workload is distributed amongst the system components. There is little agreement yet about schemes for achieving this distribution effectively.

Three schemes are being studied for distributing the processing elements and structure store modules. The first scheme [5] has the structure storage integrated within the processing elements: Advantages are simplification of the hardware structure and, under the right conditions, reduction of the required network bandwidth. However, effective distribution of the workload is difficult: In order to minimise the required network bandwidth, the location of the processing workload must exactly match the location of the corresponding structure store workload. The second scheme [18] has structure store modules and processing elements *clustered* together in relatively small numbers. This simplifies workload distribution at the expense of increasing hardware complexity and network bandwidth. The extent to which this scheme can be effective has yet to be determined, but the fundamental problem of matching processing and structure storage workload distribution remains and cannot be solved completely unless the structure store modules are entirely separated from the processing elements, as happens with the third scheme [13].

As an example of a practical dataflow computer, the prototype ring-structured dataflow uniprocessor constructed at the University of Manchester over the last decade is described in the next section [12,13].

5.2. The Manchester Dataflow Machine

In the Manchester machine, the three dataflow tasks described above (matching tokens together, finding the next instruction, and processing instructions) are implemented in three separate hardware modules. Internal activity within each module depends solely on the current input data to that module, so that successive actions may be overlapped by connecting the modules in a pipeline. One extra pipeline module is provided to queue excess tasks when highly parallel programs are running. The processor structure is thus a four-stage pipeline, as illustrated in the figure below. A separate structure store unit is attached independently to the inter-connection network. This unit comprises a microcoded processor with a large 40-bit wide data store, with facilities for deferring premature accesses (i.e. attempts to read structure elements that have not yet been written).

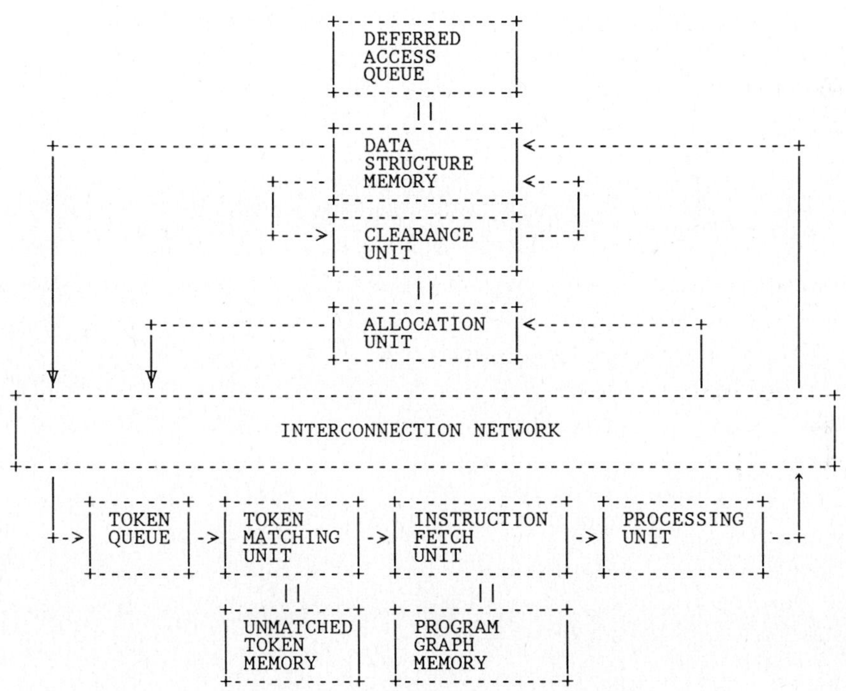

The critical part of the system is the token matching unit. The task of pairing tokens together is an act of association, so the unmatched token memory is (pseudo-)associative. It is implemented using a hardware-hashing mechanism. The average match time for the prototype version is 450 nanoseconds which limits the maximum instruction execution rate of the processing element to just over 2 million instructions per second (MIPS). A serially-activated parallel array of

20 general-purpose microcoded function units is provided in the processing unit to maintain this processing rate. The structure store consists of an *allocation unit*, a *clearance unit*, the *structure memory*, and a *deferred access queue*, all of which are connected to the interconnection network [17]. The processing ring exchanges messages with the structure store via the interconnection network, in order to allocate structures, to increment/decrement reference counts and to read/write data values. The *allocation unit* is responsible for managing storage space. The *clearance unit* performs garbage collection. The *structure memory* stores the structured data and allows asynchronous access to it in the normal data-driven fashion. When the required data has yet to be written, a read request is held in the *deferred access queue* until the data arrives. Deferred read requests for a store location will be released when the corresponding write request is processed. This scheme is similar to that proposed for the implementation of I-Structures [6]. A structure store for a larger machine would contain several units of each type, configured in a more distributed manner.

5.3. Performance

Using the three versions of the *Smooth* program introduced earlier, the following table indicates the achievable processing rate of the current configuration of the Manchester Dataflow Machine. Comparable figures for a Pascal version of the program running on a VAX11/780 are included. It will be seen that the later versions of the SISAL program are progressively faster, even though the instruction processing rate decreases (due to the increased complexity of the instructions being executed).

Program name	**Elapsed time**	**Processing rate**
Smooth_conditional	0.3137 secs.	1.07 MIPS
Smooth_concatenate	0.2640 secs.	0.90 MIPS
Smooth_vectorised	0.1757 secs.	0.74 MIPS
Smooth_Pascal/VAX	0.3100 secs.	0.32 MIPS

6. CONCLUSIONS

The implicit approach to parallel computing is essential for minimising programming effort whilst achieving maximum efficiency. It is also desirable as a means of reducing programming errors. However, attempts to realise implicit systems through "parallelisation" of existing programs have not yet been completely successful. This paper has investigated an alternative approach to implicit parallelism, using a novel, *single-assignment* programming language implemented on a fine-grain *dataflow* computer.

Single-assignment programming is similar in style to both conventional programming and functional programming (i.e. SISAL programs can be read either operationally, in the same way as, say, Pascal programs, or declaratively, in the same way as, say, programs in pure Lisp). Although not as powerful as general functional languages (e.g. SISAL does not allow the user to define higher order functions), single-assignment languages have functional semantics that allow program properties to be proved with greater ease than for conventional languages. Transformations to improve the execution efficiency of algorithms can be implemented straightforwardly.

At machine-level, the efficiency of dataflow code generated from SISAL has been shown to be comparable to that of conventional (sequential) machine-code generated from conventional high-level languages. Practical dataflow uniprocessors are achieving performances that compare well with their conventional counterparts. The scalability of these practical systems is yet to be convincingly demonstrated, but researchers in the field are confident that good results can be obtained. Plans are well advanced for experimenting with multiprocessor dataflow systems of significant size, developing and demonstrating workable schemes for workload distribution and throttling.

Overall, impressive integration has been achieved already between the high-level programming concepts embodied in languages such as SISAL and low-level implementation features on hardware such as the prototype Manchester Dataflow Machine. The imminent arrival of high-performance machines such as the SIGMA-1 system [18] being constructed at the ElectroTechnical Laboratory in Japan (expected to be operational in mid-1987 with 128 processing elements and a sustained execution rate of 50 to 100 MFLOPS) promises a breakthrough in credibility for this unconventional approach.

ACKNOWLEDGEMENTS

The authors are indebted to their colleagues, past and present, in the Dataflow Research Group at the University of Manchester. Particular thanks are due to John Foley, John Glauert, Chris Kirkham, Adrian Parker, John Sargeant and Ian Watson. There have been considerable contributions from researchers outside Manchester, especially the SISAL language design and implementation teams from Lawrence Livermore National Laboratory, Digital Equipment Corporation and Colorado State University. Construction of the prototype Manchester Dataflow Machine and implementation of the SISAL compiler were funded by the Science and Engineering Research Council of Great Britain. Applications studies have been supported by Digital Equipment Corporation and the UK Alvey Programme in advanced information technology.

REFERENCES

[1] Ackerman, W.B., Dataflow Languages, *IEEE Computer* 15/2 (1982) pp. 1087-1095.

[2] Allen, F.E. and Cocke, J., A Program Data Flow Analysis Procedure, *Communications of the ACM* 19/3 (1976) pp. 137-147.

[3] Amamiya, M. *et al.*, A List-Processing-Oriented Data Flow Machine Architecture, *AFIPS Proceedings* 51 (1982) pp. 143-151.

[4] Arvind and Gostelow, K.P., Some Relationships between Asynchronous Interpreters of a Dataflow Language, *in*: Neuhold, E.J., (ed.), *Formal Description of Programming Concepts* (North Holland, Amsterdam, 1978) pp. 95-119.

[5] Arvind and Kathail, V., A Multiple Processor Dataflow Machine that Supports Generalised Procedures, *Proceedings 8th Annual Symposium on Computer Architecture* (ACM, 1981) pp. 291-302.

[6] Arvind and Thomas, R.E., I-Structures - An Efficient Data Type for Functional Languages, *Technical Memo LCS-TM-178* (MIT, 1981).

[7] Arvind and Ianucci, R.A., A Critique of Multiprocessing, von Neumann Style, *Proceedings 10th Annual Symposium on Computer Architecture* (ACM, 1983) pp. 426-436.

[8] Arvind and Culler, D.E., Managing Resources in a Parallel Machine, *in*: Woods, J.V., (ed.), *Fifth Generation Computer Architectures* (North Holland, Amsterdam, 1986) pp. 103-121.

[9] Böhm, A.P.W. and Sargeant, J., Efficient Dataflow Code Generation for SISAL, *Technical Report UMCS-85-10-2* (University of Manchester, 1985).

[10] Chamberlin, D.D., The 'Single-Assignment' Approach to Parallel Processing, *AFIPS Proceedings* 39 (1971) pp. 263-270.

[11] Glauert, J.R.W., High-Level Languages for Dataflow Computers, *in*: Wallis, P., (ed.), *State of the Art Report on Programming Technology* (Pergamon-Infotech, Maidenhead, 1982) pp. 173-193.

[12] Gurd, J.R., *et al.*, The Manchester Prototype Dataflow Computer, *Communications of the ACM* 28/1 (1985) pp. 34-52.

[13] Gurd, J.R., *et al.*, The Manchester Dataflow Computing System, *in*: Dongarra, J.J., (ed.), *Experimental Parallel Computing Architectures*, (North Holland, Amsterdam, 1987).

[14] Kuck, D.J. *et al.*, Dependence Graphs and Compiler Optimisations, *Proceedings 8th Symposium on Principles of Programming Languages* (ACM, 1981) pp. 207-218.

[15] McGraw, J.R. *et al.*, SISAL - Streams and Iteration in a Single-Assignment Language, *Language Reference Manual* (Lawrence Livermore National Laboratory, Livermore CA, 1983).

[16] Miller, R.E. and Rutledge, J.D., Generating a Data Flow Model of a Program, *IBM Technical Disclosure Bulletin* 8/11 (1966) pp. 1550-1553.

[17] Sargeant, J. and Kirkham, C.C., Stored Data Structures on the Manchester Dataflow Machine, *Proceedings 13th Annual Symposium on Computer Architecture* (ACM, 1986) pp. 235-242.

[18] Shimada, T. *et al.*, Evaluation of a Prototype Data Flow Processor of the SIGMA-1 for Scientific Computations, *Proceedings 13th Annual Symposium on Computer Architecture* (ACM, 1986) pp. 226-234.

[19] Skedzielewski, S. and Glauert, J.R.W., IF1 - An Intermediate Form for Applicative Languages, *Reference Manual M-170* (Lawrence Livermore National Laboratory, 1985).

[20] Skedzielewski, S. and Welcome, M., Data Flow Graph Optimisation in IF1, *Lecture Notes in Computer Science* 201 (1986) pp. 17-34.

[21] Treleaven, P.C., *et al.*, Data-Driven and Demand-Driven Computer Architecture, *ACM Computing Surveys* 14/1 (1982) pp.93-143.

[22] Veen, A.H., Reconciling Dataflow Machines and Conventional Languages, *Lecture Notes in Computer Science* 111 (1981) pp. 127-140.

[23] Watson, I., Dataflow Architectures and Performance, *in*: Chambers, F.B., *et al.*, (eds.), *Distributed Computing* (Academic Press, London, 1984) pp. 21-32.

Parallel Systems and Computation
G. Paul and G.S. Almasi (Editors)

BUILDING AND BINDING SYSTEMS WITH TRANSPUTERS

Dr Chris JESSHOPE

Dept of Electronics and Information Engineering
The University
Southampton
SO9 5NH

This paper investigates some of the major issues in parallel computer design; the need for parallelism and the problems of scaling and communications. In particular it gives an introduction to the use of the INMOS Transputer and Occam as building blocks for highly parallel systems and as a glue for binding other systems in a formal and consistent framework. Two projects are described, which illustrate these two aspects of the Transputers use.

1. PARALLELISM - WHO NEEDS IT?

Recent advances in both semiconductor and computer technologies have enabled parallelism to be used as a viable technique to obtain high performance at a modest cost, in a wide range of computing systems. Before we explore these recent trends however, let us first understand why; for if, as is generally agreed, programming concurrent systems is more complex than programming sequential systems, then the programmer certainly does not need it. Who then does?

Systems designers need parallelism, as a technique to improve systems performance. We now are in an era, where the basic circuit technology speed can no longer provide the order of magnitude performance increase that the user has come to expect every five years. Technologists are approaching fundamental physical limitations, which mean that only diminishing returns in speed of operation may be expected from new generations of integrated circuits. For example, consider the improvements in basic clock speed for a range of similar architectures designed by Seymour Cray. The CDC 7600 in the late 1960s had a clock of 27.5 ns, but the following generations of machines (Cray 1 12.5 ns and Cray 2 4 ns) have failed even to double the clock rate every 5 years. The performance trend is still there, but it has been obtained by parallelism and not clock speed.

Speed of light is the major limitation, and although the trend has been to more compact implementations to minimise its impact, there are other physical constraints, which limit this process. Examples are fine line definition and power dissipation. Another solution has been to use relatively slow but dense VLSI chips and to increase performance by processing in breadth. This use of fast "on chip" processing combined with great breadth, is the philosophy advocated by INMOS with its Tansputer [1]. Unbounded parallelism however, does lead to problems. In particular a loss of communication bandwidth between distant processors, which is one of the issues addressed in this paper.

VLSI chip designers also need parallelism, to enable the efficient exploitation of the massive complexity that is to be found in these circuits. The gate, traditionally the measure of complexity of a system, is being replaced in VLSI circuits by the wire, which is adding both delay and area to integrated circuits. Parallelism provides some solutions to the problems facing silicon designers, by introducing regularity of structure and of interconnect. Current VLSI circuits contain more than a million artifacts, and in the near future it will be possible to construct large, highly complex systems, as single monolithic circuits. These circuits may well contain in excess of one billion artifacts, and without the regular structure introduced through parallelism, would be almost impossible to design. Figure 1 illustrates this with a schematic floorplan of the RPA chip, described later in this paper. Although the processors here are simple, in five years time they could be of Transputer complexity for example.

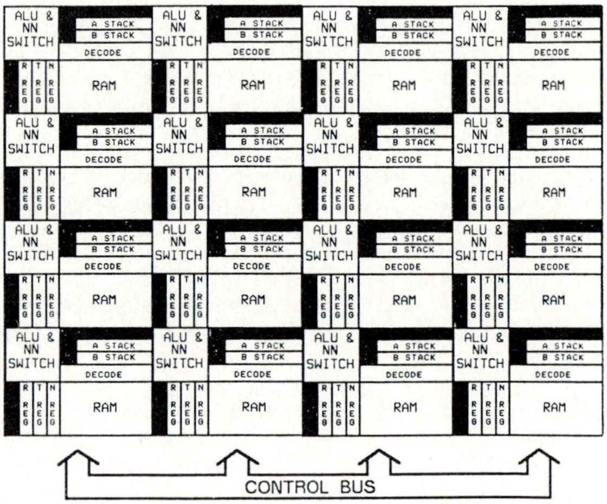

Figure 1
Floorplan of the RPA processor array chip

2. COMMUNICATIONS IN PARALLEL SYSTEMS

Communications play an important role in all well designed systems. The communications bottleneck in a conventional processor is typically the processor to memory interface, which is usually the off chip interface. Communications not surprisingly can also limit the performance of parallel machines, although here it arises in processor to processor communications. Moreover this problem is fundamental, and although it can be moved up and down the systems hierarchy, it will not go away. For example, we can trade chip and wiring complexity in a fully switched system against the large diameter of a static network.

In the latter case, when processing a partitioned data structure, one that is shared between the processors in the system, then only in the special case where each partition of the data structure is independent, will no communications be required between processors. More generally data must be shared between processors in the system and in many problems, the communications complexity can dominate the complexity of the algorithm. For example, in sorting or computing matrix products, each element in the resulting data structure requires information from all other elements in the original structures.

Such problems with global communications properties scale rather unfavourably with the extent of parallelism in the system, unless the connectivity between processors reflects that between partitions of the data structure. The Transputer for example, has four links, which could implement a 2-D grid of processors, a perfect shuffle exchange network, a butterfly network, or other topologies[2,3]. However in all cases, if the data partitioning does not match the network, then communication bandwidth will be degraded in relation to the processing rate of the system, in proportion to the diameter of the network. The diameter of the networks above varies from $\log_2 n$ to $n^{1/2}$. On these applications therefore, performance will not scale linearly with processors added to the system.

The technique which avoids this unfavourable scaling is to allow arbitrary permutations to be established between processors, using a cross-bar switch or its equivalent. Although the latter has many advantages, and allows an arbitrary scaling of parallelism, the costs of such a switch will tend to grow with the square of the number of processors in the system. The costs of the fixed networks however, scale linearly with the number of processors added to the system.

3. THE TRANSPUTER AND OCCAM

The Transputer family of products from INMOS are programmable VLSI components, that support concurrency. They combine a RISC processor, memory, and Transputer to Transputer communications. The latter are implemented over simple bit-serial circuits, enabling many such interfaces to be provided on a single chip, without incuring an excessive chip pin-out. Currently the Transputers available include a 32 bit processor with a 32 bit multiplexed address/data bus, a 16 bit processor with 16 bit address and data busses and a disc controller chip.

Two further products will shortly be added to these, a graphics (blitter) chip, and a floating point version of the 32 bit processor.

In all products, a range of speeds is available, currently up to 20 MHz internal operation. One unique feature of the Transputer products however, is that the external clock rates are maintained at 5 MHz for all parts. This greatly simplifies engineering and allows a simple chip replacement upgrade. This will also be true of the floating point version.

Transputers are designed to implement the programming language Occam [4] very efficiently, and although they will also provide efficient implementation of most modern languages, concurrency in Transputer systems is only available through Occam. Occam programs comprise processes, which are connected by unbuffered communications channels to form a network. Processes can be instructed to execute in sequence or in parallel. If the latter is chosen, then all communication between processes must be via the channels, as no shared variables are allowed between parallel processes.

All processes are constructed from three basic processes; namely input, output and assignment. Input and output are used to communicate between concurrent processes, with the input output pair across a channel being formally equivalent to an assignment, plus a synchronising event between those processes. What is more, this is the **only** synchronisation primitive implemented in the language. The model of concurrency implemented in Occam is heavily influenced by Hoare's CSP [5,6].

In any parallel system that relies on synchronisation between co-operating processes, each operating in its own time, there is the danger of an inefficient utilisation of processor resourses. The solution to this is to virtualise the execution of concurrent processes, so that more than one process can be executed concurrently on a single processor. In this way if one process is awaiting a synchronising event, then there are other processes that may compete for the processor's resources. Where more than one Occam process is running on a single Transputer, then the Occam channels are implemented by moving data within the Transputer's memory, using the same synchronising protocol as is applied to the link. Moreover the same Transputer orders are used for both situations, allowing precompiled code to have a channel assigned to a link or a memory location.

An Occam program is configured when Occam channels are assigned to the links on a physical Transputer. When this is done, the Occam program provides a static process structure, which at some level of its hierarchy is mapped onto the network of Transputers. Occam programs thus provide code for executing on Transputers, as well as information defining the network connecting them.

4. THE INMOS LINK

The operation and performance of the INMOS link is fundamental to the effective exploitation of the Transputer. All Transputer products will support communications over this asynchronous point-to-point connection, with speeds of 5,10 and 20 Mbits/sec.

Each link implements two Occam channels in opposite directions over a three wire TTL level circuit. Communications over these links are controlled by autonomous controllers, which have DMA access to the Transputer's memory. Four bi-directional communications, and processing can therefore proceed concurrently on the same Transputer chip. However, unless the messages passed over the links are large, a true overlap will not be possible, as each transfer will use a small but finite amount of processor resource. If the link bandwidth is measured as a function of message length, the classic pipeline model is seen, with a start-up without transmission, followed by a constant through-put. The granularity of a message therefore modifies the bandwidth seen. It must also be remembered that the start-up period also degrades processor performance, to such an extent that many concurrent small transfers may saturate the processor.

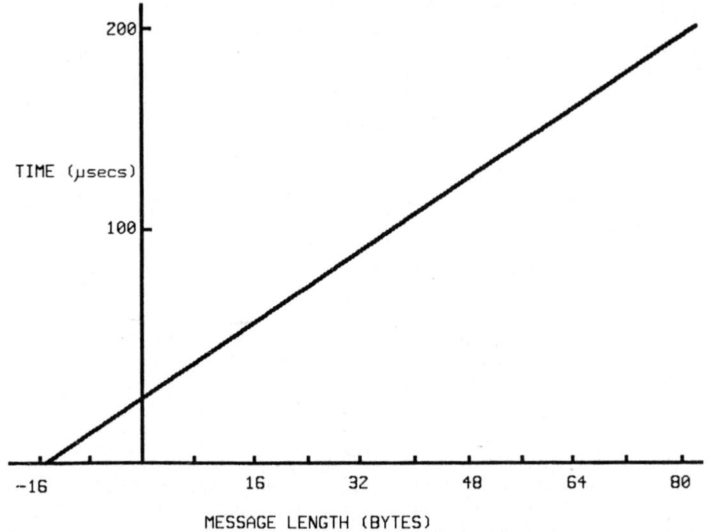

Figure 2
Performance of the INMOS link
(10MHz bit rate, 12.5MHz processor clock)

Figure 2 shows the time required to tramsmit a message of a given size on a transputer with 10 Mhz links and 12.5 Mhz processor, as found in the first T414 Transputer products. The maximum or asymptotic transfer rate is approximately 1/2 Mbyte/sec, which can be achieved in both directions over the link. A half performance message length of 13 bytes is also observed. Various processor and link rates will modify these observed parameters, with the startup time being proportional to the processor clock and the asymptotic bandwidth being to a first order, proportional to the link rate. Thus on current best silicon (20 Mhz processor and 20 MHz links), an asymptotic bandwidth of 1 Mbyte/sec should be seen, with a half bandwidth message length of 16 bytes.

The link protocol uses an 11 bit data packet, containing a start bit, a bit to distinguish data and acknowledge packets, eight data bits and a stop bit. The acknowledge packet is two bits long and contains a start and stop bit. The protocol allows for a data byte to be acknowledged by the receiving Transputer on receipt of the second (distinguishing) bit. This would allow for continuous transmission of data packets from the transmitting Transputer, providing that the signal delay was small compared with the packet transmission time.

This pre-acknowledgment of data packets is not implemented on current T414 Transputers, and an acknowledge packet will not be sent until the complete data packet has been received. However with this protocol implemented, a maximum theoretical transfer rate of approaching 2 Mbytes/sec could be obtained, although there would be degradation on bidirectional traffic, as data and acknowledge packets are interleaved.

5. TECHNIQUES FOR EXPLOITING PARALLELISM

The parameters on link communications given above, establish the granularity with which a program or its data may be partitioned for distribution on a network of Transputers. Assuming of course, that the program requires communications. Having established the granularity, there are a number of different techniques that can be applied to exploit concurrency:

5.1. The Processor Farm

This is one of the simplest methods of exploiting parallelism. It can be applied to an applications in which discreet bundles of processing can be "farmed out" to any available processor. These processes may well be identical, but must be independent. For example, in experimental high energy physics, vast amounts of data are produced from experiments. This data must be analysed for significant events. Each event may require a large amount of processing, which can be allocated to a given processor taken from a pool of processors. The allocation would typically be performed by a supervisor process. The requirement for efficient operation is therefore to have independent units of processing that are significant compared with the overhead of distributing the work and collating the results. There is still a data transmission requirement, which must be overlapped with the processing activity. The load on the supervisor will also limit the granularity of the unit of computation.

5.2. Algorithmic Parallelism

In this technique, a program or process is partitioned and are distributed across a network of processors. Each partition executes in parallel on its own data, or may may be pipelined, if there are any sequential constraints for example. The network of Transputers required for this technique must ideally reflect the data flow of the given algorithm. It should in fact form a static data flow graph of the algorithm. The granularity of the distributed processes could theoretically be at the level of a single operation, but would normally be determined by the ratio of time required for processing and communications. This is a highly effective way to program the Transputer, especially if the code and data required in each Transputer is small compared with its on chip memory, for benefits from its greater speed will be obtained. This technique has often been exploited in special purpose hardware for example in digital signal processing. However given a programmable component, such as the Transputer, many applications could exploit common hardware. The problem is, that unless the network accurately reflects the data flow graph of the application, the granularity of the distributed processes will become unacceptably large. This is due to the additional latency, larger processor overhead, and the lower bandwith, associated with data forwarding between non-adjacent Transputers.

5.3. Geometric Parallelism

The final technique for exploiting replication, involves a partitioning of data, rather than code. If a given algorithm can process a large data structure concurrently, then it may be partitioned over a network of Transputers. In this case, the algorithm normally used to process that data, would simply be replicated on every Transputer in the network. The algorithm would then be applied to the local partition of the data structure, together with any data communicated from other partitions. It is important for the reasons outlined above, that the underlying network reflect the communications patterns required between partitions of the data structure.

6. THE SUPERNODE - A SWITCHED CLUSTER OF TRANSPUTERS

The Supernode shown in figure 3 is configuration for optimising resources, especially communications, in Transputer based systems. It may directly exploit all of the above parallel processing techniques. The Supernode is a cluster of Transputers connected by switching circuits over their links, so that any network of Transputers may be realised. The square law cost argument applied against fully connecting processors in a systems has a small constant in Transputer systems, as the links require only a narrow port on the switching circuit (2 bits per link). Advantages from direct connections between communicating processes result from increased bandwidth as well as lower processor overhead.

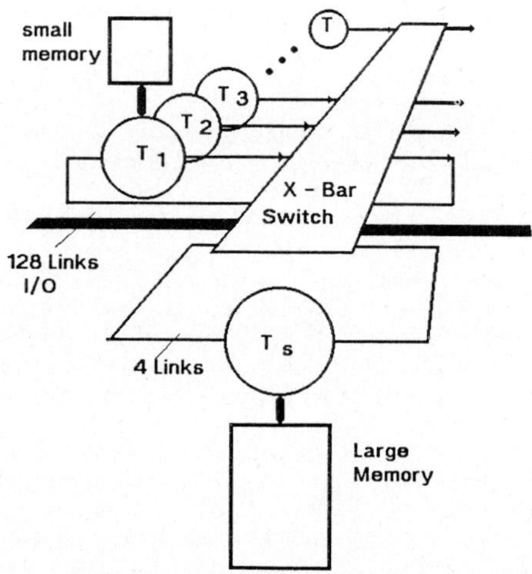

Figure 3
The structure of a single supernode

The Supernode can be considered as a Super-Transputer, for it obeys an Occam programming model, with the Occam providing Transputer orders for each component and instructions to set the switching circuits, which realise the required network of connections. Thus Occam is used to define procedure and structure.

A Supernode would typically comprise some 10-50 Transputers and would provide a powerful, standalone workstation. Larger machines can be constructed using the Supernode as a unit of replication, in regular arrays for example. Because the supernode has far more links available than the Transputer, more richly interconnected graphs may be used. Moreover by equating a Supernodes to a Transputer, we have defined a recursive strategy for constructing Transputer systems of almost unlimited size. Such a machine is being developed at Southampton University within an Esprit funded collaborative project. It will comprise some 300 Transputers, capable of being configured into an arbitrary Transputer graph and should give a performance of about a 1/4 Gflop.

7. PROCESS vs STRUCTURE PARALLELISM

In considering control and implementation, there are two methodologies for exploiting parallelism; structure parallelism and process parallelism. The Transputer and Occam efficiently exploit the later. Programming techniques for the two methodologies may be very similar and many algorithms would map equally well onto either. However for distinction, assume that structure parallelism is defined at the granularity of a single operation, and that the operations are carried out on data structures, as if simultaneously, over every element of that structure. This implies synchronisation at the instruction level. As we have seen above, process parallelism is usually defined over larger grain sizes and synchronisation between the concurrent instruction streams is performed by some explicit mechanism, a communication in Occam. Because each process involves its own instruction stream and state, an overhead is required when implementing a high degree of concurrency. The overhead is produced by the requirement to establish that instruction stream, and to maintain it state during process swapping.

Structure parallelism is used in many architectures, usually, but not exclusively in SIMD machines. APL [7] was one of the first languages to express such parallelism, which has been adopted as a basis for many later machine specific languages, such as DAP FORTRAN. Later languages such as the proposed FORTRAN 8X, allow the programmer to express the structure and concurrency inherent in an algorithm, rather than that of the hardware. The use of virtually unbounded parallelism in this approach does not incur the same penalty in overheads as found in process parallelism, as a transformation from parallel to sequential can be made at compile time for a given target architecture, and any ordering imposed can be such as to optimise access patterns into the memory system. A temporary storage requirement arises from the need to perform all operations as if simultaneously, so that complex expressions require array valued temporaries.

8. THE RECONFIGURABLE PROCESSOR ARRAY

The RPA is an architecture designed for structure processing, it is a processor array, which uses many simple processors, but which can adapt its physical structure in a limited way to accomodate a variety of data structures. This is also an optimisation on communications. Thus the RPA is designed to support structure processing over the widest range of data structures. It is like the DAP and Connection Machine, in that it is an array of single bit synchronous processing elements with a common micro-controller. It is not a true SIMD machine however, as local modification of an instructions is allowed by distributing some of the control word fields across the array.

It is well known that a synchronous structure such as this is limited in the size to which it can be extended, unless clock frequencies are reduced. There is therefore an optimal size of RPA, which will depend on the characteristics of the implementation and packaging technologies. The current architecture will support arrays of up to 256 by 256, with 16 processors per VLSI chip. The size of an RPA system however, is not limited by the size of the optimal synchronous system block, for RPA systems can be further expanded using process parallelism. The RPA exists within a Transputer's memory system as active memory, and processes executed on the RPA can be considered as extending the Transputer's instruction set in an Occam programming model. Another way of expressing this, is that the process parallelism of the Transputer and Occam is used to bind together many synchronous systems capable of efficiently executing structure parallelism.

8.1. The RPA Processing Element

The RPA array is constructed from a very flexible processing element (PE) in a two-dimensional, four-connected latice, with wrap around at both edges. A single RPA system is illustrated in Figure 4. Ideally, in a processor array for structure processing, there should be a single processing element for each element of the data structure processed. Unfortunately there is no way of knowing a priori, how large or small a data structure will be required. Indeed the structure may vary dynamically. The RPA PE has been deigned so that the array may adapt as efficiently as possible to structures of all kinds and of all sizes

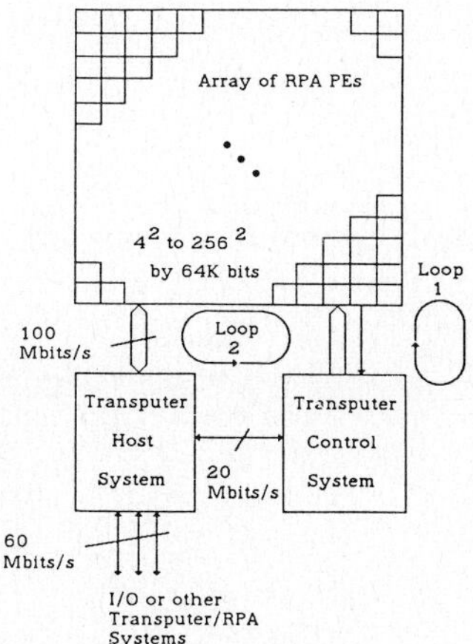

Figure 4
A single Transputer/RPA system

Data Structures larger than the array are reasonably well understood, for each processing element can process sequentially as many elements of the data structure as is required. Problems arise however, in maintaining the topology of the data structure, especially if the structure is complex. The corollary of this problem is the ability to assign more than one PE to a data structure element, and this is less well understood. In fact this represents the major departure between the RPA and other bit serial processor arrays.

The array of RPA PEs have been designed to act as a pool of virtual processors, connected according to the structure being processed. To achieve this, each PE must be considered as a bit slice of a larger processing unit, which will support a wide range of common microprocessor operations. The composite processing unit supports binary operations, a wide range of shift operations and bit parallel arithmetic operations. These processing units can be configured, dynamically if required, from any connected path of RPA PEs. The most useful configurations are closed subgraphs of the RPA array, as these support cyclic and double length shift operations in a single micro-cycle and also greatly simplify serial arithmetic, for example performing 16 bit arithmetic using 4 bit processing units.

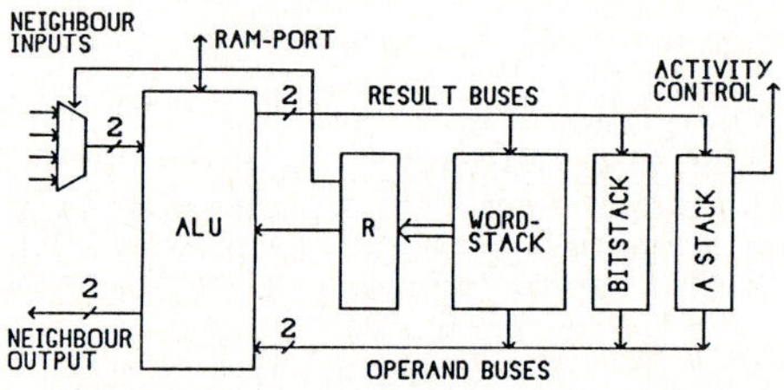

Figure 5
The RPA Processing Element

The PE has a four bus structure, as shown in Figure 4, with two operand and two result busses. The ALU provides logical and bit-serial operations, using local operands only and the neighbour select provides a means of transfering data from one PE to another. Bit-parallel arithmetic is made possible by the use of both ALU and neighbour select, which together form a fast Manchester, carry-chain adder. The key to the flexibility of the array, lies in the use of three preset control fields, which are provided in **each** PE in the array, R in Figure 4. These determine switch settings and edge effects in arithmetic and shift operations.

The storage provided in each PE is stack based. There is a bit stack and an activity stack, for storing single bits of data in a PE (words of data in a processing unit). Each comprises eight bits of data and both are identical, with the exception that the top bit of the activity stack can be used to conditionally dissable the operation of the PE. Storage is also provided for words of data in the PE (sequences of words in a processing unit). These are arranged as a stack of eight bit words in each PE, with parallel to serial and serial to parallel conversion provided by a pair of shift registers. This structure allows bit-serial (or word-serial) arithmetic to be performed, without the awkward bit reversal encountered in stack storage. Finally a single bit I/O port allows up to 64Kbits of external storage to be connected to each PE.

8.2. The RPA Control System

Processor arrays, such as the DAP and Connection Machine, generally use a single controller to control all processors in the array. This gives a very cost effective machine, by sharing a complex control mechanism between many processors. An RPA system, figure 6, departs from this control structure in two ways. Being bound by Transputers, the RPA can be considered as a MIMD system, with each "processor" containing an array of processors under SIMD control. The synchronous component of the system can therefore exploit the parallelism found in structure, such as arrays, strings, lists and trees, while the event synchronised MIMD component can exploit the irregular or independent parallelism also found in many algorithms. Secondly, as described above, each PE in a single RPA may under locally determined conditions, store or generate some or all of its control word, for use in subsequent operations. This facility maintains the advantage of fine grain synchronisation, while allowing a limited adaptability to differing processing requirements in the array.

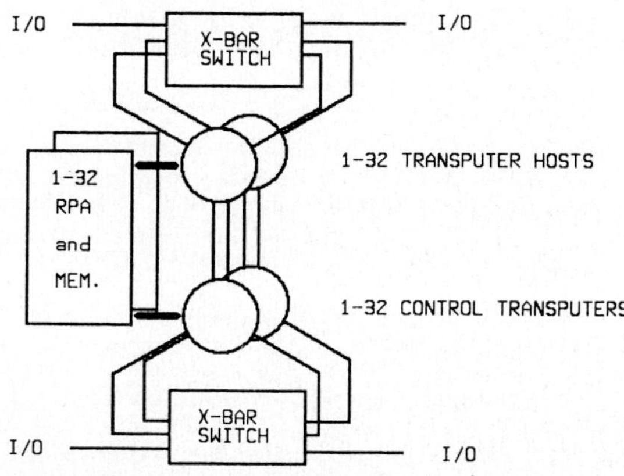

Figure 6
A Multiple Transputer/RPA system

Figure 4 shows the control structure of a single RPA, where two control loops can be identified. The first is between the array and its micro-sequencer. This is conventional; the controller supplies micro-control words and addresses to the array (a wide word data path) and receives condition signals from the array and possibly from the other devices in the system. The second control loop involves data from the array memory, which can be accessed by processes executing on the host system. This loop allows a coarser grain synchronisation that may involve events from other Transputer/RPA systems.

One of the major design goals of the RPA system has been to map this control loop into an Occam programming model, in such a way that the programmer can trade real and virtual concurrency in an application. This will allow for the code to be ported between different Transputer/RPA configurations.

9. MAPPING THE RPA CONTROL INTO AN OCCAM PROGRAMMING MODEL

The implementation alternatives in mapping the RPA control structure into Occam are determined by the granularity of processes running on the array. Should array processes be complete programs, running concurrently and perhaps communicating with the host? or should array processes be considered as indivisible extensions to the host instruction set? If we define a basic array process as being an indivisible unit of computation, so far as communication between host and array is concerned, such that the order may be modelled by the following Occam fragment,

```
-- host perception of array order
array ! something
array_process
array ? something else,
```

then any decision concerning the partitioning of control between host and array controller, is in effect a decision whether constructs containing basic array processes may be sequenced by the array controller, or by the Transputer host. (loop 1 or loop 2 in figure 3)

9.1. Autonomous Array Programs

If sequences of these basic array processes are to be determined by the array controller, allowing complete programs (processes) to run on the array, then for concurrent operation of the host and array, there must be communication between host and array, to provide the necessary synchronisation events. For example, the host may initiate action in the array and proceed. At some later stage the host and array processes synchronise by a communication and both then proceed, perhaps modifying their actions based on that communication. In this control model synchronising communications may be initiated by host or array.

If we wish to overlap processing and communication, so that efficiency is not lost in achieving synchronisation, then this model must be modified to allow both host and array to run their respective processes in parallel. To implement this model requires an array sequencer that can support multiple, concurrent processes. It would need to be interuptable, so that an array process requiring communication with the host could be suspended, while communications were proceeding, and resume on completion of the communication. However, the overheads in this process switching are large, and the microcontroller required is complex. Thus in the RPA we have opted for the alternative of indivisible array orders.

9.2. Indivisible Array Orders

This approach excludes synchronisation between processes running on the host and array, except on initiation and termination of the array. It has a number of advantages. Because there is no need for synchronisation within an array process, there is now no need for array orders to be suspended. Entry micro-routines can run to completion using a simpler micro-sequencer. Some mechanism for supporting concurrent process execution on the array is desirable however, as there may be communication, before and after each micro-routine and it is still desirable to overlap this with processing. Such parallelism may however be implemented using a single process queue, containing active processes; an interuptable sequencer would require at least two process queues, for active and suspended processes, with support for suspending and activating processes to achieve synchronisation.

Figure 7 gives a more detailed view of the Transputer control system, which contains a single multi-port process queue, through which the Transputer and micro-controller communicate. Within this implementation, array micro-code routines provide processes, which can be considered as indivisible extensions to the hosts instruction set, which map into the Occam language. PAR and SEQ constructors, and array and host processes may now be freely mixed, with communication (hidden in the example below) providing synchronising events and control flow where required.

```
-- Host/Array Process
Seq
   .
    .
     .
      Par
         host process 1
         Seq
            array process 1
            array ? something
         host process 2
         Seq
            If
               something = 'good'
                  array process 2
               true
                  array process 3
```

As well as handling virtual concurrency of array processes in a simple and efficient manner, this scheme also allows the control Transputer to look ahead in the instruction stream (subject to synchronisation), thus minimising any latency associated with the two level control structure. Sequences of array processes may be added to the process queue in the array controller and then executed from this queue in sequence by the array controller, without further intervention from the control Transputer.

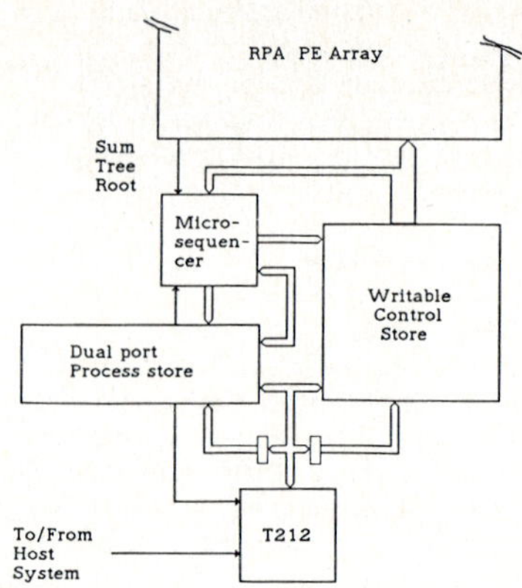

Figure 7
Implementation of the RPA control System

ACKNOWLEDGEMENTS

I would like to acknowledge the work of friends collegues and others working at Southampton and RSRE, on these two projects. Funding for the Supernode project is from the ESPRIT program, project P1085 and from the ALVEY program for the RPA project, ALV/ARCH/010/.

REFERENCES

[1] INMOS, The Transputer Reference Manual
[2] Hockney, R.W. and Jesshope, C.R. Parallel Computers (Adam Hilger, 1981)
[3] Seigel, H.J. Interconnection Networks for Parallel Processors (1985)
[4] INMOS, The Occam Programming manual (Prentice Hall, 1985)
[5] Hoare, C.A.R. Communicating sequential processes, Comm ACM 21 (1978) 666.
[6] Hoare, C.A.R. Communicating Sequential processes (Prentice Hall, 1985)
[7] Iverson, K.E. A Programming Language (Wiley, 1962)
[8] Rushton, A. and Jesshope, C.R. RPA an architecture in need of wafer scale integration, in Wafer Scale Integration (eds Jesshope and Moore, Adam Hilger, 1986) 148

SECTION 4
PERFORMANCE ANALYSIS, MODELING AND APPLICATIONS

Parallel Systems and Computation
G. Paul and G.S. Almasi (Editors)

Performance Evaluation of Supercomputers and Their Applications

Joanne L. Martin

IBM T. J. Watson Research Center
P.O. Box 218
Yorktown Heights, New York 10598

The proliferation of new architectures designed to enhance significantly current computational speeds has added a new dimension to the requirements of performance evaluation. This necessitates the analysis of applications as well as architectures, and the study of how to conform one to the other. In this paper, two specific applications are examined relative to their performance on (1) a shared memory vector architecture, (2) a shared memory scalar architecture with vectors, and (3) a distributed memory system. Application characteristics and performance results are presented for sequential and parallel implementations of the problems. Additionally, from the comparison of the parallel implementations on the shared memory vs. the distributed memory systems, it is observed that erroneous interpretations can result if communication overhead is ignored when estimating the performance of multiprocessors.

1.0 Introduction

The evaluation of supercomputer performance has received increased attention during the last decade, not only because of the extremely high cost of acquiring these systems, but also as a consequence of the proliferation of different architectural types designed to enhance dramatically the available computational speed. In reviewing the research activities and future needs in this area, a special Committee of the U.S. National Research Council recently concluded that there is a need to develop new analytical techniques that can address the special requirements of the community of supercomputer users, as well as to examine the applications to be executed on this class of machines for their contribution to overall system performance [1].

Traditional mainframe computers are based on the von Neumann structure as the single computational model. In this model, instructions are executed sequentially and are controlled by a program counter. The performance of such sequential uniprocessors has been well understood, primarily in reference to business or commercial workloads, and the expected performance can be estimated with high confidence levels if one is given specific parameters that relate to the environment and total system structure [2]. In evaluating the performance of sequential uniprocessors, emphasis has been placed on understanding the throughput, response time, and system bottlenecks - the goal being to provide a balanced system design and to allow for optimal user productivity (where productivity is defined mainly in terms of system response time and throughput rates).

Although a balanced system is still important, absolute speed is the ultimate goal of supercomputing, and this goal positions a magnifying glass over the central processing unit(s). The emphasis has shifted from system throughput as a measure of performance to the execution speed of individual problems. Applications that require execution on supercomputers (most often scientific in nature) are typically computation intensive and demand the maximum speeds achievable from the CPU(s). Consequently, when analyzing supercomputer performance, it is not sufficient to characterize a workload as being made up of classes that average specified units of service time within the processing unit(s). Rather, it is exigent to understand the quality of the individual time units. That is, although two very different applications might be grouped within the same job class because both demand high CPU utilization over the same time period, one of the applications could unfortunately outperform the other by several orders of magnitude during the time that it holds the resource. This distinction is a critical consideration in the development of approaches to supercomputer performance evaluation; in its absence we can predict characteristics of system performance (where the CPU is one resource within a total network) but cannot predict the quality or the performance of the execution time spent in the CPU.

The emergence of radically different processor architectures has exacerbated the need to evaluate approaches for performance evaluation. Some architectures remain tied to the basic von Neumann model, in that they depend on the computational structure dictated by a single, sequential program counter. Enhancements within this context include the addition of multiple functional units and pipes, and vector processing capabilities. The model of execution is not changed significantly, but the potential range of performance is expanded. With the gain in potential processing power comes a corresponding increase in potential bottlenecks. Whereas the main bottlenecks within the scalar, sequential processing system result from the time required to perform memory accesses relative to the time to perform arithmetic computations as well as from the overhead exhibited by I/O processing, vector and pipeline architectures add bottlenecks defined in terms of vector or pipeline startup times. Although vector processing helps to reduce the impact of memory access time for regular and vectorizable references to memory, the logic involved in beginning the necessary instructions introduces a possible penalty for vectors that are not structured well with respect to the memory system of the machine.

Supercomputers currently being examined by the research community (and, in many cases, being released commercially) represent divergent architectures - some incorporate vector, pipeline, and array structures into a basic von Neumann structure, whereas others employ more revolutionary techniques to enhance performance. The less radical departures include the Cray X-MP line of processors, the Cray 2, ETA10, IBM 3090, Cedar, and RP3, all of which are based on a common memory structure, with multiple processors implying multiple program counters [3-8]. The bottlenecks in these systems include, in most cases, the bottlenecks of previous generations, with additional overhead resulting from processor synchronization and communication. Dataflow architectures, the Connection Machine, Hypercubes, and GF11 represent significant departures from the von Neumann style that will require the rethinking of basic principles of algorithm design or implementation in order to achieve the performance goals of today's scientists [9-12].

Because speed is the ultimate goal, it is important to limit the cost associated with various bottlenecks as much as possible. Largely to this end, each novel architecture is optimized, or at least found to be most suitable, for a particular model of computation. As the spectrum of possible models expands, it has become necessary to limit that expansion (or at least our analysis of it) by determining classes of applications and architectures, and then by assessing the relationships among the various classes and the corresponding impacts on performance [13].

In this paper, the performance of two applications is examined on several systems, focusing attention on the need to understand the types of parallelism available in existing implementations of algorithms, as well as the need to fit algorithms to architectures according to their computational characteristics. The results presented here are not meant to provide a benchmark of the individual systems, but rather, to enable a comparison among certain classes of machine organization. The applications are abbreviated versions of large production codes, and were selected to stress the dimensions of the architectural designs.

2.0 The Applications

2.1 Overview

Performance attained by a system depends on the implementations of the individual applications that comprise the system's workload. Two documented examples emphasize the extent of this dependence. In [14], information regarding the Los Alamos National Laboratory workload was presented and analyzed. For one of the production codes considered, measurements were made on two different problem setups. Specifically, depending on the input to the program, either of two paths could be followed through the code to achieve the desired computational result. From the physicists' perspective, the different paths represented distinct computational methods, one a Monte Carlo solution technique, and the other an approach reliant on more traditional methods of hydrodynamics. From the perspective of the performance analyst, the first path yielded a computational rate of 2 MFLOPS, whereas the alternate path computed at a rate of nearly 20 MFLOPS. This difference should not be viewed as an indictment of the system on which the application was being executed, but rather, as indicative of a possible mismatch between the architecture and the application.

Another example concerns the development of a rather new technique that is attracting considerable attention and debate [15]. Computational fluid dynamics problems traditionally have used the numerical solution of Navier-Stokes equations [16]. Recently, cellular automata have been applied to the solution of these problems with reported success [17]. Although the cellular automata approach is still under investigation, it provides considerable hope for the utility of massively parallel computers in fluid dynamics - a claim less plausible for the more traditional techniques [18]. The distinction between these techniques presents a separate dilemma for the performance analyst. The Navier-Stokes implementation can well be measured in terms of attained MFLOPS because the calculations are dominated by floating point arithmetic. Cellular automata computations involve almost no floating point calculations, which means that the basic rate cannot be measured in MFLOPS. A comparison between the two implementations requires a common metric, still to be developed. As an indicator of performance, speed must be measured relative to the problem rather than to its implementation for a comparison between computational techniques to be possible.

In this section, two specific applications that were analyzed and measured on three architectural models are described. Here, an application refers to a particular implementation of a more general scientific problem. Whereas the original problem statement is independent of any notion of machine architecture, the final implementation reflects a number of choices that have been made, many of which are influenced specifically by the target architecture.

Both of the applications that are considered here are benchmark versions of large production codes. ESN is from the Los Alamos National Laboratory [19], and VA3D from NASA/Ames [20]. Although much of the computational structure remains in these versions, it should be noted that, particularly in the case of the VA3D code, the array dimensions in the benchmark version are considerably smaller than they would be in the production version. This discrepancy will be seen to have a profound impact on the achievable vector lengths, as well as on the possibility of combining vectorization with parallelization.

2.2 ESN

The physical problem of interest is in the area of transport physics. The mathematical model chosen to solve this problem involves the solution of the transport equation. The author, B. Wienke, notes that a choice has been made regarding the solution of that equation [21]. Whereas a typical method of solution involves finite difference or finite element techniques on fixed or iteratively defined meshes, this implementation discretizes some of the independent variables by the discrete ordinates method and then solves the resulting system of uncoupled ordinary linear differential equations. The numerical method chosen to affect the quadratures is an adaptive Newton-Cotes 7-point routine. ESN, derived from the SNEX code at LANL, is the final high-level language encoding of the application for the choices that have been made.

2.3 VA3D

VA3D is a three-dimensional, implicit, approximate factored algorithm [22] solving the EULER equations or the Navier-Stokes equations with a thin layer approximation. Either laminar or turbulent boundary layer computations are performed about an axisymetric, hemispherical-nosed projectile. The approximate factored algorithm is a particular form of the Alternating Direction, Implicit (ADI) algorithm after Douglas and Gunn [23]. The equations are written in arbitrary curvilinear coordinates retaining the strong conservation law form. The approximate factorization results in three one-dimensional operators, each of which contains derivatives in only one spatial direction. Central differencing yields block tri-diagonal matrices which are inverted in each spatial direction. The boundary conditions, right hand side operator and smoothing are performed explicitly.

The implicit integration requires three sweeps through the entire data base, with a block tri-diagonal matrix inverted for each point in the plane normal to the sweep direction. The solution in the sweep direction is cyclically recursive.

The decoupling of spatial coordinates provides the motivation for the consideration of parallel processing. It should be noted that the decoupling is a feature of the approximate factorization, and is not associated with the central differencing scheme. Thus any algorithm exhibiting spatial decoupling should allow the use of the same sort of parallelism.

3.0 The Architectures

3.1 Overview and Considerations

Just as the choice of implementation effects the performance of an application on a system, the architectural design of the system also contributes to the suitability of particular implementations and to the performance attained. As architectural designs have progressed from scalar to vector to parallel, new capabilities have been introduced. If used well, each new capability has the potential to improve performance and to accelerate processing speed. Each new capability carries with it, nevertheless, a new overhead - and if the capabilities cannot be used effectively, the price of enhanced computational power is the potential to fall further and further from the peak performance of a system. Although it is very tempting to quote and rely on the peak processing speeds of supercomputers (as often advertised in the popular media) there is rarely a direct correspondence between peak rate as derived from clock rate and number of pipes and/or functional units and actual net processing rate as measured on major applications [24].

Any system will have an overhead associated with accessing memory. Measurements made on a Cray-1 have demonstrated the rate of execution of a real matrix multiplication to range from 37 MFLOPS to 110 MFLOPS, where the only program change involved unrolling the loops in the Fortran program. Loop unrolling caused the ratio of floating point instructions to memory access instructions to increase from 0.7 to 1.9 [25]. Hockney has characterized the cost of this overhead in terms of $f_{1/2}$ - the relative cost of memory accesses to computation [26]. Its effects can be reduced by careful user programming in some cases, but more often by exploiting a sophisticated compiler [27]. In other cases, high efficiency can be achieved best by resorting to assembly language programming, whereby specific register allocation minimizes the number of memory references required to complete a computation.

Vector processors have the additional overhead associated with setting up and initiating vectors. This also has been represented by Hockney, as $n_{1/2}$, the vector length at which half the peak performance for a particular vector function is attained [28]. Measurements of vector startup times are based on constructing appropriate loops around basic operations, executing the loops for a variety of vector lengths, and using a least squares analysis to determine the constant factors represented by the results. An example of this method appears in [29].

For a parallel system, new overhead is introduced in the form of communication costs among processors, and other multitasking overhead that is required for synchronization of processes. The overhead for communicating among processors is given by Hockney as $s_{1/2}$, and represents the relative cost of communicating results to that of computing them [30]. When evaluating performance of parallel systems, communication costs cannot be ignored; especially when evaluating the difference between performance of an algorithm on a shared-memory multiprocessor and on a common-memory system, the contribution of data transmittal time is a very significant parameter.

In this paper, three systems are considered as a testbed for an analysis of the applications described above. Detailed machine descriptions are available for each of these systems [31-33]. As advocated in [13], the following descriptions are limited to the gross specifications that permit system classification.

3.2 Cray X-MP

The Cray X-MP/48 is a 4-processor shared-memory system in which each of the processors is a powerful vector processor. Measurements have indicated that the cost of using vectors on the X-MP is low [30]. That is, the vector start-up time is small for most vector operations, which implies that short vectors will yield good results. Similarly, there is low sensitivity to the stride of vector operations, as long as it is fixed and not a power of 2. The X-MP/48 has 8 Million Words of main memory, and is not a cache-based system. It is a register-based system. There are 8 vector registers, each of which holds 64 elements of 64 bits each. Each processor permits the simultaneous transfer of three memory items, two loads and one store between the main memory and the vector registers. This design feature, together with the fast memory available, implies a smaller overhead for memory accesses than existed on the Cray-1, which had only one path to memory. The operating system used for these tests was CTSS, as run at Los Alamos National Laboratory [34]. Multitasking is available through a set of library routines.

3.3 IBM 3090 Model 400

Like the Cray X-MP, the architecture of the IBM 3090 Model 400 consists of 4 tightly-coupled processors. Each of the four processors is a strong scalar processor that can be augmented by an attached, but integrated vector feature [35-36]. The vector feature on the 3090 provides performance enhancements for suitable applications, for an incremental increase in cost. There are 8 (or 16) vector registers, each holding 128 elements can supply up to two 64-bit (or 32-bit) operands per machine cycle. Furthermore, the 3090 system is cache-based. The fast memory of the cache implies a small overhead for accessing data stored in the cache, an advantage lost for data not resident in the cache. Measurements of the 3090 indicate that vector start-up times and vector stride considerations for data not stored in the cache are more significant to performance than in the case of the Cray system [19]. The real memory structure of the 3090 includes one 64KByte cache per processor, up to 128MBytes (16 MWords) of high speed memory, and up to 256 MBytes (32 MWords) of extended memory. A total of 2 GBytes of memory is addressable in the virtual memory system. The larger memory allows for the execution of some problems in central memory that would require specified I/O on a system with less real memory, and provides a system-managed extended memory for problems too large to fit into the main allocation. The tests reported here were executed under the MVS operating system, and the parallel results were produced by utilizing the MTF, a Fortran enhancement that provides a set of library routines to handle the parallelization [37].

3.4 lCAP (loosely Coupled Array of Processors)

Developed at IBM Kingston by E. Clementi and his colleagues, the experimental lCAP system consists of an IBM mainframe host computer, and a number of attached FPS array processors [38]. Because this system is still under development, its components change from time to time. The configuration on which these measurements were based consisted of only the host and array processors, and did not include the shared memory or fast bus connections that have been introduced more recently into the system. The intent of this analysis is not to benchmark the lCAP system, but rather, to view it as a model of a distributed architecture, whereby communication among processors takes place across fairly slow (1-3 MBytes per second) channels. Although this may be argued to be an exaggerated model of a distributed system (i.e., the communication time is very large relative to the computation time), the point considered is served well by the exaggeration. The operating system in this case is a hybrid of those provided on the IBM and FPS systems that comprise lCAP. Special routines have been created to enable parallelization in the master, and are described elsewhere [38].

4.0 Results and Discussion

Using techniques described in [25], measurements were made on the programs ESN and several versions of VA3D on the Cray X-MP. Dynamic instruction counts were tabulated, and are summarized in Table I. Because the measurements were made on the X-MP, they cannot be considered independently of the system architecture. For example, because the length of the vector registers on the X-MP is 64, the maximum vector length that can be measured is 64. Beyond that, vectors will be strip-mined and a vector of length 100 would be tabulated as two vectors, one of length 64, and the other of length 36. The instruction profile should be viewed as a snapshot of the execution of an implementation of an application on a given system. Some of the characteristics, such as relative significance of floating point operations to other instruction types, numbers of floating point operations, and vector length statistics, are extrapolated to other systems more as a trend than as absolute values. For VA3D, three serial versions of the code were analyzed to measure the impact of vector length and stride variations. VA3DO refers to the original vectorized version of VA3D, VA3DLV is a long vector version, and VA3DSR is a stride-reduced version. A glossary of terms can be found in the Appendix.

Table I. Application Statistics (as measured on the Cray X-MP; counts are in millions)

	ESN	VA3DO	VA3DLV	VA3DSR
Total Instructions	929.6	277.5	260.6	315.7
Elementwise	930.4	1320.6	1428.0	1371.3
Elementwise FLOPs	148.6	516.3	540.9	516.2
Percent	16	39	38	38
Number of Jumps	41.4	9.7	17.4	9.9
Percent of Total Instructions	4.5	3.5	6.7	3.1
Percent of Elementwise Total	4.5	0.7	1.2	0.7
Elementwise Loads	147.6	415.0	448.4	413.3
Percent	15.9	31.4	31.4	30.1
Elementwise Stores	58.5	162.2	207.9	174.4
Percent	6.3	12.3	14.6	12.7
Elementwise % Vector	0	82	83	80
Dominant Vector Length	<10	28	>64	28
Required Storage (in MWords)	.03	.6	3.3	2.6

The measurements of application statistics summarized in Table I demonstrate that ESN is a scalar code that consumes a small amount of real memory and has a considerable percentage of floating point calculations relative to other types of instructions. In contrast, VA3D is a highly vectorized program, consumes a moderate amount of storage in its original form and a larger amount in its modified forms, and is dominated by floating point calculations and the corresponding memory loads and stores. Table II presents, for each program, the number of vectors executed in four ranges of vector length. ESN had a small number of vectors, and these few were clustered in the 1-10 category.

Table II. Counts of Vector Lengths

Vector Length	ESN	VA3DO	VA3DLV	VA3DSR
1-10	66800	271400	544060	258710
11-30	192	39012407	5646217	37802086
31-63	0	0	628830	0
64	5986	3628	15834967	1827

The distinct characteristics of these codes can account for their performance on different architectures, as shown in Table III. For example, the ESN code is representative of a class of applications that is inherently scalar and therefore maps well onto a system, such as the IBM 3090, in which the primary architectural emphasis is on scalar execution. The term architecture used here refers to the broad descriptive definition constructed in [13]. The benefit of this emphasis is seen from the execution time measurements of ESN on the IBM 3090 and the Cray X-MP. Although the clock rate of the X-MP is roughly twice the clock rate of the 3090 (9.5 nsec vs. 18.5 nsec) the execution times differ by less than one percent. In contrast, the strength of the X-MP vector architecture is evident from the timing measurements of the highly vectorized code, VA3D. In its original implementation, this code has fairly short vector lengths combined with large strides. The X-MP is insensitive to either of these points, although both pose performance problems for the 3090. A slight revision of the implementation enhances the 3090 vector performance and demonstrates a significant improvement over 3090 scalar performance on this code, but does not bring the execution time to within a factor of 2 of the Cray performance. VA3D thus represents a class of applications that performs well on a Cray architecture.

Table III. Timings for Sequential Executions (in seconds)

System	ESN	VA3DO	VA3DLV	VA3DSR
Cray X-MP				
CFT1.13,CTSS				
Vector	24.6	10.3	11.1	10.6
Scalar	24.6	48.3	----	----
IBM 3090				
VSFortran VS 2,MVS				
Vector	25.2	67.6	42.2	48.2
Scalar	24.0	77.6	86.1	----

In VA3D, the vector lengths in the original program (VA3DO) are a function of the problem size and are fairly short, being dominated by a length of 28. In the long vector version, extraneous floating point operations and excess storage requirements have been traded for increased vector length, which now is dominated by vectors exceeding the maximum Cray vector length of 64. Additionally, there is an increase in the percentage of jumps executed in the long vector case. This is primarily the result of the strip-mining of vectors that occurs on the Cray for vectors longer than 64. On the 3090, where the vector registers are length 128, the overhead of this type is seen for vectors longer than 128.

The benchmark VA3D measured in these tests has arrays dimensioned (30,21,30), which accounts for the dominant vector length of 28 - taking the boundaries into consideration. A more reasonable problem in a production implementation would have dimensions of (100,64,64), yielding naturally a much longer vector length and precluding the necessity for modifying the program structure and introducing superfluous operations and artificially increased storage [39].

It should be noted that the scalar performance of VA3D on the X-MP is significantly better than the scalar performance of ESN on that system. The enhanced performance is the result of the regular structure of the code, which permits its vectorization. There is a performance difference between executing vector code in scalar mode and executing scalar code. This difference should not be ignored when evaluating the suitability of different architectures for distinct classes of applications.

In Table IV, the MFLOPS are presented for each of the programs, in vector and scalar modes, on both the Cray X-MP and the IBM 3090. Again, the strong scalar architecture of the 3090 is reflected in the performance of the ESN program, whereas the impact of the Cray architecture is seen in the VA3D performance. A significant gain in performance is observed on the 3090 for the long vector version of VA3D, although there is a small loss in the X-MP performance for that program. As noted above, the drop in speed on the X-MP is at least partially attributable to the increased number of jumps executed to handle the strip-mining of long vectors. Because extraneous operations are executed in the long vector and stride reduced versions of VA3D, MFLOPS are computed relative to the augmented number of floating point operations as well as to the original number. (The MFLOPS for the original number of floating point operations are shown in parentheses in Table IV.)

Table IV. MFLOPS for Sequential Executions

System	ESN	VA3DO	VA3DLV	VA3DSR
Cray X-MP				
Vector	6.0	50.1	48.6 (46.5)*	48.7 (48.7)*
Scalar	6.0	10.7	----	----
IBM 3090				
Vector	5.9	7.6	12.8 (12.2)*	10.7 (10.7)*
Scalar	6.2	6.6	6.3	----

*These MFLOPS reflect the rate of computation relative to the original (requisite) number of floating point operations.

Because instructions are tabulated for each subroutine or other program component, it is possible to consider the instruction profiles of the individual subroutines that will form the parallel portion of a program when it is multitasked. Such a consideration is shown in Table V, where the numbers presented reflect the instructions executed in a sequential run of the original program, before explicit synchronization instructions were included. These measurements indicate that ESN, with 99% of its sequential execution time spent in the parallel routines, has a potential speedup of 3.9 on a 4 processor system. ESN has a further advantage in its structure, in that only one synchronization is required per time step. These facts, together with the small amount of data traffic that this program requires, make ESN an excellent candidate for parallel execution on either a common memory or a distributed memory architecture.

VA3DO is a somewhat worse candidate for parallel execution. Because only 91% of the sequential execution time is spent in parallel routines, the maximum speedup that can be achieved for this program on a 4 processor system is 3.2 (Table V). Moreover, the alternating direction algorithm used in the calculation forces orthogonal sweeps through the data, resulting in the need for 4 synchronizations per time step. The amount of data transferred at each of these synchronizations is large (and will be much larger for the more realistic array dimensions previously noted), totalling more that 2 million words per time step. While the impact of this amount of data transfer is not felt in the common memory architecture, the distributed system pays a heavy penalty for the shipment of such large data blocks. Finally, there is some tradeoff in this program on a parallel, vector architecture in that the parallel routines are also the vector routines. Some speedup due to parallelization may be lost because of conflicts with the vectorization.

In Table VI, the speedup results for parallel execution on the different systems are presented. The speedup of VA3DO on the Cray X-MP is a simulated result, based on execution of the VA3DO program on the X-MP at Los Alamos National Laboratory, using a multitasking simulator [40]. The slightly lower speedup achieved on the IBM 3090 by the multitasked ESN program is under investigation. The synchronization overhead is somewhat higher on the 3090 than on the X-MP, but there appears to be another factor, perhaps relating to the cache management scheme, that is contributing further overhead.

Table V. Measurements for Parallel Routines

	ESN	VA3DO
Elementwise Instructions	930M	1321M
Elementwise Instructions in Parallel Routines	930M	1222M
Percent of Total	99.9	92.5
Percent of Execution Time in Parallel Routines	99	91
Number of Time Steps	1	10
Number of Synchronizations/Time Step	1	4
Amount of Data to be Moved per Time Step	2.5 KW	2.2 MW
Maximum Parallelism		
∞ processors	100	11.1
4 processors	3.9	3.1

Table VI. Speedups Attributable to 4-Way Parallelization

	ESN	VA3DO
Cray X-MP/48	3.7(*)	3.0(**)
IBM 3090-400	3.2	3.0
ICAP-1	3.6	(***)

(*)Los Alamos National Laboratory benchmark results [19]

(**)Simulated time [40]

(***)Not parallelized on this system

On the ICAP system, the VA3DO code was not executed in parallel, because initial estimates indicated that the expectations were too low to warrant further implementation. In an alternate approach shown in Table VII, timings were determined for the sequential execution of this program on both the host mainframe and on a single attached processor. Using these measurements, the estimates of speedup presented in Table VIII were determined. These estimates provide lower bounds for the time of parallel execution, and upper bounds for potential speedup. Estimates are given for a system consisting of M attached processors. The case M=11 is a hypothetical system configuration not realized by the current ICAP system.

Table VII. VA3DO on ICAP

	Entire Program	Serial Portion	Parallel Portion
Sequential Execution		9%	91%
Time on Host (IBM4381)	550 sec	49.5 sec	500.5 sec
Time on AP (FPS 164)	264 sec	24 sec	240 sec

Table VIII. Speedup Estimates for VA3DO on ICAP - Lower Bounds for Time, Upper Bounds for Speedup (Times in seconds)

M	Host Time	AP Time	Overhead	Total	Speedup
1	50	240	103	393	.6
2	50	120	52	332	1.1
3	50	80	34	164	1.5
4	50	60	26	136	1.8
...					
...					
...					
11	50	22	9	81	3.2

M represents the number of attached processors (APs).

In the calculations shown in Table VIII, the host time is considered to be a constant, regardless of the number of processors. Nine percent of the code will execute serially on the host, consuming roughly 50 seconds of execution time. The AP time of 240 seconds (91% of the total AP time of 264 seconds) is divided by the number of processors, and the overhead for communication of the requisite amount of data is also divided by the number of processors (since each processor is assumed to have a dedicated channel, and host/AP communication can be accomplished asynchronously). By executing a sequential version of the code on the combined host/AP system, where the serial portion of the problem executed on the host and the parallel routines executed on the AP, the overhead for communication was measured to be 393 seconds.

It has been observed that when the number of processors available in a system is chosen to equal the average parallelism in an application that is to be measured (where average parallelism is defined to be the speedup, given an unbounded number of available processors), then the attained speedup will be at least 50% of the maximum possible speedup [41]. This observation is based upon a model in which only the average parallelism in an application is considered, the amount of data transfer and communication is ignored. The validity of this model of speedup was tested well by our consideration of VA3D on the ICAP system. Assuming that the average parallelism in a code can be represented as

$$\lim_{p \to \infty} \frac{1}{f_s + \frac{(1 - f_s)}{p}}$$

where p = the number of processors, and f_s = the fraction of work that must be performed sequentially, then

$$\lim_{p \to \infty} \frac{1}{.09 + \frac{.91}{p}} = 11.1$$

represents the average parallelism in this code. From this, we conclude that with 11 processors, the speedup of VA3D on any parallel system should be greater than or equal to 5.6. If we extend the estimates of speedup on the ICAP system to include an 11-processor configuration, then the maximum speedup that could be attained, given the need for communication among processors, is 3.2 (Table VIII). The absence of communication overhead in the model implies an overestimate in the speedup prediction.

In analyses of this type, it is important to consider the tradeoffs in performance that emerge from the myriad of processor architectures. In parallel systems, one of the most noticeable differences is seen in the overhead due to communication in a shared memory vs. a distributed memory system. When comparing these two classes for their suitability to various applications, communication overhead cannot be ignored in any estimates of average parallelism in applications, and in the corresponding models of achievable speedups on the architectures.

5.0 Conclusions

The emergence of radically different processor architectures has underscored the need to evaluate approaches for supercomputer performance evaluation. To enhance the utility of the new classes of architectures, there are certain considerations that must be addressed. In particular, we need to

1. understand the types of parallelism readily available in existing implementations of algorithms,
2. fit algorithms to architectures according to their computational characteristics,
3. search actively for new algorithms, which in some cases will be radical and controversial departures from today's best science, and
4. understand how to measure performance relative to the problem, rather than to its implementation.

In this paper, attention was focused on areas (1) and (2), in evaluating the performance of two distinct applications on several systems that differ in their architectures. Area (3) is an active area of study [42,43], whereas (4) remains an unexplored research topic worthy of increased attention. Hopefully, the growing interest in the evaluation of supercomputer performance will enable these and other special requirements of the community of supercomputer users to be addressed in parallel with architectural advances.

Acknowledgements

I gratefully acknowledge the specific contributions of and many helpful discussions with a number of my colleagues. The measurements on the Cray X-MP and the simulation of the speedup on that architecture were accomplished in collaboration with Elizabeth Williams of the Los Alamos National Laboratory. The various versions of the VA3D code, as well as an understanding of the operation of that application, were contributed by David Soll of IBM Kingston. The ICAP parallelization of the VA3D code was performed with Nelson Strother of the IBM T.J.Watson Research Center.

Finally, Doug Logan, of IBM at Kingston, provided assistance with the execution of ESN on the ICAP system.

References

[1] An Agenda for Improved Supercomputer Performance Evaluation, Report of the National Research Council, 1986.

[2] Lazowska, E.D., Zahorjan, J., Graham, G.Scott, and Sevcik, Kenneth, C., Quantitative System Performance: Computer System Analysis Using Queueing Network Models (Prentice-Hall, 1984).

[3] Larson, J.L., Multitasking of the Cray X-MP-2 Multiprocessor, IEEE Computer, July 1985 (62-69).

[4] Introducing the Cray-2 Computer System, Cray Channels, Vol.7, No. 2, Summer 1985.

[5] Orszag, Steven A., John von Neumann Center for Scientific Computing, IEEE Software, Vol.2, No.6, November 1985 (63-64).

[6] Tucker, S.G., The IBM 3090 System: An Overview, IBM Systems Journal, Vol.25, No.1, 1986 (4-19).

[7] Kuck, David J., Davidson, Ernest S., Lawrie, Duncan H., and Sameh, Ahmed H., Parallel Supercomputing Today and the Cedar Approach, Science, Vol.231 (967-974).

[8] Pfister, G.F., Brantley, W.C., George, D.S., Harvey, S.L., Kleinfelder, W.J., McAuliffe, K.P., Melton, E.A., Norton, V.A., and Weiss, J., The IBM Research Parallel Processor Prototype (RP3): Introduction and Architecture, Proc. of the 1985 International Conference on Parallel Processing, Aug 1985.

[9] Arvind and Gostelow, K.P., A computer capable of exchanging processors for time, in Proceedings IFIP Congress 77, Aug 1977 (849-853).

[10] Seitz, C., Experiments with VLSI Ensemble Machine, Journal of VLSI and Computer Systems, Vol.1, No.3, Computer Science Press, 1984.

[11] Gabriel, R.P., Science 231, 975 (1986).

[12] Beetem, J., Denneau, M., and Weingarten, D., The GF11 Supercomputer, Proc. 12th Annual International Symposium on Computer Architecture, June 17-19, 1985 (108-113).

[13] Martin, J.L. and Mueller-Wichards, D., Supercomputer Performance Evaluation: Status and Directions, The Journal of Supercomputing, Vol.1, No.1 (to appear).

[14] Martin, J.L., Bucher, I.Y., and Warnock, T.T, Workload Characterization for Vector Computers: Tools and Techniques, Technical Report LA-UR-82-3213, Los Alamos National Laboratory, Los Alamos, New Mexico, December 1982.

[15] Maddox, J., Mechanizing Cellular Automata, Nature, Vol.321, May 1986 (107).

[16] Pulliam, T.H. and Steger, J.L., On Implicit Finite-Difference Simulations of Three-Dimensional Flow, AIAA 78, Jan 1978.

[17] Margolus, N., Toffoli, T., and Vichniac, G., Phys. Rev. Let., 56 1694, April 15, 1986.

[18] Rodrigue, Garry, H., Parallel Numerical Methods for Partial Differential Equations, this volume.

[19] Brickner, R.G., Wasserman, H.J., Hayes, Ann H., and Moore, James, W., Benchmarking the IBM 3090 with Vector Facility, Technical Report LA-UR-86-3300, Los Alamos National Laboratory, Los Alamos, New Mexico, 1986.

[20] AIR3D, T.H. Pulliam, NASA/Ames.

[21] Wienke, B.R., SNEX: Semianalytic Solution of the One-Dimensional Discrete Ordinates Transport Equation with Diamond Differenced Angular Fluxes, Computer Physics Communications, 38, 1985 (397-402).

[22] Beam, R.M. and Warming, R.F., and Implicit Factored Scheme for the Compressible Navier-Stokes Equations, AIAA Journal, Vol.16, No.4, April 1978.

[23] Douglas, J. and Gunn, J., A General Formulation of Alternating Direction Methods, Numerical Mathematics, Vol.6, No.5, 1964.

[24] Hack, James J., Peak vs. Sustained Performance on Highly Concurrent Vector Machines, IEEE Computer, Vol.19, No.9, (11-19).

[25] Martin, J.L., Dana, A.L., and Warnock, T.T., Tools for measuring software performance of vector architectures, in Proc. of the Symposium on Application and Assessment of Automated Tools for Software Development, November 1983.

[26] Curington, I.J. and Hockney, R.W., Synchronization and pipeline overhead measurements on the FPS-5000 MIMD Computer, in Parallel Computing 85 (M. Feilheimer, G.R.Joubert and U. Schendel, eds.) North-Holland (Amsterdam, 1986).

[27] Dongarra, J. and Eisenstat, S., Squeezing the Most out of an Algorithm in Cray Fortran, ANL Technical memo, ANL/MCS-TM-9, Argonne National Laboratory, Argonne, Illinoie, May 1983.

[28] Parallel Computers: Architecture, Programming, and Algorithms, R.W.Hockney and C.R.Jesshope, Adam Hilger Ltd., Bristol, England (1981).

[29] Lubeck, O., Moore, J., and Mendez, R., A Benchmark Comparison of Three Supercomputers: Fujitsu VP-200, Hitachi S810/20, and Cray X-MP/2, IEEE Computer, 18(12), December 1985 (10-23).

[30] Hockney, Roger W., $(r_{\infty}, n_{1/2}, s_{1/2})$ measurements on the 2-CPU Cray X-MP, Parallel Computing 2, 1985 (1-14).

[31] Chen, S.C., Large-Scale and High-Speed Multiprocessor System for Scientific Applications: Cray X-MP Series, Proc. NATO Advanced Research Workshop on High-Speed Computing, J. Kowalik, Ed., Springer-Verlag, Julich, W. Germany, June 20-22, 1983.

[32] IBM System/370 Extended Architecture Principles of Operation, SA22-7085, IBM Corporation, available through IBM branch offices.

[33] Corongiu, G. and Detrich, J., Large-Scale Scientific Applications Programs in Chemistry and Physics on an Experimental Parallel Computer System, IBM Technical Report POK41, March 1984.

[34] Fong, Kirby W., The NMFECC Cray Time-Sharing System, Software Practice and Experience, Vol.15, No.1, January 1985 (87-103).

[35] Gibson, D.H., Rain, D.W., and Walsh, H.F., Engineering and Scientific Processing on the IBM 3090, IBM Systems Journal, Vol.25, No. 1, 1986 (36-50).

[36] Bucholz, W., The IBM System/370 Vector Architecture, IBM Systems Journal, Vol.25, No.1, 1986 (51-62).

[37] VS Fortran Version 2, General Description , Order No. GC26-4219, available through IBM branch offices.

[38] Clementi, E., Detrich, J., Chin, S., Corongiu, G., Folsom, D., Logan, D., Caltabiano, R., Carnevali, A., Helin, J., Russo, M., Gnudi, A., Palamidese, P., Large-Scale Computations on a Scalar, Vector and Parallel Supercomputer, in Structure and Dynamics of Nucleic Acids, Proteins, and Membranes, E. Clementi and S. Chin, Eds., Plenum Press, NY (1986).

[39] Pulliam, Thomas H. and Steger, Joseph L., Recent Improvements on Efficiency, Accuracy, and Convergence for Implicit Approximate Factorization Algorithms, AIAA-85-0360, AIAA 23rd Aerospace Sciences Meeting, 1985, Reno, Nevada.

[40] Williams, Elizabeth and Bobrowicz, Frank, Speedup Predictions for Large Scientific Parallel Programs on Cray X-MP-Like Architectures, ICPP 1985 (541-543).

[41] Eager, Derek L., Zahorjan, John, and Lazowska, Edward D., Speedup Versus Efficiency in Parallel Systems, University of Washington, Technical Report 86-08-01, August 1986.

[42] Salem J. and Wolfram, S., Thermodynamics and Hydrodynamics with Cellular Automata, (to be published).

[43] Baudet, G.M., Asynchronous Iterative Methods for Multiprocessors, JACM, Vol.25, April 1978.

5.1 Appendix: Definitions of Measurement Terms

- Instruction Count

  reflects the total number of Cray instructions issued during the execution of the code. In this measurement, vector instructions are counted as single instructions.

- Elementwise Instruction Count

  represents the total number of Cray instructions issued during code execution, where vector instructions are counted as the associated vector length. For example, a vector of length 64 would augment this counter by the 64 operations performed rather than by the single instruction issued to execute them.

- Elementwise FLOPs

  represents the total number of floating point operations executed, where vector floating point instructions are counted as the associated vector length.

- Elementwise Percent FLOPs

  measures elementwise FLOPs as a percentage of elementwise instructions.

- Percent Vectorized FLOPs

  reflects the elementwise number of FLOPs performed in vector instructions as a percentage of the elementwise number of FLOPs. Only arithmetic FLOPs are included in this measurement (i.e., loads and stores of floating point numbers are not reflected).

- Elementwise Percent of Vectorization

  measures the number of operations (all types) performed in vector mode as a percentage of the total number of operations executed.

- MFLOPS

  Millions of Floating Point Operations per Second is the ratio of the elementwise number of floating point operations executed to the total CPU time for the code to complete. Timing was performed in a separate run from the measurements.

- Vector Lengths

  represent the number of times vectors of stated lengths were used. Note: the maximum vector length on the Cray is 64; beyond that, vectors are strip-mined.

- Sequential Time

  represents the number of CPU seconds required to execute the code sequentially.

- Parallel Execution Time

  represents the elapsed (wallclock) time for parallel execution

- Speedup

  represents the ratio of the sequential time (with no multitasking overhead) to the parallel execution time

Parallel Systems and Computation
G. Paul and G.S. Almasi (Editors)

Parallel Applications Development for Shared Memory Systems

Frederica Darema

Computer Sciences Department
IBM T. J. Watson Research Center
Yorktown Heights, NY 10598

We describe general methods that we have used to enable parallel execution of applications on *hybrid shared memory* systems. We discuss observations of parallel program characteristics and performance issues. We have used the VM/EPEX system for parallelization and execution.

1.0 Introduction

Currently a variety of MIMD architectures are being proposed and pursued as a means of providing increased computational power. The characterization of these architectures is that they employ multiple processors connected together and cooperatively working to execute the same program. Such systems, referred to as *parallel architectures*, have produced new domains of investigation, not only from the hardware point of view, but also in terms of the computational models employed to program on such machines and the mapping of applications and algorithms on a given architecture. Actually, there exists a symbiotic relation between software and hardware, in that applications are *tuned* to the architecture for optimal performance and hardware designers are guided by the requirements of applications.

The main issues in the parallel execution of a given program is how to distribute the work to be done to a number of processors and how to enable the processors to execute the computation in a cooperative way. The machine organization and architecture are crucial underlying factors in influencing the techniques used to run on that machine. We are interested in *hybrid* shared memory systems, where in addition to memory shared by all processors, local memory is provided to each processor [1].

In this paper we discuss our experience with methods to program parallel machines and the application of these methods to the development of parallel scientific applications. We have focused primarily on taking existing applications running on uniprocessors (serial execution) and make them run in parallel. We examined application programs written in FORTRAN, as this is the most widely used language for scientific applications.

We describe general methods that we have used to enable the parallel execution of the applications. We discuss the application of the tools provided by the EPEX [2-4] system and the effort to achieve parallelization. We present our observations on the parallelization issues and the emerging characteristics in the various applications. We deal with issues such as which program structures seem predominant in the parallel programs, the character of data, I/O management and debugging. We will also discuss performance issues.

Experience is drawn from parallelizing applications in the areas of Fluid Dynamics, Molecular Dynamics, Solid State Physics, Seismic, Design Automation and Graphics that use techniques such as Finite Differences and Monte Carlo, and employ numerical algorithms such as FFT's, Implicit Techniques, Linear Systems and Eigenvalue Solvers. In this paper we present our general experience on the applications that we have parallelized. Characteristics of specific applications, are given in a forthcoming paper [5]. Here only examples from the applications will be given for illustration of points.

2.0 Parallelization

2.1 Classification

Parallelism in programs can be found in many levels. There is *fine-grain* parallelism which is exhibited either as identical operations on independent data elements (vectors) or as a small number of independent statements in a program, and exploited by two approaches: vector processing and data-flow systems. At the other extreme is *coarse-grain* parallelism and exhibited by long, independent computations comprising of many millions of instructions and/or floating-point operations before there is any need to communicate between the computations. Such parallelism is exploited by distributed or loosely coupled systems.

We are concerned with an intermediate level of parallelism, where each task comprises of the order of thousands of instructions or what is referred to as *loop-level parallelism*. Such parallelism is exploited by a large number of systems emerging presently [6,7] and proposed [1]. We also will deal with parallelism issues that are exhibited in running on machines that support memory shared by all processors as as well as local (private) memory. Systems that support only local memory (distributed) or primarily local (loosely coupled) present other issues which we will not address but only occasionally for comparison.

Execution on the emerging parallel architectures has given the impetus for the development of several computational models and techniques to synchronize the processors executing in parallel, that is cooperating in the execution of a program. The synchronization techniques are tailored to the computational model. In general however, techniques used for intermediate-grain can be used effectively to handle coarse-grain parallelism; the reverse though is not true.

We would like to establish here the following terminology. *Process* generalizes the notion of a processor; it is an executed instruction stream in a program. A *section* is a part of a (parallel) program. A *task* is each of the independent instruction streams in a section . *Granularity* is the size of each task and *chunk* is a group of tasks.

2.2 Basic Techniques to discover/enable parallelism

In handling intermediate as well as coarse grain parallelism some general techniques can be applied to uncover parallelism in applications. They can be divided into two categories:

The techniques in the first category can be characterized as *mild* or *straightforward*. That is make no or minor modifications to the original serial algorithm or application program.

The second category can be characterized as more *drastic* or *innovative*. In this category belong techniques that approach the problem in a different way, devise completely new (parallel) algorithms.

In the straightforward category we distinguish the following two techniques:

- Find the independent tasks. When a specific application (program) is at hand these general classifications above translate into finding sections in the program independent from each other, and finding loops with independent iterations. Indeed the major targets of parallelization are DO-loops whose iterations are independent from each other.
- Reorganize the order of computation to create or increase size and number of the independent tasks. In the algorithm level this might mean restructuring the sequence of operations. It can be as simple as interchanging loops in the application program or as complex as modifying the method of the computation of given loops.

The following basic techniques are emerging from the second category:

- Partition the problem into subproblems (subdomains); that is apply domain decomposition. Partitioning can be either static or dynamic during execution time.
- Apply divide-and-conquer techniques to create independent tasks. That is break the problem into subproblems each of which can be processed in parallel, then combine results and process the resulting (fewer) subproblems in parallel and so on.
- Increase the parallelism and the efficiency of the computation by imposing less synchronization among the parallel processes. That is, perform non-synchronized (chaotic) computation.
- Pipeline sections of the execution of program sections that except of some dependencies can be executed concurrently; for example problems consisting of two phases or pipelining (or overlaping) computation with I/O.

These techniques surface either in coarse or intermediate -grain parallelism. Depending on the resulting granularity of the generated tasks the domain of applicability is intermediate or coarse grain systems.

3.0 Overview of EPEX (Computational Model and Tools)

3.1 Parallel Program Structures

We have used the EPEX [2-4] system that has been developed to provide the means of low-overhead parallel execution and with the assumption that the machine has a shared as well as local memory organization [1,4]. With EPEX we can simulate the parallel execution on highly parallel machines such as RP3 and codes parallelized under EPEX are portable to RP3.

In the SPMD [2] computational model that has been implemented to run parallel FORTRAN applications under EPEX, all processes participating in the parallel computation are created at the beginning of the execution and remain in existence until the end. However, during execution, at the same time different processes may be executing different instructions and act on different data. The tasks to be executed by each process are determined dynamically during execution, by the usage of synchronization directives that are imbedded in the program. In [8] is given a nice critique of the usage of SPMD on message passing, pure shared memory and shared/private (*hybrid*) memory systems.

Based on the model the following parallel program structures are encountered [2]:

- *serial sections*: are sections executed by a single process. Examples of such sections can be data initialization and I/O.
- *parallel sections*: are sections executed by multiple processes acting cooperatively. Examples of such sections are loops whose iterations are mutually independent.
- *replicate sections*: are sections executed by every process. Such sections involve relatively small amount of computation that could be executed by a single process; if however the serialization overhead is larger than the computation itself then it is more efficient to let every process repeat the computation.
- *barriers*: are points of synchronization where *all* processes running the program have to arrive before execution proceeds.
- *Shared and Private Data*: As the machine architecture supports memory accessible to all processes in read and write mode, as well as memory that each process has exclusive access, we distinguish the data in shared and private.

3.2 Expression of parallelism

EPEX provides to the user macros and synchronization routines to be inserted in the program and designate parallel execution, that is it provides tools to the user to explicitly declare the parallelism. On the other hand, no tools are provided for automatic detection of parallelism (parallelizing compiler). The parallelization detection is the responsibility of the user who uses the macros to designate parallelism. A preprocessor is available to convert the macros into (FORTRAN) synchronization routines. The synchronization routines are also available to the user for direct invocation without the preprocessor.

The synchronizations provided are such that processes at most wait for work in a given section to finish and not for every process executing the program to arrive at the synchronization point. That is we eliminate process *join* except in *barrier* points. Among the macros provided are:

- @SERBEG and @SEREND macros designate *Serial sections*; the macros bound the program section to be executed by one process only. The capability exists in EPEX to designate a specific process to execute the section.
- @DO and @ENDO macros designate *Parallel loops*; the macros are inserted at the beginning and end of the loop.
- @SHARED designates *Shared Data*:; the rest of the data are by default private.
- @BARRIER designates *Barriers*:.
- @WAITFOR designates waiting for certain condition.

The WAIT (default) option at the end of the section signifies that the execution of the section has to be completed before subsequent computation can proceed. The NOWAIT option signifies that when all the work in the section has been assigned then remaining processes can proceed to execute the subsequent section, thus it enables simultaneous execution of parts of the application program that are independent from each other. The NOWAIT option again gives flexibility in pipelining the computation of independent loops.

We have found that most parallelization directives involve the @DO, the @SERBEG and the @SHARED constructs. Hard barriers, declared by the @BARRIER macro, that force *all* processes to arrive at the barrier are not that frequent as the concern has been expressed (e.g. [8]).

Besides the high level synchronization mechanisms EPEX provides and low level synchronization. Of the low level primitives provided by EPEX the Fetch-and-Add [9] and explicit capability to set locks appear to be the most useful.

4.0 Parallelization characteristics

We have observed that many application programs that we examined were straightforwardly parallelizable, that is, used same algorithm, same program organization as serial algorithm. This is encouraging and interesting because it indicates that existing serial algorithms lend themselves to parallelization; that is *the world does not need to be rediscovered to exploit parallelism*. The underlying physical problems, typically solved in scientific computations and the numerical algorithms used, basically lend themselves to parallel execution.

Many physical problems, to solve the equations governing the system, involve mapping the physical space and fields onto N-dimensional grids and the computations can be independent for the various grid points, or grid lines, or planes. Numerous applications involving either finite difference or finite elements methods, fall in this category.

Other physical problems involve a system of particles and computations on each particle can be independent; such problems are for example molecular dynamics or particle plasma simulations. Another type of problems are ones dealing with Hamiltonians of systems; again there the computations involving Hamiltonian matrix elements are independent from each other.

To illustrate some of the techniques that we used and the observations on the characteristics of the applications we refer to an example shown in Figure 1, and extracted from a Fluid Dynamics application program (ARC3D) [10], which uses implicit methods to calculate fluid flow. In this example are shown two loops, the first loop does a smoothing of the corrections on the flow fields in the interior grid points, along the $x{=}const$ planes (the loop with respect to J) and the second does smoothing of the points next to the boundary x planes. Corresponding loops exist in the program for smoothing along the y and z planes.
In Figure 2 is shown how this piece of the program was parallelized under EPEX.

Many of the techniques we used in the parallelization of applications that we studied, fall in the category of:

4.1.1.1 Simply detect independent tasks.

For example detect parallel loops: The types of computations discussed above are expressed in the form of loops in a program. An example of such loops is given in Figure 1.

4.1.1.2 Reorganize the order of computation.

In many cases we found that this was all that was needed, essentially to bring the parallelism in the outer loop. Such exchange, shown in Figure 2 where the loop with respect to N that displays low level of parallelism was moved in so that the parallelization is done with respect to the grid points that display more (parallel) iterations. It is worth mentioning that when the parallel system supports in addition vector processing, then when interchanging loops, care should be taken so that when vectorization is displayed in the original loop structure effort should be made to preserve it; that is leave the inner loops vector, parallelize outer loops.

```
C
      JMM          = JM - 1
      DO 2 N = 1,5
      DO 2 K = 2,KM
      DO 2 L = 2,LM
      DO 2 J = 3,JMM
      EE           = -SM1/Q(J,K,L,6)
      EE4          = 4.0*EE
      EE6          = 6.0*EE
      S(J,K,L,N) = (((( (S(J,K,L,N)) +EE*Q(J-2,K,L,N))
     *                 -EE4*Q(J-1,K,L,N)) +EE6*Q(J,K,L,N))
     *                 -EE4*Q(J+1,K,L,N)) +EE*Q(J+2,K,L,N)
    2 CONTINUE
C
      DO 3 N = 1,5
      DO 3 K = 2,KM
      DO 3 L = 2,LM
      EE2          = SM1/Q(2,K,L,6)
      HEE2         = 0.5*EE2
      EEJM         = SM1/Q(JM,K,L,6)
      HEEJM        =.5*EEJM
      S(2,K,L,N) = (( (S(2,K,L,N)) +HEE2*Q(1,K,L,N))
     *               -EE2*Q(2,K,L,N)) +HEE2*Q(3,K,L,N)
      S(JM,K,L,N) = (( (S(JM,K,L,N)) +HEEJM*Q(JM-1,K,L,N))
     *                -EEJM*Q(JM,K,L,N)) +HEEJM*Q(JM+1,K,L,N)
    3 CONTINUE
C
```

Figure 1. Example of program section extracted from ARC3D [10]

There were cases however where the change was slightly more involved and we would like to mention two examples to illustrate such changes:

The first example is taken from a Molecular Dynamics application [11], which models the evolution of a system of particles and uses a *neighbor list*. That is, a pointer array exists that points each particle's neighbors; in addition the length for each set of neighbors for each particle is variable. Creating in this way the neighbor list requires the optimal buffer size but causes the computation of the list creation and the computation of the interparticle forces to be executed serially. In the parallel program a fixed buffer for each particle in the model problem was allowed. Then for each particle all of its neighbors can be found and stored simultaneously. The gain is that not only the list can be constructed in parallel but also that all the time dependent computation can also proceed entirely in parallel. The required buffer size is increased slightly from the optimal serial storage but considering that this part of the data is negligible compared to other data used in the problem, the gain in parallelism is a good trade-off.

The technique of using neighbor lists is applicable to other areas such as Finite Element methods and the parallelization remedy discussed above could also be used effectively there.

The second example is taken from the solution of a linear system of equations [12]. In this case reordering of rows and columns of the matrix was done to increase for example the number of independent pieces of the matrix that can be factorized in parallel.

```
C
      JMM          = JM - 1
      @DO 2 K = 2,KM
      DO 2 L = 2,LM
      DO 2 J = 3,JMM
      EE           = -SM1/Q(J,K,L,6)
      EE4          = 4.0*EE
      EE6          = 6.0*EE
      DO 2 N = 1,5
      S(J,K,L,N) = (((( (S(J,K,L,N)) +EE*Q(J-2,K,L,N))
     *                 -EE4*Q(J-1,K,L,N)) +EE6*Q(J,K,L,N))
     *                 -EE4*Q(J+1,K,L,N)) +EE*Q(J+2,K,L,N)
    2 CONTINUE
      @ENDO 2
C
      @DO 3 K = 2,KM
      DO 3 L = 2,LM
      EE2          = SM1/Q(2,K,L,6)
      HEE2         = 0.5*EE2
      EEJM         = SM1/Q(JM,K,L,6)
      HEEJM        =.5*EEJM
      DO 3 N = 1,5
      S(2,K,L,N) = (( (S(2,K,L,N)) +HEE2*Q(1,K,L,N))
     *               -EE2*Q(2,K,L,N)) +HEE2*Q(3,K,L,N)
      S(JM,K,L,N) = (( (S(JM,K,L,N)) +HEEJM*Q(JM-1,K,L,N))
     *               -EEJM*Q(JM,K,L,N)) +HEEJM*Q(JM+1,K,L,N)
    3 CONTINUE
      @ENDO 3
C
```

Figure 2. Example of parallelized section of ARC3D.

4.1.1.3 Computations of loops with dependencies

Were encountered and in general the parallel execution of those can be handled using locks. A case of loops with dependencies is when at some point in the loop iteration I of a loop depends on iteration I-1; for example element A(I), of array A depends on A(I-1). As computation of the two iterations can proceed independently until the point of dependence, the A(I-1) element can be locked (before the loop begins or at the beginning of the I-1 iteration) and the lock released after it has been computed; thus the process executing iteration I will wait at the point that needs to use the A(I-1) element for the lock to be released [15]. By setting locks on array elements one can handle more general and dynamic dependences between the iteration and the array elements that have to be protected. Such an example is encountered in the parallel execution of the Simulated Annealing algorithm [13].

On the other hand there are cases such as parallel prefix, parallel queues, parallel quick sort computations which do not need locks.

4.1.1.4 Chaotic approximations

We applied chaotic approximations to parallelize the Simulated Annealing algorithm, solving the *chip placement* problem. In this problem pairs of chips are interchanged and the objective is to minimize the total length of the wires connecting the chips (score function). Other approaches to this problem apply domain decomposition and assign different regions of the problem to different processors with some communication among the processors for connections among chips in different regions. We exploited the advantage of the shared memory and allowed processors to pick pairs of chips at random, and in order to minimize synchronization we allowed non-synchronized (chaotic) policy for the update of the score function.

4.1.1.5 Domain decomposition

We applied a technique akin to domain decomposition for the parallelization of a program that calculates Electronic Band Structure in Solids [14]. There the different domains are not physical regions of the problem but different quantum numbers (K-vectors) in the problem; thus we allowed different processors to act and diagonalize (independent) Hamiltonians resulting from different K-vectors. It is worth noting here that this application program could have been parallelized also in a different way, where multiple processors cooperate in the computations for each K-vector or a combination of both methods (to exploit nesting). The method we followed was dictated by the absence (at that time) of suitable parallel eigenvalue solution libraries.

4.1.1.6 Other techniques

Other techniques used were to allow replication of the computation by each of the processes to avoid overhead of serialization. An example of such replication are statements like: *JMM = JM-1*, in Figure 1. Such computation could have been done by one process only and then the result be made available to the other processes by making the variable JMM shared; however the overhead of the serialization routines that each process would execute, is much larger than the statement itself. In addition another point can be made here: The variable JMM is accessed repeatedly by multiple processes in a tight loop; that has implications in memory and network contention. By allowing the replication of the computation the variable can be private thus resulting in more efficient execution. Another technique that we used, in the same spirit, was to evaluate partial computations (e.g. sums) as locally as possible and add to the shared sum once by each process, this again is allowed by some computation replication and usage of local data as much as possible. In general we can say that parallel computation allows another computational degree of freedom, the flexibility of redundancy for efficiency.

In our applications we found cases where entire subroutines are called from within parallel loops, but found no cases where different subroutines could be executed independently in parallel; such cases can be efficiently handled in the EPEX environment. Usually independent tasks in the form of different subroutines executed by different processes are targets of coarse grain parallel systems.

From all the parallel program structures, parallel loops are the predominant targets of parallelization and therefore we will focus our discussion on our observations regarding parallel loops. We will discuss next our findings on the nature of the parallel loops encountered, based on the applications that we have examined.

4.2 Parallel Loops

In general we have seen that the parallelism is exhibited in the form of many and successive parallel loops as is shown in the example in Figure 1. Detailed statistics on the frequency of parallel loops in individual application programs is given in [5].

In addition we observe that though there are successive loops, there are limitations in combining such loops. In many cases the number of independent iterations in two consecutive loops can be different; we discuss this later on, in the section: Degree of Parallelism. More likely is that because of the physical constraints in the problem, one loop has to finish before the other starts and synchronization barriers need to be placed between calculation stages when is required to ensure proper data dependencies. Therefore not only loops cannot be combined but we also observe that the WAIT (as provided by EPEX) option at the end of the loops, is the most frequent option. In some cases the WAIT is more severe than needed. In many instances iteration I of second loop could proceed if iteration I of first loop is done. If the capability existed to enable this less restrictive waiting then process synchronization would be further decreased and the approach would result into increased parallelism; this would be akin to the data-flow approach to parallelism. It would require however, more complex and specialized synchronization constructs than the ones provided in existing systems, EPEX for example.

4.3 Distribution of the parallelism

In general we found that applications are highly parallelizable; that is they mostly exhibit sections that can be run by more than one processors. Serial sections, that is sections run by one process only, comprise a small part of the computation time. Frequently nearly 99% of the computation can be executed in parallel; at no time we found less than 90% parallelization. High percentage of parallelization is crucial for the efficient utilization of highly parallel systems; to get a speedup of 250 on 512 processors, the serial computation has to be less than 0.5%.

High percentage of parallel computation is to be distinguished here from the degree of parallelism, that is the maximum number of processors that can be employed in parallel; this issue is addressed in the subsequent section. However it should be noted here that the amount of parallelism found is higher in general than the amount of vectorization in applications; that is the MIMD (Multiple Instruction Streams - Multiple Data Streams) execution provides more flexibility than SIMD execution.

Total percentages of parallelism in the code are a good coarse measure, but need refinement. There can be multiple successive parallel loops of fine granularity as for example is exhibited in the test problem in Figure 1.

We have also observed that small granularity can be interspersed by parallel loops of large or very large grain. An example is shown in Figure 3 from the Fluid Dynamics program ARC3D, using as model problem a grid size of 30X21X30.

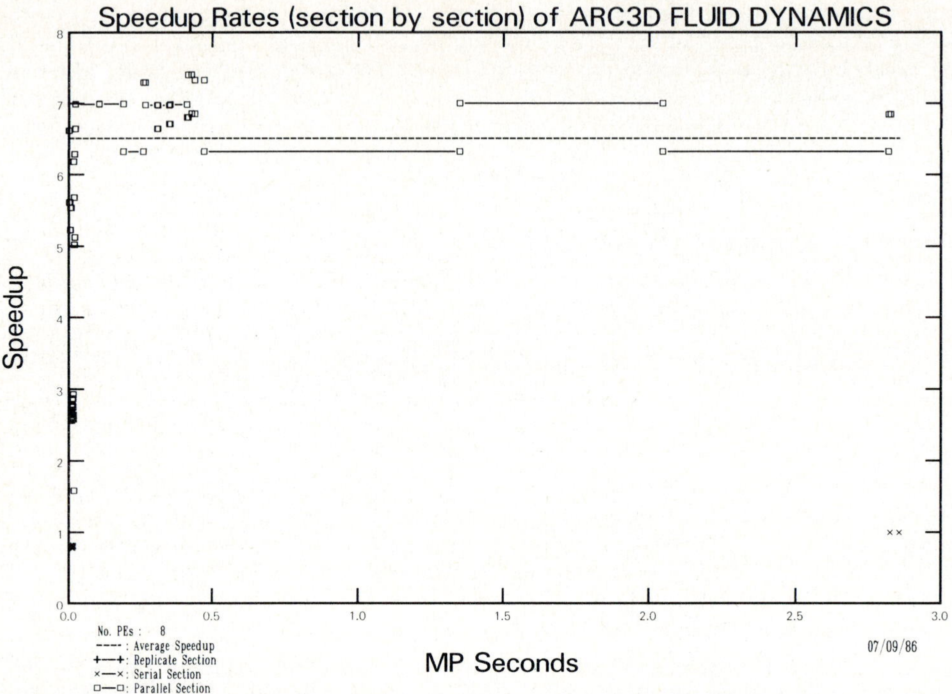

Figure 3. Execution length and speedup in section by section for eight processor run of ARC3D.

In this Figure horizontal lines connecting "square marks" indicate execution length of parallel sections. Thus it is seen that the initial phase of the computation consists of a large number of small parallel loops, while the last phase consists of three very long parallel loops. Small parallel loops increase the synchronization overhead and variation in the various parallel sections make the overhead non-uniform throughout the problem. This is an important consideration for designers of intermediate as well as coarse grain systems. Fine grain is quite detrimental for a coarse grain system because usually such systems do not provide very efficient means of synchronization. Such inefficiency would either result in parallel execution with reduced efficiency or will force execution of such parts serially, thus reducing the amount of parallelism in the program. Very large grain might be correlated with small degrees of parallelism; at least that has been our observation with some programs (for example [10] and [14]).

4.4 Degree of parallelism

The degree of parallelism is the number of independent tasks that can be executed simultaneously. For example the degree of parallelism for a loop is N, if there are N independent iterations in the loop.

We found that in in many cases the degree of parallelism in different loops in a program can vary. The variation results from the physical constraints in the problem or the numerical methods used to solve the problem. For example, in grid problems the solution involves mapping the problem onto a grid and in general the number of grid points along each direction can be different. For grid computations employing explicit methods, the computation can proceed simultaneously and independently on each spatial direction. In that case the degree of parallelism can be fixed because the parallel loop always can be with respect to a fixed direction, thus having the same number of points (in the outer parallel loop). In grid problems which use implicit methods, the parallelism is exhibited in different planes on each spatial direction that can be processed in parallel. That has the effects that each loop will be parallel with respect to a different (x, y or z) spatial direction; thus the degree of parallelism can vary from loop to loop. The ARC3D program from which the example in Figure 1 is taken displays such cases.

Another example where the degree of parallelism in the different loops varies, is in Molecular Dynamics applications; there some parallel loops involve N parallel computations on all the particles and other loops involve N-1 parallel computations on pairs of particles.

If fast turnaround of a single job is desired, then the maximum degree of parallelism should be accommodated by an equivalent number of processors allocated to the given job. If however, the objective in the parallel computation is to achieve the most efficient utilization of the parallel system then this variation has to be taken into consideration. Some tools exist to evaluate the optimal number of processors to be used for a given problem. In Figure 3 is shown how the speedup for a given number of processors can vary for the various loops and the dotted line indicates the average speedup obtained over all the problem.

4.5 Nesting

Many of the existing parallel (FORTRAN) models [2,16,17] have avoided providing mechanisms of handling nested parallelism automatically. The issues are not only how to handle nested synchronization but also how to handle the data sharing among the various levels of parallel tasks.

Is nesting necessary? It seems so. Arguments for it are: is the means to achieve high level of parallelism and exploitation of parallel libraries. We have found that existence and amount of nesting are application and algorithm dependent. For example in particle dynamics applications, loops dealing with particle kinematics do not display nesting, while loops that deal with interparticle interactions have one level of nesting. Grid computations that use explicit methods, as discussed in the section of degree of parallelism exhibit more levels of nesting; that is there are three nested parallel loops. On the other hand computations that use implicit methods might exhibit less or no nesting; the example in Figure 1, taken from an implicit type computation has only two nested parallel loops and other sections of that computation have no nested loops, unless the changes are made to the algorithm.

Nested parallelism can also enable parallel programs to exploit parallel libraries. Jackson [18] has for example found that 60% of the parallel loops in the Argonne linear algebra libraries (LINPACK, EISPACK) that involve numerical computation, exhibit also at least one level of nesting, that is at least one parallel loop within another parallel loop.

4.6 Parallelization Overhead

The parallelization overhead can be divided into two categories: The static overhead that is induced by the insertion of the parallelization directives (synchronization routines) in the program and in addition the execution time overhead which arises from resource contention such as obtaining locks.

The smaller the granularity of work, the larger the static parallelization overhead; thus overhead is tightly coupled with the degree of parallelism and the issue of nesting. If the degree of parallelism is large, even when there are few statements in the loop executed, one can assign a large number (chunk) of iterations each time a process requests work, thus reducing the overhead. On the other hand if there are nested loops, enabling all levels of nesting to be executed in parallel, can result in small granularity; it might be preferable then to have one parallel loop (the outer) and let the inner loops be executed serially. An illustration of both such cases is the example in Figures 1 and 2.

For the applications studied and the EPEX synchronization routines used, we found that the overhead of parallelization was in most cases 1% or less. In some applications where we found that the overhead was about 10%, the model problem studied was small; an increased problem size will make the work in each loop longer and/or will allow larger chunk sizes, thus reducing the overhead.

4.7 Speedup Measurements

The most common performance measurements in parallel execution are: speedup and efficiency. Usually these are measured with respect to execution time of the original (or best) serial code. An example of the speedups we obtain in the applications is shown in Figure 4 for the ARC3D application, where we plot the speedup as a function of the number of processors.

A number of points can be made from this plot. First we see that the speedup is not monotonically increasing but there exist plateaus that correspond to ratios of grid sizes and processor numbers that do not divide exactly. For larger problem sizes, typically the curves scale up so that they deviate from the linear speedup for larger processor numbers.

When the algorithm is deterministic then it is straightforward to define the speedup measurements: compute the result with the serial algorithm, compute the same result with the parallel algorithm for a given number of processors and then compare the execution times. When the algorithm is non-deterministic, for example like in the Simulated Annealing problem, where starting from a different random seed results into a different walk through the phase space of the the system, then even in the serial algorithm the results *and* running times are not fixed. We have proposed to measure the performance of such algorithms in a statistical way, that is measure speedups over an ensemble of runs and and ensemble of results [13].

5.0 Other Parallelization Issues

5.1 Data Management

As we are considering systems that support shared memory as well as private memory, two types of data exist: shared and private. Shared data are application data and data required by the synchronization routines, that can be accessed by *all* processes in a read *and* write mode, during runtime. The private data are such that each process has a copy of and has *exclusive* read *and* write access to; no other process can read or write another process's private data.

Whether the parallelization is done by automatic means of detection (compilers) or manually by the user, detection of which data are shared and which data are private are one of the most serious efforts. What makes it more difficult is when the parallelism involves either parallel loops with subroutine calls or when parallel loops are within many levels of subroutine calls.

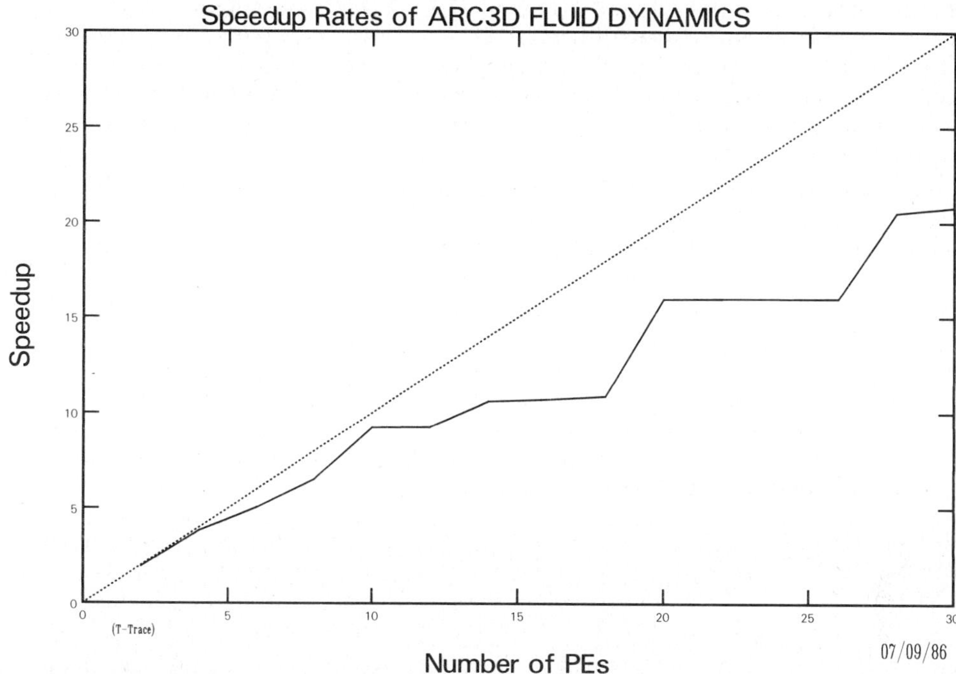

Figure 4. Speedups of ARC3D benchmark as function of number of processors.

Then the utilization of the data has to be examined at all levels; that is interprocedural analysis has to be done either manually or automatically.

For the majority of applications we studied, we have observed that parallel execution consists of loop computations acting on large (multidimensional) matrices; thus most data structures in shared memory involve matrices. In general we have also found that the majority of data are shared, frequently they comprise over 80% of the data. On the other hand performance measurements that we have made [19,20] show that the frequency of references to the the shared data is small, on the average of the order of 15% of all memory accesses.

Data sharing in a highly parallel system is an important performance issue. When many processes access close in time a set of memory locations, close in distance, congestion can occur at the memory system, that is the memory modules and the interconnecting network. This may seriously degrade performance.

Minimizing the access frequency or size of the shared data in a parallelized program is always a good strategy, since it reduces memory contention, network traffic and increases efficiency. This can be achieved by creating local copies of shared data as much as possible, though this can result in slightly more computation by each process and somewhat increased memory requirements; the optimum trade-off depends on the memory hierarchy of the system. In general we create private copies for variables such as loop bounds, which are initialized once or changed infrequently during runtime, but are read very frequently by all of the processes, as they are potential areas of memory and network contention [21]. For these we maintain shared and private copies: the shared copy may be set up by a specific process and subsequently each process makes a private copy of it.

Another example of computations that can be done locally is the formation of global sums; they should be done in such way so as to accumulate parts of them locally as much as possible, and then add them to the shared variable.

Parallelization can increase the size of both the private and shared data. The data required by the synchronization routines are in general a very small fraction of the shared data. The major increase in the amount of shared data can result from the need to expand the data so that various processes can act on independent sections. Invariably the amount of total private data increases as every process allocates a separate space on its own; thus the amount of total private space to be allocated in the system increases proportionately with the number of processes executing in parallel. Also the amount of private and shared data created, for the same application program, depends on the way the program is parallelized. In general parallelizing in the loop level, creates more shared data; coarser grain of parallelization like in domain decomposition methods ([14]), the size of the private data dominates and the shared memory is used for occasional synchronization. Considerations of that nature can affect the way a program is parallelized.

5.2 I/O Management

During execution of a program, data files are used for storing final results or for storing intermediate results in a computation for checkpointing or as scratch files; scratch files are an artifact of the limitation of the memory available in the system relative to the problem size that one wants to run.

The types of I/O, that are encountered in scientific applications, are sequential and random access. In serial execution, results can be stored in a sequential manner. As each record is computed, it is written out, then the data can be read in again for a subsequent computation. Random access I/O, that is files where each record is tagged by a number specific to the computation, are used because data will not necessarily be read in the same order as they were written.

When a program is executed in parallel, additional considerations emerge. When I/O is done sequentially to a file, then only a given process can be allowed to either read or write into the file, in order to enable consistency with *serial* execution and to maintain integrity of the file. For example, under EPEX this is achieved by designating a process with a certain identity to do the I/O. This can be relaxed when other safeguards are provided by the system or user. However the computations might require that different processes than the one that has written the file at one stage of the computation, to read the file at another stage; therefore such facility is needed and supported in EPEX for example [22].

When running in parallel, random access I/O can be used to enable multiple processes to read or write into a file, if the underlying operating system provides the support for processes to simultaneously access the file. Reading or writing into a random access file can be done simultaneously by multiple processes. Efficiency is gained in doing that, for a number of reasons: Multiple processes can read independently the appropriate data to do a computation instead of relying on a single process to do the reading and be a server. Some computations might even be impossible to do otherwise, as when each process reads it's own data they are usually read directly into its private address space; if a server process were used then a (larger) shared buffer would have to be allocated for each process running. In general at different instances different processes might need to do I/O to a file, that is, in general I/O work need be assigned dynamically.

We feel that the utilization of random access files simplifies and facilitates the parallel I/O. The alternative is to create sequential files for each record. That can be as efficient, if each record were fairly large, of the order of several megabytes, but it could be somewhat disadvantageous considering all the explicit file declarations.

There are other issues in data handling such partitioning data in a computation to minimize I/O [23]. Such issues are important and are accentuated when parallel processing enters into the picture. Though for the parallel execution of certain applications we restructured the I/O mechanisms, we made no major restructuring of the data organization for the purpose of enabling parallel execution nor we modified the data organization to minimize I/O. Such investigations are important and we intend to address them in future work.

5.3 Debugging

We found that the usage of the macros and the high level synchronization routines provided by EPEX [3], help to a great extend in the parallelization and eliminate many potential bugs. In general we found that application parallelization, though sometimes laborious, is not an insurmountable task. We discuss here some of our experiences and observations regarding debugging.

We have dealt with scientific applications that are mostly written in FORTRAN. Neither the language design nor the applications program design was intended for parallel processing. The result is that programs have been created with many branches from one point in the program to another and many conditional branches out of loops, for example. In parallelizing such programs bugs can be introduced, such as race conditions and deadlocking. For example, a shared variable, regulating a conditional GOTO, can change and can cause some of the processes (that arrived before the change) to follow a certain flow of control through the program, while others (that arrive after the change) can get directed elsewhere and of course that will result in erroneous execution. Errors of that nature are hard to debug because the work is allocated dynamically to the processes and it can cause the errors to appear only sporadically. In some cases though the bug may not be hard to find. In the case cited, if some processes follow faulty control flow and there are barriers elsewhere in the program, then such processes will not show up at the barrier and proper safeguards in the synchronization software will cause the execution to stop.

Other sources of error that are very common, is the distinction of which are the data that are shared and which are private; mistakes in either declaration can create elusive and not easy to find bugs.

Another source of grief is the fact that computations occur out of order. In the case where large sums of numbers occur then the sequence of execution changes the round off error. Thus it can be hard to detect any errors that cause differences of the order of the round off error. Another issue arises in debugging non-deterministic computations. In this case bugs might be even harder to find and more clever approaches have to be found including devising methods to make the multiprocessor computation go through the same steps as would happen in the one processor run.

In general debugging serial codes has been approached in an artistic way. Though various system facilities are provided, such as termination error messages, tracing facilities and even program dumps, applications programmers use mostly termination error messages; the majority of debugging is done by inserting in the program PRINT statements, to print strategic values that are inspected by the programmer. This can be effective in discovering some errors in the parallel program also. However when that is done, it sometimes has the effect of interfering with the original execution and in many cases the bug goes away! In addition this assumes that the parallel environment provides I/O capability by every processes. In EPEX this is not a problem, but some systems lack this capability thus depriving even this possibility of debugging.

Time stamping, that is at specific locations in the program print the time of their arrival at that point, has also been proposed [8] and seems to be a very useful tool.

One easy and prudent debugging strategy that we always followed was to compare the results of the parallel code run on one processes with the results of the original serial code. That eliminated errors that resulted from changes in the algorithm or changes due to data division in private and shared or changes to the I/O.

6.0 Summary

We have discussed a number of parallelization issues and observations stemming from our experience with a number of diverse scientific applications.

We found that many existing (serial) algorithms lend themselves to parallelization. Many times straightforward changes go a long way to uncover parallelism. The amount of parallel computation found in the applications we have considered is in general high. Parallelization can be found in many levels in a program. Intermediate level parallelism is displayed primarily in the loop level in programs. Parallel sections in the code can be interspersed by (small in general) serial or replicate sections. The degree of parallelism can vary in the different parallel sections in the same code.

Few parallelization directives seem to be sufficient for the expression of parallelism; that has the implication that few extensions to current FORTRAN language are needed to express parallel structures. Though FORTRAN was not designed for parallel execution and branching can be disruptive or even detrimental to parallelism, it is very plausible that the language can be used more effectively as program designers gain more experience in parallel programming.

Hybrid shared memory in parallel systems seems to provide flexibility and facilitates parallelization; from our experience we also feel that requires simpler synchronization mechanisms compared to distributed or message passing systems.

Debugging and the design of debugging tools is a major challenge to parallelization. Even if automatic parallelization tools become available, the need for user directed optimization and the direct development of parallel programs will make parallel debugging a ever present necessity.

7.0 Acknowledgments

I wish to acknowledge the valuable collaboration with a number of members of the RP3 group: EPEX the tool used for the parallelization of the applications was developed in collaboration with Alan Norton, David George, Greg Pfister, Evelyn Melton, Jan Stone and Tony Bolmarcich; performance tools and application measurements are a collaboration with Kimming So.

This summary work is a combination not only of my own experience in parallelizing applications but of many other people who enthusiastically used the EPEX system to parallelize their own applications; among them I express my thanks to Alan Karp of the IBM Palo Alto Science Center, to Pat Teller of New York University, and to Paolo Carnevali and Piero Sguazzero of the IBM Rome Science Center and ECSEC.

8.0 References

[*1*] G. F. Pfister, W. C. Brantley, D. A. George, S. L. Harvey, W. J. Kleinfelder, K. P. McAullife, E. A. Melton, V. A. Norton, J. Weiss, **The IBM Research Parallel Processor Prototype (RP3): Introduction and Architecture** , *Proc of the 1985 International Conference on Parallel Processing*, Aug. 1985.

[*2*] F.Darema-Rogers, V. A. Norton and G. F. Pfister, **Using a Single-Program-Multiple-Data Computational Model for Parallel Execution of Scientific Applications** IBM Research Report, RC11552, 11/19/85.

[*3*] J. M. Stone, F.Darema-Rogers, V. A. Norton and G. F. Pfister, **The VM/EPEX FORTRAN Preprocessor Reference** IBM Research Report: RC11408, 9/30/85

[*4*] D. A. George, **EPEX - Environment for Parallel Execution** to be submitted.

[*5*] F. Darema-Rogers (editor) **Applications Survey Reports I** in preparation.

[*6*] W. Crowther, J. Goodhue, E. Starr, R. Thomas, W. Milliken and T. Blackdar, **Performance Measurements on a 128-node Butterfly Parallel Processor**, Proceedings of the International Conference on Parallel Processing, Aug. 1985, p. 531.

[*7*] R. Perron and C. Mundie, **The Architecture of the Alliant FX/8 Computer** Digest of Papers, Compcon, Spring 86. Ed. A. G. Bell, IEEE Computer Society Press, Wash. DC, 1986.

[*8*] A. H. Karp, **Programming for Parallelism** IBM Palo Alto Scientific Center Report G320-3490, June 1986.

[*9*] A. Gottlieb and C. Kruskal, **Coordination of Parallel Processors: A partial Unification,** *Computer Architecture News*, Oct 1981.

[*10*] T. H. Pulliam, **ARC3D** NASA Ames Research.

[*11*] T. Y. Kwok et al., **Evidence for Vacancy Mechanisms in Grain Boundary Diffusion in a BCC Tilt Boundary**, Phys. Rev. Lett., 47, 1148.

[*12*] A. Greenbaum, **Synchronization Costs on Multiprocessors**, New York University, Ultracomputer Note #98, April 1986.

[*13*] F. Darema-Rogers, V. A. Norton, S. Kirkpartick, **Parallel Simulated Annealing Method for Shared Memory Parallel Systems** To be submitted.

[*14*] K. Pandey, IBM Research, Yorktown. Private communication.

[*15*] R. Cytron, **Compile-Time Scheduling and Optimization for Asynchronous Machines** Ph.D. Thesis, U. of Illinois, 1984, Rep#UIUCDCS-R-84-1177.

[*16*] H. F. Jordan, **Parallel Computation with the FORCE** Report #85-45, Oct. 1985, ICASE, NASA Langley.

[*17*] P. Tang, P-C. Yew, C-Q Zhu, **Processor Self-Scheduling in Large Multiprocessor Systems,** Nov 1985, SIAM Conf. on Parallel Processing for Scientific Computing, Norfolk, VA.

[*18*] D. T. Jackson: **Data Movement in Doall loops**, M.S. Thesis, U. of Ill. 1985.

[*19*] K. So, F. Darema-Rogers, D. A. George, V. A. Norton, G. F. Pfister, **PSIMUL: A System for Parallel Simulation of Parallel Programs** IBM Research Report RC11674, 1/31/86.

[*20*] F. Darema-Rogers, G. F. Pfister, K. So, **Memory Access Patterns of Parallel Scientific Programs** To be submitted.

[*21*] G. F. Pfister and V. A. Norton, **Hot Spot Contention and Combining in Multistage Interconnection Networks** IEEE Trans. on Computers, vol. C-34, No 10, Oct 1985, pp943-948.

[*22*] F. Darema-Rogers and V. A. Norton, **I/O Capabilities in the VM/EPEX System** To be submitted.

[*23*] J. L. Bell and G. S. Patterson, Jr., **Data Organization in Large Numerical Computations** Preprint.

Parallel Systems and Computation
G. Paul and G.S. Almasi (Editors)

Characterizing Overheads on VM-EPEX and Multiple FPS-164 processors

Roger HOCKNEY

Computer Science Dept., Reading University, Reading, U.K., and IBM European Center for Scientific and Engineering Computing, via del Giorgione 159, 00147 Rome, Italy

The performance and overheads of an IBM 4381 hosting single and multiple FPS-164 processors, have been measured in terms of the parameters $(r_\infty, n_{1/2}, f_{1/2}, s_{1/2})$. The performance of a large semiconductor device simulation program (FET6) has been studied on single and multiple FPS-164s. The performance can be characterized by the three parameters $(R_\infty, p_{1/2}, \text{and } \tilde{p})$, where p is the number of processors.

1. INTRODUCTION

A parametric description of computer performance has been used for some time to characterize the dependence of vector (i.e. SIMD) computer performance on vector length, using the parameters $(r_\infty, n_{1/2})$ [1]. Similarly the degradation of performance due to bottlenecks in memory access can be described by the parameters $(\hat{r}_\infty, f_{1/2})$ [2]. More recently the parameter $s_{1/2}$ has been introduced to characterize the synchronization overhead that is incurred when programming with many instruction streams (i.e. MIMD computing) [3]. Throughout these characterizations one functional form repeatedly occurs, namely $y = 1/(1 + x^{-1})$. Because of its origin we define this as the pipeline function, pipe(x), and use it to simplify the expressions.

In this paper we apply the same techniques specifically to the study of the Clementi LCAP computer system. The E1 version of this system, available at the IBM European Center for Scientific and Engineering Computing (ECSEC), Rome, Italy, comprises ten FPS-164 computers attached over channels to an IBM 4381 host. In section 2, the uniprocessor performance for both the IBM 4381 and FPS-164 is measured using the simple $(r_\infty, n_{1/2})$ benchmark [1]. In section 4, this benchmark is parallelized across multiple virtual processors, using the VM/EPEX virtual parallel programming environment [6]. This includes a measurement of the software overhead associated with the EPEX parallel @DO-loop, in a way that enables a user to assess whether parallel execution is worth while. In section 5, the same benchmark is executed in parallel across multiple real FPS-164 processors. In this case the observed performance depends critically on the number of floating-point operations executed in the FPS-164 for every data transfer from the IBM 4381 host (the variable f). This dependence is well modelled by simple expressions depending on the ratio $(f/f_{1/2})$, where $f_{1/2}$ is a hardware parameter characterizing the memory bottleneck. This leads to the suggestion that problems might usefully be classified according to their value of f.

In order to assess the performance of a complete program, we have measured both the virtual and real parallel performance of a large semiconductor device simulation program (section 6). This program FET6 has been in use for over fifteen years on traditional serial computers, and has sections that are ideally suited for vectorization, others for execution on multiple processors, and other critical sections that must be executed serially only on a single processor. In these respects the program provides a good vehicle for the study of parallel computing in its various forms. In this paper, we report only on the parallelization of part of the code to run on multiple processors. Vectorization has not been performed. In section 7, the virtual Speedup under VM/EPEX is reported for up to 30 virtual processors, and in section 8, the real performance on LCAP is given using up to ten FPS-164s.

2. UNIPROCESSOR PERFORMANCE $(r_\infty, n_{1/2})$

The performance of the IBM 4381 and the FPS-164 as uniprocessors has been assessed using the $(r_\infty, n_{1/2})$ benchmark [1]. This involves measuring the time for the following simple loop as a function of the loop-length N:

```
      DO 10 I  =  1 , N
10         A(I)  =  B(I) * C(I)                (1)
```

We shall refer to the loop-length N also as the vector length whether or not the loop is implemented by vector or scalar instructions, because the above loop defines the element-by-element multiplication of two mathematical vectors of length N. In the case of a vector computer, this loop would be executed by a vector instruction, and the benchmark measures the performance of the vector pipeline and any software overhead introduced by the compiler. In the case of a computers like the IBM 4381 and FPS-164 which do not have vector instructions, the benchmark is still a useful one, and measures the efficiency with which the compiler schedules the scalar instructions for this simple DO-loop. In either case, the benchmark measures the speed of the computer as seen by the user through FORTRAN on this simple kernel. Of course, different and more complex kernels may be used in the DO-loop, and a table of different performance figures obtained. There is value, however, in adopting the above vector-multiply kernel as a standard fixed point of comparison between computers, variations about which can be studied separately.

The time, t, for execution of the above loop consists of a startup time,t_0, and a time per element, t_e, multiplied by the number of elements, $n = N$

$$t = t_0 + t_e n \tag{2}$$

The average time per element, $\bar{t}_e$, is then

$$\bar{t}_e = t / n = t_e + t_0 / n \tag{3}$$

and the average processing rate, or performance r, is

$$r = \bar{t}_e^{\,-1} = \frac{1}{t_e + t_0 / n} \tag{4}$$

After a little rearrangement these formulae can be written

$$t = r_\infty^{-1}(n + n_{1/2}) \tag{5}$$

$$r = n / t = \frac{r_\infty}{1 + n_{1/2} / n} \tag{6}$$

where $r_\infty = t_e^{-1} \qquad n_{1/2} = t_0 / t_e$ (7)

The significance of the parameters r_∞ and $n_{1/2}$ in equations (5) and (6) is as follows. In this timing model of a DO-loop, the maximum performance occurs for infinitely long vectors and is designated by r_∞. This performance is never quite achieved for vectors of finite length, but is approached asymptotically as the vector length increases. One can tell how close the performance will be to the asymptote by comparing the vector length with the second parameter $n_{1/2}$. If the vector length equals $n_{1/2}$ then the pipeline performance will be half the asymptotic maximum of r_∞. The performance for other vector lengths can be computed simply from equation (6). The functional form of this approach to the asymptote will occur repeatedly in the subsequent discussion of computer performance, and we define it as the pipeline function

$$\text{pipe}(x) = \frac{1}{1 + x^{-1}} \tag{8}$$

The formula for the performance can then be written

$$r = r_\infty \, \text{pipe}(n \,/\, n_{1/2}) \tag{9}$$

In this characterization of performance the parameters r_∞ and $n_{1/2}$ have been chosen rather than the original timing parameters t_0 and t_e, because they are more directly related to facts about a problem that are known to a computer user. The parameter $n_{1/2}$ provides a user with a yardstick with which to compare the vector lengths that occur in his problem, and r_∞ provides a target with which to compare the actual performance of his program. The characterization also nicely separates the effects of changes in the technology used to implement a computer architecture, from changes to the architecture itself. The former, such as a reduced clock period, only effect r_∞, whilst the latter, such as a change in the number of pipeline segments, only effect $n_{1/2}$. Measurements of the above parameters have been reported for a number of pipelined computers including the Cray-1 and CDC Cyber 200 [1], the Cray X-MP [3], and the Denelcor HEP [4].

Table 1 gives values for the $(r_\infty, n_{1/2})$ benchmark on the IBM 4381 and FPS-164 for a variety of simple kernels. Based on the value of the asymptotic performance r_∞, we find that the FPS-164 is between 1.4 and 2.0 times faster than the best performance of the IBM 4381. This latter depends very much on whether the data that is manipulated is in the cache store or not. The first of the two values quoted for the IBM 4381 assumes this, and the second applies when the data is out-of-cache, and must therefore be fetched from main memory. This degradation in performance varies from negligible to almost a factor of two. A second factor influencing the performance is the increment in memory location between successive elements of the vectors, commonly known as the vector *stride*. Computer storage is usually designed to provide the speediest access to data that is stored contiguously in memory, that is to say has a stride of one. Non-unit strides usually cause a degradation of performance due to memory bank conflicts or an increase in cache misses. We have taken the single non-unit stride of eight to see this effect. The in-cache performance is only slightly reduced by this change, reflecting the fast access time of the cache memory. The out-of cache performance is, however, degraded by almost a factor of two. The corresponding degradation on the FPS-164 is about 20 percent.

Both the computers have separate floating-point multiply and add pipelines which may operate simultaneously, hence an increased performance is seen for kernels that use both pipelines. The third, fourth, and seventh kernels illustrate this for the cases of the all-vector triad, the SAXPY kernel and a first-order recurrence respectively. The asymptotic performance of the IBM 4381 is increased to between 0.8 and 1 Mflop/s, and that of the FPS-164 to 1.8 Mflop/s. As we shall see in section 5, performance is also strongly dependent on the number of floating-point operations per memory reference. The sixth kernel, the inner product -- $S = S + B(I) * C(I)$ --, shows this effect since it has one floating-point operation per memory reference, compared with only one half for the triadic or SAXPY kernels. The FPS-164 performance is proportional to this ratio, and we find that the performance on the inner

TABLE 1 - Values of $(r_\infty, n_{1/2})$ for a number of different kernels used as statement 10 in (1). Two values for each parameter are given for the IBM 4381. The first applies when the data is available in the cache, and the second when the data in not in the cache. Except where stated, the stride between successive data values is unity.

KERNEL	IBM 4381		FPS-164	
	r_∞	$n_{1/2}$	r_∞	$n_{1/2}$
	Mflop/s		Mflop/s	
A(I)=B(I)*C(I) stride=1	0.67 , 0.58	0.8 , 18	1.07	3.7
" -- " -- " stride=8	0.63 , 0.34	0.7 , 7.5	0.89	2.8
A(I)=B(I)*C(I)+D(I)	0.88 , 0.82	0.5 , 13	1.8	4.3
A(I)=A(I)+S*D(I)	0.80 , 0.79	1.5 , 5.5		
Random scatter/gather	0.69 , 0.45	1.1 , 42	0.99	3.1
Inner product	1.10 , 1.00	0.9 , 10	3.5	8.7
A(I)=B(I)*A(I-1)+D(I)	0.92 , 0.83	0.2 , 8.4	1.8	2.7
A(J(I))=A(J(I))+S	0.50 , 0.49	1.6 , 55	0.67	2.1

product is 3.5 Mflop/s or almost exactly twice that for the triadic kernel. The improvement is not so striking on the IBM 4381, but there is an increase by about 20 percent to 1 Mflop/s for the inner product.

The random scatter/gather kernel -- $A(J(I)) = B(I)$ and $A(I) = B(J(I))$ -- refers to the scattering of contiguously stored data to random positions in memory given in the index list $J(I)$, or the inverse operation of gathering randomly positioned data into a contigously stored vector. Table 1 gives the number of such scatters or gathers per second, and is the average of the scatter and the gather rate which may differ slightly. The observed rates are essentially the same as that for the standard dyadic vector-multiply benchmark. Kernel eight is a similar benchmark that involves the updating of memory locations that are specified in an index list. Since the entries in the index list are arbitrary, there may be many references to the same memory location. Such multiple requests to update the same location must be executed sequentially in order that the correct sum be obtained. Consequently the different instantiations of I in this loop may not be independent and therefore cannot be executed simultaneously by either a vector instruction or by multiple processors. Because the compiler does not know the values of the indices the loop will not be vectorized by a vectorizing compiler, and the kernel is primarily designed to show the degradation due to non-vectorization on a vector computer. However some experimental parallel computers, such as the IBM RP3, have special hardware to combine multiple requests to update the same location (the so-called combining network), and the performance of such computers should not be degraded significantly by this kernel. However neither the IBM 4381 nor the FPS-164 has either vector instructions or a combining network, and we might expect similar performance to the standard kernel. Compared to this, we find the performance of the IBM 4381 degraded by about 30 percent, presumably due to the overhead of indirect addressing. The corresponding degradation on the FPS-164 is about 40 percent.

The magnitude of the DO-loop control overhead and the access time to memory, is measured by the values of $n_{1/2}$. The in-cache values for the IBM 4381 are essentially zero, showing that the computer acts like a traditional serial von-Neumann computer with the time of execution directly proportional to the amount of arithmetic or vector length (see equation (5) with $n_{1/2} = 0$). The out-of-cache values, except for scatter/gather, are between 5 and 20 reflecting the access time to main memory for the first elements of the vectors. The FPS-164 values, except for inner product, are between 2 and 4. Loop lengths of ten times these values are required to achieve 90 percent percent of the previously quoted asymptotic rates (see equation (6)). Nevertheless these $n_{1/2}$ values are small, and the performance of both computers may be considered to be independent of loop length, except for trivially short loops.

3. SYNCHRONIZATION OVERHEAD (r_∞, $s_{1/2}$)

A simple model of MIMD computing that covers many real programs is based on the FORK/JOIN primitives. A program is considered as a sequence of serial and parallel sections, in which the work is performed respectively by either one or many processors (instruction streams or processes). Each parallel section starts with a FORK which assigns work among the p processors, and initiates the parallel computation in each processor more or less at the same time. Each section ends with a JOIN at which the processors wait until they have all finished their share of the computational work. The FORK and the JOIN are thus synchronization points in a parallel program. It is important to know the computation cost of the synchronization software and hardware that is provided on any parallel computer system, because this will influence the way in which a particular program is reorganized for parallel execution (i.e. how it is parallelized).

A benchmark has been defined for measuring the synchronization overhead [4] This involves measuring the execution time for a single parallel section and fitting it to the expression

$$t = r_\infty^{-1}(s + s_{1/2}) \tag{10}$$

where s is the amount of computational work in the parallel section measured, for example, in floating-point operations, and $s_{1/2}$ is the overhead of a FORK/JOIN synchronization, measured in terms of the amount of work that could have been done during the time of the synchronization. This is the amount of lost work, and measures the cost of synchronization in a currency that has a known value to the programmer.

As with the other 'subscript 1/2' parameters, $s_{1/2}$ is the amount of work in a parallel section that is necessary to achieve half of the asymptotic performance. Clearly it is hardly worth making a parallel section if the amount of work involved is much less than $s_{1/2}$, and really one would like to see parallel sections with $s > s_{1/2}$ if the parallel hardware is to be used efficiently. The amount of work, s, in a parallel section is often referred to as the grain of the program parallelism, hence $s_{1/2}$ is the required grain size for the effective use of a particular parallel system. In complete analogy with equations (5) and (6), the performance for other grain sizes can be computed from

$$r = r_\infty \,\mathrm{pipe}(s / s_{1/2}) \tag{11}$$

The synchronization overhead has been measured on the Cray X-MP [3], and on the Denelcor HEP [4] and [5].

4.VM-EPEX OVERHEADS ($s_{1/2}$)

VM-EPEX [6] provides a virtual parallel programming environment in which upto about 30 virtual processes called PSIMs can be created, each of which obeys the same stream of instructions or FORTRAN program. However each PSIM may take different routes through the program and, of course, operates on its own private data. Communication between PSIMs takes place through shared common variables that are accessable by all the PSIMs. This mode of programming is often referred to as SPMD or single program multiple data programming. In a real parallel programming environment each PSIM would be assigned to a different physical processor, however parallel operation can be simulated on a single processor operating under VM by assigning each PSIM to a different virtual machine. Slices of CPU time on the single processor are assigned to the virtual machines in rotation, and the CPU time used by each virtual machine or PSIM is separatly recorded. One can then imagine that the PSIMs had been operating concurrently, and conclude that the simulated elapsed time for the virtual parallel program is the maximum of the virtual times recorded for the PSIMs. There are, of course an overheads associated with running a program under VM-EPEX and it is the objective of this section to measure some of these.

One of the most frequently used parallel constructs within EPEX is the parallel or @DO-loop, for example

```
      @DO 10 I = 1, N      CHUNK = 10
             A(I) = B(I) * C(I)                    (12)
 10   @ENDDO
```

The idea of the @DO-loop is to spread the loop-index values in groups of CHUNK values as uniformly as possible across all the PSIMs. However, when a PSIM reaches such a loop it is assigned the next CHUNK values of the loop index I, executes the loop for these values, and returns to the top of the loop. It is then assigned the next CHUNK loop indices, and-so-on until its time slice is exhausted. If the body of the loop is small, as in this case, it is quite possible, indeed it is likely, that one PSIM will consume all the indices, and the concept of simulated parallelism is lost. If, however, the loop body is large, there will still remain some index values to be used. These will be computed by the PSIMs in turn as they are assiged time-slices, until all the index values have been used. This mode of operation means that the index values used by each PSIM depend on a complex interaction between the size of the time slice, the size of the loop-body, and the CHUNK size; and cannot be predicted by the programmer. Consequently all the measurements reported below have been obtained on a single PSIM.

Figure 1 shows the measured time for the execution of the loop (12) as a function of loop length. This is fitted well by the formula

$$t = 92 + 30 < N/CHUNK > + 1.4N \quad \text{microseconds} \tag{13}$$

where the $<x>$ means the smallest integer not less than x, in the above case, the number of chunks required to be taken to consume all the index values. The above expression means that there is a 92 microsecond overhead to setup the loop, a 30 microsecond overhead every time a new chunk of indices is taken, and that 1.4 microseconds are required to compute the loop body. These overheads may be identified respectively with the time to execute the DOSET and DOBEG subroutines in the following code that is produced by the EPEX preprocessor from the EPEX program (12)

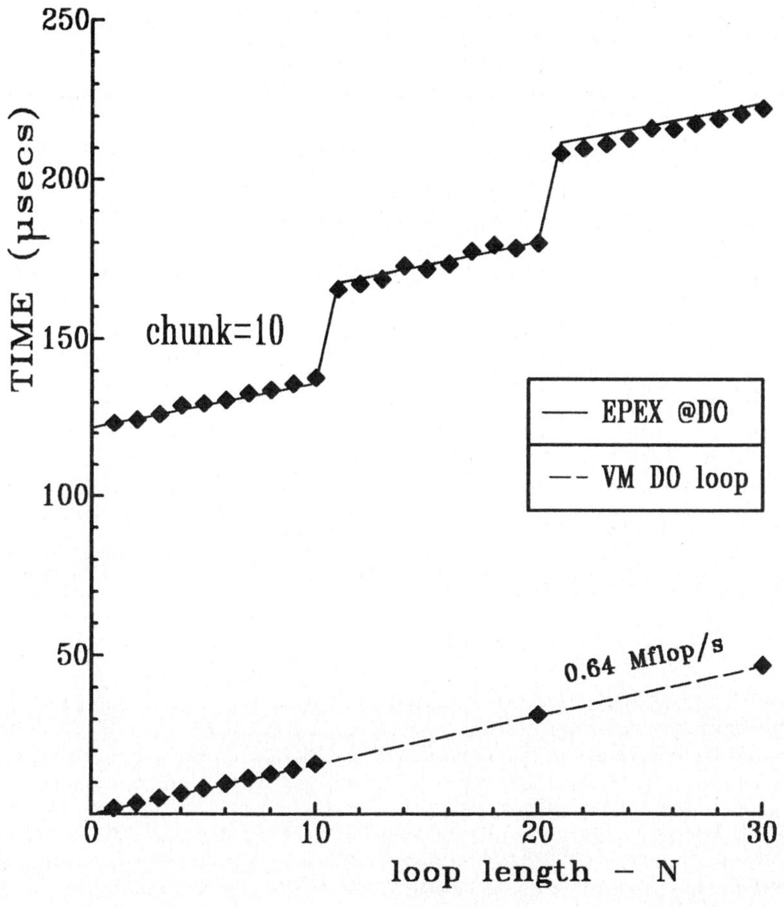

FIGURE 1

The time against loop-length graph for the ordinary FORTRAN DO-loop under VM, and the EPEX parallel @DO-loop. Note the large initial overhead of the @DO-loop, and the time delay introduced every time a new chunk of indices is taken. The measured results are fitted to the formula in equation (13)

```
          CALL DOSET   (92us)
101       CALL DOBEG   (30us)
       DO 100 I = I1, I1 + CHUNK - 1                      (14)
100         A(I) = B(I)*C(I)
       GOTO 101
```

The lower line in Figure 1 is the time for the execution of the equivalent ordinary FORTRAN DO-loop (1) running under VM/CMS with no use of the EPEX system. The slope of the line is approximately the same as that of the steps of the EPEX line, but of course has no setup or per-chunk overheads. The non-EPEX line corresponds to $r_\infty = 0.64$ Mflop/s and $n_{1/2} = 0$. The asymptotic performance using EPEX is the inverse slope of the best straight line through

TABLE 2 - Asymptotic performance r_∞ of a single PSIM using the EPEX @DO-loop and the standard vector multiply benchmark. The third column is the number of PSIMs that must work in parallel for the EPEX performance to equal or exceed that of the equivalent ordinary FORTRAN DO-loop.

CHUNK size	r_∞ Mflop/s	Number of PSIMs
1	0.032	22
2	0.061	12
5	0.135	5
10	0.227	3
20	0.345	2
50	0.500	2
100	0.588	2

the steplike timing line. This depends strongly on the CHUNK size, and we find that the asymptotic performance of a single PSIM under EPEX is

$$r_\infty = \frac{CHUNK}{1.4\,CHUNK + 30} \quad \text{Mflop/s} \tag{15}$$

Values of single PSIM performance as a function of CHUNK size are given in Table 2, together with the number of PSIMs that must be imagined to work in parallel in order that the EPEX performance equal or exceed that of the ordinary FORTRAN non-EPEX program. This table shows the importance of using a large CHUNK size if any reasonable performance is to be obtained with simple loop bodies under EPEX.

Knowing the overheads associated with the @DO-loop we can calculate the virtual performance under EPEX for multiple PSIMs. We assume that p PSIMs execute an @DO-loop simultaneously, and that there are a total of s floating-point operations to be performed. The @DO-loop distributes s/p of these operations to each of the PSIMs as a single chunk of indices, which is clearly the most efficient way of organizing the calculation. Since the PSIMs are imagined to work simultaneously, the elapsed time for the loop is the longest time of execution of any PSIM. The actual time of execution is a staircase line with an initial startup time of 122 microseconds (the sum of the DOSET and DOBEG overheads) and a step upward of 1.4 microseconds every p operations as it becomes necessary for at least one PSIM to do an extra operation. The best straight line through this staircase is given by

$$t = 121.3 + 1.4\,s/p \quad \text{microseconds} \tag{16}$$

whence we conclude by comparison with equation (10)

$$\begin{aligned} r_\infty(p) &= 0.7\,p \quad \text{Mflop/s} &= p\,r_\infty(1) \\ s_{1/2}(p) &= 87\,p \quad \text{flop} &= p\,s_{1/2}(1) \end{aligned} \tag{17}$$

Having obtained expressions for traditional serial execution on a uniprocessor and for virtual parallel execution on multiple PSIMs, one can ask for the condition which determines whether one should use the serial or the parallel system. If the amount of work to be done is s floating-point operations then the times for serial and parallel execution are respectively

$$\begin{aligned} t\,(serial) &= r_\infty^{-1}(1)\, s \\ t\,(parallel) &= r_\infty^{-1}(p)\,(s + s_{1/2}(p)) \end{aligned} \tag{18}$$

It is clear that serial operation will be faster for small values of the problem size s, and parallel operation for large values. There will be a breakeven point $s = s_b$ when the times for serial and parallel operation will be the same. Equating the equations in (18), one obtains

$$s_b = \frac{s_{1/2}(1)}{(1 - p^{-1})} = \frac{87}{(1 - p^{-1})} \text{ flop} \tag{19}$$

One can conclude from equation (19) that as the number of PSIMs, p, goes from two to infinity, the breakeven value varies from $2\, s_{1/2}(1)$ to $s_{1/2}(1)$,or from 174 flop to 87 flop. These values of $s_{1/2}$ give the problem or grain size above which it is worth considering parallelizing a problem across multiple processors using the EPEX @DO-loop.

5. IBM 4381 TO FPS-164 LINK ($\hat{r}_\infty, f_{1/2}$)

Very often the peak performance of an arithmetic pipeline is not realized because data cannot be transferred to and from memory as fast as it is needed by the arithmetic pipeline. This situation of a memory bottleneck can be approximately modelled by considering a memory access pipeline described by the parameters $(r_\infty^{(m)}, n_{1/2}^{(m)})$ feeding data to a local memory, from which an arithmetic pipeline operates described by the parameters $(r_\infty^{(a)}, n_{1/2}^{(a)})$. One may then ask what is the average performance of the combined memory and arithmetic pipeline, and describe this with the parameters $(r_\infty, n_{1/2})$. If there are f floating-point operations per memory transfer, and and it is *not* possible to overlap memory transfers with arithmetic a little algebra shows that (see [2])

$$r_\infty = \frac{r_\infty^{(a)}}{1 + f_{1/2}/f} = \hat{r}_\infty \,\text{pipe}(f/f_{1/2}) \tag{20}$$

$$n_{1/2} = \frac{n_{1/2}^{(m)} + x\, n_{1/2}^{(a)}}{1 + x} \tag{21}$$

where

$$\hat{r}_\infty = r_\infty^{(a)}, \quad f_{1/2} = r_\infty^{(a)} / r_\infty^{(m)}, \quad \text{and } x = f/f_{1/2} \tag{22}$$

In these formulae, $\hat{r}_\infty$ is the peak performance of the combined pipelines, namely that of the arithmetic pipeline. The degradation of performance from this peak is determined by the amount of computational work performed per memory reference, here measured by f, and the hardware parameter $f_{1/2}$ which in this case is the ratio of arithmetic to memory rates. The functional form of the dependence is again that of the pipeline function. Combining equations (9) and (20), one obtains

$$r = \hat{r}_\infty \,\text{pipe}(f/f_{1/2})\, \text{pipe}(n/n_{1/2}) \tag{23}$$

which shows how the peak performance is degraded by memory bottleneck (first pipe function) and inadequate vector length (second pipe function). However in this expression it must be remembered that $n_{1/2}$ is itself a function of f through equation (21)

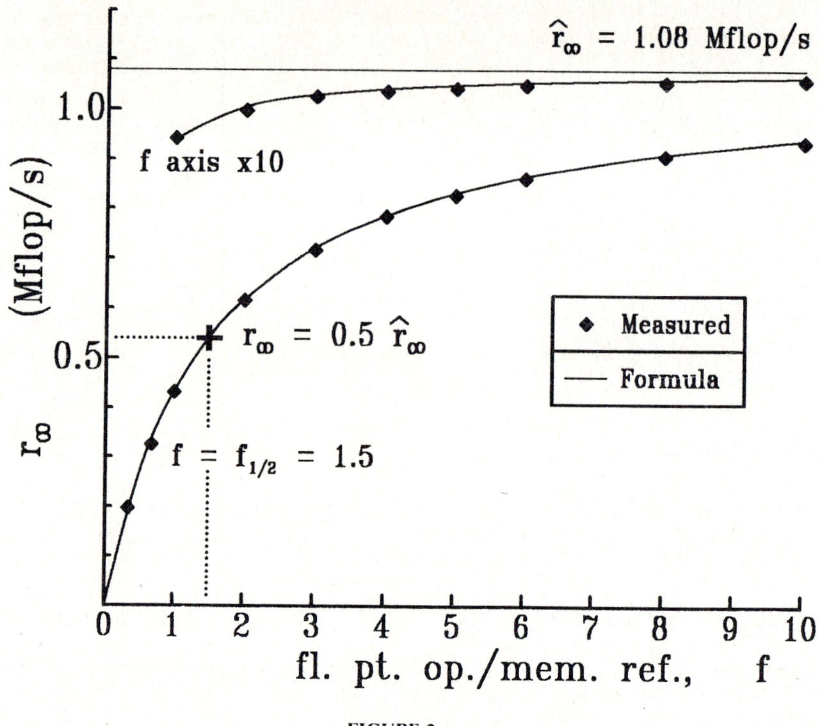

FIGURE 2

Variation of asymptotic performance, r_∞, with the number of floating-point operations per memory reference, f. $f_{1/2}$ is the value of f necessary to obtain half of the peak performance $\hat{r}_\infty$. The measured points for one processor are fitted to the formula of equation (20), with $\hat{r}_\infty = 1.08$ Mflop/s and $f_{1/2} = 1.5$

If memory transfers may take place at the same time as the arithmetic pipeline performs arithmetic, it is possible to overlap memory transfer with arithmetic [2]. In this case, a different functional form arises which we define as the knee function. This is the truncated ramp function

$$\text{knee}(x) = \begin{cases} x & \text{if } x \leq 1 \\ 1 & \text{if } x \geq 1 \end{cases} \tag{24}$$

The performance of the combined pipelines with memory transfer overlap is then

$$r_\infty = \hat{r}_\infty \,\text{knee}(0.5 f / f_{1/2}) \tag{25}$$

where

$$\hat{r} = r_\infty^{(a)} \text{ as before, but now } \quad f_{1/2} = 0.5\, r_\infty^{(a)} / r_\infty^{(m)} \tag{26}$$

Thus the effect of allowing memory transfer overlap is to half the value of $f_{1/2}$, and therefore reduce the amount of arithmetic per memory reference that is required to achieve a given fraction of the peak performance.

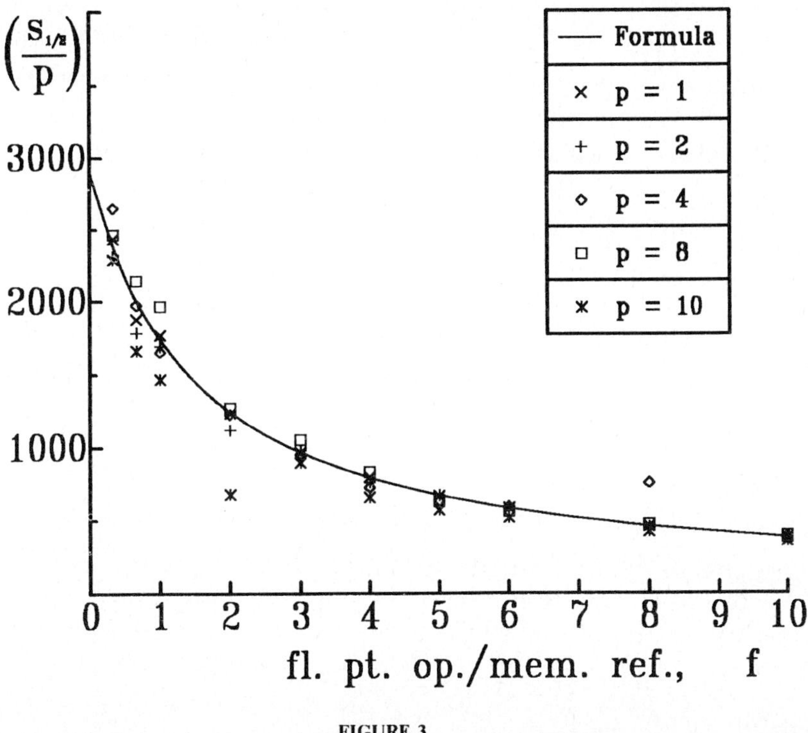

FIGURE 3

Variation of $s_{1/2}$ with the number of floating-point operations per memory reference f, for the IBM 4381 to FPS-164 link. The measured points are fitted to the formula of equation (21) $f_{1/2} = 1.5, n_{1/2}^{(m)} = 2900, n_{1/2}^{(a)} = 4$. The number of FPS-164 processors is p.

Measurements of $f_{1/2}$ have been reported for the FPS-5000 [2], and fit the above parametrization well. Figure 2 and Figure 3 show measurements of $f_{1/2}$ for the IBM 4381 to FPS-164 link on the E1 computer system at IBM/ECSEC, Rome, using the VM-EPEX software in FORTVS. Two vectors of length n, vectors B and C, are transferred as a shared memory variables from the IBM 4381 to the FPS-164, $3f$ dyadic vector-multiply operations are performed in the FPS-164 using the FORTVS code (1), and the result vector A is returned to the IBM 4381. The time for this complete operation is measured by the elapsed time clock on the IBM 4381, so that the measured time includes all the overhead associated with the transfer of data between the two machines. Measurements have been made using both single and multiple FPS-164s using the EPEX software. Unfortunately, this does not ensure that each PSIM is allocated a different FPS-164 to execute its program, in fact several PSIMs may queue to use the same FPS-164 in sequence, thus invalidating the parallel timing results. However, except in the case of 10 PSIMs, we have checked during execution that each PSIM was using a different FPS-164, and thus genuinely executing in parallel. The 10-FPS measurements should therefore be treated as suspect. In order to avoid the problem mentioned in section 4 of one PSIM performing all the work, the EPEX @DO construct was *not* used. Instead an ordinary FORTRAN DO-loop was used, the starting and finishing indices of which were calculated in the program to ensure that the work was as evenly as possible divided between the PSIMs. This strategy gives the programmer control over the program execution, and has also been adopted in the FET6 simulation program (see sections 6 to 8).

Figure 2 shows the asymptotic performance for a single FPS-164 on dyadic operations when taking data from a host IBM 4381. The results are well fitted by (20) (the full line) with

$$\hat{r}_\infty = 1.08 \text{ Mflop/s} \qquad f_{1/2} = 1.5 \text{ flop} \tag{27}$$

The measurements on multiple (p) FPS-164 can be similarly fitted to (20) but with

$$\hat{r}_\infty = 1.08p \text{ Mflop/s} \tag{28}$$

The measurements of $n_{1/2}$ (when a single FPS) or $s_{1/2}$ (when multiple FPSs) are shown in Figure 3. Single FPS-164 results are fitted to (21) with the following parameters

$$n_{1/2}^{(m)} = 2900 \qquad n_{1/2}^{(a)} = 4 \qquad f_{1/2} = 1.5 \text{ flop} \tag{29}$$

In the case of multiple FPS-164s we refer to the parameter as $s_{1/2}$ and fit to the formula

$$\frac{s_{1/2}}{p} = \frac{n_{1/2}^{(m)} + x\, n_{1/2}^{(a)}}{1 + x} \tag{30}$$

The results show much more scatter than those for performance but nevertheless the theoretical fit should be adequate for most purposes.

6. FET6 PROGRAM PERFORMANCE ($R_\infty, p_{1/2}, \tilde{p}$)

FET6 is a two-dimensional semiconductor device simulation program which follows the trajectories of a sample of the electron distribution stepwise in time, as the device operates ([8] and [9]). The interaction of the electrons with the semiconducting material is included by a Monte-Carlo procedure which selects scattering processes probabilistically using psuedo-random numbers. Either Silicon, Gallium Arsenide or Indium Phosphide scattering mechanisms may be selected. Between such scatters the electrons fly according to Newton's laws of motion with their correct effective mass. The model includes therefore the effect of electron inertia which results in velocity-overshoot phenomena. The electrostatic potential and field is recalculated at each timestep in response to the change in electron positions and resulting charge distribution. Such a model copies directly the physics of the device at the electron level, and is necessary for modelling small devices when the distance between scatters is comparable to the device dimensions. This applies particularly to devices displaying the "so-called" ballistic transport phenomenon. The model may be broadly descibed as particle or PIC-type, similar to those used for plasma simulation from which it was derived. It contrasts with traditional semiconductor models that solve the non-linear differential equations for electron density and current, and should be used in circumstances when the approximations used in deriving these differential equations are no longer valid.

The data structures used in the model are a regular square two-dimensional mesh covering the device, which is used to store both the charge distribution and the electrostatic potential; and a list of particle coordinates, containing the (x, y) positions and (k_x, k_y, k_z) momenta components for each simulated electron. Thus although the model is two-dimensional in space it is three-dimensional in k-space.

In outline the program structure (with times in parentheses) is as follows:

1. ***INITIALIZATION***

    a. ***CHARGE (0.08s)*** - the position of each particle is examined and its charge is assigned to neighbouring cells in the potential mesh.

    b. ***POT (0.40s)*** - a fast Poisson-solver POT4A ([10], using the FACR algorithm [11]) is used to solve for the electrostatic potential on the mesh from the charge distribution accumulated in step 2.

    c. ***ACCN (11.8s)*** - each particle is accelerated according to Newton's laws and scattered according to the material.

    d. ***TEST(13.2s : timestep a to d)*** - test for completion, if not return to step a.

2. ***FINISH***

The FET6 is an interesting program for computational analyses because it contains phases suitable for execution on vector computers, other phases suitable for execution on multiple processors, and others that must be executed sequentially. In the CHARGE step above there is an indirectly addressed update loop like kernel 8 of Table 1, and it is likely that many electrons may be asking to assign their charge to the same cell. Unless the computer has special provision for this situation, this is a critical section of code that must be evaluated sequentially on a single processor if correct results are to be guaranteed. On the other hand, this section can make good use of the special combining network that is provided, for example, on the IBM RP3 or NYU ULTRA computers. The POT step is a highly vectorizable section involving the calculation of multiple independent Fourier transforms and tridiagonal systems of equations. Although the independent systems could be evaluated on multiple processors, vectorization should be more efficient because of its smaller synchronization costs. In this part of the code the flexibility of multiple processors is simply not required.

The ACCN step, however, calls out for multi-instruction stream programming on multiple processors, because the Monte-Carlo nature of the scattering means that each electron will be taking a different route through the scattering subroutine. This section is therefore unsuitable for vector processing. After the electrostatic potential is calculated in the POT step, the life-histories of the electrons are independent of each, and there is no reason why $1/p$th of the electrons should not be given to each processor in a p processor system. The interaction between the electrons comes only through the overall electric field to which they all contribute in the CHARGE step. Fortunately most of the computer time is spent in the ACCN step and the above strategy has been used to parallelize the program on the ECSEC system. All steps except ACCN are computed on the IBM 4381 host by only one PSIM, and the particles are divided amongst the multiple FPS-164 computers during the ACCN step. The IBM 4381 does not have a vector feature or combining network so the CHARGE and POT steps were not altered from the original FORTRAN. However vectorization of the POT step would have been appropriate if the host had been an IBM 3090 with vector feature.

7. VIRTUAL SPEEDUP ($S_\infty, p_{1/2}$)

The parameter $s_{1/2}$ is concerned only with the timing of a single parallel section. In the case of a complete program such as FET6, one must include the time also for the serial sections. In the simplest case the time, T_p, for the execution of a complete program, or a repeated program segment such as a timestep, will be of the form

$$T_p = t_0 + t_1/p \tag{31}$$

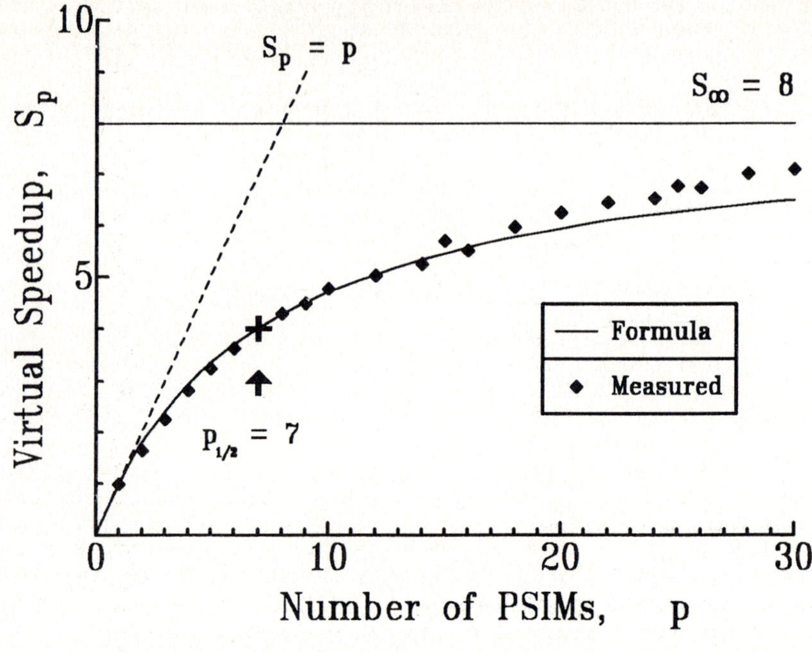

FIGURE 4

The virtual Speedup, S_p, as a function of the number of virtual processors or PSIMs, p, using the VM-EPEX virtual parallel programming environment. $p_{1/2}$ is the number of processors required to obtain half of the asymptotic Speedup, S_∞ The measured values are fitted to the theoretical formula of equation (35) with $S_\infty = 8, p_{1/2} = 7$.

where t_0 is the time for the serial sections and any constant overheads arising from the parallel sections, and t_1 is the time for the work that can be divided between the p processors, that is to say can be parallelized (for simplicity we assume that the work can be scheduled equally between the processors). The rate of execution $R(p)$ in, for example, timesteps per second is the inverse of the time of execution, and a function of p

$$R(p) = T_p^{-1} = \frac{1}{t_0 + t_1/p} = \frac{R_\infty}{1 + p_{1/2}/p} \tag{32}$$

which may be written as

$$R(p) = R_\infty \ \mathrm{pipe}(p/p_{1/2}) \tag{33}$$

where $\quad R_\infty = t_0^{-1} \quad$ and $\quad p_{1/2} = \dfrac{t_1}{t_0}$ (34)

The usual parameter that is used to compare the performance of algorithms is the Speedup [7], which is defined as

$$S_p = \frac{T_1}{T_p} = \frac{R(p)}{R(1)} = \frac{S_\infty}{(1 + p_{1/2}/p)} = S_\infty \mathrm{pipe}(p/p_{1/2}) \tag{35}$$

where T_1 and T_p are respectively the times for the algorithm to run on one or p processors. From which we conclude

$$\begin{aligned} S_\infty &= R_\infty / R(1) = (1 + p_{1/2}) = T_1 / t_0 \\ &= (\text{ fraction of original program time } \textit{not parallelized} \,)^{-1} \end{aligned} \tag{36}$$

When using EPEX, the elapsed time for simulated parallel execution is taken to be the largest virtual CPU time recorded for any of the PSIMs, and the Speedup calculated from this measurement is called the *Virtual Speedup*. Figure 4 shows the results of such measurements for FET6 using upto 30 PSIMs. The early part of the Speedup curve fits (35) well with

$$S_\infty = 8 \quad \text{and} \quad p_{1/2} = 7 \tag{37}$$

Above 20 PSIMs, however, the measured Speedup is significantly higher than the predicted curve. This effect is not completely understood but might be an effect of the IBM 4381 cache. Based on the times for the original serial program (t_0 = 1.4s, t_1 = 11.8s, T_1 = 13.2s), there is the potential to parallelize 89.4% of the program time. The measured value of S_∞ corresponds, through equation (36), to a fraction parallelized of 87.5%, showing that most of this has been realized.

8. PERFORMANCE ON LCAP

In equation (33), R_∞ is the asymptotic program performance which is theoretically approached as the number of processors increases, and $p_{1/2}$ is the number of processors required to achieve half that performance. Many parallelized programs are found to follow this functional dependence at least for small values of p. In practice, as p becomes larger synchronization and other overheads usually increase rapidly with p, with the result that there is often a maximum in the program performance, and a subsequent reduction in performance as the number of processors further increases. This observed behaviour has been fitted to the function

$$R(p) = \frac{R_\infty}{\left[1 + \frac{p_{1/2}}{p}\left\{1 + \frac{1}{(n-1)}\left(\frac{p}{\tilde{p}}\right)^n\right\}\right]} \tag{38}$$

In this formula the overhead of synchronization is represented by the factor in braces, and the rapidity with which it increases with p is determined by n which we call the index of synchronization. Clearly it is desirable for it to be as small as possible. The magnitude of the synchronization overhead is determined by $\tilde{p}$, with larger values meaning a smaller overhead. The values of these parameters are likely to vary considerably between different computer and software systems. The maximum performance occurs when $p = \tilde{p}$ and has the value

$$\tilde{R} = \frac{R_\infty}{\left[1 + \frac{n}{(n-1)}\left(\frac{p_{1/2}}{\tilde{p}}\right)\right]} \tag{39}$$

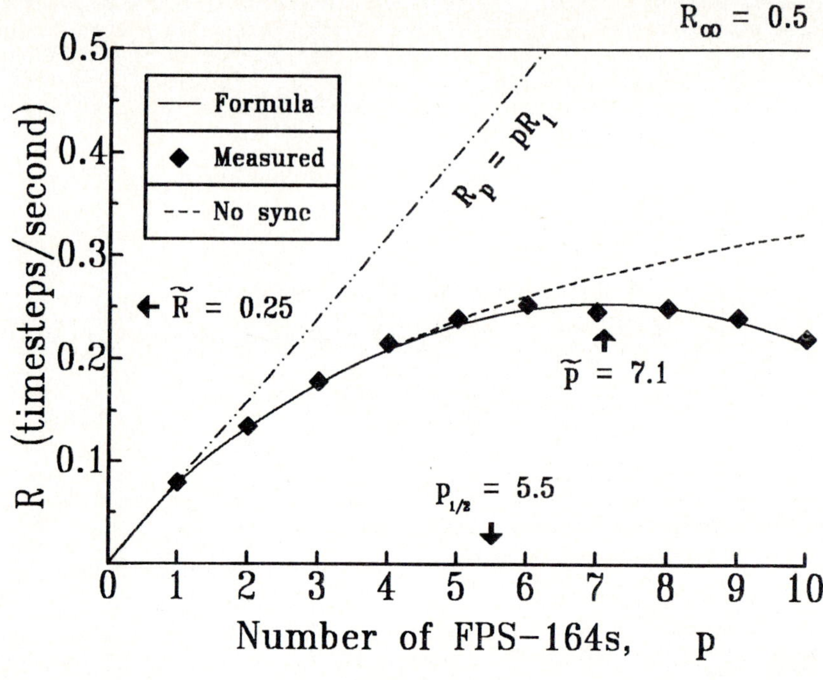

FIGURE 5

Absolute performance of the FET6 program on one to ten FPS-164s. Note that the performace reaches a peak of $\widetilde{R}$ for $\widetilde{p}$ processors. The measured values are fitted to formula (38) with $R_\infty = 0.5, p_{1/2} = 5.5, \widetilde{R} = 0.25, \widetilde{p} = 7.1, n = 5$. If the overhead of synchronization could be eliminated the performance would follow the dotted curve which asymptotes at R_∞.

Figure 5 shows actual performance measurements of FET6 on multiple FPS-164s. The timing of the parallelized program is fitted well by equation (38), in the range $1 \le p \le 10$, with the following parameters (equivalent Speedup ratios to $R(1)$ are given in parentheses)

$$\begin{aligned} &R_\infty = 0.5 \quad \text{timesteps per second} \qquad (S_\infty = 6.2) \\ &p_{1/2} = 5.5 \qquad \widetilde{p} = 7.1 \qquad n = 5 \end{aligned} \tag{40}$$

the maximum value of the performance is then, from equation (39)

$$\widetilde{R} = 0.25 \quad \text{timesteps per second} \qquad (\widetilde{S} = 3.1) \tag{41}$$

We can interpret the significance of these parameters as follows. The value of $\widetilde{p} = 7.1$ means that the parallelized program cannot usefully utilize more than 7 processors, and in this sense is reasonably well matched to the 10 processor E1 system. Values of $(\widetilde{R}, \widetilde{p}, n)$ depend on the synchronization overhead. If it were possible to reduce this substantially by additional synchronization hardware or improvements to the software, the effect would be represented by increasing $\widetilde{p} \to \infty$ and $\widetilde{R} \to R_\infty$. Since synchronization takes place on the host, this could be achieved by providing a faster host computer on the E1 system. The parameter R_∞ is thus the maximum possible performance for the program when synchronization time is negligible. Ninety percent of this performance can be achieved if the number of processors $p = 10p_{1/2} = 55$, which indicates that this particular program would benefit from the use of more processors than the ten that are available on the Rome E1 system. Thus one may conclude that the program is likely to be well matched also to the RP3 computer being built at IBM Hawthorne Laboratories, which should have much less synchronization overhead and will initially have 64 processors.

9. CONCLUSIONS

We have presented a series of parametrized formulae for the timing and performance of algorithms, which take into account the effect of vector length, memory bottleneck, synchronization and the number of processors. The advantage of such parametrized algebraic representations is that they allow simple algebraic manipulations and optimizations in the comparison of algorithms, and avoid the need to print extensive tables of numbers or graphs of, for example, performance as a function of vector length or number of processors. Comparisons can be made by looking at small number of parameters. The formulae can also be used for limited extrapolations. The identification of different terms with different effects (e.g. synchronization overhead), enables conclusions to be drawn of the effect on performance of changes in overheads, which might occur, for example, on moving to a different computer system. Measurements of these parameters have been presented for IBM 4381 and FPS-164 uniprocessors, the EPEX @DO-loop and a large semiconductor simulation program.

ACKNOWLEDGEMENTS

The author would like to thank IBM for the opportunity to visit ECSEC, and the staff there for their kind assistance in obtaining the above measurements. Discussions with Piero Sguazzero, Paolo Carnevali, Manuel Kindelan and Francesco Antonelli were particularly valuable.

REFERENCES

[1] R. W. Hockney and C. R. Jesshope, *Parallel Computers*, Adam Hilger (Bristol, 1981).

[2] I. J. Curington and R. W. Hockney, Synchronization and pipeline overhead measurements on the FPS-5000 MIMD computer, in *Parallel Computing 85*, (M. Feilmeier, G. R. Joubert and U. Schendel, eds.), *North Holland* (Amsterdam, 1986) pp. 469-476.

[3] R. W. Hockney, $(r_\infty, n_{1/2}, s_{1/2})$ measurements on the 2 CPU Cray X-MP, *Parallel Computing* **2** (1985) pp. 1-14.

[4] R. W. Hockney, Performance characterization of the HEP, in *MIMD Computation: HEP Supercomputer*, (J. S. Kowalik ed.), *MIT Press* (Cambridge, Mass., 1985) pp. 59-90.

[5] R. W. Hockney and D. F. Snelling, Characterizing MIMD computers: e.g. Denelcor HEP, in *Parallel Computing 83*, (M. Feilmeier, G. R. Joubert and U. Schendel, eds.), *North Holland* (Amsterdam, 1984) pp. 521-526.

[6] F. Darema-Rogers, D. A. George, V. A. Norton and G. F. Pfister, VM/EPEX - A VM environment for parallel execution, *IBM Research Report RC11225 (#49161)* (Yorktown Heights, 1/23/85).

[7] D. J. Kuck, *The Structure of Computers and Computations*, Wiley (New York, 1978) p. 611.

[8] R. W. Hockney, R. A. Warriner and Reiser, Two-dimensional particle models in semiconductor device analysis, *Electronics Letters* **10** (1974) pp. 484-486.

[9] R. W. Hockney and J. W. Eastwood, *Computer Simulation Using Particles*, McGraw-Hill (New York, 1981) pp. 353-408.

[10] S. J. Beard and R. W. Hockney, POT4A - a program for the direct solution of Poisson's equation in complex geometries, *Comput. Phys. Commun.* **36** (1985) pp. 25-57.

[11] R. W. Hockney, The potential calculation and some applications, *Methods Comput. Phys.* **9** (1970) pp. 135-211.

Parallel Systems and Computation
G. Paul and G.S. Almasi (Editors)

Parallelism in Seismic Computations: Two Case Studies

P. Sguazzero, M. Kindelan, A. Kamel

IBM European Center for Scientific and Engineering Computing, via Giorgione 159, 00147 Rome, Italy

Seismic prospection aims at determining the subsurface structure of the earth from indirect measurements obtained at the earth's surface. The formation of subsurface maps from surface-collected seismic data involves the use of inversion principles and of data processing techniques amongst which *seismic migration* plays an important role. A valuable tool in exploration geophysics is also provided by computerized *seismic modeling*: modeling the seismic response of several hypothesized geologic structures aids seismic interpreters in relating what is seen in the seismic data to the earth's inhomogeneities. The numerical integration of the modeling and migration equations can be achieved by *semi-spectral* (Fourier) *methods* which have proven to be accurate, capable of handling abrupt changes in the material parameters, at the expense of being computationally quite demanding. It has been common practice of the geophysical data processing industry since the late 60's to solve seismic problems by supplementing a general purpose host computer with attached array processors. More recently, vector processors have proven to be successful architectures for seismic computations. Vector multiprocessors are now an attractive option for meeting the computing requirements of the seismic industry and allow the full exploitation of the vector and parallel processing potentials inherent in seismic modeling and inversion algorithms. This work describes a vectorized and parallelized implementation of a two-dimensional semi-spectral elastic model on two computer architectures: a *tightly coupled system*, the vector multiprocessor IBM 3090-200, and a *loosely coupled system* (ℓCAP) consisting of an IBM 4381 (scalar) host and of several Floating Point Systems FPS-164 Array Processors. This paper presents also an analysis of parallel decompositions of wave equation based migration algorithms and evaluates the performance of PSPI, a frequency domain semi-spectral migration method, on the two architectures.

I. The Forward Problem: Elastic Modeling

1. Introduction

Seismic prospection for hydrocarbon detection aims at determining the geologic structure of the earth from indirect measurements obtained at the earth's surface. In seismic prospecting elastic wave fields (acoustic in first approximation) are generated at the surface, penetrate the earth, and are backscattered by the earth's inhomogeneities. The seismic interpreters then correlate what is seen in the seismic data to the earth's inhomogeneities.

The ***forward-modeling*** of several hypothesized geologic structures with the elastic (acoustic) wave equation helps the seismic interpreters in relating the recorded data to the scattering inhomogeneities. By modeling, field surveys can be simulated numerically, and computed results can be compared to field data. Forward modeling gained additional importance with the recent trend to extract more information from seismic surveys by using amplitude values in addition to travel times, and with the use of shear wave information. Modeling is often used to simulate surveys in geologic areas with strong horizontal velocity gradients. All these factors pose stringent accuracy requirements on the forward modeling tools, especially in the elastic case.

Of the different numerical methods available in modeling wave propagation we have used a ***semi-spectral*** (Fourier) method. The main drawback of this method is its high cost. However, for a specified accuracy, this approach requires fewer grid points than a finite difference method, and therefore it may be more economical despite the fact that it requires more computations per grid point. Furthermore, this method is very efficient in handling rapid space variations of the elastic parameters.

Solving evolutionary partial differential equations, like the elastic wave equations, with a semi-spectral method is a typical "number crunching" problem in scientific computation. One of the major trends in commercially available systems for scientific and engineering computation is the trend toward multiprocessor shared memory architectures, where each processor has vector capabilities (VMP). These architectures pose significant challenge to their users and impact heavily on the design of numerical software[1, 2]. The numerical algorithms must in fact be reformulated in a form that fully exploits the architectural advantages, mainly through the processes of parallelization and vectorization.

The aim of part I of this paper is to present an implementation of a semi-spectral elastic model on the vector multiprocessor IBM 3090-200 VF as well as some strategies for parallelism on a loosely coupled array processors system (ℓCAP), consisting of an IBM 4381 (scalar) host and of several Floating Point Systems FPS-164 Array Processors. The layout of part I is the following. In section 2, we describe the equations governing wave propagation, the numerical methods used to approximate those equations, and the algorithm chosen to solve them. In section 3 we describe different implementations on the two computer architectures chosen. In particular, we analyze the vectorizability of the algorithm as well as two strategies for parallelization. Finally, in section 4 we discuss the performance obtained in the various implementations.

2. *Elastic Wave Modeling*

A. Formulation

The basic equations governing wave propagation in a 2-D continuous elastic medium are the momentum conservation and the stress-strain relation [3, 4]. The linearized equations of momentum conservation are given by

$$\rho f_x + \frac{\partial \sigma_{xx}}{\partial x} + \frac{\partial \sigma_{xz}}{\partial z} = \rho \ddot{U}_x \qquad (1)$$

and

$$\rho f_z + \frac{\partial \sigma_{xz}}{\partial x} + \frac{\partial \sigma_{zz}}{\partial z} = \rho \ddot{U}_z \qquad (2)$$

where x and z are Cartesian coordinates, respectively horizontal and vertical, σ_{xx} , σ_{zz}, and σ_{xz} are the three stress components, U_x and U_z represent the displacements, f_x and f_z represent the body forces, and $\rho(x, z)$ is the density. Here, and in the rest of the discussion, a dot above a variable represents a time derivative.

The stress-strain relation in the case of an elastic and isotropic medium reads

$$\sigma_{xx} = (\lambda + 2\mu)e_{xx} + \lambda e_{zz} \tag{3}$$

$$\sigma_{zz} = \lambda e_{xx} + (\lambda + 2\mu)e_{zz} \tag{4}$$

$$\sigma_{xz} = 2\mu e_{xz} \tag{5}$$

The strain components are defined by

$$e_{xx} = \frac{\partial U_x}{\partial x} \quad , \quad e_{zz} = \frac{\partial U_z}{\partial z} \tag{6}$$

and

$$e_{xz} = \frac{1}{2}\left(\frac{\partial U_x}{\partial z} + \frac{\partial U_z}{\partial x}\right) \tag{7}$$

where $\lambda = \lambda(x, z)$ and $\mu = \mu(x, z)$ represent Lame's elastic parameters.

Conventionally, as in the acoustic case, one derives from the above equations a vector wave equation for the ***displacement*** field (U_x, U_z). However, for the elastic case, it has been reported [5] that the free-surface boundary condition for the displacements causes the Fourier method of solution of the vector wave equation to be unstable. This is because, unlike in the acoustic wave equation case, these boundary conditions involve derivatives of the solution instead of the solution field itself. Therefore, following [5], we derive a set of wave equations which contain ***stresses*** as variables instead of displacements. By differentiating equations (6-7) twice with respect to time and eliminating $\ddot{U}_x$ and $\ddot{U}_z$ with the help of equations (1-2), an alternative statement of momentum conservation is obtained:

$$\ddot{e}_{xx} = \frac{\partial A_x}{\partial x} + \frac{\partial f_x}{\partial x} \tag{8}$$

$$\ddot{e}_{zz} = \frac{\partial A_z}{\partial z} + \frac{\partial f_z}{\partial z} \tag{9}$$

$$2\ddot{e}_{xz} = \frac{\partial A_x}{\partial z} + \frac{\partial A_z}{\partial x} + \frac{\partial f_x}{\partial z} + \frac{\partial f_z}{\partial x} \tag{10}$$

with

$$A_x \equiv \frac{1}{\rho}\left\{\frac{\partial \sigma_{xx}}{\partial x} + \frac{\partial \sigma_{xz}}{\partial z}\right\} \tag{11}$$

and

$$A_z \equiv \frac{1}{\rho}\left\{\frac{\partial \sigma_{zz}}{\partial z} + \frac{\partial \sigma_{xz}}{\partial x}\right\} \tag{12}$$

The stress wave equations are finally obtained differentiating twice with respect to time the elastic stress-strain relations (3-5)

$$\ddot{\sigma}_{xx} = (\lambda + 2\mu)\ddot{e}_{xx} + \lambda\ddot{e}_{zz} \tag{13}$$

$$\ddot{\sigma}_{zz} = \lambda\ddot{e}_{xx} + (\lambda + 2\mu)\ddot{e}_{zz} \tag{14}$$

$$\ddot{\sigma}_{xz} = 2\mu\ddot{e}_{xz} \tag{15}$$

and eliminating the strain time derivatives with the help of equations (8-12). In this representation, propagation of elastic waves is governed by the equations for the stress field rather than the conventionally used vector equation for the displacement field. Equations (13-15) supplemented by (8-12) form the basic set of equations that determine the spatial distribution and time evolution of the physical variables (stresses, strains and displacements). The stresses serve as the main unknowns whereas the material parameters ρ, λ, and μ, as well as the body forces $f_x(x, z, t)$ and $f_z(x, z, t)$, are known quantities. Initial conditions of the stresses σ_{xx}, σ_{zz}, and σ_{xz} and of the stress time derivatives $\dot{\sigma}_{xx}, \dot{\sigma}_{zz}$, and $\dot{\sigma}_{xz}$ are to be prescribed. Boundary conditions (vanishing of stresses at a free surface and continuity of stresses and displacements across interfaces between different media) as well as radiation type conditions may also be needed. Once the stresses σ_{xx}, σ_{zz}, and σ_{xz} are known, the pressure p is obtained by adding σ_{xx} and σ_{zz}, the displacements U_x and U_z by integrating equations (1-2) with respect to time, and the strains by solving equations (3-5) for e_{xx}, e_{zz}, and e_{xz} in terms of σ_{xx}, σ_{zz}, and σ_{xz}.

B. Numerical Model

In order to solve numerically equations (8-15), a discretization in space and time is performed. Then, the corresponding discretized problem is solved using a procedure similar to that described in [5, 6]. This method is of the semi-spectral type, since space derivatives are computed using the Fourier method, while time stepping is obtained with a leapfrog technique. The main characteristics of the method are described in the following sub-sections.

Time marching

The stress field is stepped in discrete time, $t_n = n\Delta t$, using the leapfrog method, namely

$$\sigma(t_{n+1}) = \sigma(t_n) + \Delta t\,\dot{\sigma}(t_n + \frac{\Delta t}{2}) \tag{16}$$

and

$$\dot{\sigma}(t_n + \frac{\Delta t}{2}) = \dot{\sigma}(t_n - \frac{\Delta t}{2}) + \Delta t\,\ddot{\sigma}(t_n) \tag{17}$$

where σ stands for any of the three stress components.

It is to be noted that the initial conditions prescribe both the stresses and their time derivatives at the same initial time while the leapfrog method (16-17) needs them time-shifted by $\Delta t/2$. A different scheme (in our case a third-order Runge-Kutta) is then needed to generate initial data appropriate for time marching with the leapfrog scheme.

Spatial differentiation

The forcing terms of the three equations (17) are to be evaluated using equations (13-15) and (8-12); in particular, the spatial derivatives in equations (8-12) can be accurately computed in the Fourier (spectral) domain [6]. Substituting the spatial derivatives by their Fourier representations, equations (8-12) read

$$\ddot{e}_{xx} = \mathbf{D}_x(A_x) + \mathbf{D}_x(f_x) \tag{8a}$$

$$\ddot{e}_{zz} = \mathbf{D}_z(A_z) + \mathbf{D}_z(f_z) \tag{9a}$$

$$2\ddot{e}_{xz} = \mathbf{D}_x(A_z) + \mathbf{D}_z(A_x) + \mathbf{D}_z(f_x) + \mathbf{D}_x(f_z) \tag{10a}$$

with

$$A_x = \frac{1}{\rho}\{\mathbf{D}_x(\sigma_{xx}) + \mathbf{D}_z(\sigma_{xz})\} \tag{11a}$$

$$A_z = \frac{1}{\rho}\{\mathbf{D}_x(\sigma_{xz}) + \mathbf{D}_z(\sigma_{zz})\} \tag{12a}$$

where the operators $\mathbf{D}_\gamma \equiv \mathbf{F}_\gamma^{-1}\, i\, K_\gamma\, \mathbf{F}_\gamma$ (with $\gamma = x, z$) are the Fourier representation of the differential operators $(\partial / \partial x)$ and $(\partial / \partial z)$; $\mathbf{F}_\gamma$ and $\mathbf{F}_\gamma^{-1}$ represent the direct and inverse Fourier transform operators (efficiently implemented by the use of FFT [7]); K_γ is the operator multiplying each Fourier coefficient by its wave number, and $i \equiv \sqrt{-1}$.

Absorbing boundaries

Several non-reflecting boundary condition schemes have been recently introduced [8 – 10] to reduce wraparounds from the boundaries of a numerical mesh. In this work, an absorbing boundary condition based on the gradual reduction of wave amplitudes in the vicinity of the boundary [9] was used.

External forces

The model is driven by point sources or line sources of pressure, shear or directional body force type. These infinitely localized sources $f(x, z, t)$, are modeled by finitely localized Gaussian distributions in space $g(x, z)$, multiplied by an arbitrary time dependence function $h(t)$. Thus, $f(x, z, t) = h(t)g(x, z)$. In addition, σ and $\dot{\sigma}$ must be prescribed at time zero. In absence of source terms or body forces, the model then computes the evolution of the initial configuration. In this manner, it is possible for instance, to analyze the propagation of an arbitrary plane wave.

C. Complexity Analysis

The computational cost per time step of the semi-spectral modeling algorithm is

$$\frac{\mathbf{E}}{N_t} = 20N_xN_z\log_2(N_xN_z) + 40N_xN_z + 12N_xNSTRIP_z + 12N_zNSTRIP_x \tag{18}$$

where $NSTRIP_x$ and $NSTRIP_z$ are absorption strips widths in the x and z directions respectively.

The first term in equation (18) accounts for Fourier transformations, the last two for absorption and the second for everything else. For a medium size numerical mesh of $N_x = N_z = 256$, the cost per time step is approximately 24 × 10^6 floating point operations. Since a typical simulation run requires several hundred or even a thousand time steps, for numerical stability and dispersion control reasons, it may be concluded that the number of floating point operations performed in a medium sized 2-D problem is of the order of 10^{10}. With larger numerical mesh sizes and in 3-D modeling, it becomes essential to look for computing techniques that speed up the execution of such a code.

The computations in this code are dominated by one dimensional FFT calculations, which amount to more than 90% of the total number of floating point operations if $N_x N_z$ exceeds 128^2. FFT computation has been efficiently formulated for vector processors and, in particular, for the IBM 3090 VF [11]. The rest of the computation consists of simple vector addition and multiplications. Therefore, this algorithm is an ideal candidate for a SIMD [12] machine. Furthermore, one dimensional FFT's and vector operations appear in outer parallel loops of count N_x or N_z, thus making the code a potential candidate for a MIMD architecture [12]. An optimal performance could be achieved on a vector multiprocessor like the 3090-200 VF by splitting the outer parallel loops on several vector processors.

3. *Vector and Parallel Implementations*

A. Vectorization

A vector pipeline computer speeds up the execution of a code by performing operations concurrently, in a way similar to that used in an assembly line. Operations are divided into subtasks that are executed by specialized hardware stages organized in a pipeline architecture. Operands flow from one stage to the next, so that the various stages may concurrently process different operands. Successive stages are executed in the pipeline in an overlapped fashion on different operands. In this type of processors the elementary instructions correspond to vector operations, which operate on arrays of data rather than on single data items, and which serve the purpose of feeding data to the pipelined units at an optimal rate. If properly used, vector instructions can result in a considerable improvement of system throughput.

Vectorization of the algorithm

To obtain high performance on a vector computer, it is essential that the algorithms be designed specifically for the architecture of the computer under consideration. This can be achieved with three different approaches: 1) using a high level language, like FORTRAN through a vectorizing compiler, 2) using a low level vector machine language, and 3) using a set of routines optimized for a particular vector architecture. In the present case we have used the 3090 VF vector computer, for which a highly tuned subroutine library, the Engineering and Scientific Subroutine Library (ESSL) [13], has been developed. In particular, it contains Fourier transform routines carefully designed to optimize vector and cache performance. Since for the semi-spectral algorithm under consideration, for typical grid sizes, approximately 90% of the floating point operations required per time step correspond to FFT's, it is clear that the third approach represents the best solution for this particular problem. The remaining 10% floating point operations, which mainly consist of vector additions and multiplications, are efficiently handled by the Vectorizing FORTRAN Compiler [14].

B. Parallelization

The general model of the parallel computer architectures considered in this study consists of q equal processors, each having a private memory for local code and data, a common memory for storing global data, and an interconnection network to allow processor communication and synchronization. A program for a MIMD machine consists of a set of tasks or processes, some of which can be executed simultaneously, and of a mapping of these tasks on the processors of the MIMD machine. It is usually necessary for a process to synchronize with one or more other processes. The allocation of the tasks to the processors entails then some overhead due to communication. The over-all performance is expected to depend strongly on the granularity of these tasks, i.e., the size of work executed in parallel between synchronization points. A number of other factors influence the performance of a multiprocessor algorithm: process synchronization overhead, load balancing, shared memory contention, and additional computations needed to separate a serial algorithms into parallel components. The parallel formulations of the algorithms described below are designed to minimize interprocessor communication, hence reducing synchronization penalties. Each algorithm consists of several stages, with the most time consuming stages consisting of independent tasks (one task per processor) that can be performed with no interprocessor communication. The speedup S_q of a given program is the ratio $\mathbf{E}(1)/\mathbf{E}(q)$, where $\mathbf{E}(1)$ is the execution time of the program on a sequential base machine, and $\mathbf{E}(q)$ is the execution time on a computer with q processors each having the speed of the base machine. The efficiency of the multiprocessor when executing the program is defined as $\eta = S_q/q$.

In this section we first analyze strategies for the parallel decomposition of the semi-spectral modeling algorithm, and then discuss different approaches for the implementation of these strategies with different software/hardware configurations. In what follows we will only consider the decomposition of the time stepping part of the modeling algorithm since it is the more computationally demanding part.

Algorithm decomposition strategies

From a computer implementation viewpoint, a parallel decomposition of an algorithm breaks down to program decomposition into tasks and communication among those tasks. Generally, sequences of tasks assigned to a particular processor are not completely independent of those assigned to other processors. Processors often need to exchange information about the status of computation, and therefore a mechanism of communication among tasks is needed. To solve the problem of intertask communication two main approaches are used: (i) sharing of memory between processors (*shared memory* technique), and (ii) exchanging messages and data between them (*message passing* technique).

We will analyze two alternatives for the parallel decomposition of the algorithm: a *domain decomposition* technique, based on dividing the domain of integration into a set of subdomains and assigning the computations of each sub-domain to a different processor, and a *functional decomposition* procedure, based on partitioning the operations to be performed on the data into subsets, and assigning each operation subset to a different processor. It is also possible to look for a simultaneous functional/domain decomposition. Moreover, had we performed an additional Fourier transform with respect to time, similarly to the acoustic wave equation case analyzed in the part II of this paper, a set of independent elastic wave equations for each frequency would have resulted, leading to an additional parallelism level.

Domain decomposition

In the case of the semi-spectral algorithm for the wave equations, one can make use of the fact that with a computational grid oriented along the cartesian coordinates x and z, space derivatives operate on individual columns/rows independently of one another. Thus the problem domain can be decomposed into strips of columns or rows, depending on which partial derivative is considered, and each processor handles the operation for its strip. A switching of strip orientation from row to column or viceversa is needed whenever one needs to compute a different partial spatial derivative. Equivalently, one could transpose the computational grid and fix the strip orientation. The processors could also cooperate in the transposition. In our implementation we favored this second method keeping the strips oriented column wise as recommended for faster execution in FORTRAN.

It is worth to emphasize an important difference between semi-spectral schemes and finite-difference schemes in solving the wave equation. The first schemes are non-local, in the sense that in order to compute derivatives in the x and z directions at a given point, it is necessary to access all the data of the row and the column relative to the point. On the contrary, finite difference schemes are local and for each point, only data in a small neighborhood have to be considered. This difference has an important implication when trying to domain-decompose the algorithm. In the Fourier methods each processor needs data from other processors, and therefore this type of decomposition is in practice prevented unless a shared memory implementation is used. Domain decompositions of finite-difference schemes only require sharing the data along the boundaries of the subdomains, and therefore they may also be implemented efficiently with message-passing schemes.

Functional decomposition

This strategy for parallelization is based on the use of several processors to compute simultaneously different independent operators on the data. In this approach, it is necessary to design the algorithm carefully to fully exploit the characteristics of the available hardware. In particular, it is important to make a balanced partition of the workload between the processors, so as to maximize resources utilization, and to design an efficient synchronization scheme to insure that each processor receives the correct data, while minimizing waiting times. In the case of the elastic wave equation, functional decomposition takes advantage of the fact that there are three equations to compute the three dependent variables σ_{xx}, σ_{zz}, and σ_{xz}. Thus, each of the equations (8-17) can be handled by one of three processors, thereby speeding up the execution of the job.

A simple way to decompose functionally equations (8-12) and (13-15) using three processes ($P1$, $P2$, and $P3$) is the following:

1. $P1$ computes A_x, $P2$ computes A_z, ($P3$ is idle) *via* Eqs. (11-12)
2. $P1, P2$, and $P3$ synchronize
3. $P1$ computes $\ddot{e}_{xx}$, $P2$ computes $\ddot{e}_{zz}$, $P3$ computes $2\ddot{e}_{xz}$ *via* Eqs. (8-10)
4. $P1$ and $P2$ syncronize ($P3$ does not have to wait here)
5. $P1$ computes $\ddot{\sigma}_{xx}$, $P2$ computes $\ddot{\sigma}_{zz}$, $P3$ computes $\ddot{\sigma}_{xz}$ *via* Eqs. (13-15)
6. $P1$ advances $(\dot{\sigma}_{xx}, \sigma_{xx})$, $P2$ advances $(\dot{\sigma}_{zz}, \sigma_{zz})$, $P3$ advances $(\dot{\sigma}_{xz}, \sigma_{xz})$ *via* Eqs. (16-17)
7. $P1, P2$, and $P3$ synchronize

Synchronization is required so that processors may exchange updated data needed for subsequent tasks. This particular strategy of decomposition makes a rather efficient use of the three processors by achieving an acceptable workload balance. In step 1, $P1$ and $P2$ share σ_{xz}; in step 3, $P1$ and $P3$ share A_x, and $P2$ and $P3$ share A_z; in step 5, $P1$ and $P2$ share $\ddot{e}_{xx}$ and $\ddot{e}_{zz}$.

C. Implementations

Two versions of the semi-spectral algorithm for the elastic wave propagation, have been implemented. The first one has been implemented on the 3090-200 VF taking advantage of the Vector Feature to vectorize the inner loops of the algorithm, and using the two 3090 processors to parallelize the outer loops. The second version has been implemented on a Loosely Coupled Array Processors System (ℓCAP), consisting of an IBM 4381 (scalar) host with 10 channel-attached FPS-164 array processors, and is based on a functional decomposition of the algorithm.

In addition, scalar versions of the algorithm on the 4381, FPS-164 and 3090 have been implemented for comparison.

Implementation on the 3090-200 VF

The 3090-200 VF is a two-processor vector computer [15 – 16]. Its architecture is very well suited to the semi-spectral algorithm we are analyzing, since it permits very efficient computation of the FFT's using vectorization, and at the same time a parallel decomposition of the domain using Multitasking. In order to make an efficient use of the Vector Facility, we have used routines from the ESSL library [13] to compute the direct and inverse Fourier transforms. These routines have been designed to optimize 3090 vector and cache performance, and represent most of the computational requirements of the algorithm we are analyzing. In addition, we have used the Vectorizing FORTRAN Compiler to vectorize the remaining computations. As indicated in section 2.B, spatial differentiation in direction γ is performed by $\mathbf{F}_\gamma^{-1}\, i\, K_\gamma\, \mathbf{F}_\gamma$, where $\mathbf{F}_\gamma$ and $\mathbf{F}_\gamma^{-1}$ represent the direct and inverse Fourier transform operators respectively. For a certain array, the derivative in the z (x) direction requires the computation of a set of N_x (N_z) direct and inverse Fourier transforms of N_z (N_x) elements each. These transforms are computed using routines SRCFT and SCRFT (real to complex and complex to real Fourier transforms respectively) of the ESSL library. These routines require that the data to be transformed are stored with stride one. Therefore, when taking the derivative in one direction, say z, a single call to SRCFT and SCRFT suffices to compute the derivative of the whole array. However, when taking the derivative in the other direction, x in our example, the input array has to be transposed prior to taking the direct Fourier transform in order to place the data with stride one. Similarly, after taking the inverse transform, the data has to be transposed again to place them in their correct locations in the array. This overhead to transpose the arrays, is small compared to the time to compute the Fourier transforms.

With respect to parallelization, we have used the VS FORTRAN Multitasking Facility (MTF) [17] to divide the work between the two available processors. MTF is based on FORK/JOIN (DSPTCH/SYNCRO) primitives, to divide the program into serial and parallel sections, which are executed by either one or several processors. MTF is a shared memory version of parallelism. In our implementation, we have used a domain decomposition of the algorithm, partitioning the integration domain into two sets of contiguous rows/columns. Each one of the two processors handles then the computations in the corresponding subdomain.

Implementation on a loosely coupled array processor (ℓCAP) system

A second version of the algorithm has been implemented on the ℓCAP system at the IBM European Center for Scientific and Engineer Computing (ECSEC) described in [18]. It comprises ten FPS-164 array processors hosted by an IBM 4381 with two CPUs. Parallelism is implemented within the VM/EPEX parallel software environment [19], which provides shared memory management on the 4381 host; data passing between the host and the attached array processors is accomplished through the standard FPS software. For this system, several possible implementation strategies have been considered: in particular, domain and functional decompositions have been studied. For a detailed analysis of these alternatives see [20].

4. *Performance Analysis.*

The sustained performance of the different versions of the semi-spectral algorithm (8-17) on the different architectures for the 128^2 grid is reported in Table I. It contains the time per step in seconds, the percentage of time used in computing FFT's, and the sustained performance in millions of floating point operations per second (Mflop/s), for a resolution of 128 x 128 grid points. The Mflop/s rating is obtained using equation (18) for the number of floating point operations per time step. Equation (18) considers only floating point additions and multiplications, and therefore neglects integer arithmetic, transpositions, and loads/stores, although it is known that they play an non-negligible role in the balance.

	ARCHITECTURE	PROCESSING	TIME	FFT %	Mflop/s
A	4381 uniprocessor	Sequential	8.41	77.4	.63
B	FPS-164	Sequential (pipelined)	1.36	53.3	3.88
C	3090 uniprocessor	Sequential	.99	87.1	5.31
D	3090-200	Parallel, MTF	.53	83.5	9.96
E	3090 VF uniprocessor	Vectorized	.19	66.5	28.3
F	3090-200 VF	Vector-Parallel, MTF	.12	59.8	45.4
G	4381+ 3 FPS-164	Parallel, VM/EPEX Funct.Decomp.	0.94	53.3	5.57
H	4381 dual processor	Parallel, VM/EPEX	4.21	77.4	1.25

Table I. Performance of different implementations of the elastic modeling algorithm for the 128 × 128 grid.

For different 3090 configurations, Table II shows the sustained performance in Mflop/s obtained for different grid sizes.

Speed (Mflop/s)	*Grid Size*				
Configuration	64^2	128^2	256^2	512^2	1024^2
3090 uniprocessor	4.6	5.31	5.30	5.52	4.54
3090-200	8.1	9.96	10.13	10.38	8.02
3090 VF uniprocessor	21.5	28.3	31.1	34.3	26.9
3090-200 VF	28.5	45.4	54.2	61.3	43.2

Table II. Performance of the IBM 3090-200 VF (main storage = 64 Mbytes; extended storage = 128 Mbytes) on the elastic code for different grid sizes.

In the following sub-sections the results shown are analyzed in detail.

A. Sequential performance

The performance of the vectorized and parallelized semi-spectral algorithm, has to be compared with the performance of sequential versions of the code running on the same processor. Therefore, it is interesting to analyze first the performance of the sequential code on the different architectures, using the IBM 4381 as a reference machine.

It is observed the good scalar performance of the 3090 (Table I, case C), which has a 8 : 1 performance ratio with respect to the 4381. The ratio obtained in the computation of the FFT is similar to that obtained in the rest of the job. In the case of the FPS-164 (Table I, case B) the performance ratio with respect to the 4381 is 6 : 1, mainly attributable to a 9 : 1 ratio on the computation of the FFT's. The performance ratio for the rest of the job is 3 : 1.

B. Vector performance

Case E of Table I shows the results obtained vectorizing the algorithm on the 3090 VF. It shows very good performance results with a 3090 vector/scalar speedup of 5.3. This ratio is 7 for the computation of FFT's with the ESSL routines and ranges from 2.2 to 2.4 for the remaining computations. It is worth noting that as the grid size increases the performance improves, as shown in Table II. This is due to the fact that the percentage of floating point operations associated with FFT's computations increases with grid size and that these computations are very efficiently handled. The key factor in performance improvement here is the increased number of floating point operations per memory reference. However, for the cases in which the problem size does not fit in real storage (last column of Table II), the data must allocated to the expanded storage of the 3090 (the specific model used in these experiments had 64 Mbytes of real storage and 128 Mbytes of expanded storage). The operating system then pages the data in and out of real storage at a rate of approximatly 75 µs. per pagefault. This leads to a degradation in performance as can be observed in the case 1024 × 1024 of Table II. Nevertheless, this performance is still very satisfactory: moreover, since the operating system takes care of paging, it is possible to run very large models without explicit memory management. For comparable performance data on a different vector machine see [21].

C. Parallel performance

Let us first analyze the improvements on performance in the case of domain decomposition of the algorithm with a 128 × 128 grid. Multitasking has been used to implement the decomposition on the 3090 machine in scalar mode (Table I, case D), parallelizing parts of the code corresponding to 96% of the execution time, and leaving in sequential mode the matrix transpositions and the computation of the absorption. The speed-up (parallel/sequential) ranges from 1.6 to 1.94 for the individual sections of the algorithm leading to an overall speed-up of 1.87. In the vectorized and multitasking case (Table I, case F), the speed-up for the 128^2 grid is only 1.6, because in this case the parallel parts of the code correspond to 87% of the execution time with individual speed-ups ranging from 1.5 to 1.9. However, Table II illustrates that with increased grid sizes overall speed-ups greater than 1.75 can be obtained.

The algorithm has been parallelized using the functional decomposition technique and implemented on the Rome ℓCAP system using three array processors. Table I (case G) shows that the performance improvement from parallelism is partially offset by a large communication overhead to transmit the data between the host and the array processors. With a resolution of 128^2, the processing time per step is .8 s, corresponding to a speed-up of 1.7 with respect to the sequential case. However, with a data transmission rate of approximately 1.6 Mbyte/s per channel in the system used for these experiments, the transmission overhead is .136 s when the individual AP routines and the host routines are "linked together", or a staggering .94 s, if the routines are not linked together. The total speed-ups are, therefore, 1.45 and .78 respectively. Since the poor performance in the parallel implementation on the ℓCAP system is associated to transmission overhead, it is interesting to compute the number of floating point operations per datum transmitted. As detailed in [20], this number is $(20 \log_2(N_x N_z) + 40) / 6$, which in the case of a resolution of 128 × 128 and three processors amounts to 53 operations per datum transferred. Therefore, to obtain a better parallel/serial speed-up from the ℓCAP system on this problem using parallel decompositions it is necessary that the number of operations per datum transferred is higher than 50: this is essentially due to the fact that the single array processors operate quite efficiently on FFT-based computations. A domain decomposition technique using three or more array processors has been ruled out because of its inefficiency as detailed in [20]: however, the recent addition to the Rome ℓCAP system of an FPSBUS [22] which supports direct data transfers between the array processors is expected to reduce considerably the data transmission overhead and to render efficiently implementable also domain decomposition techniques.

II. The Inverse Problem: Seismic Migration

1. Introduction

The purpose of migration is to reconstruct the reflectivity map of the earth from the seismic data recorded at the surface. The seismic signal recorded by a receiver (geophone) is a superposition of upward directed seismic waves originating from all the subterrain's discontinuity surfaces in the rock parameters. The term ***migration*** refers to the movement of the observed wavefields to their true spatial positions. The concept of migration can be summarized in the following terms. In the process of seismic data acquisition the upward traveling waves are recorded at the surface. In the migration process these recorded waves are used either as initial conditions or boundary conditions for a wave field governed by the wave equation. As a result, these waves are propagated ***backward*** and in ***reverse time***, from the surface to the reflector locations.

Up to the 1960's migration was achieved by graphical methods. This was followed by diffraction summation and wave front migration based on ray theoretical considerations. In the 1970's several important developments took place. Efficient algorithms were developed from simplified finite-difference approximations of the wave equations for downward extrapolation. Another important processing advance was made by the introduction of Fourier transform methods. These ***frequency domain*** approaches proved to be more accurate than finite difference methods in the space-time coordinate frame.

The aim of part II of the paper is to study the inherent parallelism in wave equation based migration methods. The organization of the paper is as follows. First, the basic concepts of seismic data representation are introduced. Next, some classical migration schemes are described. This is followed by the study of the algorithms and their parallel decomposition.

A summary of results obtained implementing PSPI, a frequency domain, semi-spectral migration method, on a tightly coupled system, the IBM 3090 Vector Multiprocessor, and on a loosely coupled parallel system, the Rome ℓCAP, concludes the paper.

2. Migration of Seismic Data

A. Acquisition and Representation of Seismic Data

Reflection seismology is an echo-ranging technique. An acoustic source (shot) emits a short pulse and a set of recorders (geophones) register the reflected waves at the surface. The time series (sampled) data associated with a single shot and receiver is known as a trace. In typical marine exploration a boat tows a source and a streamer of receivers. As it moves one-half receiver interval along a seismic line, it fires a shot and records the pressure at each receiver location. A trace is thus associated with each shot and receiver point.

Seismic processing techniques have been developed for groups of traces, called gathers. One such processing step preceding migration is known as ***stacking***. It consists of the summation of the traces of each gather sharing the same common source-receiver midpoint after correcting them to compensate for the offset between source and receiver. This is known as the normal moveout (NMO) correction. When the proper amount of time shift is applied to the traces, apart from a minor distortion effect, they appear as if they were recorded with coincident source and receiver, i.e., with zero source-receiver "offset". The ensemble of summed traces is referred to as the CMP (Common Mid Point), stacked, zero-offset section. A very important benefit of this operation is the significant improvement in the signal-to-noise ratio of the CMP section in comparison with the unstacked data. In what follows we will restrict ourselves to the migration of CMP stacked data.

B. Wave Equation Migration

Migration can be formulated as a numerical solution to partial differential equations, which govern the propagation of the recorded signals from the surface to the reflector locations, in reverse time. This approach, generally referred to as wave-equation migration, consist of two steps: (1) ***wave extrapolation*** and (2) ***imaging***. Downward extrapolation results in a wave field that is an approximation to the one that would have been recorded if both sources and recorders had been located at depth z. Thus, events appearing during the extrapolation process at the current depth z at time $t = 0$ are at their correct position. Therefore, the extrapolated data at $t = 0$ are taken as being the correctly migrated data at the current depth. These data ($t = 0$) are then mapped onto the depth section at z, the depth of extrapolation. This mapping process is also referred to as imaging.

The theory of wave extrapolation is based on the assumption that the zero-offset pressure data, defined in the (x, t) domain, satisfy the scalar wave equation

$$\frac{\partial^2 p}{\partial z^2} = \frac{4}{v^2}\frac{\partial^2 p}{\partial t^2} - \frac{\partial^2 p}{\partial x^2}\,, \tag{19}$$

with $p = p(x, t, z)$, where x is the horizontal variable, z is depth, t is two-way travel time, and $v = v(x, z)$ is the velocity. The corresponding ***one-way wave equation*** in terms of the variable $P(x, \omega, z)$ obtained from $p(x, t, z)$ with a Fourier transform with respect to time, reads

$$\frac{\partial P}{\partial z} = \frac{2i\omega}{v}\mathbf{F}_x^{-1}\left[1 - \left(\frac{k_x v}{2\omega}\right)^2\right]^{1/2} \mathbf{F}_x P, \tag{20}$$

where k_x is the wavenumber with respect to x and ω is the temporal frequency, $\mathbf{F}_x$ and $\mathbf{F}_x^{-1}$ represent the direct and inverse complex Fourier transform operators with respect to the direction x. Equation (20) is the fundamental equation for downward extrapolation of zero-offset data. It is expressed in the wavenumber-frequency domain (k_x, ω), and does not have an explicit representation in the physical domain (x, t).

Migration in the (k_x, ω) Domain

We let $p(x, t,\ z = 0)$ represent the zero-offset section and $\hat{P}(k_x, \omega,\ z = 0)$ its double Fourier transform. The problem is to reconstruct the wave field $p(x, t = 0, z)$, which existed at $t = 0$ from the wave field $p(x, t,\ z = 0)$ observed at $z = 0$. We shall assume that within one extrapolation step, say from depth z to $z + \Delta z$, the velocity is constant, i.e.,

$$v(\zeta) = \text{constant} \quad , \ z \le \zeta < z + \Delta z. \tag{21}$$

Then the solution of equation (20) can be expressed as

$$\hat{P}(k_x, \omega, z + \Delta z) = \hat{P}(k_x, \omega, z) \exp \left\{ \frac{2i\omega}{v} \left[1 - \left(\frac{k_x v}{2\omega}\right)^2 \right]^{1/2} \Delta z \right\}, \tag{22}$$

in which $\hat{P}(k_x, \omega, z)$ is the zero-offset section extrapolated to depth z. This analytic solution states that P is extrapolated from z to $z + \Delta z$ by simply rotating its phase by a specified amount. Therefore, migration schemes based on this principle are referred to as ***phase-shift*** methods [23]. From $\hat{P}(k_x, \omega, z)$ we obtain $p(x, t = 0, z)$ by an inverse Fourier transform with respect to k_x and a summation with respect to ω, i.e.,

$$p(x, t = 0, z) = \sum_{k_x} \sum_{\omega} \hat{P}(k_x, \omega, z) \exp(ik_x x). \tag{23}$$

Although equation (22) is valid only under the assumption expressed in equation (21), the velocity can vary from one Δz step to another. Thus, the phase-shift method can accommodate media with vertical velocity variations, i.e., in which $v = v(z)$.

Migration in the (x, ω) Domain

As we have seen, in the absence of horizontal velocity dependence, the equation (20) which governs the extrapolation of the zero-offset seismic data has a simple analytic solution expressed by equation (22) which is not valid for velocity fields with lateral variations. In this case, the square-root pseudo-differential operator appearing in equation (20) must be approximated in some form, for instance by a quadratic polynomial (Claerbout's [24] ***parabolic*** approximation). The expansion can then be formally converted into a numerical method in the (x, ω) domain.

Another alternative is rational approximation by truncated continued fractions [8] and splitting, which results in two extrapolators

$$\frac{\partial P}{\partial z} = \left(\frac{2i\omega}{v}\right) P, \tag{24}$$

which is known as the ***thin lens*** term, and

$$\left[1 + \frac{v^2}{16\omega^2} \frac{\partial^2}{\partial x^2} \right] \frac{\partial P(x, \omega, z)}{\partial z} = \left(\frac{iv}{4\omega}\right) \frac{\partial^2 P(x, \omega, z)}{\partial x^2}, \tag{25}$$

which is the ***Fresnel diffraction*** term. Advancing to greater depths is done by applying equations (24) and (25) alternately in small Δz steps. At each step Δz, (24) advances P through the multiplication by a phasor corresponding to a shift backward in time of magnitude $\Delta T = 2\Delta z / v$. To advance P with (25), for numerical stability considerations, an implicit Crank-Nicolson difference scheme is most often used.

An alternative approach to wave field extrapolation in general media is described in [25]. At each Δz step the wave extrapolation is accomplished in two stages. In the first stage the wave field $P(x, \omega, z)$ given at depth z is extrapolated to $z + \Delta z$ by the phase-shift method using ℓ reference velocities $v_1, v_2, \ldots, v_\ell$ spanning the velocity range at depth z. This stage generates ℓ reference extrapolated wave fields at $z + \Delta z$, namely $P_1, P_2, \ldots, P_\ell$. In the second stage the definitive wave field $P(x, \omega, z + \Delta z)$ is constructed by interpolation of the ℓ reference wave fields. This ***phase-shift plus interpolation (PSPI)*** method is unconditionally stable and has good dispersion relation properties worth its relatively high computational cost (for each frequency ω, and for each step in depth, $\ell + 1$ Fourier transforms in the x direction are required).

Migration in the (x, t) Domain

Migration as a wave depropagation process is best described in the *transformed domains* (k_x, ω) and (x, ω). It was introduced however in the early 70's using paraxial wave equations in the *physical* space-time (x, t) [24, 26]. We will reproduce here these equations, deriving them from their frequency-domain counterparts.

An inverse Fourier transform of the wave field $P(x, \omega, z)$ in equations (24) and (25) results into the following two equations in terms of $p(x, t, z)$

$$\frac{\partial p}{\partial z} = \frac{2}{v} \frac{\partial p}{\partial t}, \tag{26}$$

$$\frac{\partial^3 p}{\partial t^2 \partial z} + \frac{v}{4} \frac{\partial^3 p}{\partial x^2 \partial t} = \frac{v^2}{16} \frac{\partial^3 p}{\partial x^2 \partial z}. \tag{27}$$

For gentle dips, the right hand side of equation (27) can be neglected, and it becomes

$$\frac{\partial^2 p}{\partial t \partial z} + \frac{v}{4} \frac{\partial^2 p}{\partial x^2} = 0. \tag{28}$$

Equations (26) and (27) or (26) and (28) are specialized wave equations that depropagate wave energy only within a small angle about the vertical axis, hence are called ***paraxial*** approximations: details on their numerical integration with finite difference methods can be found in [27] (pp. 211-212).

3. Parallel Decomposition of Seismic Migration Algorithms

We have provided an overview of three major methods for seismic migration. In what follows we analyze the potential of using general-purpose multiprocessors for the seismic migration problem. Optimal results are obtained through multilevel parallelism: vectorization in the innermost loops and multiprocessing in the outer loops. This paper focuses on the parallel decomposition of the outer loops. An in-depth analysis of the issues related to the vectorization of the inner loops in a frequency domain method can be found in [28].

A. Algorithmic Description of the Finite Difference Method in the (x, t) Domain

The paraxial approximation to the wave equation is the prototype of the wave equation migration methods. This equation has a limited accuracy, but serves well the purpose of illustrating the computational aspects of finite difference migration methods. The 15° paraxial wave equation (28) must be supplemented by the boundary conditions

$$p(x, t, z = 0) = f(x, t), \tag{29}$$

and

$$p(x, t = T, z) = 0. \tag{30}$$

The desired output of the migration is

$$p(x, t, z) \quad \text{with} \quad z = \int_0^t \frac{v}{2} dt . \tag{31}$$

In terms of discrete data, the function $p(x, t, z)$ is represented at the nodes of the grid $z_j = j\Delta z$ and $t^k = k\Delta t$ by a set of vectors $\mathbf{P}_j^k$, where the vectors run along the x-axis. The function p is prescribed by (29-30) at the mesh points of the upper ($t = T$) and right ($z = 0$) borders of the rectangle $(0 \leq z \leq Z,\ 0 \leq t \leq T)$ and it has to be computed at all mesh points above the diagonal

$$j = k \tag{32}$$

Using centered finite difference operators δ_t, δ_z, δ_{xx} and centering at $\mathbf{P}_{j+1/2}^{k+1/2}$, we can approximate (28) with

$$(1 - a\delta_{xx})\mathbf{P}_{j+1}^k = (1 + a\delta_{xx})\mathbf{P}_j^k - (1 - a\delta_{xx})\mathbf{P}_j^{k+1} + (1 + a\delta_{xx})\mathbf{P}_{j+1}^{k+1}, \tag{33}$$

where

$$a = \frac{v\Delta z\Delta t}{8\Delta x^2}, \tag{34}$$

which describes the relationship among four adjacent $\mathbf{P}_j^k$ vectors. Knowledge of any three of these vectors determines the fourth, but stability considerations and the location of boundary conditions restrict the unknown vector to be $\mathbf{P}_{j+1}^k$, the bottom-left component of the quadruple. If the operator δ_{xx} is approximated by a three-point difference expression (1,-2,1), then equation (33) requires the solution of a linear tridiagonal system for each gridpoint $j\,k$. For a seismic section consisting of n traces, each composed of n time samples, and an output section of the same size, the computational cost of the 15° finite difference migration algorithm is

$$\mathbf{E}(1) = 25n(n - 1)(n - 2)/2. \tag{35}$$

For $n = 1000$, $\mathbf{E}(1)$ is approximately 16 Gigaflop.

Formula (33) represents a two-dimensional first-order vector recursion. Any ordering of computations with (33) that sweeps the (z, t) plane backward in time (decreasing k indices) and downward in depth (increasing j indices) is admissible. For example, one may scan the (z, t) plane by successive "rows" $t = t^k$ (from top to bottom) or by successive "columns" $z = z_j$ (from right to left). Such scans however are eminently sequential. For the purposes of parallel decomposition, sweeping the (z, t) plane from top-right to bottom-left by ***successive diagonals*** is advantageous. The algorithm must be sequenced in $n - 2$ stages. At stage l, the elements of the diagonal

$$\mathbf{P}_j^k \quad \text{with} \quad j - k = n - (l + 2), \tag{36}$$

are computed from the already computed diagonals

$$\mathbf{P}_j^k \quad \text{with} \quad j - k = n - (l + 1), \tag{37}$$

and

$$\mathbf{P}_j^k \quad \text{with} \quad j - k = n - l. \tag{38}$$

At stage l the computations of the l elements (36) are independent, and can be carried out in parallel. On a multiprocessor with q PE's, it is natural to assign to each processor a diagonal segment of l/q gridpoints to compute. The efficiency of this parallel algorithm is rather low for the following reasons:

1. overhead of assigning diagonal segments to PE's and of synchronizing the PE's at the end of each stage

2. smaller granularity: the mean granularity is of order $O(n^2/q)$

A parallel strategy with coarser granularity is obtained (i) partitioning the (z, t) computational domain $(0 \le z \le Z,\ 0 \le t \le T)$ into the subdomains

$$D_\sigma^\tau = (Z_{\sigma-1} \le z \le Z_\sigma,\ T^{\tau-1} \le t \le T^\tau) \tag{39}$$

with $\sigma = 1, 2, ..., q$, and $\tau = r, r-1, ..., 1$, and (ii) splitting the migration algorithm (33) into qr subtasks S_σ^τ corresponding to the subdomains D_σ^τ. Since the boundary condition of the migration problem are prescribed at $z = 0, t = T$, the dependency graph of the subtasks is quite simple: each subtask S_σ^τ can start as soon as $S_\sigma^{\tau+1}$ and $S_{\sigma-1}^\tau$ have finished and have provided S_σ^τ with its own boundary conditions $z = Z_{\sigma-1}$ and $t = T^\tau$. An efficient parallel implementation of this graph is provided for example by a macro-pipeline of q processors, indexed by $\sigma = 1, 2, ..., q$, operating in an overlapped fashion on the subdomains D_σ^τ with different indices τ: for instance, while the subtask S_σ^τ is executed by processor σ, processor $\sigma + 1$ is executing $S_{\sigma+1}^{\tau+1}$. This parallel decomposition has a smaller number of synchronization events and a coarser granularity, of order $O(n^3/qr)$.

B. Algorithmic Description of the PSPI Frequency Domain Method

The limitations of the finite difference migration schemes have prompted the development of the more accurate, but more costly, frequency domain methods. All frequency domain methods start off with the Fourier transform of the seismic data in time, thus replacing independent variable t with ω. Due to the linearity of the migration problem, the calculations carried out for different ω are simply superimposed to obtain the complete solution. Furthermore these calculations are completely independent.

In the frequency domain, the migration procedure is the following. For each ω, solve the downward extrapolation equation (20) starting with the initial or surface conditions $P(x, \omega, z = 0)$. Then compute the complete solution by summing the harmonic components. Different frequency domain methods differ in the way they approximate and solve the extrapolation equation (20). In the present analysis we shall consider the PSPI (Phase Shift Plus Interpolation) method which consists of the following computational steps.

1. Get the harmonic component of the wave field as recorded at the surface $z = 0$, i.e., $P(x, \omega, z = 0)$.

2. Fourier transform $P(x, \omega, z)$ in x to obtain the plane wave decomposition $\hat{P}(k_x, \omega, z)$.

3. For each reference velocity v_r, $r = 1, 2, ..., \ell$ spanning the velocity range $v(x, z)$ at depth z, and each wavenumber k_x, compute the plane wave extrapolators

$$\exp\left\{\frac{2i\omega}{v_r}\left[1 - \left(\frac{k_x v_r}{2\omega}\right)^2\right]^{1/2} \Delta z\right\}, \tag{40}$$

4. For each reference velocity v_r, and each wavenumber k_x, multiply by the extrapolators the plane waves $\hat{P}(k_x, \omega, z)$ to obtain $\hat{P}_r(k_x, \omega, z + \Delta z)$, the plane wave decompositions at depth $z + \Delta z$ of the reference wave fields P_r, $r = 1, 2, ..., \ell$.

5. Inverse Fourier transform $\hat{P}_r(k_x, \omega, z + \Delta z)$, $r = 1, 2, ..., \ell$, thus obtaining $P_r(x, \omega, z + \Delta z)$, the downward extrapolated reference wave fields.

6. Obtain $P(x, \omega, z + \Delta z)$ by means of interpolation among the moduli and the phases of the ℓ complex reference wave fields $P_r(x, \omega, z + \Delta z)$ using weights $w_r(x, z)$ depending on $v(x, z)$ and the reference values v_r.

7. Add $P(x, \omega, z + \Delta z)$ to the migrated section.

8. Increment z by Δz, and go to step 2, until the bottom $z = Z$ of the section is reached.

When all the harmonic components $P(x, \omega, z)$ have been processed, the migrated section is completed. For a seismic section consisting of n traces, each composed of n time samples, and an output section of the same size, the computational cost of the PSPI method when $\ell = 3$ reference fields are used, is

$$\mathbf{E}(1) = (5/2 \log_2 n)n^2 + (10 \log_2 n + 94)n^3. \tag{41}$$

For $n = 1000$, $\mathbf{E}(1)$ is approximately 200 Gigaflop. It should be noted that, in the practical use, this operation count can be considerably reduced, if care is taken to bypass by example step 6, for horizontally homogeneous layers, and step 3, when the plane wave extrapolators computed for a certain depth z can be used at depth $z + \Delta z$.

A simple parallel decomposition of the PSPI algorithm on a multiprocessor with q equal PE's can be obtained by assigning to each processor the task to compute a group of $n / 2q$ arbitrarily chosen harmonic components. There are then q independent tasks that need to be synchronized only at the end of the algorithm. There is no arithmetic overhead due to the parallel decomposition. If each PE has a private memory large enough to accommodate the partial sum of its $n / 2q$ components, the tasks do not interfere with each other. Even if the components have to be stacked in shared memory (which is likely to be the case in 3-D migration), there is a very limited potential for memory conflict: indeed the processors can be conveniently delayed in order to prevent them to overwrite the same output grid point $P(x, z)$ at the same time.

It should be noted that the PSPI migration algorithm essentially consist of three nested loops and that the proposed decomposition partitions the outermost loop (in ω) : the vectorization of the innermost loop (in x or k_x) is assured by the vector structure of stages (2-7). The intermediate loop (in z) is eminently sequential, representing a downward continuation process, and cannot be parallelized except for the particular case of a horizontally stratified medium. The proposed decomposition has also a very coarse granularity: each parallel task involves $O(n^3 / q)$ arithmetic operations.

All considerations that hold for the two-dimensional case are also valid for algorithms designed for the migration of 3 and 4-dimensional data, e.g., migration before stack [29] and 3-D migration. In both cases the cost of computation increases by the size of this added dimension (at least two orders of magnitude, so that $\mathbf{E}(1) = 20000$ Gigaflop for $n = 1000$), but the parallel decomposition can be carried out as in the 2-D case [30].

Performance measurements of the PSPI code

The vectorizability and speed-up characteristics of the PSPI code were studied running it and measuring execution times on the 3090 computer in scalar and vector mode. The problem under consideration consisted of the migration of a synthetic zero-offset section of size 512^2 [31]. The vectorized version of the code was developed from the original scalar code by introducing relatively minor modifications, e.g. loop reordering, etc.. The idea was to enable the VS FORTRAN Version 2 Compiler to recognize vetorizable loops and to convert them into vector instructions.

As seen in the previous section, the PSPI algorithm consists of the three major operations: (1) Fourier transformation, (2) complex multiplication, and (3) interpolation between the wave fields.

Table III summarizes the performance data of the PSPI algorithm on the IBM 3090-200 VF. The measurements do not include I/O, the initial transformation from the time to the frequency domain, parameter initialization, etc., operations that account for less than 1% of the total execution time in the scalar version of the code. Table III summarizes the results of our measurements by showing the CPU time, in seconds, for the main part of the code and their relative importance. The best speed-up is observed for the FFT, which does not come as a surprise, as the ESSL's SCFT (single precision complex transform) is carefully tuned to the 3090 VF.

	Scalar Code(uniprocessor)		Vector Code(uniprocessor)		Vector-Parallel
	CPU (s)	%	CPU (s)	%	
FFT	1181.1	61.8	180.6	39.1	90.3
Complex Multiply	173.7	9.0	37.3	8.0	18.7
Interpolation	478.7	25.5	209.7	45.4	104.9
Other	67.5	3.9	34.4	7.4	17.2
Total	1901.0		462.0		231.1

Table III. Performance of the PSPI code on the IBM 3090-200

As we mentioned earlier, the data and the computations associated with different frequencies ω are independent. We took advantage of this to run the loop over the frequencies in parallel on the two CPUs of the 3090 VF. The software tool we used to do this was the VS FORTRAN Version 2 Multitasking Facility [17]. In the case of PSPI, we started two identical tasks that processed half of the frequencies each. We had only to make minor changes to the original scalar code. The overhead involved in this process is very small, particularly if compared to the coarse granularity of the problem. We effectively measured a twofold speed-up when running on a dedicated system using two CPUs. Using the vector structure and the parallelism inherent in the problem we measured an effective speed-up of about 8 compared to the scalar uniprocessor version.

The same problem, that is the migration of a synthetic zero-offset section of size 512×512, was run on the loosely coupled Rome ℓLCAP consisting of an IBM host 4381 supplemented by $q = 2, 4$, or 8 FPS-164 Array Processor. The parallel software tool used in this case was VM/EPEX [19] to create and manage q parallel processes as "virtual machines" residing in the host and controlling the q Array Processors through the standard FPS-164 APEX/SUM (Array Processor Executive / Single User Monitor) interface [32]: an efficient version of the migration code for the Array Processors had obviously to be generated mainly by introducing calls to APLIBR64 [33], a library of FPS-164 optimized subroutines containing a.e. the FFT. Table

IV summarizes the performance data of the PSPI algorithm on the ℓCAP system.

Configuration------ ---------Component	4381 serial	q=2	q=4	q=8
(F) Fourier T.	8987	621	310	155
(M) Complex Multiply	1582	155	77	39
(I) Interpolation	6134	737	368	184
(O) Other	1107	177	90	45
(T) Total	17810	1690	845	423

Table IV. Performance of the PSPI code on the Loosely Coupled System (ℓCAP) with $q = 2, 4, 8$ processors.

It can be noted the perfect linear speed-up using $q = 2, 4,$ or 8 Array Processors, due to the very coarse granularity of the problem. The timings of Tables III and IV cannot be easily converted into Megaflop/s rates since the highly optimized scalar/vector/parallel versions of the PSPI code used for this comparison do not conform strictly to the simple (unoptimized) operation count of equation (41): however, a rough estimate can be obtained, associating (as inferred from Table I) the speed of 0.7 Mflop/s to the (scalar) IBM 4381, and getting all the other speeds by the ratios of the timings given in the Tables III and IV.

III. Concluding Remarks

We have presented in part II of this paper an overview of seismic migration methods and analyzed their suitability for parallel processing. The frequency domain methods are easily decomposable into parallel tasks having large granularity and require very limited interprocessor communication. The finite difference methods in the (x, t) domain can be formulated as independent tasks, but the granularity is smaller and the intertask communication overhead is higher. Among the frequency domain methods optimal results (in terms of accuracy) can be obtained by the PSPI method. This algorithm can adapted conveniently to architectures ranging from vector uniprocessor to loosely coupled array of processors. Frequency domain lend themselves most conveniently to parallel formulation since there is no interdependence among data associated with different temporal frequencies.

We have also described in part I two parallel/vector implementations of a seismic modeling code based on a semispectral (Fourier) method.

These two characteristic problems indicate that in seismic computations there is a very large potential for *coarse-grain* parallelism at the *algorithmical* level, which can be enhanced by one or more suitable *integral transformations* (a.e. Fourier transforms). Parallelism appears at multiple levels which can be simultaneously exploited, rendering possible and useful the application of parallel decomposition techniques like *domain* decomposition, *functional* decomposition, and (at the lowest level of parallelism) *vectorization.*

As regards the suitability of different computer architectures to seismic problems, both *tightly coupled* systems like the vector multiprocessors (VMP) and *loosely coupled* systems can be efficiently exploited, but for *non-local* algorithms (like the semi-spectral methods) and/or time-dependent problems requiring synchronization at each time-step, a shared-memory VMP architecture appears to impose the least amount of effort in the parallel restructuring of an original serial code.

Amongst the *software tools*, VM/EPEX offers a very compact and elegant way of representing parallel algorithms, but the SPMD (Single Program Multiple Data) model subtended is probably better suited to massively parallel architectures than to the systems with few processors analyzed in this study: in this respect, the facilities offered by Fortran Multitasking match quite well the coarse-grain parallelism of seismic computations.

References

1. Hockney, R.W. and Jesshope, C.R., *Parallel Computers* (Adam Hilger Ltd., Bristol, 1981)

2. Hwang, K., *Supercomputers: design and applications* (IEEE Computer Society Press, 1984)

3. Achenbach, J.D., *Wave Propagation in Elastic Solids* (North Holland Publishing Company, The Netherlands, 1975)

4. Tolstoy, I., *Wave Propagation* (McGraw-Hill Inc, 1973)

5. Kosloff, D., Reshef, M. and Loewenhal, D., Elastic wave calculations by the Fourier method, *Bull. Seism. Soc. Am.* ***74*** (1984) 875 - 899.

6. Gazdag, J. Modeling of the acoustic wave equation with transform methods, *Geophysics* ***46*** (1981) 854-859.

7. Cooley, J. W. and Tukey, J. W., An algorithm for the machine calculation of complex Fourier series, *Math. of Comp.* ***19*** (1965) 297.

8. Clayton, R. and Enquist, B., Absorbing boundary conditions for acoustic and elastic wave equations, *Bull. Seism. Soc. Am.* ***67*** (1977) 1529 - 1540.

9. Cerjan, C., Kosloff, D., Kosloff, R. and Reshef, M., A non reflecting boundary condition for discrete acoustic and elastic wave equations, *Geophysics* ***50*** (1985) 705-708.

10. Kosloff, R. and Kosloff, D., Absorbing boundaries for wave propagation problems, *Journal of Computational Physics* ***63*** (1986) 363-376.

11. Agarwal, R.C. and Cooley, J.W., Fourier transform and convolution subroutines for the IBM 3090 Vector Facility, *IBM J. Res. Develop.* ***30*** (1986) 2, 145-162.

12. Flynn, M., Some computer organizations and their effectiveness, *IEEE Trans. Comput.* ***C-21*** (1972) 948-960.

13. Engineering and Scientific Subroutine Library, General Information, Order No. GC23-0182, IBM.

14. Scarborough, R. G. and Kolsky, H.G., A vectorizing FORTRAN compiler, *IBM J. Res. Develop.* ***30*** (1986) 2, 163-171.

15. Tucker, S.G., The IBM 3090 system: An overview, *IBM Systems Journal* ***25*** (1986) 1, 4-19.

16. Buchholz, W., The IBM System/370 vector architecture, *IBM Systems Journal* ***25*** (1986) 1, 51-62.

17. VS FORTRAN Version 2, General Description, Order No. GC26-4219, IBM.

18. Di Chio, P. and Zecca, V., IBM ECSEC facilities: user's guide, IBM Technical Report G513-4080, (IBM European Center for Scientific and Engineering Computing, 1985).

19. Darema-Rogers, F., George, D.A., Norton, V.A. and Pfister, G.F., A VM parallel environment, IBM Research Report RC11225 (Yorktown Heights, N.Y., 1985).

20. Kamel, A., Kindelan, M. and Sguazzero, P., Elastic modeling with Fourier methods on the IBM 3090 vector facility, IBM Technical Report G513-4099, (IBM European Center for Scientific and Engineering Computing, 1986).

21. Schmidt, N. and Johnson, O., A vector elastic model for the CYBER 205, (Research Computation Laboratory, Univ. of Houston, 1984).

22. FPSBUS Software Manual, Release G, 860-7513-004A, FPS.

23. Gazdag, J., Wave equation migration with the phase-shift method, *Geophysics* ***43*** (1978) 1342-1351.

24. Claerbout, J., F., Coarse grid calculation of waves in inhomogeneous media with application to the delineation of complicated seismic structures, *Geophysics*, ***35*** (1970) 407 - 418.

25. Gazdag, J. and Sguazzero, P., Migration of seismic data by phase shift plus interpolation, *Geophysics* ***49*** (1984) 124 - 131.

26. Claerbout, J., F., Toward a unified theory of reflector mapping, *Geophysics* ***36*** (1971) 467 - 481.

27. Claerbout, J., F., *Fundamentals of Geophysical Data Processing* (McGraw-Hill, New York, 1976)

28. Dubrulle, A., A. and Gazdag, J., Migration by phase shift - An Algorithmic description for array processors, *Geophysics* ***44*** (1979) 1661-1666.

29. Schultz, P., S. and Sherwood, J., W., C., Depth migration before stack, *Geophysics* ***45*** (1980) 376 - 393.

30. Hsiung, C., C. and Butscher, W., A new numerical seismic 3-D migration model on the Cray X-MP, presented at the *SIAM Conference on Parallel Processing and Scientific Computing*, (Norfolk, Virginia, November, 1983).

31. Gazdag, J., Radicati, G., Sguazzero, P. and Wang, H.H., Seismic migration on the IBM 3090 Vector Facility, *IBM J. Res. Develop.* ***30*** (1986) 2, 172-183.

32. FPS-164, Operating System Manual, 860-7491-007A, FPS.

33. APLIBR64 Manual, 860-7488-001A, FPS.